Sermons On The First Readings

Series I

Cycle C

Steven E. Albertin
Charles D. Reeb
Richard E. Gribble, csc

CSS Publishing Company, Inc., Lima, Ohio

Copyright © 2003 by
CSS Publishing Company, Inc.
Lima, Ohio

Scripture quotations marked (NRSV) are from the *New Revised Standard Version of the Bible*, copyright 1989 by the Division of Christian Education of the National Council of the Churches of Christ in the USA. Used by permission.

Library of Congress Cataloging-in-Publication Data

Albertin, Steven E., 1949-
   Sermons on the first readings. Series I, Cycle C / Steven E. Albertin, Charles D. Reeb, Richard E. Gribble.
      p. cm.
Includes bibliographical references.
   ISBN 0-7880-1967-8 (pbk. : alk. paper)
   1. Bible. O.T.—Sermons. 2. Sermons, American—21st century. 3. Church year sermons. I. Reeb, Charles D., 1973- II. Gribble, Richard. III. Title.
   BS1151 .55.A43 2003
   252'.6—dc21

                                                                    2003004797

For more information about CSS Publishing Company resources, visit our website at www.csspub.com or e-mail us at custserv@csspub.com or call (800) 241-4056.

ISBN 0-7880-1967-8   PRINTED IN U.S.A.

Table Of Contents

**Sermons For Sundays
In Advent, Christmas, And Epiphany**
Through Cross-colored Glasses
by Steven E. Albertin

**Sermons For Sundays
After Pentecost (First Third)**
Calling Others In God's Name
by Richard E. Gribble, CSC

Sermons For Sundays
After Pentecost (Middle Third)
The Justice Of God
by Richard E. Gribble, CSC

Sermons For Sundays
After Pentecost (Last Third)
Conversion To Christ
by Richard E. Gribble, CSC

Sermons On The First Readings

For Sundays In
Advent, Christmas,
And Epiphany

Through Cross-colored Glasses

Steven E. Albertin

To Harry Huxhold,
friend, colleague in ministry, and mentor,
whose passion for parish ministry,
commitment to the Word, joy in life,
and love of the gospel
have inspired and encouraged me
through 25 years of ministry.

Introduction

The title I chose for this collection of Old Testament sermons, *Through Cross-colored Glasses,* summarizes my approach to preaching the Old Testament texts here. Understanding their usage in the context of the Christian worship service is fundamental to appreciating why I have interpreted and proclaimed them the way I have.

As a youth growing up in the Lutheran Church, the Old Testament was virtually ignored in the Sunday worship service. The lectionary only included two readings, both from the New Testament, the Epistle and the Gospel. If Old Testament texts ever showed up in worship, it was usually during the season of Advent when various Old Testament texts suddenly became important because they "predicted" the birth of Jesus. During the rest of the year the Old Testament was largely ignored. I was never really quite sure why. But somehow I got the impression that it was "old" and "obsolete" because Jesus had come. Somehow I got the impression that the God of the Old Testament really wasn't the same God of the New Testament. He was angry, crotchety, unpredictable, and sometimes downright mean. That certainly wasn't the same God whom Jesus called "Father." Likewise, the religion of the Old Testament was harsh and moralistic. The Jews were hung up on trying to earn their way to heaven by keeping the commandments and all those absurd ceremonial laws. We enlightened New Testament believers had a better way, a better God, and a better religion. Of course, years later I came to see that this was nothing more than another warmed-over version of the ancient Marcionite heresy. Nevertheless, it was an impression many had and many may continue to have in the pews of Christian congregations.

In Lutheran circles with the advent of *The Lutheran Book of Worship* in 1978 and in the years leading up to its publication, that all began to change. The lectionary was expanded and greater prominence was given to a third reading, the First Lesson, which in most cases was from the Old Testament. For the first time in my life public worship was forcing me to take seriously the Old Testament. Many of my old assumptions began to crumble. My education in college and seminary continued to alter those assumptions about the Old Testament being "old" and "obsolete." Since then I have learned to call it the "First Testament" instead of the "Old Testament." Such a designation reflects my renewed appreciation of those ancient texts and their close relationship to the "Second Testament." The two go together, hand in glove. One doesn't really understand the Second/New Testament without the First/Old Testament.

These sermons assume that there is a basic continuity between both Testaments. It is the same God in both. The God whom Jesus called "Father" is also the God of Abraham, Isaac, Jacob, Moses, David, and the prophets. The God of the First/Old Testament is the same God of grace and mercy reflected in Jesus and proclaimed by Paul. That is why the First/Old Testament is read in Christian worship. That is why Christians want to recover the use and appreciation of the First/Old Testament. The story of the Second/New Testament, the story of Jesus, and the mission of the church that emerged from his life, death, and resurrection would be incomplete without the history that went before it.

But these sermons are also shaped by the context of the First/Old Testament reading in the Christian worship service. These First/Old Testament texts are interpreted and preached from the point of view of *Christian* conviction and faith and not from some other religious conviction and faith, whether it be Jewish, Muslim, Unitarian, and so on. Their use in the *Christian* worship service assumes that they must be interpreted Christologically. They are not properly understood and proclaimed unless they proclaim Christ.

This is already reflected in the structure of the lectionary. The *chief* text of every service is the Gospel. The First Lesson was selected because of its perceived relationship to the Gospel. Lectionary editors chose a particular First/Old Testament text because they saw the message of the Gospel lesson appointed for that day reflected in it. Therefore, as I read, interpret, and proclaim the First

16

Lesson, it is always done from the perspective of the day's appointed Gospel. Even more, it is always read, interpreted, and proclaimed with the assumption that "Christ" must be there in the First Lesson. And if "Christ" is not there, I must bring him there. By "Christ" I mean the Gospel, the Good News of God's unconditional love for the world in the crucified and risen Jesus Christ. No sermon is adequately preached if "Christ" is not proclaimed.

That is what I mean by the title, *Through Cross-colored Glasses.* When I preach the First Lesson, I always come looking to preach Christ. This is not some idea I concocted. This is not something I invented. The very structure of the Christian worship service and the placement of the First Lesson in the service assume this hermeneutical perspective. Martin Luther, himself a First/Old Testament scholar and great Bible teacher of his day, also assumed this hermeneutical perspective. For Luther the Word of God could not be proclaimed as the Word of God unless it proclaimed Christ, i.e., God's offer of the forgiveness of sins through the death and resurrection of Jesus. Therefore, these sermons are all preached through cross-colored glasses. I interpret and proclaim the First Lesson always looking to proclaim the "cross" of Jesus Christ. That means looking for aspects of the First Lesson that "foreshadow" the cross, details, symbols, themes, and events that signal the presence of God's grace and mercy that was finally "fulfilled" in the coming of the Christ, the Jewish Messiah, Jesus of Nazareth.

Preaching through cross-colored glasses means that these ancient texts are treated as if they are "Christian" texts. They are treated as if they themselves beg to be read from the perspective of Christ and his cross. Both the early church and the Second/New Testament emerged from a context where this claim was the source of enormous debate and controversy. The overwhelming majority of the first Christians were Jews who believed that Jesus was the "fulfillment" of all the hopes and dreams of their Scriptures, what we today call the First/Old Testament. They believed that Jesus was that Jewish Messiah for whom they had been waiting for so long. Of course, the majority of their Jewish brothers and sisters disagreed with them and expelled them from the Jewish community.

These sermons share the convictions of these first Jewish Christians: that Jesus is the hoped-for Messiah; that these First/Old Testament texts are "fulfilled" in him; that therefore these texts belong in the Christian worship service; that these texts are properly understood and proclaimed when they are read through cross/Christ-colored glasses.

Preaching from the First/Old Testament also assumes that these texts aren't just history, that they aren't just interesting stories from the past. Rather, in these stories we see the struggles of God's people as they seek to remain faithful in every time and every place. Jaroslav Pelikan in *Luther The Expositor, Introduction to the Reformer's Exegetical Writings,* points out that this is one of significant breakthroughs that Luther achieved in his treatment of the biblical narratives, both First/Old and Second/New Testaments. Breaking with the allegorical interpretation that dominated the church in the Middle Ages, Luther began to read the Scriptures as real history, history that is lived out time and time again in the life of God's people, the church. "... the history which Luther read in the Biblical narratives was not just any history; it was a special and particular history, the history of the church as the people of God."[1]

Preaching these First/Old Testament texts through cross-colored glasses means that I see in these ancient narratives the same history of the people of God that is repeated in every time and place. It is always this struggle: to believe the gospel and live life trusting it. That struggle can be found in the pages of the First/Old Testament, in the pages of the Second/New Testament, in the pages of church history ... and in the lives of the people who sit in our congregations every Sunday morning. It is has always been the same struggle. It is the conviction of this preacher that the cross of Jesus Christ, the grace and mercy of God, has always been God's response to that struggle. Even though the context is always changing, the message remains the same.

Whether you struggle to preach to a Christian congregation or whether you are sitting in the pew looking for a good word to sustain you in your faith for another day, I hope you will find these sermons helpful. Perhaps their interpretation and proclamation of the First/Old Testament through cross-colored glasses will make these ancient texts come alive. Even more, I hope they help you to realize that seeing all of life through cross-colored glasses, through the cross of crucified and risen Jesus, the Christ, the long-awaited and now-arrived Jewish Messiah, is wonderful Good News and a great way to live your life.

---

1. Jaroslav Pelikan, *Luther The Expositor: Introduction to the Reformer's Exegetical Writings* (St. Louis: Concordia Publishing House, 1959), p. 89.

The Power Of The Future

We have all had them. We all hate them. You know what I am talking about: boring history teachers. All they can do is rattle off names, dates, and places. All they expect from their students is the rote memorization of facts. When you were in their classes, you couldn't wait for the bell to ring. But the good history teacher was someone special. He/she made history come alive. The past was vital and interesting. The past was important because it helped you to understand the present. The past was important because it taught you invaluable lessons about human nature and the nature of human life. The past was important because it helped you not to repeat the mistakes of the past.

But that is all easier said than done. The more we study the past, the more it seems that for every step forward, we take two steps backwards. In spite of our desire not to repeat the mistakes of the past, we nevertheless commit them anyway. Those pat phrases about history that once seemed to be clichés now ring more true than ever before: "The more things change, the more they stay the same." "We are condemned to repeat the sins of the past."

Despite our determination to do things differently, despite our commitment to human freedom, it seems that it is next to impossible really to overcome the sins of the past. I once heard a pastor in a marriage ceremony say to the bridal couple, "By the grace of God may you grow old together." That was an understatement if I ever heard one. Given the emotional and psychological baggage that a couple brings to their marriage, given the sins they will commit against each other, and given the grievances they will hold

21

against each other, it is indeed only by the grace of God that their relationship will hold together.

Our health is continually shaped and haunted by the sins of the past. Especially as I age, I have become acutely aware of how I can't escape the consequences of the past. For all of us, as we age, the shortness of breath, the pains in our chest, the stiffness in our joints, the cancer in our organs, all are reminders that we reap what we sow. We can't escape the consequences of our choices. The lack of exercise, the one too many desserts, the over-indulgence with the wrong sorts of foods, all limit the choices of our future actions. No matter how hard we try, we can't escape the choices of the past. We are prisoners of our history. We are doomed finally to die.

Recently a popular song on the airwaves by Irish rock band U2 expressed just this sentiment. The song, titled "Stuck in a Moment and Can't Get Out of It," expresses musically the frustration of being unable to escape your mistake, your error, your failure, and to move on with your life.

Today's First Lesson from the prophet Jeremiah addresses a similar situation. It is the sixth century B.C.E. and Israel is stuck in the consequences of its past and has no future. The mistakes of the past that Israel was unable to keep from repeating have condemned it and destroyed its future. Time after time the prophet Jeremiah had warned Israel to repent and change its idolatrous and rebellious ways or it would be destroyed. In 586 B.C.E. his words finally came true. The Babylonian empire swept down and destroyed the city of Jerusalem and the magnificent Temple of Solomon. In order to further ridicule and humiliate the Israelites, its King Jehoiakim was removed, his eighteen-year-old son and next in line for the throne, Jehoichin, was deported and his uncle, Mattaniah, was installed as a flunky, puppet king by the Babylonians. In a further gesture of humiliation and ridicule, Mattaniah was given a new name by the Babylonians, Zedekiah, which translated meant "The Lord (Yahweh) is our righteousness." The name was actually an expression of ridicule and derision. It was intended to add insult to injury because it ridiculed the religious faith of the Israelites. Obviously, their God was anything but righteous with the way he had allowed his people to be so defeated by the Babylonians.

The final humiliation of the Israelites is recorded in 2 Kings 25. In a climactic gesture of degradation, the Babylonians murder King Zedekiah's children before his very eyes and then poke out his eyes. The death of his children would be the last thing he would be permitted to see in this world. And instead of putting him out of his misery and executing him, they allowed him to live out his life in prison with the vision of this painful execution seared into his memory. They had absolutely no respect for this puny, upstart nation, its incompetent king and, most of all, its God. "The Lord is our Righteousness"? Ha! This God and his people are nothing in comparison to the mighty and powerful Babylonian empire and its gods.

All the symbols of their nation and their religious faith had been destroyed. God had promised them and given them a land, a holy city, a temple, and a king. Their God was loving and merciful and worthy of their praise. But now in the rubble of Jerusalem and in their deportation to a strange and foreign land filled with foreign gods, the Israelites were faced with the biggest crisis in their history. Not only was their suffering great, but also their religious faith seemed to be in vain. What about their God? Was he weak and insignificant? Had be been defeated? Did their God even exist? Without their land, their city, their temple, and their king, they had no hope, no future, and no faith.

It is into this context that Jeremiah makes the shocking announcement that is today's First Lesson. From a section of the book that bears his name called the Book of Consolation, Jeremiah refuses to accept the evidence of the present moment. Contrary to appearances, in spite of evidence to the contrary, Jeremiah insists that God has not abandoned his people. Instead, God has promised them a new future. They will not be prisoners of the past. The days are coming when all those signs of God's faithfulness and their status as God's chosen people will be restored. They will have the land of Judah regained. Jerusalem and the Temple will be rebuilt. And the monarchy will be restored, which would include the return of a king from the line of David.

It is interesting to note how Jeremiah takes a jab at the legitimacy of the puppet king Zedekiah and all the less than honorable kings that reigned before him. Jeremiah promises that this new king will also be called "The Lord is our righteousness," which in Hebrew is also "Zedekiah." In contrast to the disgraceful treachery, intrigue, and corruption that were a part of the regime of the present Zedekiah, the new Zedekiah, the future Zedekiah, would rule with a sense of righteousness and honor that was truly befitting of his name.

Of course, it was promises such as this one from the prophet Jeremiah that sustained the Israelites through their time of exile and into the future. Despite centuries of occupation and humiliation by one nation after another, the Israelites still had hope. They did not give up. They still waited for the coming of a king, a righteous branch and true descendant of King David, who would restore their good fortunes and lead them to future greatness.

Why do we read this passage today on this first Sunday in Advent and at the beginning of another church year? The word *advent* means "coming." Of course, at this time of the year we are anticipating the "coming" of Christmas and the celebration of the "coming" of Jesus the Christ as the babe of Bethlehem. From the first days of the early Christian church, Jesus was seen as the fulfillment of this prophecy from Jeremiah. Jesus was the true Zedekiah, the one who was in every way an expression of the Lord's (God's) righteousness. In Jesus, the true Zedekiah, the righteous Branch and descendant of King David finally came. God finally kept his promises and the good fortunes of God's people were restored.

But all is not well. Just like the first Zedekiah's tarnished and fraudulent reign that was an absolute betrayal of everything right and true and just, we are still waiting for the restoration. There are times in this life when we feel as betrayed as the Israelites must have felt betrayed by their fraudulent king Zedekiah. The leaders and government officials, in whom we thought we could trust, more often than not turn out to be imposters, fakes, more interested in their own careers than serving the people who elected them. The boss we thought we could trust, the friend we thought we could count on, the spouse we thought we could believe in, the job that we thought was safe and secure, all too often turn out to be disappointments, pretenders, the betrayers of our faith, and the saboteurs of our hope.

Even worse, we seem unable to shake a past that always seems to haunt us. The Israelites were unable to escape the centuries of unfaithfulness and sin that had accumulated all around them. The sins of the fathers were finally visited upon the children. The piper finally was paid. Jerusalem, the Temple, and the monarchy were finally obliterated. Likewise, we are haunted by the past and are unable to shake its consequences. We struggle not only with our forefather's stupidity and arrogance but also with our own. America seems to be a culture gagging on its own self-indulgence. The diseases of affluence, diabetes, heart disease, hypertension, and obesity are destroying us. Our extravagance is consuming our resources and polluting our environment. Complacent with our success our children are content with a dumbed-down education, disdain hard work, and consider success to be a right. Our neglect of marriage and family finally has caught up with us, and we are plagued with divorce and broken families. And worst of all, God is the one holding our feet to the fire. As he made Israel pay for her sin, so also will he make us pay. In fact, the pain and disappointment we suffer every day are the signs that we already are reaping the fruits of our sin.

Advent is also that season of the church year when we ponder our future and the Second Coming of Christ. That means that we ponder the meaning not only of the first coming of Christ in the babe of Bethlehem but also the Second Coming of Christ, when he comes again "to judge the living and the dead." Given the predicament we have gotten ourselves into, that Second Coming seems to promise more doom than blessing, more judgment than mercy. We fear that it will be an apocalyptic holocaust and the obliteration of our Jerusalems, our temples, and our monarchies, since we have been just as inept and corrupt as the sixth-century Israelites.

But that is when we need to remember just who this "righteous Branch" is and what this second Zedekiah, the true "Lord is our righteousness," has done. It is because of the first Advent coming of this Zedekiah that we can look forward to the second Advent coming of this Zedekiah not with fear and trembling but with joy and hope. Jesus, the Zedekiah truly worthy of his name, became one of us and one with us in our sin, in the disasters we have brought upon ourselves, and in the follies we have inflicted on one another. And he carried them in his flesh to the cross where he suffered the same fate suffered by the first Zedekiah and ancient Israel and every other sinner that has walked the face of the earth. But this time there was a big difference. He suffered "for us and our salvation." As the Son of God, he suffered our fate under his Father's own wrath "for us." His death finally silenced the charges and accusations God brings against us. God so loved the world that he chose not to make the world pay but sent his own Son to pay. He suffers his own judgment on himself so that we might be free from this damnable fate. He loves the world that much.

A mother is walking down the sidewalk alongside a busy street with her toddler in hand. It is a great day. They are enjoying their stroll. Suddenly a dog barks. The mother turns and looks at the dog. Distracted she relaxes her grip on the hand of her child and he slips away and walks into the street. The mother quickly turns, realizing what has happened. She screams when she sees that her child has walked out into the street into the path of a speeding truck. The driver of the truck obviously has not seen her child. Death is certain. So the mother runs out into the street shouting at her child to run when she lunges, pushing her child out of the path of the speeding truck only to be struck dead herself. In the ultimate act of love, she has sacrificed her life for the life of her child. She is truly righteous. There is no duplicity, nothing phony or fake in this "Zedekiah." Her action has restored Jerusalem and saved Judah. She is the "righteous Branch to spring up for David." She is Jesus. She is the one who has saved the world.

Because of the first coming of Jesus, of the true Zedekiah, the authentic "The Lord is our righteousness," we can look forward to the Second Coming of Jesus. Then, when he "comes again to judge the living and the dead," he will finally set all things right in this world. Because of the Christmas we are about to celebrate, we can look forward to that future. It is a future filled with promise and hope. Because of Jesus and his death and resurrection, our sins have been forgiven. Our past need not enslave us. We no longer need be imprisoned by it. We can dare to live life differently and begin to make a new world that is not doomed to repeat the sins of the past. Our lives can be different from what we thought they had to be.

Because of what Jesus has done, you have a new future. You have a life filled with new possibilities. It is like that day when you were promoted to a new job. You now have a career and opportunities that you never had before. Your life now can be different from what it had been before. It is like that day when you received that diploma. You graduated! You now can go and do things that before were never possible. It is like that day you made those wedding vows. Those promises opened up a whole new life with new experiences, pleasures, and blessings that never existed before. You have a new future. The new future changes the way you live in the present.

The Reverend Martin Luther King, Jr., knew what it was like to have a vision of the future change the way you live in the present. In his famous "I Have a Dream" speech he spoke eloquently of having been to the mountaintop, the mountaintop of Calvary, where the cross of Jesus gave him a vision of a new future. There he saw new possibilities for the human race. There he saw a new world, where people were no longer "judged by the color of the their skin but by the content of their character."

It was 1880 in the Connecticut House of Representatives. It was a bright day in May. The legislature was doing its work by the natural light of day, when suddenly in the middle of the day a solar eclipse interrupted the light of day. Not understanding the scientific significance of this "natural" event, the people gathered in legislature panicked. There was a clamor for action. What were they going to do? The Speaker of the House took the floor and spoke.

"The Day of the Lord may be approaching and the judgment of this world may be upon us ... or it may not. I don't know. If it is not the Day of the Lord, then there is no reason to adjourn our assembly. If it is, I for one wish to be found doing my duty. I am not at all worried about what fate lies ahead for me. Therefore, let us break out the candles and continue our work."

These are the words of a man who expected Jesus to come but was unafraid. He was ready to get back to his desk and continue the legislative debate. He had a vision of the future. He was confident that the future was in Jesus' hands. That meant that there was nothing to fear. He was sure that his sins of the past could not hurt him. He knew that he could be about the work God had given to do with a sense of peace that the world could never give him. Only Jesus could give him that, only the true Zedekiah, only the one who really was "The Lord is our righteousness."

That same peace and confidence is ours. We too have a future in the hands of Jesus. Therefore, there is nothing to fear. And there are no limits to changes we can work to bring to this world.

Advent 2
Malachi 3:1-4

Be Careful What You Ask For!

It is a piece of worldly wisdom we often hear in the course of our daily conversations: "Be careful what you ask for. You might get it."

It has been a long summer drought and everyone is praying for rain. When it finally does start to rain, it rains so much that the land floods and everyone starts praying for it to stop raining. A new, small family business is ready to open its doors for the first time. Everyone is hoping for a good first day. But that first day is so successful, they are so overwhelmed with business, they are so swamped with customers that they have to close their doors to recoup their energies. The actor works hard, striving to become recognized, even famous. When fame finally does arrive, he can't stand it. He has got to fight for every moment of privacy. He no longer has a life. The man faithfully bought lottery tickets on every payday. He was so sure that if he only won the big one, his struggles would be over. He would have it made in the shade. When he finally does win the lottery, his life is miserable. Everyone has come out of the woodwork and wants a piece of his new wealth.

Yes, how true it is. "Be careful what you ask for. You might get it."

It was to a similar situation that the prophet Malachi addressed today's First Lesson. The prophet Malachi wrote the last book of the Old Testament. But we aren't even sure that Malachi was his name. The book is actually anonymous and has been called Malachi, which in Hebrew means "my messenger," because of the reference to "my messenger" in the first verse of today's First Lesson. We

29

aren't even sure of the date of the book, but it seems to have been written at the beginning of the fifth century B.C.E. in Judah. The Israelites had returned from exile in Babylon. The Temple had been rebuilt, even though it was nothing compared to the magnificent structure of Solomon. Worship life had resumed under the priests in the Temple. Modest gains in rebuilding life in Jerusalem had been achieved. But all was not well. The priesthood was troubled with corruption and immorality. The people were discouraged and disillusioned with their lives. They were filled with cynicism and wondered where God was. Life was still the same old story. The rich got richer and the poor got poorer. Good went unrewarded and evil went unpunished. People openly wondered how there could even be a God when there seemed to be so little justice in the land. They cried, "When will God set things right? When will God's people be vindicated and God's enemies punished? Life is just not fair. When does God give us what we deserve, because certainly we deserve better than this?"

To such complaints the prophet addresses today's First Lesson. He asks if they really want God to set things right? Do they really want God to keep his covenant and hold them accountable? Do they really want to get what they deserve? Do they really want "The Day of Lord" to come?

"The Day of the Lord" was an important concept to many of the Old Testament prophets. "The Day of the Lord" was that future day, as yet unspecified, when God was going to come and finally balance the scales of justice. Goodness would be vindicated and evil would be punished. God's people would be rescued and their faith in God vindicated. The enemies of God's people would be destroyed. God would finally keep his promises. All would be set right. The curtain would finally fall. The end of the whole shootin' match would finally arrive.

Do they really want God finally to set all things right? Do they really want "The Day of the Lord" to come? Well, be careful what you ask for! Malachi announces that "The Day of the Lord" is finally coming. God will send "my messenger" (Malachi?) to prepare his people for the final reckoning, for the final balancing of the scales of justice. Finally they will get what they deserve. But,

30

the prophet wonders, who can endure "The Day of the Lord?" Will anyone be able to survive this final judgment?

The sentiments of fifth-century Israel haven't changed all that much, have they? We too complain about the state of this world and our lot in life. So much of life is unfair and unjust. That guy didn't deserve to be promoted before you. It's not fair with the way some people get all the breaks. You are sick and tired of your bad luck. The rich and the famous get every advantage. Why me, Lord? It isn't fair! If God would only give you what you deserve, if God would only set things right, if God would only make this world just and fair, then you would be happy. Then you would be satisfied. Then you would be saved.

Of course, we assume (and it is a big assumption) that if God would only give us what we ask for, if God would only give us what we deserve, then we would come out ahead. We assume that God's justice is good news. We have convinced ourselves that if we only got what we deserve, then all would be well. But the words of the prophet Malachi warn us, "Be careful what you ask for. You just might get it and it won't be pretty."

What Malachi calls "The Day of the Lord," we experience in other ways. The closest thing to Malachi's "Day of the Lord" is our understanding of the Last Day, the end of the world, the Final Judgment. Of course, there are many in our world today who don't even believe that there will be a final judgment and reckoning, but they do know that they will one day die. I don't know when the Last Day will come. I don't know when the curtain will fall and the show is over. I don't know when the whole shootin' match will be over. It could be next week, next month, next year, next decade, next century, next millenium or ... your next breath! That makes this whole matter of "The Day of the Lord" a whole lot more relevant.

Some years ago I came across a wonderful yet hard-hitting publicity poster that The Episcopal Ad Project was selling to congregations to be used in their advertising. It was aimed at people who had drifted away from the church. It addressed the anxiety that every human being feels about the Last Day. At the center of the poster was a large picture of six men carrying a casket up the stairs into a church for a funeral. Printed over the picture were these words: "Will it take six strong men to bring you back to church? ... The Episcopal Church welcomes you back no matter what condition you are in, but we would prefer to see you breathing." We used that poster in an evangelism campaign to the neighborhood of my previous congregation. Needless to say, the poster got everyone's attention.

Perhaps some of you have driven through rural areas of the Midwest or the South and seen one of those religious billboards on the side of the road. They attempt to put the "fear of the Lord" in your heart as they remind us of the Last Day: "What if Jesus returned right now?" I remember as a youth my mother trying to put some fear into the hearts of my brothers and me to prevent us from being tempted by too may worldly amusements: "What if Jesus returned ... and you were smoking a cigarette?"

Johnny and his wife went to the funeral of cousin Billy at that little country church just down the road they admired. But when they went inside, it was not as it appeared to be. The preacher shouted and screamed at them and all the other mourners. "It's too late for Billy. He might have wanted to believe. He might have wanted to accept Jesus. He might have thought about going to church. But he can't now. It's too late for Billy."

Johnny mumbled to his wife, "This is terrible. How can this be of any comfort to anyone?"

The preacher went on, "It may be too late for Billy, but it's not too late for you. If you get right with God, if you accept Jesus, if you get your fanny back in church, you still have time! Now is the time. Do it!"

On the drive home Johnny continued to complain to his wife. "That is one of the most insensitive, manipulative, and inappropriate funeral sermons I have ever heard. Who would ever want to go to that church? How could Billy have ever put up with preaching like that? What did you think?"

Choosing her words carefully, she said, "Yes, it was insensitive, manipulative, and inappropriate. But worst of all ... it was true!"

"Be careful what you ask for, you might get it," the prophet Malachi warns us. Do we really want God to give us what we deserve? Do we really want God to set everything right? Do we really want God to bring down the curtain and settle the whole shootin' match? All of us are sinners. All of us have fallen short. Can any of us hope to endure?

It sounds as if the prophet is warning us. It sounds as if we are all doomed. But as we look more closely at the words of the prophet, we see that he is *not* talking about annihilation but about purification! Before the great and terrible Day of the Lord arrives, God is going to send a messenger who will be like a refiner's fire and fullers' soap purifying us, preparing us, getting us ready to survive. This final reckoning will not be certain destruction but the beginning of a new life!

A refiner's fire might look like destruction, but it is not. Its white-hot flames threaten to sear us to death. But this is the heat that melts away the dross and the slag and purifies a precious metal. The refiner's fire eliminates the impurities and gives us pure gold and silver. The fullers' soap in the ancient world was not the fragrant and gentle concoction our world calls "soap." This soap was harsh. It may have burned. It was abrasive. But when properly applied, it cleaned. It washed away the impurities. It purified. The prophet announces that this coming messenger, though threatening and ominous, ultimately works for the good of God's people, getting them cleaned up and prepared for the big day when God comes to settle accounts. The refiner's fire and the fullers' soap will make that day a blessing for God's people.

The New Testament believes that the promise of this coming messenger, this preparer for the Day of the Lord, was fulfilled in John the Baptist. He announces that the Day of the Lord is at hand. God is finally coming to settle the score with all the evil and corruption of this world. Like a refiner's fire and fullers' soap, John tried to get his hearers cleaned up and purified so that they would survive this great and terrible Day of the Lord. Repenting of their sins and submitting to his extraordinary baptism was the way of getting ready for this final reckoning.

John's baptism was not Christian baptism. It was not even your run of the mill first century Jewish baptism. Baptism and other such ritual washings were not unusual in the Judaism of the day. Proselytes, converts to Judaism, submitted to washing to signify the change in their lives. Even ordinary Jews would frequently submit to various kinds of ceremonial washings in order to become ritually pure and able to perform some religious ritual. John's baptism was different. Everyone needed to submit to it, not just a few proselytes. It was done only one time, not every time you needed to be ritually purified. This was a unique, special, and unprecedented baptism because something unique, special, and unprecedented was about to happen. The Day of the Lord was almost upon them. Everyone needed to get their act cleaned up. Everyone needed to confess their sins. Everyone needed to be ready.

And then one day Jesus showed up. And everyone, including John, was surprised when Jesus asked John to be baptized. This was not the way things were supposed to be. Jesus was the One everyone had been waiting for. Jesus was the One who was going to usher in the Day of the Lord. Therefore, if anyone was to be baptized, it ought to be Jesus baptizing John! John's baptism was for sinners who needed to get ready for the Day of the Lord and not for someone like Jesus who is the manifestation of the Day of the Lord. But Jesus would have it no other way.

Jesus has been sent by his Father to love the world. Jesus loves the world by choosing to join us in the midst of our sin and brokenness. Jesus takes upon himself the sin of the world. So Jesus submits to John's baptism, a baptism intended for sinners, and continues through his public life the process of taking upon himself the sins of the world, a process that takes him all the way to the cross. There he suffers what we deserve. There Jesus suffers the terrifying judgment of the Day of the Lord for us ... and our salvation. He suffers in his own body the judgment and death that we deserve so that we don't have to get what we deserve.

This is Good News. Whenever Jesus' story is told and what it means for us is proclaimed, it is Good News. The gospel is proclaimed. We are promised that because of him, our sins are forgiven. We won't get what we deserve. Instead we receive the mercy of God. And when the Day of the Lord finally does arrive for us, whether it is the last gasp of the cosmos or the last gasp of you and me, it will be Good News. Our sins are forgiven. We have nothing to fear.

When we trust that Good News, a new life begins. It is a new life of repentance and faith. Christian repentance is different from the public examples of repentance that have been in the media recently. Race car driver Al Unser, Jr., admitted that he had a drinking problem. He was very sorry. He decided to go into treatment. If he hadn't made that decision, he may have lost his car and perhaps his career. NASCAR driver Tony Stewart publicly apologized for punching a reporter. With all the bad publicity he had received, he had to be repentant and make the apology. Again, if he had not, he may have lost his ride. Perhaps some of you saw it in the news. The Gary School System acknowledged that it had improperly prepared and "coached" students to take the ISTEP tests. In other words, this wasn't just a case of the students cheating. The school system cheated. They had to repent. They had no choice. Otherwise they would have lost their accreditation and tons of money. In each one of these cases, someone got caught. Repentance was part of "let's make a deal." "I will repent and then you won't punish me."

But this is not the kind of repentance practiced by Christians. It is nothing like "let's make a deal." I don't know of another organization in our community that begins their meetings like we do. If you go to a Rotary or Kiwanis meeting, to the local scout troop meeting or the board meeting of a corporation, you can be sure that those meetings will always want to put their best foot forward. They always want to look good. Acknowledging mistakes, errors, and failures is forbidden. To begin your meeting with them seems especially foolish and disheartening. But not the Christian Church! We start our meetings precisely by doing the foolish and forbidden. We begin by publicly acknowledging everything that is wrong with us through the Brief Order of Confession and Forgiveness. We drag out all the dirty underwear and skeletons in the closet. We can dare to pass through a refiner's fire and fullers' soap because we trust that we will be forgiven. We trust the gospel and its

35

promise that there is no sin too awful for God to forgive. To demonstrate that hope and confidence, we begin our worship by making the sign of the cross "in the name of the Father and of the Son and of the Holy Spirit." We come here looking for mercy. We come here trusting the gospel, believing that God will forgive us no matter what. And we are not disappointed! Our sins are forgiven. We are purified by the refiner's fire of God's grace and cleansed by the fullers' soap of God's mercy.

"Be careful what you ask for. You might get it." What sounds like a warning is a warning, if what we ask for is only justice. If all we want from God is that we get what we deserve, we are at least living dangerously. At most we are inviting our own destruction. But God has taken the initiative to reverse this dismal state of affairs. In his grace and mercy he has chosen not to give us what we deserve. From the promise to Abraham to the coming of Jesus to the word and sacrament ministry of this congregation, God wants to be gracious and merciful to his people. Trusting that promise, we don't need to be careful what we ask for. We can boldly put our claim on God's mercy. We can dare to ask that he not give us what we deserve. And as we gather here in worship, to hear his word, to eat at his table, and to be washed in his bath, our daring pleas and bold requests are not disappointed. Graciously we are cleansed and purified by the refiner's fire and the fullers' soap.

Why Rejoice?

I recently saw a survey conducted by the Muzak Holiday Channel concerning the most popular Christmas songs played at this time of the year. They are 1) "The Christmas Song," 2) "White Christmas," 3) "Winter Wonderland," and 4) "Silver Bells." It is interesting to note that they are all secular songs that focus on the "warm fuzzies" and sentimental feelings of the season. There are no Christian or religious songs here.

The songs reveal what is really at the center of this annual orgy of self-indulgence. Our culture no longer even calls it "Christmas" but instead prefers to call it "The Holidays." The songs urge us to be full of joy and merriment because of how we have been blessed. It is because of all those good things that fill our lives *now* that we ought to be joyful and to sing merrily those wonderful "carols of the season." We are encouraged if not pressured into spending and buying gifts, often beyond our means, as a way of assuring ourselves that life is really pretty good. Self-aggrandizement becomes self-congratulation.

The traditional, explicitly Christian carols that we sing at this time of the year also express our joy and happiness, but with one *big* difference. In these songs the source of our joy is not in the blessings of the *now*. We are not rejoicing because we are able to buy gifts and afford a lavish Christmas dinner. No, the source of our joy is strangely in the *past*! It is an event that took place 2,000 years ago: the birth of a child in an obscure place in an obscure time, laid in a manger because there was no room in the inn. That is the source of our joy now.

How odd!

The same could also be said of some of the best "praise songs" of the Christian tradition. Contrary to many of the sappy and sentimental "praise songs" that get sung in churches today, songs that solipsistically whine "I feel happy because I feel happy," the best and most enduring praise songs of the church base their joy not in the feelings of the moment but in an event of the past. In fact, some of these songs emerged from situations where the *now* was a living hell and anything but something that would fill your heart with joy.

In this congregation we love to sing the African-American spiritual "I'm So Glad, Jesus Lifted Me." It is filled with hope and joy and marked with a lively rhythm and an upbeat melody. The irony of the song is that it is a song that was first sung by blacks struggling with the suffering and oppression of their slavery. Their *now* was miserable. Yet, they could sing with joy because of something that happened in the past. That past event was the resurrection of Jesus.

One of the great, classic "praise songs" of the Christian tradition is "Now Thank We All Our God." With a deep and poetic lyric and a powerfully uplifting melody, it expresses an abundant joy and certain confidence in God. But the irony of this song is that its author, Lutheran pastor Martin Rinkert of Eulenburg, Germany, wrote it during the darkest days of the Thirty Years War. As this religious war raged around him, thousands of people had fled the countryside into the supposed safety of the city of Eulenburg. As a result the city was overcrowded and the services were stretched to the limit. Soon the Black Plague broke out and people began to die in droves. At one point Pastor Rinkert was conducting fifty funerals a day. Finally, he lost his own wife to the dreaded plague. In the midst of this terrible suffering, when everything in the present moment was drenched in misery, he wrote this marvelous and joyful song. His reason for joy had nothing to do with the *now* but had everything to do with the *past*. It had everything to do with what God had done in Jesus Christ. And it was because of that event of the past that he could find reason to express his joy in the present. His feelings of the moment were filled with sorrow and pain. He had lost those most dear to him. Nevertheless, he had a reason to rejoice. It had nothing to do with the present and everything to do with what God had done in Jesus Christ.

How odd!

We see this same odd joy reflected in today's First Lesson from the prophet Zephaniah. It was sixth century B.C.E. Judah and the religious reforms instituted by King Josiah had failed. The prophet had already uttered some scathing oracles of doom announcing the coming "Day of the Lord" when Israel would be destroyed. The "Day of the Lord" finally did arrive in the devastating assault of the brutal Babylonian army on Jerusalem. Everything that mattered to Israel was obliterated. The signs of its divine election, the evidence that God had chosen them, the Temple, the city of Jerusalem, and the Davidic monarchy were all destroyed. It was a political and social crisis. Most of all it was a religious crisis. How could they continue to believe in a God who had allowed the very signs of his existence to be destroyed? How could such a God be trusted? Did such a God even exist? And if he did, he was either a puny weakling or a fickle monster. It was the greatest crisis and darkest hour to have ever come upon God's people. It was a time for the people of Israel to weep and gnash their teeth.

It is this context that makes the words of the prophet Zephaniah in today's First Lesson so utterly amazing. In this uninhibited spurt of enthusiasm he utters a magnificent song of joy. Contrary to appearances, in spite of the pain and sorrow that must have torn his heart and the hearts of those around him, contrary to the experience of the *now*, independent of the suffering of the present moment, Zephaniah sings for joy!

How outrageous! How amazing! How odd!

It is interesting to examine the basis of Zephaniah's joy and optimism. It defies the logic of common sense. First, Zephaniah simply announces that God has already removed his judgment against Israel. Even though the rubble of the Temple and the city of Jerusalem lie all around him, he insists that things are not what they appear to be. In fact, they are just the opposite. Even as the Babylonians are carrying off the Israelites to their captivity in Babylon, Zephaniah insists that the disaster is already over. The deliverance and liberation from captivity is about to happen. It is just around the corner.

And what is the basis of this hope and joy? The future! He is absolutely certain that one day in the future God will keep his promises, rescue his people, and destroy their enemies. He is so confident that it is as good as accomplished. Therefore, let the party begin now!

He utterly refuses to base his faith on the reality of the present. He rejects the experiences of the moment. His joy is solely based on the future. Today we might call such people fools or deluded or crazy. Where are the men in the white coats? Let's get him committed! But to the people of Israel he was a prophet. He was speaking for God. They believed him ... and rejoiced!

How out of step! How peculiar! How odd!

It is for the same reason that so many consider the church's celebration of the season of Advent to be so completely and utterly odd. The same could be said for the Christian Gospel. Both refuse to ground their message and hope in the vagaries and peculiarities of the present moment.

With the celebration of the season of Advent, the church refuses to be caught up in our culture's annual self-indulgent plunge into the excesses of the *now*. Our culture, insofar as it is even familiar with the word "advent," seeks to collapse it into the season of Christmas. I even once had a conversation with a Lutheran pastor of a large and successful church who had decided to turn the four weeks of Advent into the four-week season of Christmas and to move the season of Advent (he preferred to call it "pre-Christmas") back into mid-November. How sad!

The parties, the gift-giving, the festive lights, the rich foods, the sentimental songs, all are ways of assuring ourselves that life is good. We have "made it." And God bless America! We deduce our relationship with God backwards from our experience of the present. And since all of us want to believe that God is good and likes us just the way we are, it is so important to "celebrate the holidays" and to have a "merry Christmas."

But letting the season of Advent remain Advent and refusing to collapse it into the season of Christmas is important. It is not just that we want to spoil everyone's desire to get an early start on celebrating Christmas. No, on the contrary, it promises truly to let Christmas be Christmas and have its joy be grounded on something more permanent and enduring than the fleeting fluctuations and permutations of the *now*.

Just when we thought we could turn Advent into Christmas, in rushes John the Baptist. Dressed in his animal skins, munching on locusts and wild honey, and screaming, "You brood of vipers!" he is not the kind of guy you want to have come to your holiday party. The Christian lectionary during the season of Advent is dominated by the imposing and disturbing figure of John the Baptist. He is about as far from jolly old Saint Nick as you could imagine. His abrasive appearance in our Advent Gospel readings is intended to remind us that, if there is a reason to rejoice during this season, it is not because life is good and all is well and God bless America!

On the contrary, this fiery prophet reminds us that all is not well and that we had better stop pretending that all is well. The signs of "the End" and that this world is under the judgment of God are everywhere. There is that lump in your breast, the blood where it isn't supposed to be, the pink slip when you arrive at work, the bodies of babies in dumpsters, the depressing litany of divorces, the continuing wars and rumors of war, the economic prosperity that is a pipe dream for all too many and a fleeting illusion for others. If we are to be joyful in this season of Advent, if we are to be joyful in any season, why? What is the basis of our hope? The fiery and disturbing words of John the Baptist insist that it can't possibly be *now* because *now* is still so flawed and so far from perfection. The four-week season of waiting we call Advent refuses to let us give into our culture's mad rush to turn Christmas into a month-long celebration of excess. It reminds us that the source of our joy can't possibly be the blessings of the *now*. The basis of our joy and hope is in what is *coming*, in what is *not yet*.

John the Baptist points to the "Coming One," to Jesus. As Luke's editorial comment at the end of today's Gospel reminds us, John the Baptist's raging against the complacency and whitewashing of the present was ultimately heard as "good news"! Why? Because all he wanted to do was to focus his hearers' hearts away from

41

themselves and the illusions of the present moment and onto Jesus. He is their only hope. He is the only reason to rejoice. And he will not disappoint them.

Like the prophet Zephaniah before him, John the Baptist calls our attention to the One who is coming. Zephaniah did the same thing when he called his hearers to look away from the destruction of the moment and the rubble of Jerusalem to the future, to the coming Day of the Lord, when at last everything would be set right for God's people. Their days of forever being the doormat of other nations would finally be over. Their days of disappointment and frustration would finally end.

That day of liberation and deliverance, that Day of the Lord, finally did come — in Jesus. Jesus, the Immanuel, the "God with us," came to suffer the shame, the humiliation, the failure, the sin, the rejection that has always plagued God's people and us. In Jesus, God suffered "for us" and "with us." He exchanged our plight for his blessing. During Advent we are reminded that the reason for our joy lies not in the blessings of the *now* but in the *One who is coming*. Advent reminds us that the *now* is so broken that our hope must come from someplace else, from some *one* else. Christmas celebrates that this *one* has come. And he has carried with him to the cross everything that is wrong with *now* and suffers the consequences. When he is raised "on the third day," at last we can be sure that we have been delivered. Everything that is wrong has been defeated. It is at last time to rejoice!

The season of Advent reminds us that we now live "between the times." The Day of the Lord has come in Jesus. God's enemies have been defeated. But all is still *not yet* accomplished. We now live in the "not yet" waiting for that Last Day when Jesus will "come again" to complete finally the victory that has already begun.

It reminds me of being up early in the morning just before sunrise. It is still dark. But as I begin to see the first rays of light begin to illuminate the horizon, I am certain that the sun will soon appear and a new day will begin. I now live in joyful and certain anticipation of what is to come. I live "between the times" of night and dawn.

It is like waiting for the airplane to arrive. The runway is still empty, but you know that it is on time and it will soon be touching the earth. You live in joyful anticipation of the arrival of your friend. You live "between the times."

You have just discovered that your wife is pregnant. For the next nine months you will be living "between the times" in joyful anticipation of a new baby. Until she actually begins to "show" the new baby in a growing tummy, you wait. You are excited with joy, a joy that will be confirmed in the future. Every day is filled with joyful anticipation of the new life that will grace your family.

This future-based joy of the season of Advent permeates the scripture readings of this third Sunday in Advent. This joy is reflected in the fact that the tradition of the church has always called this Sunday *Gaudate Sunday*, which in Latin means "Rejoice!" You might see an Advent wreath in some churches with a pink candle. That pink candle is lit on this third Sunday in Advent to reflect this joyful spirit in a season that is reluctant to shout for joy while it waits for Christmas.

The joy we emphasize on this Gaudate Sunday is similar to the joy expressed by the Israelite exiles in the sixth century B.C.E., by the first-century hearers of John the Baptist, by the seventeenth-century inhabitants of plague-ridden Europe, and by the eighteenth-century African slaves in America. Like them, the source of our joy is not in the experiences of the *now* but in the reality of what God has done in the past and promises to do in the future. They invite all of us, the dying, the lonely, the poor, the sick, and the broken to join them in songs of joy. Our joy and faith need not be undermined by the sufferings of this present moment. Because of the Jesus who *came* and who *will come* to at last set all things right, we can *rejoice now* in the present!

Therefore, joy can permeate all of our life. As I keep on reminding everyone who comes to Christ Church, everything here is a "get to." There are no slavish "have to's." What we have to offer is a gift. It is free. God's love comes with no strings attached. Therefore, we confess our sins, we bury our dead, we work at our jobs, we serve our neighbors, we give away our money, we offer our Christmas gifts, and we sing our Christmas carols — with joy!

43

And that joy is based not on the superficial, emotional whimsies of the present moment but on what God has done in the past and what he promises to do in the future independent of anything we do. When I look at the daily fluctuations and inconsistencies of my own life, this is certainly good news!

Because of the One who *came* and who *will come*, we also have our eyes opened to see how he continues to *come* now in the present. Words that sound all too ordinary and human now are heard as God's Word. Ordinary bread and wine, simple water from a faucet, now are "the means of grace," the very tools God uses to heal and redeem this world. Even in the midst of tragedy and suffering we can rejoice now, not because we are naïve and foolish but because the basis of our joy is what God has done in Christ and not our feelings in the present moment.

There is probably nothing in our recent experience that has caused us to question the goodness of God more than the tragedy of 9-11, the terrorist attacks on the World Trade Center and the Pentagon. Where was God as those towers came crashing down and thousands lost their lives? I have seen several e-mails and newspaper and magazine accounts that have tried to answer that question. Most of them have been inadequate. Many have tried to argue that God really was there doing good — as the police and firemen helped thousands to escape, as the thousands of volunteers stepped forward to help victims, as many had their lives saved because they missed a doomed flight or were late to work that day. But I find such explanations arbitrary and inadequate. Such explanations seem to be nothing more than desperate attempts to "get God off the hook" and still make him look good. Let's face it. The suffering and evil of 9-11 was monstrous. There is no way around it.

Where was God that day? In the aftermath of the clean-up, some creative iron workers probably portrayed it best when they welded together a huge steel cross from the wreckage and placed it in the middle of the rubble. Where was God for all those people who lost their lives? God was there with them in the midst of the deadly wreckage. God suffered with them on the cross. When Jesus died on the cross, he suffered with and for everyone who has ever had to suffer the irrational suffering of this world gone mad. The basis of our hope and joy in these moments of pain and suffering is only there, in him, in that great event of the past and in his promise to come again to make it all right.

One late night, I was watching one of the newscasts from "ground zero." Most of the time the media in the interest of "good taste" had not reported the gruesome details of the recovery of human remains. But one uncensored "live report" got on the air late one night. I have seen no report of it since. According to the report, 23 bodies were recovered all huddled together in a circle, all holding hands, in a stairwell, all crushed to death. What were those 23 people doing all gathered together holding hands? Were they praying? Were they crying? Could it be that they were singing? Could it be that a song of joy was on their lips and in their hearts? Could it be that like so many of God's people before them, they were free from the suffering and pain of the *now* and were able to rejoice by looking forward to that day when Jesus would come again to make all things right at last? Only God knows for sure. But if it were so, it would not be new. God's people have always known why they rejoice.

The Regenerating Power
Of A Little One

Regardless of the size of a town, it is important for the residents to have a sense of civic pride. Zionsville has a brick street and a quaint nineteenth-century village that makes us proud. Indianapolis has the Motor Speedway, the Colts, and the Pacers all representing the presence of professional sports in this town. It seems that in America these days no major city can consider itself "major league" and "first class" without such professional sports. Every year the mayors of the competing cities in the World Series or the Super Bowl usually bet some symbol of their civic pride against the opposing city. This belief that cities need to have professional sports has led one city after another to use public tax dollars to build fabulous new stadiums to keep their teams. In recent years the citizens of many of these cities have begun to question the wisdom and legitimacy of using public money to fund private professional sports. The Twin Cities may lose their baseball team because they have refused to be blackmailed by the Twins. Many of my relatives in Wisconsin are still complaining that their tax dollars went to build the new Miller Park for the Brewers. It's easy to get cynical about professional sports in this kind of world. "Civic pride" seems to be nothing more than a way to shame the public into coughing up more money for millionaire players and owners.

That is probably one of the reasons why I have always been a fan of the Green Bay Packers. It is not only because the Packers are from my home state but because here is a team that represents the "little guy." The Packers reside in the smallest town in America to have a major sports franchise. Green Bay has only a little over 100,000 people. In addition, the Packers are the only professional sports franchise in America that is owned by the fans, the people of Wisconsin, and not a rich and powerful businessman. When the Packers play an opponent, it symbolizes more than just one team against another. It is small town America against the depersonalized big city. It is the little guy versus the big guy. It is David versus Goliath. It is the underdog against the rich and powerful.

This desire to support the underdog and the "little guy" is reflected in today's First Lesson from the prophet Micah. Micah was a prophet from the countryside. He was anti-big city and never hesitated to criticize the corruption of the big city, Jerusalem. Therefore, we should not be surprised that he seemed to take great delight in reminding the Israelites that the future, great Davidic King, the long-awaited Messiah who would finally restore David's kingdom in all its glory, would not come from Jerusalem. Rather he would come from that little hick town of Bethlehem. Sure, David had been born in Bethlehem, but Jerusalem was his city. Jerusalem was the city that symbolized the great achievements of his reign and not the little town from which he came. But Micah loved the underdogs and the little guys and he was convinced that the future Messiah would be an underdog and not a big shot. He would come from "you, O Bethlehem of Ephrathah, who are one of the *little* clans of Judah."

The same theme is portrayed in today's Gospel. There we see that this Davidic King would continue to reflect God's partiality for the little ones, for the underdogs. In today's Gospel, Mary visits her cousin Elizabeth to tell her the good news of her recent pregnancy and impending special birth. While there, she sings that song that has captured the imagination of Christians for centuries, The Magnificat. In that song she sings joyfully of what God is going to do through the one now in her womb. Through him God will continue his partiality toward the little ones and underdogs. Through him (Jesus) God will continue to reverse the world's pecking order and its understanding of greatness.

*He has scattered the proud in the thoughts of their
    hearts.
He has brought down the powerful from their thrones,
and lifted up the lowly;
he has filled the hungry with good things,
and sent the rich away empty.*

— Luke 1:51-53

In this season of Advent we are continually reminded that these hopes of both Micah and Mary were fulfilled in the birth of Christ. However glorious we might want to make our celebration of Christmas, the biblical narrative of these events continually reminds us that the birth of this great Davidic King took place in the little backwoods town of Bethlehem. Even more, the Messiah came as a baby, as a little one, as one of the least of human beings, born in the most humble and ordinary of circumstances. Today as we conclude the season of Advent and enter the holy days of Christmas, we are reminded that God made his entry into human history as "one of us." And ironically it was as a "little one," not only as the babe of Bethlehem but as that ordinary carpenter's son from Nazareth, that Jesus had the power to change the world.

It is the seasons of Advent and Christmas and passages like this from the prophet Micah that remind us that the vulnerability of this little child reflects the unique power that the "little ones" have to change the world. The Christian Gospel proclaims that it is not the power and strength of muscle and intimidation but the power of love that saves the world. Love often looks weak and vulnerable. Love chooses not to coerce or strong arm but to lay aside its muscle in order to win the hearts and lives others. There is nothing so weak and vulnerable in this world as a baby. But yet it is a baby, this baby born in Bethlehem, the hick town, "one of the little clans of Judah," who has the power to change the world. This baby will eventually bring the powers of this world to their knees, melt their hardened hearts, and disarm their malice not with swords and guns but with the disarming strength of his seemingly weak love.

It is no accident that the long-awaited Messiah makes his entry into the world as a little baby. It is a foreshadowing of the power of

49

his kingdom. It is a foreshadowing of his coming kingdom's most glorious moment, his death on the cross. Love can be no more weak and vulnerable than that. Yet there is nothing else in this whole universe that has the power to change the hearts and lives of people so completely.

Now I want to tell you a story that portrays the amazing power of the "little ones," of a baby, to change the hearts and lives of people. It is not written by the prophet Micah. It doesn't even appear in the Bible. But it portrays a truth that is biblical. It could have been told by Micah. It vividly portrays the "regenerating power of the little one," of a tiny, vulnerable baby, to transform a harsh and hard world into a world of tenderness and compassion. In its own unique way, it portrays what it meant for God to be born in Bethlehem, "one of the little clans of Judah." It is a short story written by nineteenth-century American author Bret Harte, titled "The Luck of Roaring Camp."

The story takes place in 1850 in a rough and tumble mining camp in the California Gold Rush town called Roaring Camp. I suppose the place was called Roaring Camp because it was such a loud and rowdy place filled with characters who were crude and coarse.

The story begins when one day the camp was filled with all sorts of commotion and excitement. The whole camp was assembled before a crude cabin set at the edge of the camp. The miners were all intense and serious, mumbling something about Cherokee Sal. You see, Cherokee Sal was the only woman in Roaring Camp. And she was a coarse and sinful woman, a woman who was practicing the world's oldest profession among the residents of Roaring Camp. Cherokee Sal was a woman of ill-repute, a prostitute.

Why was there all this commotion about Cherokee Sal? Because Cherokee Sal was inside that cabin and she was in the midst of childbirth. It was not uncommon to hear about deaths in Roaring Camp. But births? This was truly an extraordinary occasion.

The men gathered outside that cabin didn't know what to do. They were shaken by this extraordinary event. One of the most gruff, coarse, and profane residents of Roaring Camp, but also one of its more prominent citizens, was a man by the name of Kentuck.

50

He stepped forward and decided that another fellow by the name of Stumpy ought to play the role of surgeon and midwife because, it was rumored, he had a family somewhere in his distant past. Stumpy reluctantly consented and went inside to do his duty.

All the camp, approximately 100 men, waited impatiently outside. They were a rough, hard drinking, heavy smoking, gutter-talking bunch of characters. They had all come to make their fortunes in Roaring Camp. But now they were all mesmerized by this birth that was about to happen to Cherokee Sal. They waited all night, when suddenly near dawn they heard a sudden cry, the likes of which they had never heard before. Together they all jumped up and started shouting and yelling for joy. Guns were fired into the sky. A baby boy had been born. But sadly in the midst of all the pain, Cherokee Sal had died.

The men of Roaring Camp were fascinated with this newborn child. Curiously they all filed through the small one-room cabin to catch a glimpse of this strange, new life. Each offered the child a gift ranging from a silver tobacco box to a golden spur. Then came the coarse and rough Kentuck. Harte writes:

> As Kentuck bent over the candle-box half curiously, the child turned, and in a spasm of pain caught at his groping finger and held it fast for a moment. Kentuck looked foolish and embarrassed. Something like a blush tried to assert itself in his weather-beaten cheek. "The d-d little cuss!" he said, as he extricated his finger, with perhaps, more tenderness and care than he might have been deemed capable of showing. He held that finger a little apart from its fellows as he went out and examined it curiously. The examination provoked the same original remark in regard to the child.
>
> In fact, he seemed to enjoy repeating it. "He rastled with my finger," he remarked holding up the member, "the d-d little cuss!"
>
> Kentuck was obviously moved by the experience. That night he walked back and forth in front of the cabin until he finally got enough courage to knock on the door.

It was opened by Stumpy. "How goes it?" said Kentuck, looking past Stumpy toward the candle box. "All quiet," replied Stumpy. "Anything up?" "Nothing." There was a pause, an embarrassing one, Stumpy still holding the door. Then Kentuck had recourse to his finger, which he held up to Stumpy. "Rastled with it, the d-d little cuss," he said and retired.

Cherokee Sal was buried and Roaring Camp was forced to make a decision. What were they going to do with this baby? They didn't want to send him to another camp. They decided against getting a female nurse. No decent woman would ever come there anyway. And they didn't want any more of that other kind of woman. Finally, Stumpy agreed to do the job of raising the child. But in reality the whole camp pitched in.

Surprisingly the child thrived in Roaring Camp. For a while he was variously called "The Kid" and "Stumpy's Boy." Finally it was decided that the boy needed a name. It was decided to call him Tommy Luck because "luck" was something that was on the mind of every man in Roaring Camp. The men even decided to have a christening ceremony for "The Luck." In all seriousness someone played the preacher. There was even a choir. Stumpy announced the christening.

"I proclaim you Thomas Luck, according to the laws of the United States and the state of California, so help me God." It was the first time that the name of the Deity had been uttered otherwise than profanely in the camp. Tommy Luck was christened as seriously as he would have been under a Christian roof, and cried and was comforted in an orthodox fashion. And so the work of the regeneration began in Roaring Camp.[1]

An amazing thing then happens in the story. Roaring Camp is changed or "regenerated," as Harte puts it. The cabin is remodeled. The camp is cleaned up. Shouting and yelling are prohibited within earshot of the child. It is quite a change, especially for a place called Roaring Camp. Profanity is given up. No one is allowed to hold the child without a bath. Some even take to singing lullabies to put the child to sleep. The miners even begin to pick bouquets of wild flowers to adorn the "corral" of Tommy Luck. The camp is so intent on cleaning up its image that there is talk of building a hotel and inviting some decent families to come and live in the camp ... for the sake of "The Luck."

But in the spring of 1851 tragedy struck. A sudden flash flood arose and washed away part of Roaring Camp, including the cabin where Stumpy and The Luck were living. Stumpy was eventually found downstream — dead. But there was no Tommy Luck. The men of Roaring Camp thought all was lost, when suddenly a relief boat arrived from downstream carrying a man and an infant nearly exhausted. Rushing to the boat, they saw old Kentuck lying there, cruelly crushed and bruised, almost dead, but still holding tight in his arms — The Luck of Roaring Camp. As they looked at this pair, they thought that the child was dead. One said, "I reckon he's dead." But Kentuck opened his eyes and said feebly, "Dead? Yes, my man, and you're dying, too." A smile lit the eyes of the expiring Kentuck. "Dying," he repeated, "he's taking me with him. Tell the boys I've got Luck with me now." And the strong man, "clinging to the frail babe as a drowning man is said to cling to a straw, drifted away into the shadowy river that flows forever to the unknown."

Tommy Luck, a little newborn baby, changed the lives of old Kentuck and Roaring Camp. Bret Harte calls it "regeneration," being born again. I call it an example of the power that the "little ones," the least and the most insignificant, a baby born in Bethlehem, "one of the little clans of Judah" have to change and transform lives.

On this fourth Sunday in Advent we look forward to the birth of a baby, not laid in a cigar box but in a manger, born not in the backward town of Roaring Camp but in the little and insignificant town of Bethlehem. This baby didn't just save the town of Roaring Camp from its crude and rowdy ways but saved the world from its sin. This baby was not just the child of Cherokee Sal but the child of an unwed, teenaged mother. And this child didn't just bring good manners and civility to a crude bunch of miners. He brought light to a world shrouded in darkness.

It is amazing, this regenerative power of such little ones. Can you imagine it, babies changing people's lives? But that is what God is up to in this child, just a baby, from "one of the little clans of Judah."

---

1. Bret Harte, *The Outcasts of Poker Flat and Other Tales* (New York: Penguin Books, 1961), p. 107.

A Dirty Christmas

Under every Christmas tree in the midst of the brightly wrapped packages, the choo-choo train winding through that picturesque winter village, and the glorious Christmas creche with the virgin Mary and Joseph, the shepherds, and the baby Jesus ought to be *a pail of dirt*. And that dirt ought to be really dirty dirt, not like that sanitized stuff you buy at the local garden shop. No, that dirt ought to be the real grubby, crumbly, filthy dirt, the kind that lies around a construction site or in a dump. We need to place that pail of dirt out there in front of the tree where everyone can see it. Why? Because that pail of dirt, more than the bright lights, the bows, the ribbons, the gaily wrapped gifts, and even the cute little manger scene, reminds us of what God is really up to at Christmas.

Yes, it does take the innocent and uncluttered vision of a little child to see once again what God did that holy night in Bethlehem. That became abundantly clear to me many years ago when the nursery school children at my church went to visit a local farm on a cold, damp day in December. The purpose of the field trip was to have the children experience firsthand what it must have been like for Mary and Joseph to be turned away from a warm, clean room at the inn and to have to spend a cold night in the barn. The children went up to the farmhouse, knocked on the door, as if it was the inn in Bethlehem, and asked if they could come and spend the night. The lady who answered the door told them (of course, this all had been pre-arranged by the nursery school staff) that there was "no room in the inn." But there was room out back in the barn. So the children and the staff went around to the barn in the back, trying

55

not to get stuck in the muck of the barnyard. When they finally arrived at the barn, they got to see the animals housed inside.

The reaction of the children to this field trip was most revealing. Most of the children were quite disgusted with the whole thing. Some had to be coaxed even to enter the barn. They just couldn't get over the filth and dirt inside. The animals were muddy and smelly, hardly the freshly scrubbed creatures we see standing around the manger in all the Christmas storybooks. And, of course, there was the manure, the stinking and slimy manure. And think that Jesus was born into this! The children were shocked!

When the staff reported this incident to me, I too was shocked. Why? Because I too had overlooked the significance of the fact that Jesus was born in a barn and laid in a manger, because there was no room in the inn. Too young to have their vision skewed by years of Christmas glitter and glamour, these nursery school children were able to see the unvarnished truth of Christmas. They were able to see how dirty it really is.

It is precisely in the dirt that we discover what is so special and so amazing about the birth in Bethlehem. Dirt, manure, terrible smells, these are not the things we usually associate with the presence of God. But Christmas announces to us that this is the kind of God we have. And it is the dirt of Christmas that makes this God so wonderful.

If God would have come in the midst of fire and smoke, in thunder and lightning, in an earthquake or flood, do you think anyone would have been surprised? Of course not! When we speak of the holy and almighty God, the creator of heaven and earth, it is these awesome images of power that come to mind. In the Old Testament, the holiness of God is often revealed in powerful and frightening ways. God comes walking in the Garden of Eden in the cool of the evening and Adam and Eve are scared. They run and hide in the bushes. God appears to Moses in the burning bush and Moses is frightened. When the prophet Isaiah encounters God in the Temple, God appears in the midst of fire and smoke and Isaiah is frightened.

The holiness of God is a powerful and terrible thing for us sinful mortals. And that is what makes Christmas so amazing and filled with wonder. In this birth of a baby God finds another, very different way to come among us. God doesn't shout. God doesn't use blinding light or deafening wind. There is no fire and smoke. Instead there are the cries of pain as a woman gives birth to a child and the cries of a newborn baby in the night.

This is certainly not how the people of Israel had always thought their long-awaited royal descendant of King David would come. Their expectations were fueled by such texts as tonight's First Lesson from the prophet Isaiah. Isaiah appears to quote a royal enthronement ritual that was used every time a new king came to power. In our country, the Supreme Court Chief Justice inaugurates a new president on the steps of the Capitol in Washington, D.C., at the beginning of a new presidential term. The event is filled with high hopes and expectations for our new leader. In similar fashion, in ancient Israel the priests and other religious leaders began the reign of a new king by conducting an inauguration ritual. As with the advent of any new leader, the people's hopes and expectations were reflected in this ritual. Perhaps this king would not be just another scoundrel like so many of the kings that went before him. Perhaps this king would finally fulfill the hopes and dreams expressed in the words of this ritual. Perhaps he would truly be the noble and regal figure worthy of his position.

> *Wonderful Counselor, Mighty God, Everlasting Father,*
> *Prince of Peace.*
> *His authority shall grow continually, and there shall*
> *be endless peace*
> *for the throne of David and his kingdom.*
> *He will establish and uphold it with justice and with*
> *righteousness*
> *from this time onward and forevermore.*
>
> — vv. 6-7

But the birth of this baby in Bethlehem did not fit these regal expectations. This birth did not seem to be very becoming of the Wonderful Counselor, Mighty God, Everlasting Father, Prince of Peace. The birth in that dirty barn was not very regal or presidential and certainly not godly.

It is not easy for us to know what this meant to God, what must have gone through God's heart and mind when he decided to come into this world in circumstances like this. Perhaps it was something like this.

If you have ever lived in a more southern climate than Indiana, you will know what "lovely" creatures roaches are. I know that, if you are anything like me, you hate roaches. But suppose for a moment that you love roaches. And you want to tell them that you love them. But every time you get near them, they scurry away to hide behind the refrigerator or under the couch. Finally, it dawns on you that, in order for them to understand that you are not coming to kill them but to love them, you must come to them as a roach. Then they won't blink an eye. Then you can slip among them unnoticed. Then you can frolic with them in the garbage cans and the drainpipes. But what a coming down this is ... to become a roach! What a humiliation!

The birth in Bethlehem was this same sort of coming down, a falling off, a humbling, a humiliation. We are shocked, amazed, befuddled that God world love us so much that he would be so humiliated as to come into a smelly and dirty world, to be born in the midst of manure and filthy animals.

But what do we do with Christmas? It's not just the commercialization that takes the wonder out of Christmas. Rather, it is all of our attempts to make Christmas holy again, to glorify it, to set it apart, to make it something more fitting the glory and power of God. Nobody is supposed to cry at Christmas. Everybody is supposed to be happy and joyous. It's a time for peace and good will. There is no time for tears and pain. And so we work overtime, even frantically, to cover up and deny those very things that make us human beings and not rocks. Everyone has got to have the "Christmas spirit." And that means pretending that everything is wonderful even when it is not. And if we fail to pull it off, we complain about having "missed Christmas." The rest of the year may have its share of hurt and pain, but not at Christmas. Christmas has got to be "holy," "sacred," different from the rest of the year.

Even the Christmas story, the story of that dirty birth, is made holy. We build a fence around it and remove it from the ordinary,

58

dirty world in which we all must live. And so it is a birth totally unlike any other birth in this world. There are no sounds of pain from a mother in childbirth. The stork must have delivered this baby. And the donkey talks and perhaps some other animals, too. A drummer boy appears on the scene. The shepherds are squeaky clean. And the three magi, who were actually some sort of bizarre magicians or sorcerers, become three kings.

And then, of course, we have our Christmas trees with their shining lights, decorations, and ornaments standing there in all their isolated glory reminding us that this time is like no other time. On this night there is no place for sorrow or pain. Grieving and weeping are not welcome. Everything must be neat and clean, shiny and new. Dirt is definitely out of place.

But if there is anything that Saint Luke's account of that birth in Bethlehem ought to make clear it is that Christmas is just the opposite of what our world and we want to make it. Christmas is about pain. A woman gave birth that night. Christmas is about God in the midst of dirt. That child was born in a barn, not in the clean and pleasant confines of the local inn.

But it is precisely in the debunking and dismantling of our Christmas mythology that we can begin to behold the true wonder and glory of Christmas. There is incredibly good news for us in this dirty Christmas. In this all too ordinary birth in Bethlehem we meet God, not in his terrible and frightening holiness that makes us sinners shake in our shoes but in his loving and merciful holiness, a holiness that is truly unlike anything else in this world. It is in this all too ordinary birth in Bethlehem and not in some stuffy royal court where having one hair out of place makes us feel like fools that God comes to meet us. Who of us would set aside our power and privilege and enter this world in the midst of the dirt and stench of a barn?

We wouldn't do it any more than we would want to become a roach. But God did. And that is the Good News! Why? Because when we find ourselves cold and dirty, when we find ourselves bogged down in the quagmire of a life that has never seemed to fulfill our dreams, when our eyes are filled with tears of pain and disappointment because another year has passed and the problems are still there, all we need to do is look to the dirty birth in Bethlehem. That child *is* Emmanuel. "God *is* with us" right smack dab in the midst of the dirt and the pain, to assure us that there is nothing too dirty to separate us from his love. God is with us to love us. And in this child God has chosen to carry all of our sins and grief, all of our dirt and pain, all of our sorrow and tears, all the way to the cross where at last they will be destroyed, once and for all.

So, in the meantime, don't be afraid to have your Christmas be a little dirty. Don't be afraid to let your house get a little messy. And don't be afraid to cry. Don't feel you have to hide your hurt and pain. Don't think that you have to pretend that everything is perfect when you know it isn't. That isn't real life. Real life is dirty. But because of that first dirty Christmas, there is still a reason to smile, to brush aside the tears, and sing a Christmas carol. For when we remember that the baby was born in a smelly, dirty barn in Bethlehem, we know that our God isn't going to let real life and a little dirt get in the way of his loving us.

And by the way, when you go home to sit under your Christmas tree in all of its glory, remember the dirt. You might even want to put a pail of dirt under your tree to remind yourself why that Christmas tree is so gloriously decorated at all.

Christmas 1
1 Samuel 2:18-20, 26

The Making Of A Holy Family

How many times have your heard people say at this time of the year, "Christmas is about family. Christmas is for children"? Even though as Christians we know that this is not the case, we are not surprised that some people in our society talk this way, given the fact that children are the center of family life the year round. That is especially the case in a suburban community like Zionsville. So much of life here revolves around family and children. Families move here because of the good schools for their children. That demand in turn drives up the prices of real estate, increases the cost of living, and puts more stress on families. I continually hear parents complain about how frantic their schedules are as they try to provide every opportunity and privilege for their children.

Our congregation a few years ago purchased an in-depth sociological study of the Zionsville community. It was filled with all kinds of statistics revealing not only the usual demograhic statistics of the community, but also the residents' attitudes and values. The study revealed that one of the major needs of the community was good financial planning, because the parents wanted the financial security to provide for the needs, especially the educational needs, of their children.

When one takes a look at the whole of American society and not just suburbia, one gets the impression that in this country parents will do almost anything to make their children happy and successful.

Today's First Lesson calls our attention to a family that had an outlook on life that was very different from what we find in America at the beginning of the twenty-first century. Here we meet the family of Elkanah and his wife Hannah and their son Samuel. Perhaps you remember the story from your days in Sunday school. Elkanah and Hannah had been married for many years but were unable to have children. The couple prayed fervently to God to give them a child. They were so desperate that they promised to give their child back to God, to "lend" him to the Lord, instead of keeping and raising him in their own home, if God would give them a child. Eventually they were blessed with the birth of a son. They named him Samuel. When he was three, they took him to the temple and gave him to the priests to be trained for a life of service there.

Today's First Lesson recounts Hannah making her yearly visit to the temple to give her son the gift of a little robe she had made for him. It is a very simple and tender picture of a mother expressing her love for her son. But to our modern eyes the tenderness of this picture begins to fade when we realize that this yearly visit would never have even been necessary if Hannah had not already taken the drastic action of giving her son away. Contrary to our world, where our children are constantly worshiped and adored, here we see a parent whose focus was not on pampering her son but on worshiping God. Hannah's willingness to give her son to the Lord and only to be able to visit him occasionally in the temple is stunning when compared to how parents treat their children today.

It used to be that parents were proud when their son or daughter entered a religious vocation. In the Roman Catholic Church, it was a source of pride when a daughter became a nun or a son a priest. Even in Protestant families it used to be considered a great honor if a son would go into the ministry. I left home at the age of thirteen to go to a boarding school where young men had already made the decision to enter the ministry. Parents were honored when their sons showed such interest in a religious vocation. But the world has changed dramatically. Today I often hear of parents who are "disappointed" when a son or daughter gives up the opportunity for a successful career to enter the ministry. They fear that their son or daughter has become some sort of religious fanatic foolishly giving up fame and fortune for a life of service.

But this story is even more disturbing. In the past in this country when a young person chose "a religious life," it was assumed that he/she had at least some say in this vocational decision. No one dared to make the decision for them. But here Hannah makes the decision for her son. He is too young to be consulted. No one asked this three-year-old what he felt about this. If a parent were to do this today, you can just imagine some social worker screaming, "Child abuse!" The television cameras from *60 Minutes* would show up looking to do a segment on this weird religious cult. The neighbors would call the police, all too willing to turn these abusive parents in to the authorities.

A story like this reveals that the gap between the world of the Bible and ours is huge. It doesn't even fit into our worldview. The scriptures report this story without flinching. They don't so much as bat an eye. From the scripture's point of view this is not a story about child abuse but about faithful religious commitment and a mother's love for her son.

Why was this strange reading from 1 Samuel ever chosen for today? One reason is obvious. The life of young Samuel seems to parallel the life of young Jesus in several ways. Similar phrases are used to describe each. Both grew in stature and in favor with God and the people. Hannah's song of praise upon the occasion of Samuel's birth seems to be similar to Anna's song of praise that she sang to the infant Jesus when he was brought to the temple for his presentation. And Hannah's song expresses many of the same sentiments and images used in Mary's great song, The Magnificat, which she sang after finding out from the angel Gabriel that she was about to give birth to a most miraculous child.

But there is also a big difference between these two families and how their family life is reported by the scriptures. The decision of Elkanah and Hannah to "lend" their son Samuel to God goes smoothly. There is no family conflict. Samuel grows in stature and favor and seems to have no disagreement with his parents about his life of service in the temple. Hannah's annual visits to carry to Samuel the little robe she had made for him are portrayed as the tender episodes of a harmonious and wholesome family life. But we do not see that same harmonious picture in today's Gospel.

There we see a family in conflict. There we see a collision between Jesus' emerging sense of vocation and his parents' expectations of how a twelve-year-old ought to behave.

This conflict is similar to the struggle that every parent has with his/her children. It is sometimes hard to accept when you consider all the blood, sweat, toil, and tears that go into parenting, all the sleepless nights up with sick kids, the changing of soiled diapers, the sacrifices of time, money, and energy all because "we want the best for our kids." We do all these things for our children so that they can leave us. Such is the irony of parenting. Good parenting means that you have done a good job in preparing your children to need you no longer and to leave home and establish their own lives. It is not always easy for parents to let go after investing so much in their children.

Is that at the root of this conflict in today's Gospel? I suppose some of those dynamics may have been present, but there is a much bigger conflict going on here. This is not just about the collision of wills. This is not just another chapter in the continuing saga of every family, where the desires of controlling parents collide with a budding teenager's first attempts at independence. The conflict here is much greater. This conflict is ultimately cosmic. In this little family we catch a glimpse of what will one day a be conflict for the salvation of the world.

Luke's picture of the Holy Family makes it clear that this family is the ideal Jewish family. From the beginning of Jesus' life, all the Jewish traditions of presentation and circumcision were carefully observed. Now at the age of twelve, Jesus is taken to Jerusalem for what may have been his bar mitzvah. We are given the impression that this was not the first Passover that this family went to Jerusalem to observe. The bottom line is clear. Jesus was a "kosher Jew." He was brought up to honor and observe the Jewish law. His parents were making it clear to him that they loved and honored the law and expected Jesus to do the same.

Therefore, when Jesus willfully chose to separate himself from his parents, he wasn't just being a rebellious teenager asserting his independence. He was thumbing his nose at the Jewish tradition. He was challenging and questioning the value of his "kosher" identity and the very importance of everything his parents had taught him. When Jesus defied this kind of life defined by Jewish law, he was not just defying his parents and community custom. He was defying God. And worse yet, he defied God in the name of God! What nerve! What audacity! Yet, isn't that what was behind the most important words of today's Gospel, when Jesus said, "Did you not know that I must be in my Father's house?" Or as some of the other translations of this passage put it, "Did you not know that I must be *about my Father's business?*"

This is the only incident from Jesus' youth recorded in the New Testament. It certainly portrays the growing independence of a young Jewish teenager. But on a deeper level it reveals Jesus' growing sense of identity and mission. It is an identity and mission that is sending him in a very different direction. He senses that he is different from other Jewish boys his age. He is critical of his own parents, not just because he is a teen starting to sow his wild oats and beginning to separate from his parents. No, Jesus senses that his "family" is bigger and higher and more significant than his relationship to Joseph and Mary. His "family" and "father" and mission are now so much more important than his ties to his earthly parents. He senses that he is being pulled in another direction and the One pulling him is not only divine but in some sense his very own "Father." And this mission puts him at the same time at odds with God's own law.

Mary and Joseph did not understand the significance of what Jesus was doing and saying. They must have been deeply troubled by Jesus' behavior and especially these words about his "Father's house." Here they had been trying to do their best and be good Jewish parents by keeping all of the laws and traditions, bringing their twelve-year-old son to Jerusalem for Passover, but then they discover that it was not good enough. In fact, they had missed the point altogether. This son of theirs was now claiming to belong to someone else, to another Father and family — God's. How could they dare to disagree with God?

Mary and Joseph must have been feeling the same kind of failure and frustration that parents feel today. Like them, we love our children. We try to do what is best for them. But then we feel guilty when our schedules are so full of activities that there is no time to pass on the faith. We try to teach our children right from wrong and the importance of praying and going to church, but then wonder if they have really made it a part of their hearts or whether they are just "going through the motions." And then when they behave so badly or disappoint us in some other way, we wonder if we have totally failed.

Passing on the Christian faith is the most important gift we can give our children. Recently I reminded two couples who had their children baptized that this was the most important responsibility in their already huge job of parenting. There is no greater gift to give their children than the gift of Christian faith. In the Baptismal liturgy they would be asked to promise to do that. And then we, the rest of congregation, would pray for them. Why? Because the job is so difficult that they are going to need our prayers. And most of all they will need God's mercy because of the mistakes and failures they are sure to make.

The baptismal parents are always rather stunned and surprised when I point this out to them. Baptism is supposed to be a joyful and upbeat occasion. This is a time for celebration, but then the liturgy pours water on their party by reminding them of how difficult this business of being a parent will be. In fact, the most important business of all, passing on the faith to their children, will be so difficult that they will need not only our prayers but also God's forgiveness.

In the same way Mary and Joseph must have been stunned and surprised when Jesus "talked back" to them. Here they thought they were doing everything right only to find out that they were wrong. Jesus rebuked them for not knowing that he must be in his "Father's house." Their stunned silence was a tacit admission of their guilt. They had been exposed. It was obvious that they "didn't get it."

But there is another surprise in this story. Despite this act of defiance and Jesus' gentle "rebuke" of his parents, he does return home to Nazareth with them. He is "obedient" to them. Luke says, "Jesus increased in wisdom and in years, and in divine and human favor." It seems that even though there was this one incident of youthful defiance, Jesus still chose to return home compliant and submissive. Why? Could it be that this is one more signal of the meaning of Jesus' birth as the "Immanuel," of God coming to be with us, literally to be one of us? Even though this incident clearly revealed Jesus' growing self-understanding as the "Son of God," being the Son of God did not mean that he fled the dirt and grime of ordinary human life. On the contrary, being the Immanuel, "God with us," meant that he chose to join Mary and Joseph and all the far from perfect parents of this world in the many broken and fractured imperfections of human life, including our sin, and carry them all the way to the cross. In the Gospel of Luke, Jesus will only make one more trip to Jerusalem. On that second trip he will suffer the consequences of his return to Nazareth, of his choice to become one with his parents and us. He will be arrested, crucified, and die.

At the cross Jesus suffered the consequences of his loving choice to join us in our broken humanity. There he suffers the ultimate fate of his holy mission. There he exchanges his holiness and righteousness for our failed attempts at parenting and passing on the faith to our children. Everything that is wrong and broken with our unfulfilled lives he carries to the cross and suffers the fate we deserve. But that is not all there is. "On the third day" he is raised by his Father from the dead, triumphant, mission accomplished. The mission he began to explore that day in the Temple in his "Father's house," at the tender age of twelve, was finally finished. His "Father's business" of forgiving sinners, which would be at the center of his adult life, was vindicated. That day in the Temple when Jesus defied his parents and claimed to be part of something that contradicted not only the law of his people but the law of God reached its climax on Jesus' return trip to Jerusalem. There on the cross and then at the resurrection Jesus fulfills his "Father's business" and his mission, so that the church today can say to disappointed and imperfect parents, "Your sins are forgiven."

It is this divine mercy, it is this exchanging of the forgiveness of sins among family members, that finally makes families "holy." It is the holy love of Jesus that promises to give parents the courage and the strength to carry out their vocation. It is the mercy of the heavenly Father offered "in the name of Jesus" that promises to give families the power to resist the skewed and perverse values of so much of family life today. Perhaps then the example of Hannah in today's First Lesson will no longer seem so strange. Perhaps then parents will be willing to give their children back to God. That may not necessarily mean giving your children to a religious vocation, but it does mean that parents will show their children in their words and actions that trust in the mercy of God is indeed the most important thing in life. Then bringing children to Baptism is a priority and not an afterthought. Then taking time out of the busy daily schedule for Sunday school, confirmation classes, family prayer, and talking about the faith are necessities.

If parenting is raising your children to leave home to live lives of their own, then Christian parenting is also raising your children to leave home. But "leaving home" means learning to trust God and his mercy. "Leaving home" means trusting your Father in heaven more than anything else. "Leaving home" means trusting your heavenly Father in preparation for that day when you will go to your heavenly home forever.

Such parenting is not destructive of family life. If anything it helps the development of a healthy family life where parents and children love and care for one another. It certainly was not destructive of family life for Hannah and Samuel. Hannah still loved Samuel and Samuel still loved his mother. Such love was exchanged in the tender scenes that we see described in today's first reading.

It was not destructive of family life for Mary, Joseph, and Jesus either. It is no accident that the New Testament is totally silent concerning the events of their family life from Jesus' birth until Jesus' adulthood, except for the incident reported in today's Gospel. The New Testament is silent because their family life was so ordinary, so mundane, so down-to-earth, just like the daily routine of our family lives, that it did not warrant any special reporting.

But this silence is important! Why? Because that is exactly the point! It is in the ordinary routines of daily life that families are made holy. It is in ordinary routines of the everyday that the business of our Father gets done. It is there just like in the families of Jesus and Hannah before us, that people are loved, cared for, and forgiven. It might seem too ordinary, so unspectacular, but it is at the heart of a holy family.

Never Just Words

"Sticks and stones may hurt my bones, but words can never harm me."

There has never been a bigger lie that has ever been so widely perpetuated. A friendly playground game erupts into a fight and insults fill the air. One of the combatants defiantly shouts, "Sticks and stones may hurt my bones, but words can never harm me." Even though such words attempt to minimize the harm inflicted by such insults, in fact they reveal just the opposite. These words have wounded him deeply.

Words are never *just words*. Words are immensely powerful. They don't just convey neutral information. They also the have the power to build up and to destroy. They can bestow value and take it away. They can motivate and deflate. One thing is clear. Words are never just words.

Think of the great coaches of the twentieth century, coaches like Vince Lombardi, John Wooden, and Knute Rockne. One skill they all possessed was the ability to use words effectively. They knew that words are never just words. Words rightly used can pack enormous power. They build up. They can tear down. They can motivate players to do great things, virtually to "run through walls" for their coach and their team.

Think of a teacher you admire, a friend you value, a lover you treasure, or a parent you love. I am sure that one of the things that has made them special to you is that they all can use words so well. Their words not only can cut you to the quick, their words can also convey value and meaning to your life. What they say to you "turns on the lights," makes you smile, and helps you realize how special you are. Words are never just words.

As the parent of a daughter who was born profoundly deaf, I have had to struggle in ways that I never anticipated with the importance and power of words. The most important thing that deafness deprives you of is not just words but the language that comes with words. Without words and language it is difficult to understand this world in which we live. Basic information about life remains inaccessible. But even more than conveying information, words help us to build self-understanding and self-awareness. Without words it is difficult to communicate what most of us take for granted: that we are valuable, important, loved by those who care for us. Cut off from a world that they often cannot understand, a world that speaks in words they cannot understand, the deaf often become shy, withdrawn, and reclusive. That is why the development of words and language, even if they are in the "foreign language" of sign, is one of the most urgent educational tasks in raising deaf children.

Words are never just words. They are never just marks on a page, sounds in the air, or graceful gestures on the hands of the deaf. They are essential to the creation of human community. They help us to understand the world around us. They shape the development of our personality. They are essential to the development of our self-worth. They are part of what makes us human.

Words are also very important to the life of the church. Words are not just important because the church is a social gathering in which people communicate and try to understand each other. That could be said of any human organization or club. Words are not just important because we read a book filled with words called the Bible almost every time we gather. Every organization has its sacred texts and organizational documents. In the case of the church, words are of the very essence of our existence.

For Lutherans the Augsburg Confession Article 5 reminds us that the church is the creation of words, in fact, a very special kind of word, God's word. It says that church is where the Gospel is purely proclaimed and taught and where the sacraments are rightly administered in ways that are consistent with the Gospel.

The implications of this definition of the church are significant. It reminds us of what is necessary to the nature of the church and what is peripheral. The church is not a building. It is not just another club or an association of like-minded people. The church is not defined by a constitution, by-laws, a style of worship, quality of music, or ethnic tradition. Rather, the church is an "event" that "happens" in the midst of people, when a certain kind of word is "spoken." When the gospel "happens," there is the Christian church. When the sacraments are administered in such a way that this gospel is reinforced, there is the Christian church. Regardless of the denominational label on the door or in the constitution, there is only one church. That church happens when this special word called "the gospel" is rightly proclaimed, taught, shared, acted out, administered, or however it might "happen" in the midst of people. In the church, words are never just words. Words and particularly "the Word" of the gospel are the very life-blood of the church and without which it is no longer the Christian church.

But the word that creates the church is a very special kind of word. It is called the "Gospel," which means "Good News." This kind of word is "good news" as opposed to other kinds of words that are "bad news." For some denominations this distinction between the "bad news" and the "good news" is essential to the distinction that is at the heart of how we understand God and God's relationship to the world. That distinction is the distinction between Law and Gospel.

God relates to the world in two distinct and very different ways: through Law and Gospel. When God speaks, it is in either Law or Gospel. From the biblical point of view and especially from the point of view of the Old Testament, God's "word" is not just spoken language but God's acting in the world. In the Hebrew language the word for "word" and "action" is identical. Therefore God's word is also God's action in the world. When God speaks, God also acts. That action is either Law or Gospel.

The Law is the way God runs the world. The world knows all about the Law. Through the Law, God governs and protects. Through the Law, God rewards goodness and punishes evil. The Law is always conditional. "If" you do such and such, "then" such

71

and such will be your reward. "If" you eat your spinach, "then" you get dessert. "If" you study hard, "then" your grade will improve. "If" you eat too many fatty foods, "then" you will get heart disease. "If" your company does not make a profit, "then" you go out of business. The law always "challenges" and "accuses." We never are able to satisfy its demands. Ultimately through the Law, God exposes our sin, reveals that we are never able to please him and that we are under his judgment and sentenced to die. The Law either drives us to despair or turns us into hypocrites pretending that we can live up to its demands. Therefore, ultimately the Law is always "bad news."

But this is not the only word of God. It is also not God's last word. The "other" word of God is the Gospel, "Good News." It is "good news" because in it God unconditionally, without strings attached, offers us his grace and mercy. Instead of conditions, instead of declaring "if ... then," it declares unilaterally "because ... therefore." "Because I love you, therefore you are the apple of my eye." "Because of Jesus' death and resurrection, therefore your sins are forgiven." The Gospel is Good News because it offers us a gift we do not deserve. It never accuses but always comforts. The Gospel like the Law calls for change, but the change is always a "get to" and never a "gotta." The Law demands our works. The Gospel offers us a gift, invites us to have "faith" in that gift, and promises through that gift to change our lives. The Christian faith believes that the Gospel is God's "last word" to us. Where the Law "hides" God's true nature, the Gospel "reveals" God's true nature which is love.

Today's First Lesson from the book of Jeremiah is pure, unadulterated Gospel! In so many ways it seems so out of character for Jeremiah. So much of the book of Jeremiah is filled with the Law, with Jeremiah's rants and raves, his anger and judgment against the sin of Israel. Much of the book of Jeremiah is directed at Israel as it expresses God's anger and disappointment with their immoral lives, their idolatry, their unfaithfulness to the covenant, and their infatuation with the ways of the world. But this section of the prophet is so very different. It comes from a small section of the book that scholars have named "The Book of Consolation." In these chapters the mood and message of Jeremiah dramatically change. The rants and raves become the promises and offers of God's grace and mercy.

Our text from Jeremiah is filled with one image after another each portraying the abundant grace and mercy of God. The prophet announces that it is time for the people to rejoice and sing aloud their praises to God. Why? Because God is going to be doing some wonderful things for them. The prophet piles up one image after another, all of which are intended to portray his love for them. God is the shepherd who will gather his scattered flock, the people of Israel. Their weeping will turn to joy because in the midst of their desert-like lives, he will bring them to water. Their lives will be blessed with plenty and abundance. Their father will reclaim them. They will enjoy all the rights and privileges of being the firstborn child. And when these promises are fulfilled, the people will get down, party, sing, dance, and celebrate like they have never done before. In that day their lives will at last be full and satisfied. There will be no more longing for something better. Talk about the Gospel? Talk about the "Good News"? This is it!

But what is especially shocking are the circumstances under which these words were first spoken. Jeremiah is daring to make these incredible claims about God and the future of Israel at a time when such words and sentiments seemed absurd. These words were probably spoken at the time when the nation lay in rubble. The Babylonians had swept into Judah and Jerusalem, burned the city, destroyed the Temple, and carried off the king and the key leaders into exile. The nation was devastated. In the eyes of the world, she was an ugly duckling, a puny upstart nation that had been properly put in its place by one of the truly great nations of the ancient world. Nevertheless, even though Israel had deserved this fate, God still loves her. Even though there was no merit or worthiness in her, God cannot turn his back on her. Even more, God promises to treat her with all the extravagant generosity and love he can muster.

This is the kind of love that the world has such a difficult time understanding, let alone appreciating. This is the kind of love that the world finds so difficult to express. The love that God has for this world and for his people is love that has no agenda. There are no ulterior motives. There are no strings attached. Contrary to the love of this world, love that loves only the lovable, this love loves the unlovable. Even more, the beloved becomes lovable because of the love of the lover. It is the decision of the lover to love the beloved that makes the beloved lovable. Israel was the ugly duckling, in ruins, destroyed, exiled, and broken. There was nothing attractive about her. And what made her plight even more devastating was that she had brought this fate upon herself. She had thumbed her nose at God. Look where it got her. Nevertheless, God chooses to love her simply because he wants to. Unlike the loves of this world where "I'll love you if you love me" or "I love you because of what you do for me," God's love embraced Israel even at the darkest moment in her history, even when she was most unlovable.

Of course, there have always been those who are utterly cynical about the possibility of such love. The philosopher Ayn Rand, writing some fifty years ago, attacked the whole notion of love. For her there was no such thing as selfless, altruistic love. All love has a vested interest. We love because it interests, benefits, and satisfies us. Everything we do in life is meant to benefit our self-interest. I think in many ways Ayn Rand was right. So much in life that pretends to be genuine selflessness is in fact self-interest disguised as love. People can be charitable but only when the lights and cameras are there to capture their generosity for the paparazzi and a tax deduction is available to lessen the IRS's take. People feed the hunger and house the homeless, but always want to make sure that they get credit for it. So much for selflessness! The real driving force is "What's in it for me?" Ayn Rand was right, *except* when you come face to face with texts like today's First Lesson. This kind of love wouldn't show up on her radar screen. She would find this kind of talk unintelligible. This love is like no other. There is no agenda, no self-interest, no "what's in it for me?" This is the love that can only come from God!

This is Good News! This is the Gospel! This is the good word that is at the heart of the Bible from beginning to end. This is the word that we see God speaking in the pages of scripture and in the lives of all those people who fill its pages. From Abraham, Isaac, and Jacob to Moses, David, and the prophets, we see God's word shaping people's lives, rescuing them from their own follies, delivering them from the hands of their enemies, not because they deserve it but because God chooses to love them. The word of God is never just words. It is never just marks on a page or sounds falling from human lips. It is God in action, choosing to love and save a world that is in big trouble.

We are currently in the midst of the season of Christmas, that season of the church year that is filled with an acute sense of fulfillment. The hopes and dreams of all the years have come to fulfillment in the birth of Christ. Today's Gospel from the opening prologue of the Gospel of Saint John announces that the Word of God has come among us. The Word that was there at the beginning of the creation of the world, the Word that sustained the people of Israel through the centuries, the Word that revealed his loving heart repeatedly to his chosen people, has at last become one of us. "And the Word became flesh and lived among us, and we have seen his glory, the glory as of a father's only son, full of grace and truth" (John 1:14).

Through this Word, God continues to do the unthinkable. God continues to love the unlovable. That is the message of this season of Christmas. That is the message of the life of Jesus. That is the message which is at the heart of the mission of the church. As we listen to the words of Jesus and see how he behaves and what happens to him, we see the Word of God in action. We see Jesus, the Word of God made flesh, transform the lives of people. We see that words are never just words that are weak and powerless but are the very means by which Jesus changes the world. The people that the world had discarded as ugly and worthless, the blind, the deaf, the diseased, Jesus treats differently. Jesus speaks and his word heals. People who were social outcasts, people like Zacchaeus, that little tax collector from Jericho who sat in a sycamore tree, people who were despised and rejected by the religious and social establishment, Jesus welcomed and took out to dinner. The twelve disciples were an unimpressive bunch of fisherman, tax collectors, and uneducated working folk. Nevertheless, Jesus calls them to be his disciples, no questions asked. There are no try-outs to endure, entrance exams to be taken or obstacle courses to be overcome. Jesus simply decides that he wants them. It is simply a unilateral action. His love for the unlovable makes them the beloved. From Jeremiah to Jesus it has always been this way with the word of God, making something out of nothing, proving that words, especially this "Word made flesh," are never just words.

That same incredible word takes shape in our lives. As Saint Francis once said, "Preach the gospel always, use words if necessary."

Married for over a half of century, a husband tenderly cares for his wife. Afflicted with Parkinson's disease she trembles, drools, mumbles, and needs her diapers changed several times a day. But he loves her and tells her that she is beautiful. She smiles and cries.

A teenager has come home from school in tears, rejected by her friends or those whom she thought were her friends. Though she is depressed and bedraggled, her mother hugs her, wipes away her tears, and tells her that she is the apple of her eye. The tears dry and a smile brightens the once darkened and saddened face.

It is another round in the endless rounds of debate and anger that seem to be destroying this marriage. And then she hears from him words she can't ever remember hearing from him. "I'm sorry. Forgive me." And the angry debate melts into a forgiving embrace.

Words are never just words. Words filled with the love of Christ can transform the world.

On this table are bread and wine, just ordinary bread and wine. There is nothing special or supernatural about them. But once these words are spoken, "This is my body ... This is my blood ..." everything is changed. Suddenly these words together with this bread and wine have the power to heal broken hearts and mend torn lives. These words are never just words.

In the font is water, just ordinary water, the same kind of water that comes out of your faucet in the kitchen sink or the spigot in the backyard. There is nothing special or supernatural about it. But once these words are spoken, "In the name of the Father, the Son and the Holy Spirit," everything is changed. Suddenly these words together with this water have the power to give a new life, a fresh start, and an opportunity to be born again. These words are never just words.

Ordinary people are gathered here in this place this morning. There is nothing special about us. We all have our skeletons in the closet. We all have our fears and worries. None of us sports wings and haloes. But once these words are spoken, "The peace of the Lord be with you ... and also with you," Jesus is among us. The hands we have shaken and the bodies we have embraced are not just ordinary flesh and blood but the flesh and blood of God. Sins have been forgiven. Love has been bestowed. The unlovable have become the beloved. These words are never just words.

When those Israelites first heard Jeremiah utter the words of today's First Lesson, they must have thought he was crazy. Broken, disgraced, humiliated, and carried off into exile in Babylon, they had hit rock bottom. They were sure that they were the ugliest of the ugly ducklings. But these words were never just words. They packed power. They were comfort and consolation. They sustained them through forty years of suffering in Babylon and for centuries beyond. They brought them joy in the midst of sadness. And one day that same "Word became flesh and lived among us" in the birth, life, death, and resurrection of Jesus. The good news is that this Word continues to be among us in the mission and ministry of this congregation and Christ's church everywhere. That Word is never just another harmless puff of hot air. That Word is the presence of the living God who is here to speak new life into our bedraggled lives.

Jeremiah believed that the day was coming when this Word would finally make all things right for his people. And when that day arrived, it would be a moment of joy, a time for dancing and singing and feasting and celebrating. That day is now here. Jesus, the Word made flesh, is alive and among us. Let us rejoice and sing. Let us dance and celebrate. It is time to do what the prophet said would happen every time this word is proclaimed and believed. I invite you to rise and join me in the party as we sing these words of the prophet Jeremiah from today's First Lesson in the words of the joyful canticle, "Listen! You Nations." As we sing these words, remember that words, these words, the words of the Gospel, are never just words but the very presence of the living, breathing, loving, almighty God. They can change everything!

Don't Forget Your Nametag!

I'm glad to see that so many of you are wearing your nametags this morning. We have been struggling for some time to get you to wear them and it seems as though our latest solution is working. Putting the nametag table right next to the greeters so that you can't miss them as you walk into the church seems to do the job. Having everyone wear nametags is important to us because at Christ Church we don't want people to feel anonymous, disconnected, alone. In this church relationships matter. Relationships are at the heart of what we are about. It is through relationships with other people that we not only get connected to other people but also get connected to God.

It is difficult to have a meaningful relationship of any kind with another person without knowing his/her name. A name is a "handle" by which we can get another's attention. When someone knows our name, he or she has a "handle" by which to single us out and grab our attention. Therefore, *don't forget your nametag!*

But at Christ Church we also want relationships to move past the nametag level. And to help make that happen we have become a Christ Care Small Group Ministry congregation. Last spring four of us went off to St. Louis to be trained as Christ Care Equippers in order to come back and implement the ministry. We have just finished training our first class of Christ Care Small Group leaders. Today we are commissioning them as they finally begin their small groups. They are looking for you to sign your name to one of the small groups listed today at the sign-up table in the narthex. Christ

Church has invested a lot of time, money, and energy in this ministry because people matter. We don't want anyone here to feel alone or disconnected. We want people to know that we not only know their name but care about them as well. And a small group is a great place for that to happen.

We all know that you don't have to be on a desert island to feel alone. Sometimes being in a large crowd, even in the midst of thousands of people, can be a terribly lonely place. You know what it feels like. You are attending a large athletic contest. Thousands of people are around you. You don't know anyone. You feel terribly alone and isolated. But then someone comes up behind you and taps you on the shoulder and calls out your name. You turn and recognize the face of a long lost friend. And suddenly you are no longer alone. You belong!

You have just moved to a new town. There are neighbors all around you. But you don't know anyone. You don't even know the neighbors living on your street. You feel terribly alone. You might as well be on a desert island. But then you hear that knock at the door. As you open the door, standing there is a strange lady holding a plate of freshly baked cookies. "Hello, my name is Patty. I'm your neighbor from across the street. Welcome to the neighborhood. And what is your name?" And you exchange names. Suddenly strangers are on their way to becoming neighbors and maybe even friends. And it all started because people were willing to share their names.

Perhaps some of you have seen Tom Hanks in the popular film of a couple of years ago titled *Castaway*. Tom Hanks is a Fed Ex manager who is the only survivor of a plane crash in a distant part of the Pacific Ocean. He is washed up on the beach of an uninhabited island. After wandering around the island for a few days and discovering that he is the only person on that island, you can just see and feel the fear and panic overcome him. Will he be forgotten? Will no one ever find him? Will his fiancé and friends forget he ever existed? In order to keep his sanity and humanity he creates a relationship, a friendship, with a volleyball. And in order to have this relationship, he has to give the volleyball a name. He calls it "Wilson," because it was a Wilson volleyball. The name is important because it gives him a "handle," a way to have a relationship with this inanimate object. He needed this relationship with "Wilson" in order to maintain his humanity and his sanity.

This is not all that unlike the situation of today's First Lesson. It was the sixth century B.C.E. Israel was in exile. They had lost everything. Everything that her name stood for was gone. There was no Temple, no king, no holy city. There was no more sacred soil to call her own. She had been carried off to a distant land for the expressed purpose that she be forgotten. And without a name by which to be remembered, she would have ceased to exist. In this historical situation, the words of the prophet are incredibly bold and daring. Claiming to speak for God, it was as if he was saying to them, *"Don't forget your nametag!"*

He tells them to remember who they are. God has not forgotten them. God still remembers who they are. God still remembers their name. "I have called you by name; you are mine!" The prophet reminds them that God has created them, formed them, and redeemed them. The words he uses would have meant much to sixth century Israelites. These words would have reminded them what God has done for them in the *past*. He was the God who had chosen them as he chose Abraham. He was the God who had redeemed them from bondage in Egypt. He was going to do it again. In fact, God was doing the same thing for them right *now* in the present. The great Persian King Cyrus at that moment was conquering Babylon and bringing the Babylonian Empire to its knees. Egypt, Ethiopia, and Seba were at that moment being conquered by Persia. God was using these conquered nations to ransom his people from exile. God was using this foreign king, this "chosen one," Cyrus, to set his people free. Cyrus would shortly allow the exiled Israelites to return to their homeland.

Finally, the prophet reminds the people what God *will* do in the *future*. In that day God will once again gather together all his people from the four corners of the world and reunite them as one people. No watery flood or burning desert would prevent God from gathering together his people.

Given the circumstances, this is truly a startling promise.

81

A similar promise is offered in today's Gospel, Luke's account of the Baptism of Jesus. As God reminded the Israelites in exile that "I have called you by name. You are mine," he does the same here to Jesus. "You are my Son, the beloved; with you I am well pleased." Jesus was beginning his pubic ministry. He was beginning his long walk to Jerusalem and the deadly fate that awaited him. In the face of all kinds of opposition, Jesus' ministry would be marked by this message: "The Kingdom of God is here. Repent and believe the good news." This would be no small task. As Jesus soon discovered after his baptism, there would be a constant temptation to abandon this task. So, here at the beginning God reminds Jesus of his identity. He has a name. He is the Son of God. Jesus, don't forget you who are. Don't forget your nametag! Remembering who and whose you are will give you the strength to complete your mission.

Jesus' baptism is a picture of our baptism. Even though at our baptism the clouds didn't open, a dove didn't descend, and we heard no voice booming from the heavens, the same promise was given to us. When the water was poured and those words were spoken, "I baptize you in the name of the Father, the Son and the Holy Spirit," it was as if we were there with sixth century Israel when the prophet on behalf of God proclaims, "I have called you by name. You are mine." It was as if we were there in the Jordan River with the Baptist and the heavens opened and the voice said of us, "You are my beloved sons and daughters; with you I am well pleased."

On that day we received a new name, a name that can define our identity forever. But Baptism is more than a name-giving rite. Baptism is more than the dedication of a child to God and naming him/her John or Mary. Baptism is God giving us a new name. From now on we will be known as Christs, Christ-ians, the chosen ones, sons and daughters of God, princes and princesses. From now on God is our Father, Jesus is our brother, and all the Christians on earth and in eternity are our family.

Even more, because we have been named after Jesus, we can now make the sign of the cross on our breast and forehead to remind ourselves of who we are. We can always be sure where our lives are headed. Because of this Baptism and the granting of this new name, this new identity, Jesus' fate and destiny are now also ours. We can live our lives giving ourselves away as he did. And when we breathe our last, we will not be dying alone. We will die "with him" and therefore will be raised "with him."

No one or no thing can take this name from us. This promise defines who we are forever. When the prophet encourages those sixth century exiles by chanting, "Fear not ... I have called you by name; you are mine," we are also included. "Fear not," people of Christ Church. We have nothing to be afraid of. God will never forget who we are.

So, when we leave this place and go back out into the world, don't forget your nametag! I'm not talking about that piece of paper stuck to your clothes with your name on it. I am talking about the name you received at your Baptism. And because of that name, it is no longer going back to business as usual. Everything now has changed.

I hate shopping for a new car. I remember a couple of years ago, when I was shopping for my last car and how uptight I was. I remember walking into that car dealership looking for a late model used car. And there he was, just as I feared: the ever present used car salesman who ran up to me, enthusiastically offering me a handshake, making sure I would not elude his presence and said, "Hello, my name is _____! And who are you?"

Instinctively, I recoiled. I didn't want to give him my name. I wanted the comfort of anonymity. I wanted to stay in control. To give him my name meant I would be giving up some control in this potential transaction. I wasn't about to do that. I hesitated. I hemmed and hawed. My wife finally jabbed me in the ribs, chiding me for being so rude. And I told him who I was.

My real problem was that I was afraid. I was afraid that, if I gave him my name, I would lose control. I was afraid that if I lost control, then I might not get the best deal. I was afraid of being taken advantage of, and of coming in second in this game of one-up-manship, of who can get the best of the other. I wanted to be a winner, but if I didn't give him my name, this negotiation was dead in the water even before it started. If you aren't willing to share yourself, if you aren't willing to give your name, you will finally be a very lonely person. You not only will not be able to buy a car, you will never be able to get along with others in this world. You will be a very lonely person. You might as well live on a desert island.

But we know who we are! We are Christ's. God has called us by name. We are his. We can never lose that name to anyone or anything. God himself stands behind us. Regardless of winning or losing, regardless of whether we get the best deal or not, we will always be the apple of his eye. Therefore we can afford to offer ourselves to others. We can give our names. We can dare to care. We can dare to become weak and vulnerable for the sake of someone else. We can, how else can you say it — love!

Isn't that what love is? Putting aside our own interests for the sake of someone else? We can dare to do that now. We can dare to take the risks of service. We can dare to go against the grain, to do what is right and not necessarily what is popular. We can dare to introduce ourselves to others, even to strangers, even to those whose language or culture or skin color is different from ours, even to used-car salesman, without fear or worry. Why? Because we know who we are; because *we remember our nametag!*

Love For Herbert And Dorothy

The miracle that Jesus performed at the wedding at Cana in today's Gospel is recalled in the prayer that begins the Rite of Marriage in the *Lutheran Book of Worship*:

> *Eternal God, our creator and redeemer, as you glad-*
> *dened the wedding at Cana in Galilee by the presence*
> *of your Son, so by his presence now bring your joy to*
> *this wedding. Look in favor upon _____ and*
> *_____ and grant that they, rejoicing in all your*
> *gifts, may at length celebrate with Christ the marriage*
> *feast which has no end. Amen.*

Some might say that we start the Rite of Marriage with a prayer referring to a place where Jesus performed a miracle because Jesus needs to perform another miracle, if this marriage is to survive in this day and age. The institution of marriage is not having an easy time of it in our society today. The divorce statistics are depressing. One in every two marriages ends in divorce. People are so suspicious of entering into marriage that they have their lawyers draft "prenuptial agreements" to safeguard their financial interests. Many couples choose to live together without the benefit of marriage in various kinds of "trial" arrangements because they are afraid to make the commitment. Even when marriages survive, few of them seen to thrive. Many fall far short of the dreams and expectations with which they began.

Let me tell you the story of Herbert and Dorothy. They resemble one of those typical couples of middle-class, suburban America pursuing the American Dream in their typical suburban home with two cars in the garage, two kids in hand, the latest electronic gadgets in the house, and lots of debt. They feel blessed and wouldn't think of missing church to thank God for their blessings. But as is always the case, things are not what they appear to be.

There they are sitting in church, close to the front, all dressed in their Sunday best. Dorothy wouldn't have it any other way. All prim and proper, glancing from one side to another to see who is looking. Dorothy sings the songs with gusto and enthusiasm. In her operatic voice she seems determined to lead the congregation in singing. But the rest of the family is not as enthusiastic. The kids seem to be more interested in fidgeting, poking one another, and coloring their coloring books. And as for Herbert, relieved to have the two kids sitting between him and Dorothy, he seems bored by it all. He dutifully participates in the service, but his voice is barely audible and he lacks enthusiasm. He is doing his duty.

After the service Dorothy seems to know everyone, even their names, greeting everyone with appropriate one-liners. And when they reach the pastor at the sanctuary exit, Dorothy blurts out, "Good morning, Reverend. I loved your sermon. It was so inspiring. Herbert, the kids, and I wouldn't think of missing one of your wonderful sermons. Church is important to our family."

The kids and Herbert almost seem embarrassed by Dorothy's effusive praise. Nervously offering a perfunctory handshake, they can't wait to get out the door, that is, if Dorothy ever decides she has had enough of the latest parish gossip.

Once in the family car, Dorothy can't stop her cackling. That's what Herbert calls it when, with obvious displeasure, he finally interrupts his wife.

"Dorothy, we have all had enough. Please stop your cackling. I frankly don't care about what goes on at church with all your friends. And I certainly don't want to hear about it."

Dorothy was silenced, but only temporarily. In a few minutes her verbal reportage erupted again, but this time it was no longer about the latest events at church but instead about the latest developments in the neighborhood.

"Herbert, did you hear about the new family that moved in that two-story house on the corner? They moved here from Chicago and have two little girls. Did you see that new car they drive? Wow, that is some car! And I hear that they hired a professional designer to decorate the inside of the house. And did you see the way those two little girls dress? Sandy, from down the street told me ..."

Obviously frustrated, Herbert almost shouts, "Dorothy, please be quiet! I don't want to hear about the new neighbors and the latest juicy tidbit from Sandy. I just want to get home to watch the football game."

"But, Herbert, I just want to tell you what's going on. I just want to keep you informed. Herbert, I just want to talk with you. Will you talk to me? Herbert, please talk to me. Herbert, you are my husband. Can't I talk to you?"

But Herbert has nothing to say, hands on the steering wheel, intent on getting home as quickly and as efficiently as possible. Finally he mutters, "I just want to get home. The game starts in five minutes."

When they finally pull into the driveway, the kids scramble out of the car, relieved to escape the obvious tension. Herbert methodically gets out of the car and walks into the garage, when he stops, turns, and with guilt in his voice speaks rather matter of factly, "Dorothy, are you coming?"

"Yes, Herbert, just give me a couple of minutes."

Herbert disappears into the house. Dorothy sits alone in the car, staring into the future, tears beginning to cascade down her cheeks, wondering what went wrong. It wasn't supposed to be this way. She thought she had everything: a house in the suburbs, two beautiful children, and husband. But Herbert never seems to want to talk with her. He never seems to have time to interact with her. His mind and attention are always some place else.

They have been married for fifteen years. She has made a nice home for the family. They hardly miss a Sunday at church. And she always has so many things to tell Herbert. But he never wants to listen. Maybe he will this time. She thinks to herself, "Maybe if

I talk to him about the football game, maybe then Herbert will talk with me."

So, with a new sense of determination, she enters the house calling out, "Herbert, who is playing today? Tell me about it, Herbert. Herbert, who do you think will win? Herbert, do you have a favorite team?"

"Dorothy, please be quiet. I can't hear the play-by-play announcers. This is the biggest game of the season. I don't have time to talk now."

Dorothy and Herbert seemed to have everything. They seemed to be the ideal family. They had all the trappings of the perfect marriage. They even went to church together. But the truth of their marriage was very different from the trappings. The truth of the matter was that, even though they were married, they were living a divorce. The kids knew it. Herbert knew it. Anyone who knew them knew it. Except for Dorothy. She was living in denial. And her endless chattering and filling the air with the white noise of perpetual talk helped her to avoid the long silences that separated her and Herbert, the long silences that betrayed the truth: they were husband and wife in name only. They no longer loved one another. They were going through the motions.

The brutal truth is that Herbert and Dorothy, like so many married couples, struggle to keep up the semblance of a happy marriage but in fact are lonely, desolate, devastated, disappointed, and afraid to admit it. They strive to look good. They make their contrived visits to church on Sundays, pretending to be the happily married couple and the smiling, happy family when in fact they are living a lie.

Because of the disappointing history of so many marriages, because marriage has often been filled with as much disappointment as blessing, it is surprising that it is such a frequently used image to describe the relationship between God and his people in both the Old and New Testaments. In the New Testament, Paul occasionally refers to Jesus as the groom and the church as his bride. In the Old Testament, the prophets often refer to the covenant that God made with the Israelites as the equivalent of a marriage.

88

The image of marriage is also at the center of today's First Lesson. The prophet speaks to Israel in the midst of the crisis of the Babylonian exile in the sixth century B.C.E. The exiles have begun to trickle back from Babylon. When they finally saw the rubble of Jerusalem, they were once again confronted with the brutal reality of their fate. Everything that had been the concrete evidence of their chosen status as the people of God had been destroyed. The city, the Temple, and the monarchy had crumbled into ashes. They had once been proud to be called the Children of Israel. But that was no longer a name of which to be proud. Instead they were derided, ridiculed, and called "Forsaken" and "Desolate." They were the laughingstock of the ancient world. Any pretensions to grandeur now seemed a joke. They were a two-bit bunch of has-beens. They had been pushed all over the landscape of the Middle East, humiliated by the mighty Babylon, and now were free only because another nation, Persia, had crushed Babylon. In order to humiliate the conquered foe Babylon further, Persia decided to let prisoners such as Israel go home.

To add further insult to injury, the prophets insisted that Israel had brought this fate on itself. Israel was not simply the innocent victim. This suffering had been self-inflicted, brought upon them because they had turned their back on the God who loved them. Like Herbert and Dorothy, their marriage was sick, dysfunctional, not just in need of some therapy but of a resurrection. Like Herbert and Dorothy, their future seemed hopeless. Like Herbert and Dorothy, they were powerless to extricate themselves from this predicament.

But the prophet refuses to accept the inevitable. The prophet sees things differently. Contrary to appearances, he will not allow Israel to wallow in self-pity. Israel may feel like the ugly ducking or the girl who will never get a date or be asked to the dance. Just like Herbert and Dorothy, Israel may seem stuck in its quiet desperation. But the prophet is determined to have the last word.

The prophet announces that not only does he see things differently, so does God. Like a handsome, young beau courting his damsel in distress, God does not see an ugly duckling. Instead God sees a beautiful girl, a princess, a lovely maiden, whom he wants to woo, court, romance, wine, and dine. God does not see "Forsaken" or "Desolate." Instead he sees a beautiful woman who needs a new name more fitting her status as the beloved of God. Bursting with enthusiasm, the prophet announces that from now on Israel will be called *Hephzibah*, "My delight is in her," and *Beulah*, "Married." Israel is no longer the abandoned ugly duckling left standing alone at the dance. She is no longer the old maid, forever a spinster. No, she is the star of the ball. She is the love of God's life. She is "married" to the Creator of heaven and earth. She is the Bride of Heaven.

These words of the prophet remind me of one of my daughters' most favorite of the Disney animation films, *Beauty and the Beast*. They love it so much that they own a video of it and never seem to tire of watching it, even now as maturing, young women. At the center of that story is a beautiful young woman by the name of Belle, the fairest young woman in the whole village, and her love for the Prince, who had been turned by a magical spell into a nasty-looking Beast. When she first tells him of her love for him, the Beast can't believe it. All he can say is, "Who? Me?" He can't believe it because he had so long been rejected and despised by others who were horrified by his ugly appearance. But slowly, as the story unfolds, the Beast is transformed by Belle's love for him. He becomes confident, tender, and caring, so unlike the brutal beast he had become. He changes because he believes Belle and the good word she has for him. She thinks he is beautiful. She tells him. He believes her and it changes him.

See, it is true! Beauty is in the eye of the beholder! Belle sees beauty in the Beast. Believing that what she saw in him was true, he was transformed.

The prophet also believes that beauty is in the eye of the beholder. And when the beholder is God, it means everything. When God announces his love for Israel, these are no ordinary words. These words of love have the power to transform Israel. They are the words of a suitor pursuing his bride. They are the words of the lover for the beloved. They are the tender words of courtship as God romantically pursues his people.

The New Testament declares that these tender words of love have come true in Jesus Christ. Christ is the love of God incarnate. Christ is God's word of love with skin on.

90

I don't think that it is insignificant or accidental that the first miracle that Jesus performs in the Gospel of John, the turning of water into wine, *happens at a wedding!* The human experience that most closely reflects God's love for the world in Jesus Christ is marital love.

In the Lutheran marriage rite, when the man and woman exchange vows, they pledge to love each other with no strings attached, unconditionally. There is no mention of conditions or requirements to be met. The man does not say to the woman, "I will love you as long as you are pretty." The woman does not say to the man, "I will love you as long as you keep your weight down." On the contrary, the man and woman promise to love until death parts them, just as the prophet declared God's unconditional love for a people returning from exile. In the same way, in Jesus Christ God loved the world unconditionally, without qualification, all the way to the death of the cross. In Christ God gave himself away and suffered for the sake of the beloved, for you and for me. It is not that we were worth living. It is not that we were attractive, handsome, or beautiful. No, it is God's decision to love us that makes us lovable.

The nature of God's love for the world is so stunning and so unique that the New Testament virtually has to invent a new Greek word to describe this love. Unlike our often pedestrian English language, the Greek language has several different words to describe the various kinds of love which human beings can express. There is *philos*, the love of one friend for another, brotherly love. There is *eros*, the erotic and sexual love that the sexes have for each other. There is *storge*, the love one might have for ice cream or a sirloin steak. But most unique of all there is *agape*, the love of God for the world in Jesus Christ, the love that is so special that this rarely used Greek word for love, *agape*, becomes one of the most important words in the New Testament.

Agape love is unlike any other kind of love. Other kinds of love only love the attractive, the handsome, the beautiful, the pleasing, those that are *worth* loving, and those that *deserve* to be loved. But *agape* love cares for the unlovable and the unattractive, for those who can give you nothing in return, and for those who may

91

even be your enemies. The *agape* lover loves simply because he wants to, simply because he chooses to love another. That and only that makes the other the beloved.

The prophet expresses *agape* love when he announces that God doesn't see his people as "Desolated" or "Forsaken." In spite of all the evidence to the contrary, in spite of their desolate and devastated condition, God still chooses to love them. God still chooses to look at the ragtag and broken Israel and see not "Desolated" or "Forsaken" but Hephzibah, "My delight is in her." *Agape* love no longer sees the defeated and abandoned Israel, the ugly duckling and laughingstock of Middle Eastern nations and declares Beulah, "married." It is *agape* love that looks at the unfaithful, idolatrous, and adulterous Israel that all too often went "whoring after other gods" and sees not an adulterer, who has been humiliated by exile in Babylon, but a lover who is his wife and the delight of his heart.

It is *agape* love that moves God to send his Son to suffer and die for a sinful world, even though it has rebuffed his love time and time again, even though it is utterly unlovable. It is *agape* love that motivates Jesus to embrace sinners relentlessly even though they have played coy and hard to get. It is *agape* love that costs Jesus his life. But on "the third day" Jesus is raised from the dead. His love cannot be buried. His love cannot be thwarted. His love is alive and through the power of his Spirit it continues to seek out those who are sure they are "Forsaken" and "Desolate" and convince them that they are Hephzibah and Beulah.

It is *agape* love that moves God to look at the Herberts and Dorothys of this world, at people like us whose marriages more often than not resemble the lie being lived by Herbert and Dorothy, and still love them. Despite our forsakenness and desolation, despite the fact that we don't deserve one bit of it, God pours out his *agape* love. He looks at us and declares Hephzibah, "My delight is in her (you!)." Even though we are often alone, cut off and isolated, even from those we thought were most dear to us, God's *agape* love won't be thwarted. We are the love of his life. We are Beulah, "Married!"

This changes everything. When we believe that we are Hephzibah and Beulah, we can't help but be different. In *Beauty and the Beast*, Belle's love for the Prince/Beast transformed him from an ugly, brutal thug into a gentle giant, even though his external appearance remained repelling.

Can you imagine what such *agape* would mean for Herbert and Dorothy? Dorothy was miserable in her loneliness and did not have the strength to admit it to anyone or to herself. But what if Dorothy knew that she was not alone, that she would never be abandoned, that she was the "delight" of God? She then might have the strength to admit the truth about her marriage. She then might be able to see Herbert with the same eyes God has seen her. She then might be able to give Herbert the love that he truly needs. Then she might be able to stop talking and truly listen to Herbert. Then Herbert might be able to see that loving and being loved by Dorothy are more important than watching a football game.

Can you imagine what such *agape* love can do for us in our lives? We might be able to see others with the same eyes that Christ has seen us. We might be able to give to others the *agape* we have first received from God. We can look at the rival who threatens us and befriend him. We can look at the friend who betrayed us and forgive him. We can look at the enemy who hurt us and instead of "getting back and getting even," we can declare Hephzibah, "My delight is in you!"

And then just like at the wedding at Cana, miracles can happen. Not only is water turned into wine, but hurts are healed, conflicts are resolved, enemies become friends, and, yes, even the Herberts and Dorothys of this world rediscover their marriage. And going to church on Sunday is no longer an excuse to look good and impress the neighbors. And talking together is no longer an inconvenience or an obligation. Instead such actions are genuine expressions of *agape* love because Herbert and Dorothy have discovered, perhaps for the first time, that there is love for Herbert and Dorothy. It is God's love. And there is no other love quite like it. And God's love makes all the difference in the world. It can help even Herbert and Dorothy learn to love one another again, as husband and wife.

93

The Good News And The Bad News

Have you ever had someone come up to you with a message and then introduces it by saying, "I've got good news and bad news; let me give you the bad news first"? For example, the bad news is that terrorists attacked our country on September 11. The good news is that it has led to a resurgence of patriotism and a healthy sense of civil religion. The bad news is that you have cancer. The good news is that this is an early diagnosis and there is a good prospect for cure. The bad news is that you spent your last dollar on a lottery ticket. The good news is that it is a winning lottery ticket. The bad news is that a snowstorm is coming. The good news is that school has been cancelled. The bad news is that the picnic was rained out. The good news is that the rain has ended the drought and your garden now will thrive.

No one ever wants to hear bad news. No one wants to be a bearer of bad news. But when you know that good news is coming, when you know that your last word will be not bad news but good news, then bad news is so much easier to take.

Today's First Lesson is a good example of just this kind of bad news/good news phenomenon. There is both bad news and good news here. However, it is because of the good news, that the bad news is not just easier to take. No, even more, the good news transforms the bad news into a surprising blessing.

It is approximately 520 B.C.E. and the Israelites are returning from exile in Babylon. They have begun the massive job of rebuilding the walls of Jerusalem. Ezra, an Israelite priest, has been sent by the Persian King Cyrus, who had defeated the Babylonians resulting in Israel's release from captivity, to inspire the Israelites in this undertaking. He intends to do that by teaching them the Torah, the books of Moses including the Sinai Covenant. Today's First Lesson recounts the occasion of its first reading to the Israelites gathered in Jerusalem. You might say that the reading was a kind of pep talk, a half-time locker room oration, intended to encourage and motivate the dispirited Israelites. Ezra reads from the Torah and reminds the people of all the great things God has done for them in the past.

Immediately the people began to weep. Why such sorrow? Why was this such bad news? The reading reminded them that this horrible fate they had suffered in Babylon was self-inflicted. They had brought all this suffering on themselves because they had failed to keep the Torah. That is why God had sent them into exile. They had turned away from God and his ways. The consequences of their disobedience were the destruction of the Temple and the city of Jerusalem, the loss of the monarchy, and forty years in exile. It was bad news to be reminded once again that they had paid dearly for their unfaithfulness. It is no wonder that they wept.

But Ezra also has good news for them. In fact, Ezra encourages them not to mourn and weep but instead to rejoice, feast, party, and celebrate. Why? Because this is a holy day, a special day, a day like no other. And what makes this day so special is that the Torah Ezra read to them not only exposed their failures but also recounted God's mighty acts of deliverance and salvation. The Torah also included the account of God's providential care of Abraham, Isaac, and Jacob. It recounted the sojourn of God's people in Egypt. And most of all it recounted their miraculous deliverance from bondage in Egypt in the Exodus. This is good news because it reminds these troubled Israelites, who surely must have been wondering if God cared for them any more, that God truly is gracious and merciful, slow to anger, abounding in steadfast love and, most of all, keeps his promises. And as sure as they heard Ezra read the Torah before them in Jerusalem, they can be sure God will keep his promises again. "The joy of the Lord is your strength." And that good news makes all the difference in the world. The bad news has been trumped. The good news has the last word. God will save his people. They can count on it.

Here we see in this simple report from the rarely read book of Nehemiah a wonderful truth about the word of God. The word of God is always both good news and bad news. It is always both Gospel and Law. Like those fifth-century Israelites who gathered that day in Jerusalem to hear the words of Ezra, so also we gather in this place every sabbath to hear the word of God. And that word, just as it was for those ancient Israelites, is both good news and bad news. Like a two-edged sword it cuts and heals. It kills and makes alive. It accuses and forgives.

The big temptation is that we skip hearing the bad news. We always want to run to the good news, ignore the bad news, and think that sparing ourselves such pain has got to be an improvement. But such a shortcut is dangerous. We run the risk of missing the true healing power of the good news. It turns the good news into "cheap grace" or a simple "getting off the hook." It is like slapping a bandage on a wound that has never been cleaned. The bacteria have only been covered up and are still free to grow and spread their deadly infection. Such a cover up never faces the truth. It only postpones the dangerous consequences. So also proclaiming only the good news and at the expense of the bad news, pretending it doesn't even exist, only postpones disaster.

Unlike other communities and organizations, when we gather here for weekly worship, we do not avoid the bad news. We face it head on. We relish confronting it face to face. If you have ever been to the meeting of a civic organization or club, to the Rotary, the Boy Scouts, or the annual stockholders meeting, you will notice that they always begin by trying to paint a rosy picture. It is almost seems as if it is forbidden to acknowledge all the mistakes, failures, and disappointments. The dirty underwear is to be kept out of sight. Bad news is to be avoided at all costs. Bad PR! Can you imagine starting the monthly Boy Scout Troup meeting by calling attention to all the scouts who failed to earn merit badges, by citing the mistakes of various patrols, and by pointing out all the scouts who received demerits? This is no way to start a meeting, especially if parents or visitors or prospective members are there. We don't want to air our dirty underwear. We want to put our best foot forward. We want to impress them. This is no time for bad news. Only good news will be tolerated.

But that is not how the church functions. When we began our worship this morning, we started with the Brief Order of Confession and Forgiveness. We started by confessing our sins, our failures, our mistakes, and our crimes. There is no spin. There is no pretending. There are no qualifications. There are no excuses. We have failed.

> *We confess that we are in bondage to sin and cannot free ourselves. We have sinned against you (God) in thought, word and deed, by what we have done and by what we have left undone. We have not loved you with our whole heart; we have not loved our neighbors as ourselves.*

What a way to start a meeting! That hardly seems like the way to impress visitors who have come to check us out. It would seem far wiser to put our best foot forward and show them how good we are. But here we strangely start by listing and acknowledging our failures, our sins. Talk about bad news! Why would anyone want to come to a place that starts its public gatherings like this?

Worse yet, this seems like some crass form of bargaining, like some sort of "let's make a deal" with God, some sort of "tit for tat." Is this wallowing in the bad news the price of admission? Is this something that we "have to" do in order to get God's forgiveness? If so, this is terribly depressing. It seems downright manipulative. It seems to be daringly arrogant to think that we can somehow bribe God into forgiving us by the length or sincerity of our confession.

But that is not at all what the Brief Order of Confession and Forgiveness is about. If anything, it is just the opposite. This recitation of our sins and shortcomings is not a "have to" that we "must" do in order to get something. Rather it is a "get to," something we willingly and joyfully do because of what is already ours. Yes, dare we say it, confessing our sins, airing our dirty underwear, bringing the skeletons out of our closets, is a privilege.

But how can this be? If anything, this seems like bad news. Isn't it terrible, a travesty, downright bad news, that people like us are such rotten sinners? Who in their right mind would ever want to be a part of a group that seems to be so distant from perfection? Who wants to tell the world their problems? Isn't it actually embarrassing that we mess up so badly, when the rest of the world is determined to put its good foot forward? Shouldn't this stuff be covered up?

But this is not what it appears to be. This is not a telling of the bad news *in order to* receive the good news. This is not "let's make a deal." We come to this place not to earn our forgiveness but to be assured of our forgiveness. We come to this place because our sin has put that forgiveness in doubt. Our conscience bothers us. We know that we have done wrong. We feel badly about it. So, we come here to be assured of God's forgiveness. We crave hearing the Good News of the Gospel and hearing once again that our slates are clean. Trusting that it will happen, we willingly tell the truth. We willingly confess our sins. This is not a reward to be earned but a gift to be opened. This is an opportunity to get it off our chest and off our conscience and on to the back of Jesus. We have heard Jesus tells us that he wants to carry our sin for us. The only way that we can do that is to acknowledge it, confess it, and give it to him.

Liturgically, the Brief Order of Confession makes that clear. This is no "let's make a deal." This is no divine bribery. This is a joyful expression of our faith and our freedom. We came here to tell the truth and get the pain and burden of our sin off our back and on the back of Jesus. That is why we make the sign of the cross on our bodies. That is why we invoke the name of the Triune God. This is the name of the God we have come to know in Jesus. This the name of the God who first claimed us and made us his own in our Baptism ("I baptize you in the name of the Father, and of the Son, and of the Holy Spirit"). Now, we have come to this church to hear him speak to us again. And he does. We hear the bad news and the good news. We willingly acknowledge the validity of the bad news (we are sinners!) and joyfully claim the offer of the Good News (our sins are forgiven!).

Isn't that exactly what happened in today's first reading from Nehemiah? The people willingly came to hear Ezra read them the Torah. They knew that the Torah was surely going to bring bad news. It surely was going to expose and accuse them for all their shortcomings. Nevertheless, they got on their knees. They raised their hands.

"Give it to us, Ezra. We are ready. We can't wait to hear the bad news."

And as they heard it, they wept. They mourned. They were sorry and filled with remorse. But there was not only bad news here. There was also good news in the Torah. And after hearing the good news, the good news of God's grace and mercy for his people, Ezra urges them to rejoice and celebrate. Even though they had deserved that terrible suffering of the Exile, they now are freed and forgiven. That was the good news of this day. That was the good news of Torah. Such good news inspired them to do what seemed impossible, to rebuild the walls of Jerusalem and the Temple.

But the joy the people experienced that day in Jerusalem when Ezra read the Torah to them still was incomplete. The walls of Jerusalem and the Temple were eventually rebuilt. Those were wonderful accomplishments and great joys. But life was still far from perfect. During the next 500 years Israel still had to struggle. The nation was never quite able to get out from under the domination of one great world power after another. Their joy was never complete. They never quite seemed to arrive. For every step forward they seemed to take two backward. And to continue moving forward, to continue to be sustained as a people, to continue to keep faith in the face of so many setbacks, Israel gathered to hear again and again God's word, just like that day in Jerusalem when Ezra read it to them. They knew that they needed to hear both the bad news and the good news again and again. They knew that it had to be God's word in all its fullness, both the bad news and the good news. No shortcuts. No abbreviations. No abridged versions. They needed the whole word of God to sustain them.

Today's Gospel recounts another reading of God's word to his people. It had been 500 years since Ezra read the word to the people in Jerusalem. For 500 years God's people had been hearing the good news and the bad news. This time it was the local synagogue in the small town of Nazareth. Hometown boy, Jesus, son of Joseph the carpenter, who had become somewhat of a celebrity, had returned and had been invited to take his turn reading the word and offering a commentary. It was nothing out of the ordinary. All the Jewish men of the synagogue took their turn at this. They were proud of their famous resident and wanted to hear what he had to say. But they were not prepared to hear what Jesus had to say.

Jesus took the scroll and started reading what was probably the appointed reading for the day, a portion of the prophet Isaiah, chapter 61. This passage spoke of the grand and glorious Year of Jubilee, that future time when God was finally going to come and set all things right. In that time God would personally send an anointed, messianic leader to "bring good news to the poor ... proclaim release to the captives and recovery of sight to the blind, to let the oppressed go free, to proclaim the year of the Lord's favor" (vv. 1-2).

It was promises like these that had sustained the Israelites for centuries. At the time of Jesus the Israelites were still waiting. Judaism was filled with all sorts of versions of what it would take to bring about the Year of Jubilee and the coming of the messiah. The Zealots believed that it would happen through the power of the sword and armed rebellion. The Pharisees believed it would happen through the religious reform of the people and the keeping of the Torah. The Essenses had given up on the masses and believed that it would only happen by fleeing to the desert and establishing a pure, monastic community of Torah keepers.

But now Jesus, hometown boy made good but still just one of them, still just the son of Joseph, the carpenter, still just that kid they remember playing in the dusty streets of Nazareth, made a most incredible claim: "Today this scripture has been fulfilled in your hearing" (Luke 4:21). Jesus claimed that the Year of Jubilee, the messianic, age was here *now*! He was the chosen one for whom they had been waiting. He was the one who would finally bring about the liberation and vindication for which they had been thirsting for so long, for at least 500 years, for at least since the days of Ezra, and even long before that. Of course, this was too much for the people of Nazareth. They knew too much about the ordinary kid from their

101

town. This was too much to swallow. This was blasphemy. So they drove him out of town and would have killed him had he not miraculously escaped.

As Jesus' life and ministry unfold in the pages of the New Testament, we see Jesus actually living out these words from the prophet Isaiah. We see him setting free all kinds of people who had been captive to various oppressors. The blind are given sight. The deaf can hear. The lame can walk. The dead are resuscitated. Jesus, the ultimate friend of sinners, embraces those whom the rest of society had shunned and excluded. And most of all, Jesus dares to announce that their sins are forgiven.

Jesus claims to be the ultimate Good News from God. He dares to overrule God's own "bad news" judgment of sinners by welcoming and forgiving them in the name of God. The defenders of the righteous judgment of God were convinced that Jesus was a blasphemer, undermining the integrity of God's expectations of his people. So, in the name of God, they had to put Jesus to death. And they did it on that awesome and awful Friday on a hill outside of Jerusalem. They thought that they had ended this foolishness once and for all. But we know that this wasn't the end of the story. "On the third day," he was raised from the dead. God raised him. God vindicated his claim to be the messiah and to be able to do the things he did.

Jesus suffered on the cross the ultimate bad news for us. He silenced its criticism. He ended its crushing judgment of sinful humanity in his own body. And because of his resurrection, it at last became clear to his followers that what he first claimed that day in the synagogue of Nazareth was true. The Year of Jubilee had arrived. Jesus had saved the world in a way no one had anticipated. God had kept his promises. And most of all, the Good News for which this broken and frustrated world had waited so long had finally arrived. God's love is reliable. God can be trusted. No one or no thing can separate us from that love. The bad news of our sin and guilt has been overcome by the Good News of Jesus' death and resurrection.

Ezra had declared similar good news 500 years before: "The joy of the Lord is your strength." This good news strengthened the

Israelites to rebuild Jerusalem and the Temple. In the same way the Good News of Jesus' resurrection sustained the first Christians in their mission to an often incredulous and hostile world. In spite of the opposition, first from the Jewish community and then from the Gentile world, those first Christians boldly went into the world proclaiming both the Good News and the bad news. It is clear from today's First Lesson that proclaiming this twofold, double-edged, bi-vocal word of God was nothing new. God's word had always functioned this way. Therefore, Christians could dare to tell the bad news because the Good News was even better.

Trusting the Good News of God's love in Jesus Christ, we have nothing to fear. We can dare to tell the truth in ways that the rest of the world is afraid to do. There is no need to lie, cover-up, pretend, deny, or equivocate. The debacle at Enron and the recent collapse of other such huge corporations under the cloud of executive corruption should remind us all that the world is filled with thieves. In fact, we all are thieves. Not one of us has clean hands. Our society is filled with sick and broken marriages. Even the most healthy of relationships has its skeletons in the closet. There is no such thing as a "normal" family because every family is afflicted with its own unique brand of dysfunction. Christ Church, like every Christian congregation that has ever existed, is far from perfect. The bottom line is that we are all sinners. And sinners rightly ought to tremble in the presence of a righteous God.

This is the bad news. But the bad news is not all there is. There is also the Good News of God's love for sinners just like you and me. In fact, it is the sinners, "those who are in need of a physician," to whom God is partial. It is for people just like us with all of our flaws and embarrassments that Jesus came. It is "for us and our salvation" that Jesus lives. And because of that, Ezra was right: "the joy of the Lord is (our) strength."

Empowered by such good news, the sixth-century Israelites were able to do what few thought was possible: confess their sin and then dare to rebuild Jerusalem and the Temple. Empowered by the same good news we can do the same. We can afford to gather here every week and face the bad news head on. There is no need to equivocate, dissemble, or rationalize. We can fess up to our sins without blinking. And we do it because we "want to." We do it because we also know and trust the Good News of God's mercy. And trusting the love of God means that there is no need to do anything else than tell the whole truth and nothing but the truth. And then, buoyed by this truth, we can dare to go out into the world free to tackle head on all the bad news in this world, trusting the Good News that, regardless of our failures or successes, we are always the beloved children of God.

Can you imagine the healing that could happen, can you imagine the pain that people could have been spared, if the people of this world would only honestly face the bad news? Can you imagine all the hurt and devastation that could have been avoided, if the executives of Enron had told the truth about its finances? Can you imagine the suffering that families could have avoided, if someone had only stopped enabling the addict in their midst and forced him to face the truth about his addiction? Can you imagine the marriages that could be saved, if the couples would only end the denial and seek counseling? Can you imagine how much better our country might be, if more citizens would stop being "the silent majority" and start holding their government and politicians accountable? Can you imagine how much better our schools would be, if more parents would actually take time to support their children and their teachers?

Then Jesus' words would start coming true already *now*, just as he declared that day in the synagogue in Nazareth. Then the Year of Jubilee would actually be taking shape among us here in this place and this time. Then the messianic age would be happening among us now. Then that hope uttered by Ezra some 2,500 years ago in the city of Jerusalem would actually be a reality. Then we would be able to testify to the fact that "the joy of the Lord is (our) strength."

Such a life is possible when the word of God is proclaimed among us in all its fullness, both the Good News and the bad news. Because of the Good News we can dare to face the bad news. And because we can face the bad news, when we hear the Good News, the Good News of God's grace and mercy for bumblers like us, it will be the greatest news we have ever heard!

The Cure

"The land of the free and the home of the brave." So ends our national anthem sung today at many large public gatherings in our society. It was originally penned in a time of war and has continually reminded us that this is a nation where people will bravely fight to defend their freedoms. But in this day of post-modern relativism, when there are very few causes left which anyone will bravely defend, "freedom" still remains as the great American ideal. If there is any great ideal worth fighting for, it is our "right to freedom." What that always means isn't clear, except that we all want to be "free" to choose for ourselves. This is the age of choice! We want to be free to choose our friends, whom we will marry, what food we will eat, the cars we drive, our recreations and careers. We may not always get what we choose, but at least we have the right to try.

One of my daughters just returned from Europe, after spending two months of study and travel in Austria. Austria is no third-world country and the standard of living is comfortable. Nevertheless, after two months of being disconnected from America, upon her return she was shocked once again to walk into one of our supermarkets and be overwhelmed with all the "choices" we American consumers have. It took travel abroad to open her eyes to what we have come to accept as a right: freedom of choice!

Freedom of choice has permeated every part of our lives. We live in a consumer society in which we have the right to "choose" what we want. We choose our religion. We choose our style of spirituality. We choose the God we will worship. We choose the church to which we belong. We go "church shopping." In this nation of consumer religion, we "choose" a church by testing its worship services, trying out its programs to see if they meet our needs. If we like what we have discovered, we "sign up." We make a commitment. We "purchase" religious services. We decide to become a disciple. We join a church.

But the Bible has a very different perspective on life and our relationship to God. That is very clear in today's First Lesson. In these opening verses of the book of Jeremiah, the prophet reports to us the account of his "call" to become a prophet. One thing immediately stands out. Jeremiah did not "choose" to become a prophet. Becoming a prophet was not some sort of "career move." On the contrary, it was just the opposite. This "prophet thing" was all God's idea. "The word of the Lord" came to him. This wasn't the result of some personal search for God. Jeremiah doesn't have a "choice" in this matter. God is the one who takes the initiative. God is the one who makes the choice. God is the only one who is truly free here.

Jeremiah's response is all too human. Even though this was a time in history that would find our modern obsession with personal freedom unintelligible, Jeremiah was still human enough to know that he valued his freedom. Had he wanted to be a prophet, he would have signed up. He would have gone to seminary or prophet school. This wasn't his idea. So, all he could do was offer excuses. He was not qualified for this. This job never showed up on his career aptitude test. Besides, he was too young. He was only a boy. He didn't know how to speak well. He did not want to have any part of this "speaking for God" stuff.

But God won't take "No" for an answer! God "put out his hand and touched my mouth." God is in charge here. This is no time for excuses. Even if Jeremiah doesn't think he is qualified for this, it is no problem for God. God will put the words in his mouth. God will tell him what to say. God will help Jeremiah with what Jeremiah thought was impossible. And what God promised happened. Jeremiah's excuse making disappeared. His opposition melted away. And Jeremiah became a prophet, one of the greatest prophets in the history of Israel. And the book, which follows these verses in today's First Lesson, is a testimony to that fact.

But it almost didn't happen. Jeremiah first needed to be changed. He needed to be transformed. He needed to be "cured" of the disease, of that universal human disposition shared by all of us, the need to be in control, the need to believe that we are free to choose. In short, Jeremiah's excuses, rationalizations, and self-justifications needed to be overcome. Jeremiah needed to be set free, to be cured, of his slavery to himself, of his need to be in charge and have the last word. Jeremiah needed to be freed from sin. And, as we see in today's text, God is the only one who can do that. The book that bears the name of Jeremiah is living proof of how God "cured" Jeremiah of his reluctance to trust God and changed this self-conscious young boy into a mighty prophet.

This account of Jeremiah's call and his liberation from his old way of life is also a picture of what God continues to do among us today. Ironically we, too, are enslaved to our freedoms, to our desire to be in control, to our insatiable hunger for self-fulfillment, to our sin. God is the only one who can cure us. And God does that every time his Word is proclaimed, every time the Gospel of Jesus Christ is announced and the sacraments are administered.

To help you see *how* God does this "curing," I want to tell you the story of Martin. Martin was a very sick man. Like Jeremiah before him, Martin was afflicted with a disease. It controlled him. It distorted his view of life and himself. It seemed like an expression of freedom but in reality it prevented him from seeing and admitting the truth about himself. It forced him into always making excuses for himself. Martin was afflicted with the dreaded Yahbuts Disease. But Martin didn't know it. He thought his Yahbut's Disease wasn't a disease at all. On the contrary, he thought it was a natural part of life.

The signs of Martin's Yahbut's Disease began to appear when he was a young boy in grade school. His affliction hardly seemed to be an affliction at all. Instead, it manifested itself as an uncanny ability to wiggle himself out of the most embarrassing situations. It first appeared in these "Yah ... but ..." conversations he had with those around him.

107

"Martin!" his mother shouted. "Did you push this cookie jar over and make this mess on the kitchen floor?"

"Yah," Martin replied, "but someone had just freshly waxed that floor. When I stepped on the chair to reach the cookies, the chair slipped. Yah, I made the mess, but it's the slippery floor's fault and not mine."

"Martin!" his father shouted. "Did you leave the television room in a shambles when you went to bed last night?"

"Yah," Martin answered, "but I was going to clean it and remembered that you told me I had to go to bed at 8:00, and it was just 8:00 when I thought of it. So, I thought I had better get to bed like you said."

Martin had lots of these "Yah ... but" conversations with his parents. Martin always had an answer. Martin always had an excuse. He always found some way to justify himself. It was becoming clear. Martin had Yahbut's Disease!

Martin's teachers also got involved in these "Yah ... but" conversations with him. "Martin, is it true that you don't have your math work done in time?" asked his teacher.

"Yah," Martin replied, "but it's not my fault. You see, my mother made me clean up the cookie crumbs from the kitchen floor and that was just when I was working on my math assignment. If you don't believe me, you can call her and ask!"

It was clear that Martin now had a full-fledged case of Yahbut's Disease. Martin had an excuse for anything and everything. He always had a justification for what he did. And his excuses and justifications were always perfectly logical. Martin was never wrong and always right. Just ask him! The problem was that this never-being-wrong-and-always-being-right got to be an obsession with Martin. It was taking over his life. It would eventually destroy him, if something was not done to cure him of this dreaded disease.

Then, one day Martin bought a new sports car. His friends who knew anything about sports cars were shocked!

"Martin, oh, Martin!" they sighed. "Why did you buy this model? Don't you know, Martin? It's a lemon! Everyone knows that, Martin. Oh, boy, Martin, now you have made a real mistake!"

"Is that all you know about sports cars?" Martin sneered back. "I've read all the magazines on this particular model. This one has got the best rating of all the sports cars. It gets more miles to the gallon. It handles, accelerates, and corners well. It's got more interior room. It's got great resale value. It ..."

Martin stopped for a moment and thought and thought and thought. And then Martin, thoroughly afflicted with Yahbut's Disease, made a regrettable decision.

"Get in," he told his friends. They got in and away Martin sped in his new sports car. Up and down the streets he flew, weaving his way through traffic, squealing around the corners and screeching away from the stop lights like a maniac. Martin was having the time of his life showing off his car and justifying his choice, proving his friends wrong, defending his freedom ... when the familiar wail of a police siren sounded behind him.

"Martin, I'm going to have to ticket you for speeding and reckless driving," the policeman said.

"Yah, Officer, but I was just giving my friends a ride to show them what a great choice I made," Martin politely responded.

"No 'Yah ... buts,' Martin. No excuses. You must appear in court before a judge at 9:00 a.m. Monday morning either to pay your fine or to contest this ticket."

Martin was shattered. He knew that there was only one honest plea he could make. He was guilty! But people afflicted with Yahbut's Disease can't admit their guilt. They can't even say the word. They have got to stay in control. There had to be a way out of this. "Guilty!" The word stuck in his throat. He could never say that word.

Monday morning arrived and Martin, accompanied by his court-appointed defense attorney, was called to appear before the judge. Martin didn't want an attorney. He wanted to defend himself. He was free to defend himself and wanted to show the judge how the officer was wrong and he was right. Why did he need this attorney? Didn't the judge think he was capable of defending himself?

Things got even more confusing when the attorney asked him a question that caught him completely off balance. "Martin, are you guilty? No excuses, just tell me the truth."

Martin seemed baffled by this question, squirmed a little, and then tersely responded, "Yah, I got caught speeding. I was going a little fast, but, you see, I was just showing my friends the new sports car I bought and what a good deal I got and ..."

"Stop it, Martin!" interrupted the attorney. "This is no time for excuses. Face it, Martin. You got caught. You are guilty."

But Martin shot back, "What kind of defense attorney are you? You're supposed to defend me, prove my innocence. You are the strangest defense attorney I've ever met. And now you want me to admit my guilt without even trying to defend me?"

Silence. And then the word Martin didn't want to hear. "Yes," said the attorney.

"This is crazy! I won't do it. I'm no fool."

The attorney spoke softly. "Just trust me. I will defend you, but not like you think I should. No more 'yah ... but's.' No more excuses. Just admit your guilt and trust me to help you."

"No way! Once the judge hears me admit my guilt, I'm doomed. He will surely fine me, maybe even put me in jail. No. I can't do it. I can't risk it."

But the attorney would not be dissuaded. "Martin, you can trust me. Just no more excuses. No more 'yah ... but's.' Just trust me and admit your guilt. I will be able to save you."

Martin was bewildered. "I don't get it. I have never heard of a defense like this one. This is no defense strategy at all! 'Just trust me,' he says. Oh, boy, Mr. Defense Attorney, you must have some very special kind of connections with the judge," sputtered Martin with disbelief.

"I do," said the attorney, not blinking an eye.

"Martin," inquired the judge, "how do you plea? Guilty or not guilty?"

Martin was still unsure. Should he or should he not? Could he really trust the strange strategy of this utterly odd attorney? Could his promise be true?

"Martin, I don't have all day. You are holding up the court." The judge was getting impatient. "Martin, guilty or not guilty?"

"Just trust me." "Very special connections to the judge?" Maybe the promise was true.

"Ahh, emm, sir, ... I am ... *guilty* ... as charged." Somehow Martin managed to get *the word* out.

Then Martin heard something that utterly shocked him. "Yah, Martin, you are guilty, but ... I am going to declare you innocent of all charges," said the judge, rather matter of factly.

Martin couldn't believe what he had just heard! "Yah ... but!" That had always been his line, but now the judge was saying it! What was going on here?

Not believing what he had just heard, Martin asked, "But how you can you declare me innocent of all charges after you have heard me admit my guilt?"

With an equally puzzled look on his face, the judge responds, "But, Martin, didn't you know? Your defense attorney is my son, my only beloved son! Anyone who trusts my son, anyone who is a friend of my son, they are okay with this court ... and me! Yah, Martin, you are a traffic offender, but you also have my son as your defense attorney! That's all that matters. You trusted him enough to stop your excuse making. You trusted him enough to tell the truth. Well, that's enough for me. Martin, you are innocent, acquitted of all charges. Case closed."

When Martin had entered the courtroom that day, he was a sick man. He was thoroughly infected with Yahbut's Disease. He couldn't help but make excuses. He always had a reason for always being right and he was never wrong. He always had to have his own way. That day a destructive word had been rattling around inside his head: guilty! People with Yahbut's Disease can never say that word. But that incredible defense attorney was able to deliver on his promise. And the judge said those wonderful words he never thought he would ever hear without first having to prove himself: "You are innocent, acquitted of all charges. Case closed."

Such words are powerful. They can change people's lives. They did.

The very next day at work Martin's boss stormed into the office and shouted, "Who turned in this sloppy piece of work?"

The office was quiet. Everyone in the office knew who was responsible: Martin. But Martin always had excuses. He always had a reason as to why it was not his fault. Silence. Then the workers heard words that they had never ever before heard from Martin's lips, "I did, sir."

That weekend Martin and his wife entertained some of their friends at their home. One of his friends quipped sarcastically, "Martin, oh Martin. Where did you get this new television set?"

"From Best Buy," Martin answered.

"And what did you pay for it?"

"500," Martin said sheepishly.

You could tell that his friend was listening with unrestrained glee. He finally had one up on Martin. "You paid $500 for that set? I can't believe it, Martin. You were taken! I got one just like it at Circuit City for $100 less!"

Martin stiffened. His face turned slightly red. His friends were expecting another round of "Yah ... but's." But Martin remembered those words of the judge and his son, the attorney, and relaxed. "It sounds like you got a really good deal, a better one than mine. Congratulations!"

It was round 20 of Martin's "Yah ... but" argument with his wife, when Martin said something his wife had never heard him say before. "I'm sorry. You're right. I'm wrong. Please, forgive me."

Martin had been set free. The endless rounds of "Yah ... but" ended. The deadly hold of Yahbut's Disease, of sin, had been broken. He was a new man. Those words he heard that day in the courtroom changed his life.

So also for Jeremiah on that day when, out of the blue, God called him to a task he thought was impossible. Jeremiah had good excuses. He, too, was afflicted with Yahbut's Disease. But "the Lord put out his hand and touched my mouth." And Jeremiah heard the same kind of incredible promise that Martin heard that day in court, the same kind of incredible promise you hear every time you come to this place! God is gracious and merciful. God has chosen you. You're the apple of his eye!

That is why God has sent us his defense attorney, his beloved son, to be with us, to comfort us, to rescue us, to forgive us, to cure us of the dreaded and deadly Yahbut's Disease. People, you are cured, forgiven, free. You no longer need to make excuses. No more "Yah ... but's." You don't have to be consumed with defending yourself. Instead you can admit the truth. You can dump all that guilt and fear on Jesus and begin to be that new person God has made you to be in Jesus Christ.

A Holy God And A Holy People

Perhaps some of you saw the pictures in the newspaper or on television when officials in New York City revealed six different architectural renderings for the new World Trade Center. Each of the six different proposals more than replaces the square footage of the collapsed twin towers. The twin towers will not be replaced. In fact, in each one of the proposals the exact spot where the twin towers stood remains vacant and unused. Some sort of memorial for the victims of September 11 is planned for the space. One of the officials said that this space will never be used for commercial property. It will always be set apart and reserved in memory of those people who lost their lives on September 11. It is *sacred and holy* ground!

This secular understanding of "holy" is very similar to the Bible's understanding of "holy" and especially this passage from the prophet Isaiah.

In the Old Testament the word *holy, qadosh*, is derived from the verb *qad* which means to cut off and set something apart, to cut off and reserve it for special use. Of course, when one speaks of "the holy," one must always begin with God. God is cut off, set apart, totally unique. There is no one or no thing in the entire universe that is like God. In Israel holy places, spaces, and objects were set apart and removed from the ordinary, everyday, and profane places of life. The Holy Place and the Holy of Holies in the Temple in Jerusalem were clearly set apart and separated from the ordinary. Certain people could only enter these places at special times of the year.

The practice of Holy War in the Old Testament is especially illustrative of what it means to be "holy." The practice of Holy War is one of the most difficult concepts for us to understand and appreciate today. That the Israelites would carry out a holy war and destroy an enemy in the name of God seems brutal and barbaric. But a closer look at Holy War reveals that it is not what it appears to be. Other nations might engage in a Holy War to enhance their national wealth and power. They would carry home the booty and spoils of war to build their treasuries and arsenals. But not Israel! Their God was holy, like no other god. And they were a holy people, like no other nation. Therefore, when the Israelites would make Holy War, it was conducted like no other nation. They fought for the glory of their holy God and not for their own wealth and power. Therefore, in Holy War they were required to make *cherem*, i.e., destroy all the booty and spoils that they captured. The booty and spoils were *dedicated, consecrated, set apart* for God by being totally burned and destroyed. The Israelites were prohibited from keeping it for their own personal use.

Today's Old Testament Lesson from Isaiah 6 is one of the most important passages in the Bible in helping us understand the nature of God's holiness. Here we truly see a God who is set apart, totally unique, and unlike anyone or anything in this universe. The Isaiah 6 text would surely be the delight of a Hollywood special effects director given the opportunity to portray the spectacular and supernatural phenomena of this passage. This scene reminds me of a scene in the famous George Lucas film of the 1980s *Raiders of the Lost Ark.* Perhaps some of you remember how the very presence of God was portrayed at the end of the film when the lost Ark is finally discovered. God is portrayed with the same kind of blinding light, thundering noise, and earth-shattering transcendence that is reflected in the prophet Isaiah's vision of God in the Temple.

Isaiah's vision is certainly a unique experience. There is smoke. There is an earthquake. The very doors of the Temple shake in their hinges. There are these strange six-winged, snake-like creatures called seraphs flying about the place. Two wings cover their eyes because in the Old Testament God is so awesome and terrible that no one can dare to look him in the face. Two wings cover their feet (actually a Hebrew euphemism for genitals) because they are ashamed to be in the presence of such a Holy One. And with two wings they flutter around the sacred space as they chant this eerie song praising the God before them: "Holy, holy, holy is the Lord of hosts; the whole earth is full of his glory."

God is present sitting on his throne. But outside a reference to the hem of his robe, his appearance remains a mystery. Isaiah either cannot or will not describe it. God is so unique, so unlike anything in human experience, so utterly other, so set apart and so holy that he is beyond words.

The holiness of God also has an ethical and moral dimension. God is the essence of moral and ethical perfection. That has very specific and negative consequences for Isaiah. In the presence of the holy God, Isaiah is acutely aware of his unholiness. He feels that he is an unclean man with unclean lips in the midst of an unclean people. In other words, in the presence of the righteous and perfect God, Isaiah has an acute sense of his own sinfulness. In the presence of such perfection, he can only sense his imperfection. He is afraid, filled with terror, concerned for his very life. Being in the presence of the holy God is *not* good news. It is *not* comforting. It is frightening, scary, deadly.

Though few if any of us have ever had an experience like Isaiah's, our experiences of the presence of God are still similar to Isaiah's. When we sense that we are in the presence of divinity, we, like Isaiah, shudder. We sense our inadequacy. We feel accused, guilty, and the need to justify ourselves.

In this sanctuary we have a sacred space, set aside for holy use. As a result we don't feel comfortable using it for recreation or for a party. We sense that we should respect the altar, the pulpit, the font, and the sacred space around them. This is hardly the place for a card game or a dance party. This space should be "respected," treated with a little "fear and trembling."

God knows and my children repeatedly remind me that I am far from resembling divinity. Nevertheless, as the pastor I represent God and his presence. So when the pastor shows up, people can't help but feel slightly nervous and act a tad differently. People always feel a little threatened, a little ill at ease, perhaps even a little guilty in the presence of the pastor. When the pastor approaches, someone always sounds the alarm. "Here comes the pastor. Watch your language. Clean up your act."

I would be a rich man if I had a dime for every time this has happened to me. I'm walking through the grocery store and bump into someone from church. It may have been the farthest thing from my mind, but I always seem to get a litany of excuses as to why they haven't been in church lately. I guess the presence of the pastor automatically makes people feel guilty.

Have you ever heard one of those omnipresent "Saint Peter Jokes"? You know how the jokes go. Someone arrives at the gates of heaven and Saint Peter must decide whether to admit them into heaven or not. The jokes always assume that admittance depends on the merits of one's behavior. It seems that arriving at the gates of heaven and being in the presence of God puts everyone on the defensive. God is about righteousness. Morality and good works matter. Usually the punch line has something to do with that expectation.

That is also Isaiah's experience of being in the presence of God. He is overwhelmed with his sense of sin. Unlike our culture's emasculation of sin, where it has simply become a matter of making a mistake or an error or slip up or "getting caught in a naughty," Isaiah's sense of sin means that his relationship with God is in trouble. His sins are more than minor slip-ups. They are signs of a fracture in his relationship with God. Sin is ultimately a theological problem and not just a human problem. Therefore, being in the presence of this holy God, who is the ultimate expression of righteousness and ethical purity, terrifies Isaiah. He, a sinner, has seen God. He, a man with unclean lips in the midst of an unclean people, is in big trouble. As a sinner, in the presence of the holy God, he is doomed.

But then the text takes a surprising turn. There is one more dramatic event that must take place. It is an utter and complete surprise. Without warning or explanation, one of the seraphs flies to Isaiah holding in a pair of tongs a white hot burning coal from the altar in the Temple and touches it to the lips of Isaiah. In this dramatic gesture Isaiah miraculously is not burned and destroyed but is purged and cleansed of his sin. Isaiah was convinced that the holiness of God was bad news for him. But in fact it was just the opposite. The holiness of God is good news. That which sets God apart, cuts God off, makes God like no other, is God's grace and mercy. That which makes God utterly unique is not just that he reads the riot act to sinners. There is nothing unique or unusual about that. Everyone in the world thinks that is what God is like. What makes God utterly unique is his desire to be merciful and forgiving of sinners. That is what the holiness of God is all about. That is the holiness that God reveals to Isaiah.

This encounter with the grace and mercy of God changes Isaiah. It transforms him. It is a life-changing experience. It sets Isaiah apart. It cuts him off and makes him different. It makes him holy. Isaiah is now all too willing to be a prophet for God. "Here am I; send me!"

We see that, in this text from the prophet Isaiah, God's holiness is two-sided, bi-focal, "a two-edged sword," as Saint Paul sometimes describes it in the New Testament. This is the distinction between Law and Gospel. God's holiness is expressed as Law and Gospel. As the Law, God's holiness exposes our sin and drives us to our knees with fear and trembling. But as the Gospel, God's holiness overcomes the Law and its deadly criticism, silences its accusations, and forgives our sins. The Gospel is God's last word to us. It is this expression of God's love and mercy without any merit or worthiness in us that makes God unique, so special, so set apart, so different, so unlike any other ... so *holy!*

What makes God holy is his grace and mercy. That holiness is what sets God apart in the Old Testament and in the New Testament. That holiness is also at the heart and center of Jesus' life and ministry. What is at the heart of Jesus' holiness? The Golden Rule? The Great Commandment, to love God and neighbor? The Great Commission, to go and make disciples? No. At the heart and center of Jesus' life and ministry is this simple announcement. At the beginning of the Gospels of Matthew, Mark, and Luke, Jesus begins his ministry by saying it all: "The kingdom of God is at hand. Repent and believe the good news!"

119

Jesus is the incarnation of the kingdom of God. Watch him. Listen to him. See what happens to him and you will see what the kingdom is all about. You will see the holiness of God. That holiness is evident in Jesus' life of incredible grace and mercy, his forgiveness of sinners, his willingness to befriend outcasts in the name of God.

The proper response to this kingdom is repentance and faith. It is a repentance that is not just recognition of one's sin but a total re-orientation of one's life. Isaiah not only recognized that he was lost, a sinner, a man of unclean lips, but also he recognized that God was calling him to be a prophet. It totally changed his life. He could not resist. "Here am I; send me!" That is repentance.

The response to the kingdom of God and the gracious holiness of God is also faith. Faith trusts that this searing, white-hot holiness of God will not destroy us but purify us. Faith trusts that God has overcome his judgment and anger and instead has forgiven us. Faith trusts that God's last word to us is a wonderful promise. God is not our enemy but our friend.

In today's Gospel, Peter encounters the twofold holiness of God. When at Jesus' direction the disciples reap a miraculously large catch of fish, like Isaiah, Peter responds to this holiness with fear and trembling. In the presence of such divine holiness, Peter is acutely aware of his sin. He is not worthy to be in the presence of such holiness. But Jesus overcomes Peter's fear by comforting him with a holy word of grace and mercy. "Do not be afraid; from now on you will be catching people." This cowering sinner Jesus chooses to make one of his disciples. There is no test for worthiness. There are no hoops to jump through. There is only Jesus' gracious offer and gentle affirmation of Peter.

Did you recognize the words that were chanted by the seraphs in Isaiah's vision? "Holy, holy, holy is the Lord of hosts; the whole earth is full of his glory." These are the same words that we regularly sing as part of our Communion liturgy. The seraphs sang them as they praised this holy God who is like no other. We now sing these same words as we come forward to this altar to encounter once again the holiness of God. Like Isaiah, God will place the white-hot burning coals of Jesus' body and blood to our lips. Like

Isaiah, we will be seared, purified, and forgiven our sins. The holy God will make us a holy people, set apart, sacred, and special, like no others, because we have been forgiven.

Erika Kirsten Wujek also encountered the holiness of God and became a holy person this morning at this font. She received *holy* Baptism. When water was poured and God's promise was spoken, she was there with Isaiah in the Temple. She was there with Peter at the Lake of Gennesaret. She had her lips, heart, and body seared with the white-hot mercy of God's love. The creator of the universe, who is beyond the most distant galaxy and further than the deepest black hole, has decided to touch the life of this little child in this small Indiana town and make her a holy person, a saint, set apart, special, forgiven.

Let me tell you a story of holiness, God's holiness and our holiness. It is a story about the difference that God's holiness can make in our lives. It is a story told by a friend of mine who is a pastor and in the business of sharing the holiness of God.

> *I have had the opportunity to see this difference in the life of a seventh grader by the name of Matt. Matt was one of some seventy students participating in an all-night youth lock-in at a church in St. Louis where I was youth director. The rules for the evening were clear. No alcohol, drugs, or unruliness were allowed. The due consequences for breakage would be "home you go" regardless of the hour.*
>
> *It was midnight and the kids were settled in for watching a movie. I retreated to my office to prepare for our next devotional activity, when, lo and behold Mark (one of the youth counselors) came in with Matt, a small but always energetic seventh grader.*
>
> *"He's gotta go home, Pastor!" Mark exclaimed. "I caught him drinking during the movie!"*
>
> *Mark held up a little bottle of whiskey, the kind served on the airlines.*
>
> *"Is it true, Matt?" I asked. "Were you drinking?" But he was silent.*
>
> *"Send him home!" Mark shouted. "We have to make an example of him. Send him home."*

"That's enough, Mark," I said sharply.

I turned to Matt again. "You know what we said about drinking ... don't you?"

His silence persisted.

"We said anyone who drinks would be sent home."

Still, he said nothing. He did not even have the wherewithal to look at me. As much as I hated to do it, I picked up the phone to call his home. It was now about 1 a.m., mind you. I got Matt's mother (who understandably was not very happy) and explained all that had happened. She pleaded with me to let him stay, which I thought was a little strange. But I insisted that she come and take him home, which she did.

While the kids went to their next activity, I returned to the office. Pretty soon I heard a terrible commotion. It was Mark, and Matt was with him.

"Matt's back," he said. "And he wants to speak with you. Whatever you do, don't let him back!"

"That's enough, Mark," I snapped, gesturing with my hand that he chill out.

"What is it, Matt?" I asked.

Still not able to look me in the eyes, he spoke, "Pastor, I left without saying I'm sorry ... so I'm saying it now. I'm sorry."

I gently lifted his chin until my eyes met his. "You're forgiven, Matt. You know that, don't you?"

"I know," he said. And the hint of a telltale smile told me that he really did.

Mark blurted out again, "Don't let him...!"

"No, Mark!" I cut him off.

Looking Matt straight in the eyes, I asked, "So, what do you want to do now?"

"Oh," he said with the greatest of ease, "I want to go back home."

"You do?" I asked.

"Yah," he said. "It would send the wrong message not to."

"You're probably right," I said. "But you do know you're welcome to come back ... for future activities."

"Oh, yes!" he said and with great certainty.

*Matt walked out the door. Mark and I looked at
each other half stunned by what we had just witnessed:
repentance and responsibility, borne of forgiveness.*

*It was now the time for our last devotional activity
with the group. They were still very angry with me for
sending Matt home. But then, Mark and I told them
about what Matt had done — how he came back to say
he was sorry, and how for **their** sake (so that they would
not get the wrong idea about forgiveness and the kind
of responsible repentance it breeds) he decided to go
home. I am convinced that no amount of explanation
on my part could have ever brought that message home
to the kids. It took the life of a Christian, of a Christian
they knew, warts and all. It took Matt to bring the message home....*[1]

That night at the youth lock-in, Matt, Mark, the pastor, and
those seventy youth encountered the holiness of God. The holiness
not only exposed sin, but more importantly it granted forgiveness.
It was a holiness that surprised. It was unique. It was unantici-
pated. It was the gift of *a holy God* that for that night at the church
lock-in created *a holy people.*

---

1. Quoted from Reverend Steve Kuhl in *The Olive Leaf*, March 2002 Newsletter
   of Mount Olive Evangelical Lutheran Church, Mukwonago, Wisconsin.

No Middle Ground

It was the dirty secret. We were never supposed to talk about it openly. When it was discussed, it was in hushed whispers behind the closed doors of private homes. No, it had nothing to do with sex. It had to do with why my best friends would never eat meat on Fridays. It had to do with that strange ritual called the Rosary. It had to do with those strange women dressed in black and white who looked like penguins. I grew up in a small southeastern Wisconsin town in the 1950s where the majority of the population was either Lutheran or Roman Catholic. Even though the Protestant Reformation had taken place 400 years before on another continent, even though religious wars were no longer being fought, there was still a big chasm between us. We played together in the neighborhoods and on the playgrounds, but we still regarded one another with cautious suspicion. I still remember the shame Lutheran or Catholic parents would feel if one of their children married someone of "the other faith." Some regarded it as near apostasy. Some thought it was tantamount to denying the faith. Some thought it warranted family schism. Such concerns seem almost quaint today when many parents are thankful if their children just marry a Christian, let alone a Christian outside of their denomination.

In that small town I had lots of Roman Catholic friends and I do not remember a single incident where we ever exchanged sharp words, let alone sharp blows, over religion. It's not that our religious faith didn't matter. It did. Most of us regularly went to church on Sunday. Our parents and extended families continually reminded us of its importance. Nevertheless, we reached our separate peace,

125

our secret armistice, by everyone tacitly agreeing to an unspoken treaty. We would never openly talk about religion. Even though we went to our separate churches, even though some went to parochial school, even though some wouldn't eat meat on Fridays, even though some would never even think of uttering the word *Rosary*, we never asked why. We never talked about going to church. In a way we pretended that religion and God didn't exist or, if they did, they didn't matter. For the sake of peace, for the sake of the pick-up softball game on the vacant lot down the block, we had carved out our "middle ground," our "naked public square," where not only did religion disappear but also where God did not exist. It was a godless neutral ground where God was not allowed to make any claims or demands on us, let alone offer any promises of grace or mercy.

That "middle ground" served us well fifty years ago and enabled us to be friends and conduct our ball games, but the problem has not gone away. The debate is no longer between Protestants and Catholics but between those who believe that religion is purely a private and personal matter and those who believe it has public and civic consequences. It was interesting to see how this was an issue in our last election. When Al Gore chose Joe Lieberman to be his vice-presidential running mate, much was made of Lieberman's Jewish faith and that he publicly called for a return to religion, morality, and God in public life. The Democrats weren't about to let the Republicans be the only ones who could talk publicly about God and religion. Then after Bush's election, his selection of John Ashcroft to be Attorney General set off a storm of controversy led by those who feared that Ashcroft would let his administration of the law of the land be skewed by his conservative Christian beliefs. The on-going debate over prayer in the schools, vouchers for private and parochial schools, homosexual marriage, alternative lifestyles, abortion, and so on, has exposed the fact that Americans still can't agree on the role of religion in public life. The debate over the first amendment still rages. Does it mean the "dis-establishment" of religion, where religion is excluded from public life, or does it mean the "free exercise" of religion, where the government actually encourages public religious life but never expresses a preference for one form over another?

126

I suspect that most of us have already worked out our separate peace. For the sake of our own peace of mind and of conscience, we have convinced ourselves that it is actually possible for us to live our lives in a kind of "middle ground" where God and religion are irrelevant. Therefore, many of our prayers talk as if God is absent, as if life is godless, as if we are alone and need God to be "present" with us. We pray for God to be with us "all the time" and "wherever we go," as if there are times and places where God has been "absent without leave" and no longer with us.

Such attitudes are quite understandable because there often are those "dark and tragic" experiences of life that seem to be bereft of God's presence. So much of life seems to be perfectly explained by the laws and principles of natural science without the need to invoke the divine presence. There are our own moral lapses and failures which would make us cower in shame and fear were we not able rationalize that we live in some "middle ground" where God is not present to scrutinize us.

More than once I have reminded someone, who rejoices that God is with them wherever they go, that this is not necessarily good news. There are times, especially in the midst of our moral lapses and ethical shortcomings, that the idea of the presence of God makes us shake in our shoes. We would prefer that such moments go unnoticed by the deity.

It is understandable that we would create this sort of "middle ground," but it is not biblical. The radical monotheism of the Bible knows of no such world. This entire world is God's. God is not occasionally absent, attending to more important things in heaven. God is not occasionally asleep at the wheel. God did not create this universe and then walk away from it, leaving it to fend for itself. On the contrary, God not only created everything that is but also is continually involved in its daily operation. God governs and protects. God rewards and punishes. Even the impersonal laws and principles of the natural world are the means by which God continues to manage his creation. There is no "middle ground," "neutral space," or "naked public square" from which God is absent or, worse yet, has been banished.

This perspective on God's relationship to the world is especially evident in the Old Testament prophets. Today's First Lesson from the prophet Jeremiah is a classic example. The prophets such as Jeremiah were not just predictors of the future. Although the prophets often boldly speak of the future as "foretellers," their primary role was to speak of the present. They were fundamentally "forthtellers," daring to be able to understand what God was really doing in the present. They claimed to be able to see what God was actually doing now in the ordinary events of human history. And what they saw was often very different from what those around them saw. God was not absent from this world. All of life belonged to God. God constantly related to this world in one of two ways. God was either blessing or cursing. There was no "middle ground." There was no "naked public square." God ruled. God governed. And God did that either by blessing or by cursing.

This either/or perspective on God's relationship to this world is clearly evident in the prophet Jeremiah's words in today's First Lesson. "Those who trust in mere mortals" are cursed by God. Because their hearts do not trust God but the strength of human flesh, they are doomed to live life as if they were in a parched, uninhabited desert. But those "who trust in the Lord," their lives are blessed. Their lives will bear fruit, just as water brings life to plants in the midst of summer heat and enables them to bring forth a bountiful harvest. There is nothing to fear, nothing to be anxious over, and nothing to worry about because God is taking care of them.

Jeremiah's determination to bring God's word to bear on every situation in life, his refusal to allow God to be banished to some private or personal sphere of life, and his desire to put all of life under the microscope of God did not win him many friends. Even though this was a world removed from ours by two and a half millennia, people did what we still do: they carved out their "middle ground" where God was absent and not able to bother them. The religious establishment had confined God to the cult, to the temple, to the liturgy of worship and prayer. God was confined to the personal sphere of religious life. Therefore the religious leadership didn't need to address the sensitive political and social issues of the day. Perhaps fearing for their own welfare, they were content to keep God out of public life and in the temple. It was convenient not to raise the tough and embarrassing moral questions concerning social injustices or the immoral conduct of the king and his chronies. In contrast, Jeremiah's criticism in the name of God of the perverted religious life of Israel was relentless. He called the religious establishment to account. They could not ignore the injustices around them. As a result, he made few friends and stirred up lots of enemies.

Likewise, Jeremiah directed his ire at the political establishment that also had carved out its "middle ground," immune from the claims and demands of God. The king and his ruling class were all for religion and God as long as they stayed in the temple and the worship cult and didn't meddle with the ambitions of the regime. The kings were more interested in playing the games of political intrigue and protecting their power and privilege than in being faithful to God and the covenant God had established with Israel. Jeremiah would not tolerate such "middle ground." God could not be controlled or manipulated. God's claims on Israel were total. He saw things differently than the political establishment. The growing threat of foreign nations was a sign of God's imminent judgment on an unfaithful and disobedient nation. This was not a time for more military and political alliances but a time to return to God. Without such a renewal of faith, the nation was doomed.

To demonstrate the dark fate that awaited Israel dramatically, Jeremiah engaged in some attention-getting public actions. He publicly smashed clay pots, declaring that this is what God was going to do to Israel through the invasion of Babylon. He walked around Jerusalem carrying a yoke on his back and announcing that Israel was going to be yoked and enslaved by the coming invasion. Israel could not escape God in some fictional "middle ground." God was the Lord of all of life. There would be no way to evade his coming judgment. Both the political and religious leadership would pay a price for their sin.

Today's First Lesson reinforces just such a view of reality. Jeremiah insists that God is continually testing the heart and soul of humanity. If people trust in God, they will be blessed with an abundant and fruitful life. If they trust the lies and perversities of "mere mortals," they will suffer the consequences. They will be cursed, condemned to "be like a shrub in the desert, and shall not see when relief comes. They shall live in the parched places of the wilderness, in an uninhabited salt land" (v. 6).

Such "politically incorrect speech" was not welcome and Jeremiah paid a price. He was beaten, chained in stocks, publicly mocked, ridiculed, and thrown into a well with the hope that he would be permanently silenced. Such was the fate of being a prophet, for daring not just to be a "foreteller" but a "forthteller," for daring to tell the truth about the current state of affairs.

In today's Gospel, Jesus also reflects such a view of God's relationship to this world. This brief passage from the Gospel of Luke parallels the famous Sermon on the Mount in the Gospel of Matthew. This passage, however, has been traditionally called "The Sermon on the Plain." Jesus' words reveal that he like Jeremiah believes that there is "no middle ground." Humanity can't escape the claims and demands of God in some "middle ground," secular space, or "naked public square." We live under either the blessings or the curses of God.

In this way Jesus sounds just like so many of the prophets before him. But Jesus goes beyond such prophets as Jeremiah by claiming the authority to reverse and undo the way blessings and curses were understood both by the prophets and by the world. Jeremiah would agree with our world's understanding of blessing and curse. Poverty, hunger, sorrow, hatred, and ridicule are not blessings. Jeremiah and the gurus of our world might disagree on how one becomes blessed or cursed. Jeremiah would see it as being dependent upon our trust in God. The successful of our world would see it as being dependent on good luck and hard work. But they would both agree that it is cursed and wretched to be poor, hungry, and hated.

But not Jesus! He reverses every common sense notion of what it means to be blessed and cursed. Contrary to the brawny individualism of a Jesse Ventura, contrary to the successful entrepreneurialism of a Bill Gates or a Ted Turner, contrary to the U. S. Marines' search for "a few good men," Jesus curses the rich, the satisfied, the joyful, the self-sufficient, the popular, and the famous. Jesus curses those who have picked themselves up by their bootstraps and made something of themselves. If he were using Jeremiah's words, he would probably say, "Cursed are those who are 'like a tree planted by the water, sending out its roots by the stream (whose) leaves shall stay green' and even in the midst of drought 'bear fruit.' "

His reversal continues as he blesses those who, according to every common sense understanding of the word, are cursed.

> *Blessed are you who are poor,*
> *for yours is the kingdom of God.*
> *Blessed are you who are hungry now,*
> *for you will be filled.*
> *Blessed are you who weep now,*
> *for you will laugh.*
> *Blessed are you when people hate you,*
> *And when they exclude you, revile you,*
> *And defame you on account of the Son of Man.*
> *Rejoice in that day and leap for joy....*
> — Luke 6:20-23

And what even makes Jesus' claims even more outrageous is that he makes them in the name of God. Like Jeremiah and the prophets before him, Jesus was a "forthteller." He claimed to be able to understand what God was up to in this world. And it was not what anyone else expected.

Implicit in Jesus' outrageous claims about what was a curse and what was a blessing was a claim for himself. He was claiming to have the divine authority to reverse the very notions of blessing and curse. Such a reversal was at the heart of the startling, new kingdom that Jesus was bringing into this world. In this kingdom Jesus blesses what the rest of the world would only consider a curse. In this kingdom Jesus enables one to see the hollowness of the world's love of wealth, power, and prestige. What appears to be blessing is in fact a curse.

It was making claims like this that got Jesus into trouble. Just like Jeremiah and the prophets before him, what Jesus said and did was "politically incorrect." But worse than that, it was heresy. Therefore, in the name of God, Jesus had to die. And he did. On the cross he suffered the fate of those who dared to defy not only laws of this world but also the laws of God. And when Jesus died, it surely looked like his enemies were right. Jesus was a heretic, a blasphemer. His notions of blessing and curse were wrong.

But then, surprise! On the third day he was raised from the dead. Jesus lives! And it is clear that the audacious claims that Jesus had made not only for himself but also for his kingdom are true. In Jesus and his kingdom, God is indeed doing a new thing. As the Son of God, Jesus is the one who has been divinely authorized to turn this world upside-down and inside-out, to turn blessings into curses and curses into blessings.

Where does that put us? If there is indeed no "middle ground," no godless secular space, no "naked public square" where we can flee the presence and claims of God, then we are in trouble! Why? Because more than we would ever want to admit, Jeremiah's indictment of ancient Israel is also true of us. We put our "trust in mere mortals." We cling to our riches, our reputations, our political and social alliances at the expense of what is right, true, and just, at the expense of God. If there is no "middle ground," if God is never absent and is always there with us looking over our shoulder, then, when we are lying, cheating, gossiping, lusting, and stealing, we are in big trouble. If there is no "middle ground," then we can hardly have a clean conscience when so much of the world is hungry and starving.

The truth is that, because there is no "middle ground," we are in a big mess. Saint Paul is right. "All our righteousness is as filthy rags." Luther had it right when on his death bed, confronted with his mortality, his sin, his brokenness, he uttered, *"Wir sind Bettler, nicht wahr?"* "We are all beggars, aren't we?" We don't have a leg to stand on.

But because there is no "middle ground," there is also Good News! And the Good News is that there standing with us under the curses and in the midst of everything that is wrong with us and this world is the one who has been divinely authorized to reverse those curses. There is not only no place in this world that can escape the divine curse, there is also no place in this world that has not been rescued by the divine blessing. Despite the curse, despite God's disappointment with our trust of mere mortals and other assorted idolatries of this world, despite God's own righteous anger with our sin, God's heart is ultimately love. God ultimately wants to rescue us from this plight.

Even Jeremiah, after seeing his warnings of doom come true and Israel destroyed by the Babylonians and carried off into exile, refused to believe that God had given up on his people. Faced with such destruction, he concluded his ministry proclaiming the gracious promises of God. God's love will ultimately triumph. God's curses will one day be trumped by his blessings. God will make a new covenant with his people and remember their sin no more.

Of course, that hope proclaimed by Jeremiah did come true in the one who speaks to us in today's Gospel. Because there is no "middle ground," no space in this universe from which God has been banished, God in Christ comes to overthrow the curse, to reverse the judgment and forgive our sins. God in Christ comes to reach us with his blessing wherever we are in this world. Because there is no "middle ground," there is no desert, no plight, no disease, no poverty, no despair, no shame, no persecution, no disaster, no sin, and no curse that God in Christ cannot bless. Because there is no "middle ground," there is no dark lonely night, no hospital ward, no unemployment line, no bankruptcy proceeding, no chemotherapy treatment, no divorce court, no cemetery that cannot be transformed by the blessing of Christ. The crucified and risen one, the one who dared to bless those whom not only the world but God had cursed, comes to do the same for us.

And the Good News gets even better. When you leave this building after the worship service is completed and go out to the parking lot and into the world, a world that often seems utterly godless and devoid of anything that might remind you of the presence of God, remember there is no "middle ground." God in Christ is with you as you enter that hostile world. That promise of Christ transforms that world into a different kind of place. It is now fertile ground. It is now a field waiting to be harvested. It is now a place to carry out the mission of God. As you walk out the doors of this building, realize that you are now entering the mission field. Because there is no "middle ground," everything that lies before you is God's mission field. You have nothing to fear. You are that "tree planted by water, sending out its roots by the stream. (You) shall not fear when heat comes, and (your) leaves shall stay green; in the year of drought (you are) not anxious, and (you do) not cease to bear fruit" (v. 8).

With a promise like that, bring on the world! There is no "middle ground"! You have nothing to lose and everything to gain!

Forgiving And Not Forgetting

Someone has wronged you, betrayed you, stabbed you in the back. You are angry, fuming, ready to strangle them. You complain to a trusted friend about what has happened to you. The friend listens patiently and then offers you his/her sage advice. "Steve, you have got to move on with your life. Continuing to stew about this is just going to eat you up. Why don't you just *forgive and forget?*"

Forgive and forget! Ask someone at the coffee shop or at the water cooler in the office what forgiveness means and that is probably what he will tell you. To forgive means to forget about it. To forgive means to stop remembering the hurt or the injustice done to you and put it behind you. To forgive means to move on with your life and live as if the hurt never happened.

People who offer such advice probably think they are being helpful. They probably think their advice is even comforting. They think that forgetting is at the heart of forgiveness. But how mistaken they are! To think that forgiving is forgetting is perverse. It distorts the true nature of forgiveness. It trivializes the hurt that it is meant to heal. It deprives forgiveness of its true redeeming power. And ultimately such forgetting is humanly impossible. We might think that we are being helpful and comforting by telling someone to forgive and forget. But we are actually saddling them with a huge burden and an impossible demand.

A recent event illustrates just this point. The notorious Oklahoma City bomber, Tim McVeigh, announced to the media that he was not going to prolong the appeal of his death sentence. He hated

135

life in prison. He just wanted to be executed as soon as possible. He got his wish on June 11, 2002. What made this announcement so bizarre was that he also requested that his execution be televised to all of America. Pundits have speculated as to why he made this request. Was this another act of defiance on the part of this unrepentant terrorist? Was this his way to undermine the validity of the death sentence by showing to everyone its brutality? Some of the more adventuresome talk show hosts speculated that we ought to make his execution available on a pay-per-view basis and then give the money to the victims' families. I was also surprised to find out that over 250 people were granted "ringside seats" to view the spectacle.

This all goes to show that people just can't forgive and forget, especially the families of the victims. The hurt inflicted by Tim McVeigh was just too great to forget. The only way to bring closure to this experience and healing to the pain of the victims' families is to see justice done. The killer must pay for his crime. There will be no forgetting. In fact, to forget would imply that the lives of those victims didn't matter. To forget trivializes the lives of those who died in the bombing disaster.

Probably the place where the advice "forgive and forget" seems most absurd is in the context of family life. Try to tell brothers and sisters to "forgive and forget" after they have just had a bitter disagreement. They can't simply just "forgive and forget," because they have got to keep living every day under the same roof with this person whose very presence continues to remind them of the hurt that was inflicted on them.

Try to tell a wife or a husband to "forgive and forget" when their spouse has been unfaithful to them. A grievous betrayal has been committed. A sacred trust has been violated. If the marriage means anything, the sin cannot simply be forgotten. To forget means that those marriage vows weren't all that important to begin with. Because the marriage meant so much, the hurt cannot simply be forgotten. That is why the wounded spouse demands justice. She has a right to demand her "pound of flesh." Or he has a right to make her pay for her betrayal. To tell them to "forgive and forget" somehow makes a mockery of their marriage and belittles the depth

136

of their pain. Unfortunately, in such back and forth sparring, each trying to assert one's rights, each seeking to get what one deserves, each looking to "get back and get even," the marriage is often destroyed. But could it have been any different? Was there ever really any other choice when it is so impossible to "forgive and forget?"

If there was ever anyone who had every right in the world to "get back and get even," to get his "pound of flesh," and to make his demands for justice, it was Joseph in today's First Reading. Today's reading is from near the conclusion of the dramatic story of Joseph and his brothers. It is a wonderful Horatio Alger type of story where the loser becomes a hero. It is a story that has captured the imagination of many ever since those days when they first heard it as a child in Sunday school or dressed up in costumes to portray it in Vacation Bible School.

Joseph had been "wronged" by his brothers. Jealous of Joseph's ability to interpret dreams and of his popularity with his father, Jacob, the brothers fake Joseph's death and sell him into slavery. Joseph gets carried off to Egypt where he undergoes an amazing series of successes and failures. He manages to become a leading servant in the house of a wealthy Egyptian by the name of Potiphar. But when he refuses the seductive advances of Potiphar's wife, who then falsely accuses Joseph of improper sexual advances, he is thrown into prison. But while in prison Joseph's extraordinary ability to interpret dreams leads to his miraculous release and his eventual rise to second in command in all of Egypt. It is indeed a marvelous story of a slave's improbable rise to power. It is no wonder that Tim Rice and Andrew Lloyd Weber took the story, put it to music, and made it one of the most popular musical's of the last generation, *Joseph and the Amazing Technicolor Dreamcoat*.

Meanwhile, back at home there is a great famine in the land. Joseph's family is on verge of starvation. Jacob has heard that there is plenty of food available in Egypt and sends his sons to purchase some. When the brothers arrive in Egypt, they do not know that they will be dealing with the brother they had sold into slavery. Joseph immediately recognizes them but chooses not to reveal his identity to them. Surely, Joseph remembers what his brothers had done to him. Surely, Joseph remembers the hurt and pain they had unjustly inflicted upon him. Surely, Joseph has thought about "getting back and getting even," about settling the score with his despicable and hateful brothers, about getting his "pound of flesh" and making them pay for what they had done to him. Perhaps that is why Joseph repeatedly "tested" his brothers by imprisoning them as spies, placing money in their sacks then accusing them of theft, and finally planting a silver cup in Benjamin's sack in order to justify the arrest of Jacob's youngest son. Joseph is torn between wanting to help them and wanting to pay them back.

That brings us to the beginning of today's First Reading. The brothers are completely at the mercy of Joseph, who they still do not know is the brother whom they had so grievously wronged. But Joseph knows who they are and Joseph remembers. These are the brothers who hated him, who had wanted to kill him, who had sentenced him to a life that was supposed to have been worse than death. He had every right in the world to demand justice, to seek his pound of flesh, to "get back and get even." And if he had done that, none of us would have blamed him. For we know that most of the time that is precisely the way we treat others who have wronged us. We have a right, a holy right, a godly entitlement to justice!

Finally, Joseph just can't keep his secret any longer. He reveals his identity: "I am Joseph." But the question still remains. What will he do to his enemies? That they were his brothers, of his own flesh and blood, made their betrayal of him even more despicable. And his brothers know it. They are scared, frightened, fearful of what Joseph has every right to do to them. "But his brothers could not answer him, so dismayed were they at his presence."

Joseph could have just forgotten what had happened. "Oh, just forget it guys. What you did to me doesn't matter because I really didn't care all that much about you and my father. We can't live in the past. So let's just move on with our lives. Forgive and forget!" But Joseph didn't say that, because he couldn't say that. His family and especially his relationship to his father had meant far too much to him to say now that it didn't matter.

"Come closer to me," Joseph tells his brothers. The terror must now have been pounding in their hearts. This is the brother whom they once tried to kill. This is the brother who is now one of the most powerful men in the world. And now he wants to see the whites of their eyes. He wants them close enough to hear the words they were terrified to hear: that he had not forgotten what they had done to him.

"I am your brother, Joseph, whom *you* sold into Egypt."

Joseph was not going to forgive and forget. Joseph was not going to let sleeping dogs lie. Joseph remembered. And they, like we, are sure that he is going to make them pay for what they had done.

And that is when the story shocks and surprises us! Right when we expect this story to end like all the other great stories of human life, where the scales of justice are balanced, where good is rewarded and evil is punished, where getting back and getting even is all that matters, this story takes an unexpected twist. Joseph does not forget the past but *remembers it in a new way!* He looks back on what his brothers did to him, their hatred, their selling him into slavery and all of the intervening years of turmoil, and sees it in a new way. He sees it as God's way of preserving their lives!

"God sent me before you to preserve life."

For if Joseph had not been sold into slavery, he would never have made it to Egypt where he could rise to his important position and be able to save his brothers and beloved father, Jacob, from starvation. What the brothers had meant for evil, God has transformed and redeemed for good!

Joseph had been transformed by the grace of God so that he could remember his past in a new way. Because God had rescued him from one catastrophe after another, he was able break this world's vicious cycle of always having to "get back and get even." He no longer had to count his brothers' sins against them. He no longer had to make them pay for what they had done to him. Instead, he could now *forgive* them!

What Joseph did seems humanly impossible. He willingly forgoes and gives up his right, his God-given right, to seek justice! Any anger and disgust he had with his brothers he chooses to keep to himself. He is the one who suffers and not his brothers. He pays rather than his brothers. He sacrifices. He "bites his own tongue" and "bites the bullet" instead of taking out his anger and wrath on

139

his brothers. He could have made his brothers pay for their crime, and no reader of this story would have blamed him. But that would have been still more of the "same old same old." It would have been just one more chapter in the same old story of the world's captivity to the cycle of vengeance and getting even. But the cycle had been broken for Joseph. God had reversed the inevitable for him. God had redeemed his damnable story of treachery and betrayal and turned it into a marvelous story of rescue and redemption. As the direct beneficiary of such divine intervention, Joseph too had been changed and transformed. He too could now become a partner with God in reversing and changing this world of paybacks and revenge by forgiving. He, like God, could choose to remember the past in a new way.

In the surprising forgiveness of his brothers by Joseph, we see a foreshadowing, a foretelling, of the same kind of forgiveness God worked in Jesus and continues to work among us today. Through Jesus' death and resurrection God forgives the sins of the world. This forgiving, like Joseph's forgiving, is not forgetting. God is not some sleepy old man in the sky who is oblivious to our sins. God is not like some enabling parent who always overlooks the alcohol abuse of his teenager. God is not happy with our sin, our betrayals, and our violence. But God loves us. Therefore, he will not just look the other way and pretend these things never happened. He cannot and will not forget our sin. But then what does he do with our sin? Like the sins of Joseph's brothers, it demands justice. Someone must pay. The consequences cannot just be ignored.

So, like Joseph, God chooses to forgive not by forgetting but instead by remembering in a new way. Instead of holding our sins against us and making us pay, God "bites his tongue." God "bites the bullet." God chooses to give up his right to demand justice from us. Instead God is the one who "pays." God is the one who sacrifices. God is the one who suffers. And God does that by directing his anger with our sins and his hunger for a "pound of flesh" upon himself, upon his "only begotten Son," upon the crucified Jesus. Jesus dies "for us" and suffers the punishment intended for us. And our sins are forgiven.

Every time we begin our worship on a Sunday morning with the words of confession and forgiveness, the story of Joseph's forgiveness of his brothers and of God's forgiveness of the world through Jesus' death and resurrection are acted out again in our midst. Our sins are not forgotten. God remembers them. "If we say we have no sin, we deceive ourselves, and the truth is not in us." We remember them. "We confess that we are in bondage to sin and cannot free ourselves." But then we are told the glorious good news that God has chosen to remember them in a new way. What we intended for evil, God has turned into good. How? He "has given his Son to die for us and, for his sake, forgives us all our sins."

God in his mercy chooses to remember our sins in a new way and forgives us.

Once Joseph realized this, everything changed for him. He was able to break the "same old same old" cycle of revenge and "getting back by getting even." He was able to be a partner with God in changing the world. He forgave his brothers. Likewise, because God has chosen to forgive but not forget our sins, we can join Joseph in changing the world. We can forgive and break the painful and deadly cycle of "getting back and getting even" that so torments this world of ours.

This is the new kind of life that Jesus describes in today's Gospel. These are not demands that we "gotta" do in order to be a disciple of Jesus. On the contrary, they are gifts, possibilities, opportunities, where we can partner with God through Jesus in redeeming the world. What the world meant for evil, destruction, hatred, cursing, abuse, exploitation, and violence, we can change and transform into goodness and life. By refusing to demand our "pound of flesh," by refusing to "get back by getting even," but instead choosing to "bite the bullet," to turn the other cheek, to be generous, to love our enemies, to be merciful as our Father is merciful, and to forgive but not forget, a new world begins to take shape in the midst of the old. The kingdom of God begins to arrive. And what the world meant for evil, God has transformed into good.

The Living, Reliable Word

(*Holding up a Bible*) This is the most important book ever written. We could not imagine the Christian Faith without it. We call it the "sole rule and norm" of our faith. We all want to read it and feel guilty when we don't. We can't imagine having a worship service without reading from it. We want it on our coffee tables for everyone to see. We record our family genealogies inside its cover. We make sure each one of our children has his or her own copy. In court we swear on it. We love to quote from it. The Good Book has more authority than any other book ever written on the face of the earth.

Why? Why is it so important? It surely is great literature. It is filled with great history. It narrates fascinating stories. But none of these reasons can adequately account for its significance. If we were to take a survey of the rank and file of the American population, most would probably say something like this when accounting for the Bible's fame: It tells us what we gotta believe, gotta know, and gotta do in order to be saved.

It is one of the great ironies of our day that many so-called "liberals and conservatives," even though they have dramatically different approaches to the Bible, agree that this is the purpose of the Bible. The Bible tells you what you gotta believe, gotta know, and gotta do to be saved. They just come at it in dramatically different ways. On the one hand, the so-called "liberals" take very little of the biblical text literally. They are always trying to "get behind" the literal words of scripture to what "really happened."

143

This is so important to them because, if they only knew what actually happened, then they would finally know what they "gotta believe, gotta know, and gotta do." On the other hand, the so called "conservatives" take the biblical text very literally. There is no need to "get behind" the words of the text because those words already tell you exactly what you "gotta believe, gotta know, and gotta do" to be saved.

The problem with this kind of understanding of the Bible is that, whether you are a liberal or conservative, whether you take the words of the Bible literally or figuratively, you never seem to know enough. The Bible becomes the rule that you can never quite seem to live up to. The Bible becomes the accuser you are never quite able to please.

This became abundantly clear to me once in a Sunday school staff meeting. Do you remember that popular game of some years ago, Trivial Pursuit? During that same period of time there were also various Christian versions of the game. One of those was a game called Bible Trivia. I decided that playing this game would be a good activity for our Sunday school staff. The game had three different levels of difficulty. At first I thought we could play the medium difficulty level. But then I thought we had better play it safe and not embarrass anyone and play the easy level. The most difficult level was out of the question. Surely the easy level ought to be difficult enough for us to have fun and still learn something. Boy, was I wrong! It didn't take very long to see that even the best of us didn't know a lot of Bible trivia. (Is that why they call it "trivia," because it isn't very important?) The game turned into a nightmare for the staff and made all the teachers feel dumb and stupid, as if their knowledge of the Bible was woefully inadequate. They soon wondered how they could be good Christians and why they thought they could ever teach Sunday school since their Bible knowledge was so poor. I decided then and there that I would never use that game again.

Unfortunately that game reflected an understanding of the Bible that is widespread in our culture. It assumed that "faith" is basically a rational exercise. Faith is knowing and accepting various kinds of information and facts contained in the Bible. The game assumed that the Word of God is basically information that tells us what we "gotta believe, gotta know, and gotta do." This understanding of the Word of God unfortunately has been more influenced by Greek philosophy than by the Hebrew way of looking at life and the world. The Greeks looked at life, and the world, as if it was an object to be observed or a specimen to be examined, measured, and weighed. To the Greek point of view, the Bible is like an object in a test tube to be tested and measured. But the Bible came from a Hebrew context. Jesus was first and foremost a Hebrew. The Hebrews had a very different view of life and the world than the Greeks. For the Hebrew the world is alive. It is not so much an object to be controlled and observed as it is a "person" with whom to interact.

This different perspective is especially clear when it comes to the Hebrew understanding of "the word." The Hebrew expression for "word" is *dabar,* which can mean either "he says" or "he acts." The "word" is not a lifeless object but a living address similar to interaction between two people. The Word of God is God in action doing, creating, and making things happen.

For example, in Genesis 1 it is the Word of God that creates the world. God says, "Let there be," and there is. God simply speaks and the world happens. In Genesis 3 after Adam and Eve have eaten of the forbidden fruit and are hiding in the garden in the evening, God comes walking through the garden. He speaks. He utters a word. "Adam, where are you?" This question is not so much a reflection of God's ignorance of Adam's whereabouts, as it is God demanding an explanation for Adam's disappearance. The Word is a living, dynamic address and in this case, a word that challenges and accuses.

In Genesis 12 Abraham receives a very different kind of Word of God. Out of the blue he receives a promise, i.e., that God has chosen him, that he will be given a land that will belong to him, and that he will have children through whom he will be a blessing to all the nations of the world. Faith here is not simply accepting the accuracy of the information but trusting the reliability of a promise. A few chapters later in Genesis, God comes to speak this same word again to Abraham. Again the Word is a living address and not

145

dead information. It was a hot day when three strangers who gave him a most unusual message visited Abraham, sitting in the shade under the oaks at Mamre. Even though aged Abraham and his wife Sarah were on the verge of giving up on the promise God had given them, these three visitors, who turned out to be God himself, reassured Abraham that Sarah would indeed give birth to the promised son the next spring. God came to deliver a word not by sending a book or a letter or an e-mail but personally through three living human beings.

In today's First Lesson we see another example of God's Word. Once again, it is a living, dynamic personal address. The prophet Isaiah, like all the other prophets of ancient Israel, dared to speak on behalf of God. When the prophets spoke, they didn't first sit down and write it out. It wasn't dictated to a stenographer. No, the prophet stood on the street corners, in the thoroughfares, and in the courts of the kings of the ancient world shouting, preaching, and proclaiming his message to the people. It was a living, dynamic, personal word from God.

The context of today's First Lesson is like so many of the passages from the latter half of the book of the prophet Isaiah. Israel is in exile in Babylon. They have lost everything that had made them a nation, their king, their Temple, their capital city, and their land, to the Babylonian hordes. They know that they have suffered the consequences of their sin. They know that they have brought this on themselves. It seemed that God has finally given up on them. But faced with this dismal and hopeless situation, the prophet refuses to give up. He refuses to give up because he is convinced that God won't give up. God will not abandon his word. God will never break his promise. The Israelites can count on the word God has given to them. Then using an illustration from the natural world around him, the prophet proclaims that, as sure as the rain and snow fall to the ground and cause the seed to sprout and bring forth new plants, Israel can count on God to deliver them from their predicament in exile. They can count on God for their deliverance. There will be a new exodus. Just like the first exodus from Egypt, God will rescue his people again, but this time from Babylon.

The word of God is spoken through the mouth of a living person. The prophet speaks a word that is alive and dynamic. It is a promise calling for the faith and trust of its hearers.

The Word of God is most vividly expressed in the person of Jesus Christ. Jesus is the Word of God. Jesus is the Word of God "with skin on." The opening chapter of the Gospel of John puts it most vividly. Jesus literally is the Word of God in human flesh. In him the Word of God literally came to dwell among us, "full of grace and truth." There is no Word more living and dynamic than a human being. That Word is Jesus.

When Jesus speaks the word of God in his ministry, it is a dynamic, life-changing thing. When Jesus calls fishermen to be his disciples, he uses just two words. He simply says, "Follow me," and it changes their lives. He simply says a few words and the blind see and the deaf hear. When Jesus tells stories, he uses parables to change his hearers' lives. These stories don't just serve as packages to deliver religious propositions. Rather they are personal addresses, hearing events, that create a new vision and a new world for their hearers. Jesus speaks of a Samaritan who stopped along the road to nurse a robbed and beaten traveler back to health. He speaks of a farmer who sows seeds, suffers enormous losses, and nevertheless enjoys a bumper crop. He speaks of a father welcoming home a lost son. Through these words God's living Word breaks into the hearts and lives of people and changes them.

And even Saint Paul, whose words and phrases often seem complicated, convoluted and abstract, resorts to a dynamic, interpersonal relationship to portray his central metaphor for the Word of God, justification by faith. In the courtroom of eternity a sinner stands guilty before the judge. But the judge surprises everyone by speaking a word, by making an announcement, by declaring a judgment that no one expected. This sinner is declared innocent, forgiven, justified. The Word of God is a living, dynamic, life-changing event.

But when God speaks his word, he is always doing one of two things. On the one hand, God's word can challenge, confront, accuse, and expose us for the sinners we are. That is what God's word did when in the Garden of Eden God demanded, "Adam, where are you?" That is what Jesus did when in the Sermon on the Mount he radicalized the demands of the commandments. When he asked, "You have heard that it was said, 'Thou shalt not kill,' " you can be sure that most of his hearers were certain that they had never broken this commandment. But when he said, "But I say to you that whoever insults his neighbor is a murderer," you can be sure that every one of his hearers was shaking in his boots. This living Word of God had grabbed them by the throat.

On the other hand, God's word can offer love and mercy, unconditional comfort and grace. This is the word the prophet speaks in today's First Lesson when he assures his discouraged hearers that God will still rescue them. This is the Word that became flesh, was crucified, and is risen in Jesus Christ. This is the word that announces God's love for sinners. This is the word that silences the criticism and accusation of God's "other word" and instead offers freedom and liberation. This is the word that promises the love of God with no strings attached.

We call these two words of God Law and Gospel. We cannot ever talk about the word of God without always making the distinction between these two kinds of divine speech. We must always ask, "Is this word of God addressing us as Law or Gospel?" If it is the Law, it will be language that challenges and accuses us. It will be words that evaluate us on the basis of our performance. It will expose our sin. But if it is the Gospel, it will comfort and bless us unconditionally. The Gospel is the divine speech that offers us the love of God, no questions asked. It pronounces us saints. What makes us Christians is that we believe that God's word of Gospel has overcome God's word of Law. What saves us is that we trust the promise of the Gospel in spite of all kinds of reasons not to. The Gospel is God's last word. It is the word that reflects God's true will for the world. It reveals to us the true heart of God. And that heart is love.

The Bible is certainly God's word. It is God's word in written form. It is the "rule and norm" of our faith. We declare it "inspired" by God. But here again the distinction between Law and Gospel is essential. The Bible is both Law and Gospel. It both kills and makes alive. But the Bible is God's word "for us" and is the "rule and norm" for our faith and life because the Gospel is at the heart of the Bible. The Gospel is what the Bible is ultimately all about. We stake our lives not on the threats of the Law but on the promises of the Gospel. The Bible is the world's most important book for Christians because it is the oldest historical witness to God's gracious and merciful acts in history. It is the oldest historical witness to God's grandest act of grace, the life, death, and resurrection of Jesus Christ. The Bible is so important because there we meet Jesus, the Gospel in human flesh.

Martin Luther once used a homely and down-to-earth image to explain the significance of the Bible. At Bethlehem Jesus was held in a manger, a feedbox for animals. Luther taught that the Bible, the written word of God, is like that manger because the Bible holds Christ, the living Word, God's dynamic address to us, the Word of God "with skin on." But we don't worship the manger. We worship the Christ who came *in* the manger. But there is no Christ without the manger. Likewise, we don't worship the Bible. We worship the Christ *in* the Bible. But there is no Christ without the Bible. The Bible is just another book without Christ.

The manger was made of wood, ordinary wood. It probably had splinters. The nails may have been rusty. The angles may not have been perfect. In other words, that manger at Bethlehem reflected all the quirks, idiosyncrasies, and imperfections of human life. But at the same time it was the most important manger in the universe, because it held the infant Jesus. The Bible likewise reflects all the quirks, idiosyncrasies, and imperfections of human life. But it is the most important book ever written because it is filled with God's own Spirit, because it contains the power to save us, and because it holds Christ!

All the adjectives that we usually heap on the Bible, that it is inspired, reliable, infallible, trustworthy, and so on, are all intended to do one thing: to assure us that we can count on it and the Christ it brings to us to be sufficient to save us, just as the prophet says in today's First Lesson. We can count on it to save us, just as we can count on the rains and the snow to water the earth and make it bring forth living things. It has the power to renew our faith, to forgive our sins, to raise us to new life.

That same written word that we meet in the Bible, we also meet in ritual and sacrament in the life of the church. As we come to the table to eat and drink, we don't just eat and drink ordinary bread and wine. No, there we meet God in Jesus actively speaking and acting to give us new life. We can count on Holy Communion to accomplish that which God says it will accomplish. It will forgive our sins. It will give us eternal life. It will give us the peace our restless hearts have been seeking.

Today we celebrated the Baptism of Ian Jakob. In the water of the font God spoke his living and reliable word to Ian Jakob. God acted in that word and put a claim on Ian Jakob. For the rest of his life Ian Jakob will always be a son of God, even though just like us he will often struggle to believe it. As sure and as certain as the rain and the snow come down from heaven bringing water and life to the earth, Ian Jakob can be certain for the rest of his life of God's love for him. That water in the baptismal font was just ordinary water from a faucet. But when it was used together with God's living and reliable word, it took on new power and significance. Ian Jakob can count on it. It will accomplish what God wants it to accomplish, namely, the eternal salvation of Ian Jakob.

But that living, reliable word of God doesn't just meet us in the written form of the Bible or in the ritual forms of the sacraments of Baptism and Communion. That word also encounters us in real, live human beings. And I am not just talking about my sermons. One of the great fruits of the sixteenth-century Protestant Reformation was the concept of "the priesthood of all believers." The priesthood of all believers is not about institutional or legal power. On the contrary, the priesthood of all believers is about the Gospel. It declares that every baptized Christian is a priest and has the power to work for the salvation of every person. The priesthood of all believers means that every Christian has the power and authority to speak the word of God to anyone. Every Christian now has the power and authority to forgive the sins of others in the name of God and on behalf of God. Speaking the word of God is not just the private privilege of preachers like me. No, getting to speak the word of God is the privilege of every Christian. It is something you also have been authorized to do because God has claimed you in your Baptism.

When we speak the living, reliable word of God, it inevitably moves its hearers to repentance and faith. Those who hear it and trust it now have a new relationship with God. Hearing the word of God is similar to what happens when you are walking down the sidewalk and someone calls out your name. You stop in your tracks. You turn around and walk in a new direction toward the sound of this new voice. The power of the word of God you heard is so winsome, so captivating, and so liberating that it changes the direction of your life.

When God speaks his lively and reliable word, it is similar to an old-fashioned romance when a lover gets on his knees before his beloved to win her affections. He speaks "sweet nothings" and waxes eloquently about his love for her. He begs her to marry him. So, when she finally says, "Yes," to his proposal, her life is changed forever. In the same way God courts us. Through his living, reliable word he tries to win our affections and trust. As members of this priesthood of believers we too have been authorized to speak the word of God to one another and to the world. We have been called to woo and win them for God.

Through our words and deeds we get to proclaim the word and change the lives of people. In a world where everyone is in constant competition always trying to one up the other, where everyone is always keeping score, where the competition can easily turn us into monsters, we can assure one another with the merciful word of God. We can declare, "You are the apple of God's eye. You are God's beloved child, the love of his life. The self-doubt that has been raging in your heart can now end."

Ashamed and embarrassed by what the world merely calls "failures and shortcomings" but what we know is actually "sin," we are offered this good word from God: "Because of and in the name of Jesus your sins are forgiven."

Mourning our loss and burdened with grief, we stand at the graveside in the cemetery struggling to find some way to say goodbye to our loved one. Then we hear those glorious words, "Neither death, nor life, nor angels, nor rulers, nor things present, nor things to come, nor powers, nor height, nor depth, nor anything else in all creation, will be able to separate us from the love of God in Christ Jesus our Lord" (Romans 8:38-39). The living, reliable word of God has touched us and comforted us.

The prophet had absolute confidence in the power of the living, reliable word of God to do what it is supposed to do.

> *So shall my word be that goes out from my mouth;*
> *it shall not return to me empty,*
> *but it shall accomplish that which I purpose,*
> *and succeed in the thing for which I sent it.*
>
> — v. 11

And what is that purpose? To assure us once and for all that even in the midst of our exiles God has not forgotten us. God will keep his promise. God will save us, no questions asked, no "ifs, ands, or buts," no strings attached, unconditionally. As sure as rain and snow will water the earth and make it bring forth and sprout, you can count on it — the living, reliable word of God.

**Transfiguration Of The Lord
(Last Sunday After Epiphany)
Exodus 34:29-35**

Going To The Mountaintop

Have you ever been to the mountains? I mean real mountains and not these little hills we have in Indiana. I am referring to real mountains like you find in the American West, the Rocky Mountains. Have you ever been on those magnificent towers of stone and ice, capped with snow, so high that they seem to scrape the sky? On top of such mountains heaven and earth almost seem to meet. On top of a mountain it seems that you are closer to God.

In the ancient world that is exactly the way people thought of mountaintops. They literally were holy places where heaven and earth met. That is why the Aztecs and Incas in South America either built giant pyramids or went to mountaintops to make their sacrifices to the gods. They wanted to be closer to heaven. In Genesis 11 is that not why humanity built the Tower of Babel? They wanted to get closer to heaven and the gods so that they could make a name for themselves. Sometimes I wonder if that is why we moderns build these magnificent skyscrapers hundreds of feet into the sky. If they are not an attempt to get closer to God, then surely they are monuments to our own attempts to be more like God.

In today's lessons such mountaintops are also places for some very special encounters between the divine and the human. In the First Lesson Moses and the Israelites are camped out at the foot of Mount Sinai. Moses has just completed his second trip up and down the mountain. After his first trip up and down the mountain, Moses returned with the stone tablets on which God had written his covenant with Israel. But Moses, upon seeing the golden calf, the idol that the Israelites had constructed in Moses' absence, smashes the stone tablets in rage, grinds up the golden calf into fine dust, mixes it with water, and forces the Israelites to drink it as punishment for their idolatry. Moses then returns to Mount Sinai for a second time and has the covenant with God renewed. When he comes down the mountain a second time, something is very different. This time Moses' face is shining with such a bright light that the Israelites, are frightened. They couldn't look at his face without being blinded.

Moses had truly been in the presence of God and the blinding light blasting forth from his face was proof. Every time the Israelites looked at Moses' bright face, they knew that they were in the presence of one who had been in the very presence of God on the mountaintop. And they were frightened by it and wanted to hide. That is why Moses developed this unusual ritual. Every time when he was in the presence of Israel and was not speaking with God, he covered his face with a veil. Only then could the Israelites bear to be in the presence of Moses and not be so frightened. But his shining face, even though veiled, was a sign to them that he was speaking for God.

Today's Gospel and its account of the Transfiguration of Jesus also takes place on a mountaintop. Here too a strange and wonderful encounter between the divine and the human takes place. Like Moses, Jesus glows with a blinding light. A voice from the heavens announces that Jesus is the very Son of God. Jesus has a conversation with Moses and Elijah, two great leaders of the Old Testament one of whom was assumed directly into heaven. When Peter and the disciples saw all this — on a mountaintop of all places — they knew they were in some place special. They knew they were in the very presence of divinity. They had had a mountaintop experience.

Both mountaintop experiences seem unreal, supernatural, surreal, not of this world. Both mountaintop experiences literally were occasions when the divine met the human. Heaven met earth.

Peter was so impressed that he tried to preserve the experience by offering to set up a tent for Jesus and his two visitors. Perhaps they could turn this into a tourist attraction. They could invite travelers and pilgrims to join them on the mountaintop for a divine/

human encounter. They could even charge admission. By seeking to preserve this experience by setting up tents for Jesus, Moses, and Elijah, Peter is no different from us. We too attempt to preserve the memory of a mountaintop experience by keeping a trophy, a blue ribbon, or a photograph. Even though the memory of those mountaintop experiences will fade over time, the trophies and photographs will help us to remember and relive the thrill of the mountaintop experience.

But I must admit that I have never had a mountaintop experience like these. I have never heard voices from heaven, seen great historical characters from the past, or observed someone glow in the dark. It is strange and supernatural events like this that make the Bible an odd and unbelievable book. I don't live in a world like this. I suspect that you don't either. And when we hear stories like this read in Sunday worship in our church, it contributes to the unreality of our faith. We want to believe in God. We want to believe the Bible. But because the world of the Bible and its God and stories like this one seem so farfetched and unrelated to our world, it all seems so weird, so odd. If God inhabits a world like this, then we live in a world without God. Our religious faith seems to be nothing more than a game we play on Sunday mornings and then ignore the rest of the week.

Is there any place where these strange stories about the transfigurations of Moses and Jesus intersect with our world? Where might we have a similar mountaintop experience today? Where might we have a similar divine/human encounter? Where might we behold Jesus or Moses in all of their transfigured glory?

Let me begin with the story of Jesus' transfiguration. There is a helpful clue there that can help us see the relevance of both of these stories. When that divine voice from the cloud speaks and essentially repeats the words spoken at Jesus' baptism ("This is my Son, my Chosen"), it adds these significant words: "Listen to him." Then the whole supernatural experience abruptly comes to an end. The disciples are left with the same old ordinary Jesus. Moses and Elijah are gone. The cloud has dissipated. There is no more glowing light. There is only that very ordinary carpenter's son from Nazareth.

155

And that is exactly the point of it all. This whole bizarre experience now emblazoned in the memories of the disciples is intended to remind them of the importance of listening to Jesus. If they are ever again to return to the mountaintop for such a divine/human encounter, it will be when Jesus speaks. It will be through the Word of Jesus that they will once again get to behold the truth of Jesus' divine identity in all of its blazing glory. It will be when Jesus speaks that they will "see" the glory of God and know that they have been in the very life-giving presence of God.

But where and when does that happen in our world? Our world is cluttered with lots of words and lots of talk. Many of those words and much of that talk claim to speak for God. But the message that many of those words and much of that talk convey is disturbing and threatening. They reveal a God who is not very pleased with us and with what we have done with this world. They reveal a God who demands that we measure up. Therefore, unlike Peter and the disciples, we would rather flee than relish such a moment.

But if we look closer to what Jesus actually was saying, we see something different. Luke notes that Jesus was talking with Moses and Elijah about "his departure which he was about to accomplish in Jerusalem." The Greek word Luke uses for "departure" is the same word for "exodus."

Luke is making a very important point here. After this transfiguration experience on the mountaintop, Jesus turns toward Jerusalem and begins the last and most important chapter of his life: his arrest, death, and resurrection. By calling them his "exodus," Jesus is comparing what he is about to do with his life to what God did for the Israelites in the exodus of the Old Testament. The first exodus resulted in the liberation of Israelites from slavery in Egypt. Now in this second exodus God was once again going to work a miraculous act of liberation. This time, however, it would affect more than just one nation. This time it would mean the liberation of all of humanity from all the powers that threaten it.

It is no accident that every year on this last Sunday in the season of Epiphany, as we enter the season of Lent and our march to the cross and the empty tomb, we hear this story of the transfiguration of Jesus. The "exodus" of which Jesus spoke with Moses and

Elijah will be accomplished in the events that lie ahead. Jesus goes to the cross and suffers the fate of humanity. "On the third day" Jesus is raised from the dead and the powers of sin, death, and God's own judgment on this crooked world are broken. And in the proclamation of the Gospel, in the spread of the Easter message, we are told that God did all of this *for us and our salvation!*

There, did you hear those words? Did you hear that message? Did you hear about the "exodus" that was accomplished *for you, for your benefit?* Did these words of Good News rattle your eardrum and send an impulse to your brain that was interpreted as Good News and believed by your heart? If so, you have not just heard the preacher speak; you have heard Jesus speak. You have heard God speak. You have been there with the Israelites and heard Moses speak with his veil removed. You have been to the mountaintop. You have been in the very saving and life-giving presence of God!

Even though there has been no blinding light, no voice from a cloud, no appearance of Moses and Elijah, no Moses with his glowing face covered with a veil, you have been to the mountaintop. You have participated in a divine/human encounter. You have been to where heaven and earth have met.

You may be rubbing your eyes and asking yourself if you are missing something. How could listening to the preacher possibly be a return to the mountaintop of the transfiguration? But again, look carefully at the text of Luke. After the divine voice said, "Listen to him," all the supernatural razzle-dazzle disappeared. All the disciples had left was the ordinary Jesus.

The point the divine voice was making was clear. In the future, that is precisely the way God is going to appear in our midst. It will be in the ordinary and mundane that Jesus will take us to the mountaintop. Jesus will continue to appear to us not in the razzle-dazzle of some supernatural experience but in the ordinary and mundane of the everyday. Wherever Jesus speaks his life-giving word of mercy, there we are once again with Peter and the disciples and Moses and the Israelites on the mountaintop and in the presence of God. When Jesus speaks to us and offers to us his life

157

at this simple table in ordinary bread and wine, in this bath of ordinary water, in the words of forgiveness and absolution you heard from this ordinary human being, your pastor, and sometimes even from the members of your family, from your neighbors, or from your enemies, you are on the mountaintop! You are in the presence of the transfigured Jesus. You are at the foot of Mount Sinai with Moses, veil removed, face glowing, speaking the very words of God.

There is another powerful story in the Old Testament that shows us how God can appear to us and take us to the mountain through very ordinary human beings. Let me take you to Genesis 33 and the account of the dramatic reconciliation of two estranged brothers, Jacob and Esau. Prior to this dramatic moment, the story of Jacob and Esau has been a sad story of betrayals, lies, and deceptions. Twice Jacob had deceived his father in order to steal blessings that had rightfully belonged to his twin brother Esau. Finally, fearing for his life, Jacob fled some distance to his uncle Laban. After living in this distant land for more than fourteen years and marrying two women, Jacob decides that it is time to go home to see his aging father before he dies. In Genesis 33 he is getting close to home. His brother Esau learns of his approach and goes out to meet him. Jacob learns Esau is coming and is nervous, if not frightened. This is the brother he had cheated. This is the brother he had betrayed. He was sure that his brother would be angry and want to even the score. So Jacob sends ahead various groups from his entourage to appease, if not intimidate, Esau. Perhaps Esau would think twice before striking back at Jacob.

Finally, in one of the most dramatic scenes in all of scripture, the two brothers finally meet face to face. Jacob expects anger and revenge from his brother Esau. But instead he is surprised with an embrace of forgiveness from his estranged brother. All Esau wants to do is welcome him home. There will be no bitter recriminations from the past. There will only be mercy and forgiveness. Jacob is shocked. And then in some of the most memorable words of all of scripture Jacob says to Esau, "To see your face [of mercy] is to *see the face of God.*"

158

In this ordinary encounter with this ordinary human being, Jacob "sees the face of God." What makes this ordinary human encounter so extraordinary is Jacob's experience of such extravagant and undeserved mercy from his estranged brother Esau. In the embrace of his brother, Jacob has been to the mountaintop.

In the same way the mountaintop experiences continue for us. We "see the face of God," we are in the glorious presence of the transfigured Jesus, we are at the foot of Mount Sinai shielding our eyes from the blinding brightness of Moses' face, when we experience the undeserved surprise of God's mercy. When husbands and wives, brothers and sisters, friends and enemies refuse to "get back and get even" and instead choose to forgive, they have been to the mountaintop. They "see the face of God" in their forgivers.

In today's Second Lesson Paul takes the "mountaintop experience" one step further. Paul reminds us that as members of the Christian community and the beneficiaries of God's mercy in Christ, we get to "reflect" that same mercy in our lives and actions to others. We are like mirrors that reflect the bright, transfigured glory of Christ to others in our words and deeds of mercy.

Our congregation's mission statement develops that same image: "Servants Proclaiming, *Reflecting*, Celebrating Christ." This is quite a bold claim when you think about it. Through the ministry of this congregation we get to reflect the same glory the Israelites saw in Moses at the foot of Mount Sinai, the same glory the disciples saw in Jesus on the mountain of the transfiguration, and the same glory Jacob saw in the merciful face of Esau. Just think of it. Through our ordinary lives and the all-too-flawed ministry of this congregation we are privileged to do something very special. We can take the world to the mountaintop!

Sermons On The First Readings

For Sundays In
Lent And Easter

One Heaven Of A Party

Charles D. Reeb

To Brandy
my loving wife and very best friend

Preface

It has been said that writing a book is like birthing a child. For obvious reasons, I do not know (and will never know) what it is like to birth a child, but I certainly know what it is to conceive an idea, as well as to nurture and love it, until it is ready to be born. Such has been my experience in writing this collection of sermons. It truly has been a "labor" of love. Yet it is important to understand that the birthing process is not accomplished alone. You need the support of caring people to ensure that your "baby" will be happy and healthy.

My deepest gratitude goes out to those persons who supported and encouraged me through this process. Many thanks go to the members of my family for their love and support, especially my mother Jane Reeb, and my sisters Jill and Nancy. My mother's profound influence upon my life and faith and my sisters' cheers enabled me to write this collection of sermons. I also thank my wife Brandy. Her love, persistent patience, and endless encouragement gave me the strength to complete this collection. Thanks also go to the Reverends Allen Johnson and Sue Haupert-Johnson for their gift of friendship. They provided me with much needed comic relief while I wrote these sermons.

I am especially grateful to Reverend Ed Beck of Desert Garden Church in Sun City West, Arizona, and Reverend Bill Barnes of St. Luke's United Methodist Church in Windermere, Florida. Their invaluable feedback, wisdom, and gentle opinions helped to shape this manuscript. I also must thank Dr. Claudia Slate for being my "grammatical consultant" and Lea Ellen Dewitt for performing the necessary administrative tasks that accompany such a project.

I would be remiss if I did not thank my heroes. I could never have written these sermons without their influence upon my life and ministry: my late father, Paul Reeb — thanks for being the best father a son could have; the late Reverend Brad Dinsmore — thanks for introducing me to the power of preaching; Dr. Riley P. Short — thanks for showing me what it means to be a pastor; Dr. William L. Self — thanks for being my guide on the homiletic journey; Dr. W. Waite Willis, Jr. — thanks for helping to shape my theology; Dr. John K. Bergland — thanks for feeding my soul with wisdom; Dr. G. Gil Watson — thanks for showing me what it means to love a congregation.

Finally, I would like to thank the saints of The First United Methodist Church of Lakeland, Florida, who graciously listened to many of these sermons. Every pastor should experience the kind of love and support that this remarkable church lavishes upon its pastors.

Introduction

Is There Any Word From God Today?

Duke Chapel at Duke University in Durham, North Carolina, is a majestic cathedral gathering more than a thousand worshipers most Sundays. Distinguished preachers are often invited to preach. Following a Sunday service, I was greeted by the New Testament scholar W. D. Davies, a colleague from the Divinity School faculty. Both of us are confident about the power of the gospel and the rightness of a preached Word. "How are they to believe in one of whom they have never heard? And how are they to hear without someone to proclaim him?" (Romans 10:14). We commented on the sermon and shared our esteem for the preacher. Then with neither praise nor blame, Dr. Davies commented, "Preaching looks so easy to do. But it isn't, is it?" Every preacher knows the truth of that!

Ministers who are expected to preach, week in and week out to the same hearers, especially know the truth of it. If Barth is right, and I think he is, that folks come to church seeking a Word from God — that they come asking, "Is there any Word from God for me today?" — then we can only wonder: *Who dares to preach?*

Protestants believe that the saving presence of God is experienced not only through the bread and wine at the table, but also and more so through the Word of God faithfully preached and rightly heard. The gifted theologian and Christian martyr Dietrich Bonhoeffer boldly said, "The preaching of the Word of God *is* the Word of God!" Proclamation in Advent and Christmastide heralds the Word made flesh, full of grace and truth. The Sundays of Lent and Eastertide offer a challenge and opportunity to lift up the Presence of the Risen Christ; *Word of God for us; saving Word of God for us.* We are saved by faith through this grace of God present in Word and Sacrament.

Divine Presence In Preaching

Have you ever attended a meeting when no one else was there? There may have been a room full of people, yet no real meeting of hearts and minds. Everything was polite and courteous, no rude turning away, just folks being present without any genuine presence. Jesus spoke of this saying, "You have ears to hear, but never hear." Have you been in a meeting where both speakers and hearers were vitally engaged? Ears really heard. Words brought laughter and/or tears. Eyes became windows into soul. In that moment you knew you were "meeting" and afterwards could say, "We have met!"

I thrill to the times when I experience *Meeting and Presence* in a preached word. The scriptures have been read, prayers prayed, and the preacher is proclaiming the gospel. Then one becomes aware of the Other Voice speaking. "How silently, how silently, *the wondrous gift is given.* God imparts to human hearts the blessings of his heaven. No ear may hear his coming, but in this world of sin, where meek souls will receive him, still the dear Christ enters in."[1] This is language of the boundary, a meeting between creature and Creator, between you and your God. It's like the murmur of a gentle breeze, like the still, small voice naming you and calling you. Hearts are strangely warmed. In the theology of preaching, this is referred to as "Word Event." It is a language happening-saving word that is happening now.

A characteristic of Dr. Billy Graham's preaching is the boldness with which he proclaims the Bible as the Word of God. We shared table fellowship at a luncheon that honored him during one of his crusades. I found an opportunity to ask this question: "Dr. Graham, when you preach, you evidence confidence that you are proclaiming the very Word of God. How do you know that it is indeed God's Word and not your own idea?" He didn't hesitate when he answered, "Oh! It is when one person there, twenty people there, many people there, but when at least one person no longer hears my voice, but hears the Other Voice speaking."

But more should be said. Christian preaching which is worthy of the name will lift up the life, death, and resurrection of Jesus Christ. It offers him as Kyrios (saving grace). Kerygma (literally

166

proclamation) in the New Testament announces the saving acts of God in Christ. It proclaims, but also addresses the hearers, expecting a response. It is witness here and now. Christian preaching bears witness to the might and right of God in Christ. It is not primarily the preacher's own ideas. Every address given as "Preached Word" should offer Christ. Thus, the task for preaching is not so much to say what no one has yet said; instead, it is to bear witness to what Christ wants everyone to see and to hear.

Faced with the awesome responsibility of preaching, one needs the help of God. Yet we do well to guard against invoking the aid of the Holy Spirit too soon. Let us never claim inspiration before the text has been well studied. Luther confides that he once entered the pulpit expecting that the Spirit would give him utterance. He said that what he heard was, "You've been lazy this week, Martin." When a young rabbi asked an old rabbi, "How can I faithfully preach the Torah?" the old rabbi replied, "Turn yourself into a giant ear."

Tests For True Preaching

Since the dawning of the Age of Reason (fifteenth century), the concept of revealed truth and divinely inspired word has been challenged. Confidence (faith) is placed mostly in truth that can be tested and measured. This has prompted this question about *Word of God for me*. How does one measure it?

Hundreds of criteria are employed when sermons are considered and discussed. Here are some of them: It's brief and to the point. It holds my interest. It's easily understood. It rebukes sin. It lays down the law. It's inspiring. It lets me laugh. It makes me cry. It's relevant to today. It is faithful to tradition. It is well studied. It convicts sinners. It gets a response. It brings persons to Christ. It confronts evil. It teaches virtue. It gains a favorable verdict. It's sincerely believed by the preacher. It's faithful to the scriptures. It leads to the increase of faith. It's appropriate for the time and place. It's inclusive.

After forty years in the desert places, where a preacher prepares to preach ("in the desert of my heart, let the healing fountain start"[2]), I have come to honor almost every test and measure for the preached Word. There are three that I find most important:

Is it faithful to the scripture? Some sermons that begin with a text, quote verses of scripture, and tell Bible stories, still fail this test. They simply do not proclaim the controlling message of the text. Some sermons, focused on a topic, are faithfully biblical, even though no scripture is quoted and no text employed. A helpful assumption is that the Bible knows more about life and death than I do. It raises more important questions than most anyone asks and gives better answers than any self-help book.

Is it faithful to the hearers? A saintly woman, who had been in church every Sunday for many years, remarked that one particular preacher was outstanding. "What was there about this preacher that made him special?" she was asked. "Oh, he cares for our souls," she said. Content, style, and language should be right for the audience, but genuine love and respect for the people will cover a multitude of weaknesses. A hireling cares nothing for the sheep. Care of soul never goes unwanted.

Is it sincerely believed by the preacher? Integrity and truth are in short supply these days. "Don't believe everything you hear. Only believe half of what you read," is common counsel. People used to say, "If you can't believe the preacher, who can you believe?" The deceptions of the hope hustlers and preaching profiteers have shamed preaching and burdened the church. Still, truth remains the powerful ally of credibility. Montaigne, in his essays, says truth is supreme among all virtues. Preachers who regularly pretend may be amusing and interesting but are seldom believed. Sincerity in a preacher is instinctively seen and known by hearers, sometimes before a word is spoken. It's true that some charlatans are believed for a while, but "you can't fool all of the people, all of the time." Preachers will not always be right. They can always be forthright.

Hospitality At The Holy Desk

One can say many good things about the young preacher Charley Reeb. The sermons that follow attest to his homiletic skills. There is one controlling idea. Everything relates to what went before and builds on it. His subject is easily understood and relevant. These sermons reflect unity and movement. The illustrations, taken from both classical and common sources, as well as personal experiences, are worth the price of the book. I'll buy any book of sermons that gives me one or two good illustrations that are fresh and believable. Reeb is a master at illustrating his points.

Those of us who are privileged to hear Charley preach know that this preacher loves to preach. He reminds me of a young thoroughbred racehorse in the starting gate, eager to go and ready to run to the wire. One can only be impressed with his presence in the pulpit. I've heard him often. I have never left saying, "I wish he would have given us a bit of himself." Neither have I left wishing he had been better prepared. His willingness to stay on task in the preparation of sermons has brought this book into being.

One Sunday, Reverend Reeb's subject was "Invitation." That day, both the sermon and the preacher exemplified the power and persuasiveness of *hospitality*. In the university the very best teachers reflect hospitality in the classroom. The professor may be demanding and uncompromising, but there is respect and welcome for every student, and it calls them forth.

The quality of friendship at the pulpit translates into *hospitality at the holy desk.* In Aristotle's classical teaching of rhetoric, he names three essential qualities for the speaker: kindliness, wisdom, and verve (he called it manliness in his time). The first essential is kindliness. Hostility, rancor, bitterness, or anything else that puts an edge on you, will quickly turn others away. I think you will experience the warm-hearted friendliness of Charley Reeb in these sermons, even as he comes close to the nerve. I'm proud to say, Charley is my friend.

John K. Bergland
Retired Professor of Preaching
Duke Divinity School

Dr. John K. Bergland is a retired United Methodist minister. He served churches in Montana, Ohio, and North Carolina, and on the faculties of United Theological Seminary in Dayton, Ohio, and Duke Divinity School, Durham, North Carolina. At Duke he was professor of preaching and associate dean. For six years he authored "Sermon Starters" in the *Circuit Rider*. He compiled and edited four volumes of the *Abingdon Preachers Annual* (1991-1994). Since retirement he and his wife Barbara have lived on their cattle ranch in North Carolina and their winter home in Lakeland, Florida. In Lakeland, they attend First United Methodist Church where Charley Reeb is one of the ministers.

----

1. Phillips Brooks, "O Little Town of Bethlehem," *The United Methodist Hymnal: Book of United Methodist Worship* (Nashville, Tennessee: The United Methodist Publishing House, 1989) #230.

2. Attributed to W. H. Auden.

Come Clean

There is an old story about a mother of eight who walked into her house after visiting with a neighbor and found her five youngest children huddled together in the middle of the living room. On closer examination, she discovered that her children were gathered around a family of skunks. Utterly shocked, she screamed, "Run, children, run!" Responding to their mother's command, each child grabbed a skunk and ran.[1]

This story is a poignant parable of our sinful nature. Like giddy children huddled together around something unique, sin has a way of fascinating each of us. Like Adam and Eve in Genesis, it is the mysterious and forbidden fruit which is most attractive. In fact, sin can be so attractive that when we are told to run away from it, we cannot help but pick it up and take it with us, choosing to forget the unbearable stench it sprays over our lives. So even with love, advice, wisdom, warnings, and even screams, we apparently are unable to leave our sins behind.

Our inability to relinquish our sins makes the beginning of Lent very challenging. In order to prepare for the resurrection of Christ, we are encouraged to "give up" something. Unable to give up our sins, we dance around the edges of our weakest areas and lift up some token sacrifice, like chocolate or meat, and feel pretty good about "the cross we bear" until Easter.

However, the prophet Joel does not let us get away with our pseudo-sacrifices. Joel ushers in a wake up call, a reality check. Joel calls us to a true, honest, veneer-breaking repentance. And this call to repentance is nothing short of ominous, for Joel paints a picture that we do not want to see. A trumpet blares. A warning is made. The clouds turn threatening. Our phony pretenses dissolve into the darkness. And our only hope is found in the words that echo in the midst of the gloom: "Return to me with all your heart, with fasting, with weeping, and with mourning" (v. 12). Yet even these words are terrifying because they mean we must return to God vulnerable and exposed.

There was an assumed rule that I recognized as a child. Whenever someone in our family saw an important person come up the driveway, he or she was legally, ethically, and morally responsible to scream, "Fire drill!" Whoever was within earshot of those resounding words was obligated to find anything on the floor that did not belong — like clothes, dishes, magazines, newspapers — gather them up and run to a back room, throw the junk inside, and close the door. Each of us was then required to regroup, slap on a smiling face, wait for the door bell to ring, and when the front door was opened say, "Oh! What a surprise! Come in and see us as we always are." Sound familiar?

Many times we do that to God. When the Lord comes knocking on the door of our hearts, we plead, "Please don't ask me to open that back room in my heart and reveal all the trash I have accumulated. Please don't ask me to 'rend my heart' and allow that sinful junk to spill out. They are my secrets, and I am afraid of what you will see." As a result, we continue to gather our skunks, run to a back room in our hearts, and seek to hide them from God.

Our reluctance to return to God with *all* of our heart stems from the fear in confronting the truth within ourselves. It is difficult to probe below the surface and take a hard look at our sins. It is easier to bask in the light of denial than to stare into the darkness of truth. It is more comfortable to look the other way than to come face to face with painful reality. And, understandably so, because for some, the painful reality is the jealousy, resentment, and anger that is eating away at their souls bit by bit. For others, it is the destructive habits that wear them down to complete helplessness. Still, for many, it is the lonely and bitter life of living only for themselves. In short, returning to God with all of our heart may mean returning to God with a deteriorated heart.

The contemporary theologian Frederick Buechner gives us insight into the destructive nature of sin when he writes:

> *The power of sin is centrifugal. When at work in a human life, it tends to push everything out toward the periphery. Bits and pieces go flying off until only the core is left. Eventually bits and pieces of the core itself go flying off until in the end nothing at all is left ... sin is whatever you do, or fail to do, that pushes [God] away, that widens the gap between you and [God] and also the gaps within yourself.*[2]

This is not anything new for the majority of us. Most of us are aware of the tremendous gap between what we are and what we are called to be. It takes little self-examination to realize how far we have fallen short of the glory of God. But what is difficult for us to learn and accept is what it takes for us to be free from sin's shackles. What is difficult for us is to get our minds around the fact that returning to God with all of our heart is all about surrendering.

It has been said that "genuine religious conversions are blessed defeats."[3] This means that we must come clean, confessing and exposing our whole hearts to God, even those areas we have hidden away. We are called to do this *not* because God is angry that we have been hiding something. God is intimately aware of what we have tried to keep hidden. We are called to come clean because confessing and exposing requires us to let go of the ownership of our hearts and allow God to take over. It requires us to let go of pride and take comfort in our complete dependence upon God. It requires us to let go of sin and embrace the healing that comes through God's forgiveness in Christ.

When we come before God open and vulnerable, we need not be afraid. For God's promise in Joel is that God is "gracious and merciful, slow to anger, and abounding in steadfast love" (v. 13). I relish the words, "abounding in steadfast love." To me, they mean that God does not give up on us and is always willing to pour out gifts of love and grace lavishly. All we must do is receive them.

I heard about a woman who opened herself to God's abounding love and received far more than she ever expected. She had

173

become active in a church and was beginning to release sins and wounds from a checkered past. She was reluctant, however, to bring her bleeding heart to God; yet as she felt the love and acceptance of the congregation and God's Spirit, she began to experience the freedom that comes from trusting in God's mercy. Soon she felt ready to express her liberating faith through the sacrament of Baptism. Her pastor was so excited about her transformation that he planned a baptism unlike any other. When the day came for her baptism, the whole congregation gathered in great anticipation. At the appointed time, the pastor, who usually baptized by sprinkling, took a jumbo-sized cup, dipped it in the baptismal font, and said, "I baptize you in the name of the Father!" — and poured the entire cup over her head. He took another cupful and said, "And of the Son!" — and poured it all over her head. Then he took the third cupful and said, "And of the Holy Spirit!" — and poured the water all over her head. The woman was drenched. The water was heard trickling off her hair and clothes and on to the floor. But she was not uncomfortable. In fact, she was relieved. She stood in front of the chancel soaking wet and leaned over to whisper in the pastor's ear, "Now I know Jesus loves me."[4]

What holds you back from a fresh new baptism of God's Spirit? Why not return to God with all of your heart and experience the abundance of God's steadfast love? Return to God with all your sins and bathe them in the lather of God's forgiveness. Return to God with all your vulnerabilities and be drenched in God's acceptance. Return to God with all your tears and allow God's warm blanket of grace to dry them all. Come clean and be made clean.

---

1. *Just for Laughs* (The Christian Communications Laboratory, 1982), p. 132.

2. Frederick Buechner, *Wishful Thinking: A Theological ABC* (New York: Harper Collins, 1973), p. 88. Used by permission.

3. Attributed to C. S. Lewis.

4. Story shared with me by a colleague.

One Heaven Of A Party

Moses saw that look in their eyes. He saw that glimmer of hope on their faces. For when those words dripped like honey from his mouth, the people of God dreamed about what it was going to be like. At first glance, they really do not seem to be very exciting words, but for those who had been toiling in the wilderness, these words were like living water to a parched soul: "When you have come into the land that the Lord your God is giving you as an inheritance to possess, and you possess it, and settle in it ..." (v. 1).

When those words tickled their eardrums, all kinds of thoughts blossomed in their minds: thoughts of a land of their own with crops as far as the eye could see, thoughts of luscious food that would nourish their bodies, and thoughts of living life without fear or famine. They had waited so long for that moment when they would be able to say good-bye to the same old manna and enter the Promised Land. So with high hopes and delightful dreams they went forward, anticipating how Moses was going to complete the sentence: "Is he going to tell us to throw a party? Is he going to tell us to gather all the food and wine and eat and drink until our heart's content? Don't we deserve a little celebration, considering all we have been through?"

God wanted them to have a celebration but probably not the kind for which they were hoping. Moses instructs the Israelites that the first thing they are to do when they come into the Promised Land is to take their first fruits and present them to the Lord. That sounds fair enough. God was going to give them this land, so the least they could do is say a little prayer before the big banquet. But

175

just a prayer over the food was not all God expected. In verses 11 and 12, we find that Moses tells the people that after they present the food and thank God for it, they are to celebrate by giving it all to the Levites, aliens, orphans, and widows. How's that for a celebration — taking the first bounty you have been dreaming about for years and giving it away to the needy?

I think it is fair to say that when we imagine a celebration, this is not the image that comes to mind. Extravagance and indulgence, these are the things we envision at a celebration; a time to spend money on a nice dress or suit and show up ready to forget the cares of the world for a little while. But gathering up all the food from lavishly decorated tables and driving to a nearby mission to feed the hungry is usually not an activity which appears on an engraved invitation.

What is God saying to us through this challenging text? In order to receive the full impact of Moses' words to the Israelites, we need to appreciate the essence of "celebration" as it comes to us in this text. In effect, God was telling the Israelites through Moses to give out of their fullness, which is what celebrating is all about. The Israelites were being told that when they entered the Promised Land and were filled with joy and bounty, they were to let it spill over so others would share it too. Then they would experience what it means to celebrate life.

Honestly, I wonder if the Israelites were spiritually and emotionally ready for this kind of generosity? This is a probing question for those of us who live in a consumer culture. It seems that in our world a desire to experience the joy of giving is a rare virtue. Our culture spreads the gospel of greed, and many people are converted to it daily. Since childhood, the words, "That's mine, not yours," have shot from our mouths in one form or another. Ownership and possession seem to be what everyone is selling their souls for these days. "The one with the most toys wins." Is this not right? But there is a price to be paid when living a life governed by having and not giving. And the price is having an unbearable itch that is never scratched. The price is realizing that all our possessions will never bring lasting fulfillment. The price is the disappointing discovery of having gone against our creative destiny as those who bear the image of God.

When Jesus told the parable of the rich fool, he was offering this very insight. In the parable Jesus communicates how tragic it is for a person to be void of generosity. Jesus describes a man whose foolish greed caused him to miss out on life's most meaningful action: giving. The man looked upon all of his inherited possessions and became obsessed with hoarding them. At the end of the man's life, Jesus asked the inevitable question, "The things you have prepared, whose will they be?" (Luke 12:20). This pointed question reminded the greedy man that it was useless to keep all of his possessions, for he could never take them with him.

C. S. Lewis wrote of waking up in the middle of the night and not being able to fall back asleep. At the time, he was a bachelor and a college student and remembered how dark and still his dorm room was at Magdalene College. He recalled how there was no way for him to experience anything outside himself. He felt alone in a black hole. Suddenly, it dawned on him that what he was experiencing was the logical end to a self-centered life.[1] And "So it is with those who store up treasures for themselves but are not rich toward God" (Luke 12:21).

This is the very thing from which God was trying to protect the Israelites as they entered the Promised Land. God realized that receiving so much after they had gone without for so long might cause them to become dangerously independent. God realized that their tendency might be to store up their bounty selfishly and forget those who were unable to gather food for themselves. God realized that if they failed to remember that what they possessed was not their own, but only entrusted to them, they would probably fail to remember that *they* were not their own and be on their way toward ruining what they had been graciously given.

I have always been deeply struck by the damaging effects of selfishness. If we stop and think about it, selfishness is the cause of more pain, chaos, and destruction than any other human vice. All it takes is some overblown pride fertilized by blind insensitivity for corruption to rear its ugly head. History teaches us this. How many individuals, cultures, and civilizations have been destroyed by the simple, yet consuming demon of selfishness? We know this demon exists in our own hearts. After we have hurt a loved one, we look surprisingly at the wounds we have inflicted and confess, "I do not know what happened. I do not know what got into me. I guess I did not think how it would affect you." And we realize that, for a little while, we were not ourselves, and it scares us.

We were not intended to live only for ourselves. We were created as images of a generous God. The eloquent preacher and writer John Claypool shares an insight about our connection to God through generosity:

> *I never tire of contending that generosity is the most basic of all the virtues. In the time before time, the Bible suggests that God said, "This wonder of aliveness is too good to keep to myself. I want others to get in on this ecstasy and to experience this wonder." This is the biblical answer to the question, "Why something and not nothing?" Creation is at bottom an act of generosity — God sharing the bounty of what he was and what he had.*[2]

When reflecting on this great truth, we should conclude that we are never more like God than when we are generous. When we give with grateful and joyous hearts, we are somehow sharing with God the ecstasy of generosity. And as we allow ourselves to share what we have, we are imitating the very character of God.

The glorious gift of creation beckons us to reflect the generosity of God. Unfortunately, many of us do not take the time to notice. Consider trees. We walk and drive by them everyday, but do we ever consider how they inherently share and give back to the world in which they live and grow? Gaze at a tree sometime and reflect on the beauty, food, shade, and shelter it gives. Climb a tree and remember how it becomes fuel to warm us, timber to house us, medicine to heal us, and material to clothe us. Yet that is only the beginning. Remember that a tree serves as a homegrown air-conditioner by absorbing enormous amounts of heat. In addition, an average shade tree serves as a humidifier for our environment, releasing 75 to 100 gallons of water into the air per day. A tree is also an air-filter, removing one-quarter pound of dust particles from the air everyday. And that is not all. An average tree supplies all the oxygen needed by ten people in one year and removes carbon dioxide from the atmosphere.[3] A tree demonstrates the generous cycle of life. It receives life and gives back life. Is it any wonder that the psalmist compares those who follow the laws of God as "trees planted by streams of water, which yield their fruit in its season" (Psalm 1:3)?

I read a true story about a woman who yielded her first fruits in a very generous way. The story attracted so much attention that it appeared in the *Boston Globe*. The story began with her entering a Hyatt Hotel with her fiancé to plan their wedding reception. They looked over menus filled with sumptuous gourmet food. They pored over a wide variety of china and silver. They even studied catalogs of flower arrangements. When they finally made all their selections, they received the bill. As they looked at what they owed, they discovered that they had very expensive tastes. The bill came to $13,000. They winced a little, wrote a check for half that amount as a down payment, and went home to work on wedding announcements.

A day or two after the announcements were mailed, the groom got cold feet and the wedding was canceled. When the distraught bride returned to the Hyatt to collect her refund, the events manager poured salt on her wounds by telling her that their contract with the hotel was binding. They could only receive $1,300 dollars back. She only had two options: forfeit the rest of her down payment or go ahead with the reception.

An incredible idea swept over this disappointed would-be bride. She thought to herself, "Why not go ahead with the reception?" But wait, whom would she invite, and what would she be celebrating? Suddenly, she knew exactly whom she would invite and why she would invite them. Ten years before, this same woman was down and out, living in a homeless shelter. Fortunately, she was eventually able to find a good job and, over time, set aside a sizable nest egg. Standing in the lobby of the Hyatt, she remembered this and had a gigantically generous notion that she would use her savings to throw a big bash for all the homeless people of downtown Boston. She sent invitations to rescue missions and homeless shelters and made sure everything was ready.

So in June of 1990, the Hyatt Hotel in downtown Boston hosted a party of Kingdom-like proportions. People who normally dug through garbage cans for scraps of food savored the taste of chicken cordon bleu. Those with ragged and torn clothes were served hors d'oeuvres by waiters in tuxedos. Bag ladies, vagrants, and addicts lived like royalty for one night by drinking champagne, eating wedding cake, and dancing to big-band music until well after midnight.[4]

As the hostess looked upon the celebration and experienced the ecstasy of generosity, I imagine she felt a little of what the hymn writer felt when he wrote these words:

> *O Love that wilt not let me go,*
> *I rest my weary soul in thee;*
> *I give thee back the life I owe,*
> *That in thine ocean depths*
> *Its flow may richer, fuller be.*[5]

Try generously giving away the first fruits of the life God has given you. And as you share a laugh with a lonely person, see contentment from a hungry person, receive a hug from a wounded person, you just may close your eyes, hold back a tear, and pray, "Lord, now I know what you mean."

---

1. Copyright 1993, 2000, John Claypool. All rights reserved. Reprinted from *Stories Jesus Still Tells* by John Claypool; published by Cowley Publications (p. 15), 907 Massachusetts Ave., Cambridge, MA 02139, www.cowley.org (800-225-1534). Used by permission.

2. *Ibid.*, p. 120. Used by permission.

3. James Earl Massey, *Sundays in the Tuskegee Chapel: Selected Sermons* (Nashville: Abingdon Press, 2000), p. 62.

4. Philip Yancey, *What's So Amazing About Grace?* (Grand Rapids, Michigan: Zondervan, 1997), pp. 48-49.

5. George Matheson, "O Love That Will Not Let Me Go," *The Covenant Hymnal: A Worship Book* (Chicago: Covenant Publications, 1996).

Falling Into Faith

Woody Allen once quipped, "If there is a God, he is the ultimate under-achiever." This statement is a stinging indictment, especially for those who have high expectations of God. Some may even find it offensive. It is unthinkable that God would want to do less than the very best for the world. However, these deflating words are not too distant from the attitude of Abraham at the beginning of Genesis 15.

Abraham has waited expectantly for the child that God has promised him and anticipated the joy of a son who would continue the lineage of the Hebrews. But his patience and anticipation run thin. He has experienced the days turning into weeks and weeks turning into months and months turning into years and, still, no son. So when a word from God is revealed in a vision which speaks about the promise of great rewards, Abraham can't help but protest, "What do you mean, a reward? How can you say you will give me anything when you have not kept your promise of a son? Because you have not kept your promise, a slave born in my house is to be my heir. I must say that I expected more from the Creator of the universe."

If we are honest, there are times when Abraham's protest is our protest. Deep disappointments compel us to shake a fist at God for not fulfilling our expectations. Circumstances in life have not turned out the way we had hoped. Our lives have not turned out the way we had planned. Dreams have been shattered. Promises have been broken. Goals have been admired but never realized. Honest and earnest prayers appear to have no results. Life just doesn't work out the way it was supposed to, and we are angry — angry with God, angry with life, and angry with ourselves.

In Arthur Miller's play *The Price,* there is a scene where a couple is reminiscing about their lives together. As they reflect on their past, they sense what a disappointment their lives have been. They recall all the goals which were never realized. Climactically, the wife says to her husband, "Everything was always temporary with us. It's as if we were never anything. We were always just about to be."[1]

We have all been there: waiting desperately for the fruition of a hope but never seeing it come to pass. It is very agonizing and painful. We can only stand on our tiptoes for so long. Soon our hope shrinks before our growing disappointment, we become hopeless, and an existential doubt settles deep within our spirit.

God heard and felt a similar hopelessness in Abraham, so God led him outside to count all the beautiful stars. As Abraham gazed at the sky dotted with dazzling bits of light, God shared with him that his heir, his very own son, would produce as many descendants as there were stars in the sky. At this point, we would expect Abraham to chime in with the cynical sigh, "Promises, promises." That is what most of us would have done. But this time, Abraham's response was different: no complaints, no questions, no doubts, only belief that all of God's promises would be fulfilled.

As we follow this dialogue, now is the time some may ask, "What just happened?" One moment Abraham is a pouting protestor, and the next moment he is a bonafide believer. One moment we are living vicariously through Abraham as he complains to God, the next moment Abraham accepts God's promise and a big crown of righteousness is placed on his head. Did we miss something? What caused Abraham to move from doubt to faith so swiftly? The passage does not appear to help us in any way. For after God shares with Abraham the promise, scripture simply reads, "And (Abraham) believed the Lord" (v. 6). That's it. God said it. Abraham believed it. That settles it. Or was there more to it than that?

Maybe pivotal pieces to this sacred conversation are missing from the text. Perhaps God answered all of Abraham's questions and doubts about the delayed promise, and Abraham was satisfied.

Or maybe God led Abraham beyond the stars and gave him a big glimpse into the future filled with a great land and a blessed ancestry and said, "If you will just believe, all of this will be yours." These are not bad explanations. If they were true, they would certainly make it easier to understand Abraham's abrupt faith. But all we have are the words, "He believed the Lord: and the Lord reckoned it to him as righteousness" (v. 6).

What exactly happened that special night under the stars? I believe the key to understanding this remarkable transformation is to shift our focus from Abraham to God. After all, this is where the scripture is leading us. For Abraham to believe God in spite of his circumstance was nothing less than a miracle. The brilliant Old Testament scholar Walter Brueggemann put it this way: "[Abraham] did not move from protest to confession by knowledge or persuasion but by the power of God who reveals and causes his revelation to be accepted."[2]

This idea of faith is foreign to many of us because we typically see faith as something that we provide, instead of something that God gives to us. But faith can only happen when we allow God to give it to us. We come to faith through God's initiative, not ours. When we gain this understanding, we begin to see faith as giving in to the power of God and permitting that power to have control over our lives. The eloquent preacher John Claypool remembers when he had this epiphany regarding faith. He stated, "Faith is not believing in the unbelievable, nor is it committing intellectual suicide and taking a leap in the dark. But faith is response on our part to the inthrust of God."[3] I believe this is what happened to Abraham. God "inthrusted" power and promise upon Abraham, and Abraham gave in and gave up. He finally arrived at the place where he waved the white flag of surrender and confessed that he needed God's power more than he needed his own agenda.

Sometimes it takes a great deal of time before we learn what it means to have faith. Why do you think we often hear of people who came to faith when they were in the midst of great despair or anguish? It is not that God wills pain or suffering on anyone, but often people are more open to the power and purposes of God when pride and selfishness are weakened.

"I am in deep," I cried out to God
"I am deeper," God replied
"How deep?" I asked
"Let go and see," God sighed[4]

Henri Nouwen beautifully illustrates faith as letting go when he recounts his experience of seeing a German trapeze troupe perform. After the breath-taking performance, Nouwen sat down with Rodleigh, the leader of the troupe, and asked him how he was able to perform with such grace and precision. Rodleigh explained: "The public might think that I am the great star of the trapeze, but the real star is Joe, my catcher ... The secret is that the flyer does nothing and the catcher does everything. When I fly to Joe, I have simply to stretch out my arms and hands and wait for him to catch me ... The worst thing the flyer can do is to try to catch the catcher. I am not supposed to catch Joe. It's Joe's task to catch me."[5]

Such insightful truth applies to the principle of faith. Often times, we misunderstand faith as the ability to grab on to God by affirming certain beliefs about God. But that requires intellectual work, which can be stimulating, but it is not faith. Faith is allowing God to grab you, wherever you may be. For instance, when Jesus called the disciples, he did not say, "Before you can be my disciples, I need to tell you who I am and then find out if you believe me." On the contrary, he simply commanded, "Follow me!" And the belief and understanding came only after they "gave in" and followed him. To use a metaphor, falling in love does not require an intellectual understanding or belief in love. The power of love does not invade only those who believe in it or desire it. In fact, love often comes unannounced. Even cynics have come to rest in the arms of love. Later, those same cynics come to know and believe in love's power. The same could be said of God. Assuming that we must provide intellectual assent to everything we can discover about God in order to have faith presupposes that we are able to figure everything out. What a ridiculous notion! We are not capable of grabbing God by our own efforts or mental gymnastics. We are only capable of allowing God to grab us.

When we begin to understand faith in this manner, Abraham's "change of heart" becomes clear. Abraham attained righteousness through faith not because of what he did but what he refused to do. Instead of controlling his life and destiny and taking God on his own terms, he accepted God on God's terms and rested in the truth that God's plan and promise was paramount, even if the timetable seemed uncertain. Abraham understood that "hope is trusting that something will be fulfilled, but fulfilled according to the promises [of God] and not just according to our wishes."[6]

For Abraham, God was more than a vehicle for a promise. God was the Lord of his life. This is evident in Abraham's attitude and strength in the midst of his barren situation. When Abraham first believed, his circumstances did not change immediately. Sara did not come leaping to him exclaiming she was pregnant, nor did a baby fall from the starry sky. But Abraham's attitude changed. Instead of waiting in protest, he waited in hope. We see this in verse 8 when Abraham asks, "O Lord God, how am I to know that I shall possess it?" For Abraham, the question was no longer if or when, but how. Abraham was now confident that God's promise for him would be fulfilled. He prepared himself through faith to receive it and looked toward the future with a renewed confidence.

When we open our lives to God's gift of faith, the promises of God take on a whole new meaning. The profound statement of faith in Hebrews becomes flesh in us: "Faith is the *substance* of things hoped for, the conviction of things not seen" (Hebrews 11:1). Our faith becomes a living out of the expectation that God's promises will be known by us in the future. Through our thoughts, attitude, and actions, we become the very substance of that for which we hope. Our faith provides us with a vision of what God desires for us and the strength and conviction to live out that vision.

In *The Baltimore Sun*, there was an article about an artist suffering from macular degeneration, a disease which deteriorates the eyes and affects vision. You would think that an impairment of this kind would be an artist's worst nightmare, but not for Sophia Libman. Ironically, the disease has helped her become a better artist. Because she is not able to see details, her ability to capture the essence of what she paints has increased. Her work has become more truthful, unencumbered by decoration. Her condition gives her the ability to envision and paint only the essentials.[7]

When we fall into faith, our wishes, expectations, and timetables for life become blurred and God's vision for our lives comes into perfect focus. Our agendas move to the periphery to make room for God's power, purpose, and plan for us. Soon we are able to see God's will for our lives, and we begin to live out God's promises.

Haven't you waited long enough? Haven't you listened to the promises of God long enough? Isn't it time for you to follow Abraham's lead and open yourself to God's power and plan for your life? So why not let go and find faith. Give up and find God. Give in and find power. Fall back and find a future.

1. Maxie Dunnam, *Pack Up Your Troubles: Sermons on How to Trust in God* (Nashville, Tennessee: Abingdon Press, 1993), p. 79.

2. Walter Brueggemann, *Interpretation: A Bible Commentary for Preaching and Teaching-Genesis* (Atlanta, Georgia: John Knox Press, 1982), p. 145.

3. John R. Claypool, *The Preaching Event* (Waco, Texas: Word Books, 1980), p. 101.

4. Poem by Charles D. Reeb.

5. Henri J. M. Nouwen, *The Only Necessary Thing: Living a Prayerful Life* (New York: The Crossroad Publishing Company, 1999), pp. 195-196.

6. Henri J. M. Nouwen, "A Spirituality of Waiting," *Weavings* 2, no. 1 (January-February, 1987), p. 10.

7. Originally published in *Circuit Rider*, copyright The United Methodist Publishing House, Charles D. Reeb — January/February 2002. Article in *The Baltimore Sun* written by Holly Selby.

The Invitation

I don't know about you, but I love receiving invitations. They make me feel special because they are deliberate and have me specifically in mind when sent. Now, sometimes invitations can be disappointing, especially when they have a hidden catch like, "Come to the wedding, but don't forget a gift," or "Come on vacation with us and maybe you will want to buy a time share." Invitations quickly lose their appeal when there is an agenda hidden behind them. But generally speaking, receiving an invitation means someone has taken the time to think of you and wants you to be part of something special.

What is the greatest invitation you have ever received? Do you remember it? Well, there is an invitation which will beat your greatest one hands down. For there are invitations, but there is also The Invitation. The Invitation promises more than just a good time or a wonderful experience. The Invitation is filled with more joy, fulfillment, and hope than any person or setting could ever give you. There are no hidden fees or agendas, and it costs you nothing. The Invitation is what many of you have been waiting for your whole life. Sound too good to be true? Well, it's not, because this invitation is not of this world.

The Invitation comes from God through many sources, but today The Invitation comes through the prophet Isaiah. Obviously, there is nothing new about The Invitation. It is timeless. It was originally extended to the people of God as they wandered in the wilderness, trying to find the way. Soon they became so desperate that they were grasping at anything and everything which looked like an answer. Remember the golden calf and the invitation to follow Baal? So God clarified The Invitation often but never more clearly than through Second Isaiah. Listen to the clarion call:

> *Ho, everyone who thirsts, come to the waters; and you that have no money, come, buy and eat! Come, buy wine and milk without money and without price. Why do you spend your money for that which is not bread, and your labor for that which does not satisfy? Listen carefully to me, and eat what is good, and delight yourselves in rich food. Incline your ear, and come to me; listen, so that you may live.* — Isaiah 55:1-3a

Since the period of the Israelites, The Invitation has been offered down through the centuries to those seeking to find the way: from prophets to peasants — from Paul to Priscilla — from mothers to monks — from Augustine to Wesley — from Billy Sunday to Billy Graham. Many servant followers have been the mouthpiece of The Invitation. Some have accepted The Invitation; others have rejected it. But The Invitation always stands, for it is the greatest invitation ever given to humankind.

Let me share with you for whom The Invitation is intended. The Invitation is for all who have been searching for meaning and fulfillment but have never found it. The Invitation is for those who have always desired so much more out of life. The Invitation is for those who feel empty, lost, and without hope. The Invitation is for those who continue to thirst and hunger for ultimate satisfaction. The Invitation is for those who have ever cried out, "What is the point of my life? Is there more to life than carpools, meetings, paying bills, and growing old?" For God's invitation is to experience an abundant life — the kind of life which only God can provide. And The Invitation is officially extended to you today. So the question is: What will you do with The Invitation?

Maybe your first inclination is to wait for a better invitation. This is what the Israelites seemed to do throughout their history, much to their disappointment. So I don't recommend it. But if you insist on looking for a better offer, you will be in good company. You can always find those who are looking for better invitations,

188

and you can always find what first appears as a better invitation. In fact, our whole culture is built around the desire for a better invitation. Advertisers make billions each year accommodating our desire for a better invitation. Therefore, we are an inviting culture.

We don't even need to leave our homes for our culture to invite and entice us. All we have to do is turn on the television or computer and go to the mailbox, and we will find invitations galore. When I returned to the pulpit from Atlanta some time ago, there were over 200 new e-mails on my computer. I wish I could tell you I had 200 close friends, but if the truth be known, eighty percent of those e-mails were advertisements — each one promising a new and improved, a more exciting, wonderful life. They guaranteed a better belly, a better bottom, a better boat, and a better business.

Have you checked your mailbox lately? Have you seen the sacrifice of the trees? And for what? Junk mail and advertisements. And some are very slick with their invitations. I received one that was packaged in an imitation overnight envelope. Written upon it for all to see were the words, "Urgent delivery for Charles D. Reeb, open immediately." It got my attention! So I tore it opened and discovered a new, exciting, once-in-a-lifetime offer for a credit card!

What about those fancy catalogs? Did you know there are 10,000 plus companies in America in the mail order business? They mail out over 13.5 billion catalogs each year.[1] And these catalogs are very inviting. Beautiful people without an ounce of fat modeling clothes, attempting to convince me that if I wear these clothes I will look exactly like them. Who are they trying to kid? Men in fancy garments doing yard work with not a drop of sweat on them and huge smiles on their faces, as if wearing that jacket makes you euphoric over yard work. Then there are the catalogs advertising all those cutting-edge gadgets and toys which are so essential to our existence on earth. For instance, I saw one catalog advertising a gizmo that will put "Caller ID" on your television screen so that you don't have to strain yourself getting out of the recliner to see who is calling. This is an essential household item.

Then there are the invitations on television. If you watch even a modest amount of television, you know that the answer to all

189

your problems seems to be a new automobile. Pardon the pun, but cars are the new "vehicles" of salvation. There was an advertisement for a certain type of automobile which claimed that the car will not only transform, but transfix you. When you feel the leather seats, hear the state of the art stereo system, and sense the power of the engine, all of your problems will dissolve. You will be elevated to another dimension. You will ride in a state of complete ecstasy. But have you seen anybody smiling in traffic lately? Or is the new smile the lifted middle finger?

We cannot forget the fast food companies. Those dealers in grease spend over 50 billion dollars annually in advertising. All of us have had our mouths watered by the bigger than life hamburger on the television screen. Oh, and don't forget the large fries and soda. Just forget that a Big Mac has enough calories for two meals. They just "love to see you smile" as you respond to their invitation.

If you speak honestly to advertisers, they will tell you that their goal is to convince you that you cannot live without their product. And we're convinced! In fact, advertisers are so convincing that someone has said, "No one ever lost money underestimating the intelligence of the consumer." Another put it this way: "The only reason a great many American families don't own an elephant is that they have never been offered an elephant for a dollar down and easy weekly payments."

We are convinced that we cannot live without these invitations. In fact, some are so convinced that they pray each night before they go to bed:

> Now I lay me down to sleep
> I pray my Cuisinart to keep
> I pray my stocks are on the rise
> And that my analyst is wise
> That all the wine I sip is white
> And that my hot tub's watertight
> That racquetball won't get too tough
> That all my sushi's fresh enough
> I pray my cell phone still works
> That my career won't lose its perks

My microwave won't radiate
My condo won't depreciate
I pray my health club doesn't close
And that my money market grows
If I go broke before I wake
I pray my Lexus they won't take.[2]

Many people live in the illusion that they cannot live without more. And as long as there is money to be made from gullible consumers, our culture will continue to accommodate and perpetuate this illusion by inviting us to have more, purchase more, and obtain more. We have been convinced that the more we have, the happier we are. But you and I know this is one of the greatest delusions humankind has ever produced. For many people are making a good living but living poor lives. There are many people who have much but love little. There are many people who look slick, and appear to have everything they desire, but inside they are decaying and rotting because they have been sold a bill of goods that "more will make them happier." But no matter the invitations we have received in the past, there is nothing big enough, powerful enough, thrilling enough, or pleasurable enough to satisfy our deepest thirst and hunger.

Need examples? Consider Howard Hughes. All he ever wanted was more money, so he parlayed inherited wealth into a billion-dollar pile of assets. All he wanted was more fame, so he invaded the Hollywood scene and became a filmmaker and star. All he wanted was more sensual pleasures, so he paid handsome sums to try to satisfy his every sexual urge. All he wanted was more thrills, so he built and piloted the fastest aircraft ever known. All he wanted was more power, so, in secret, he dealt political favors so masterfully that two U.S. presidents became his pawns. All he ever wanted was more and more and more. He was absolutely convinced that more would bring him complete satisfaction. Unfortunately, history proves otherwise. In his final years, he was emaciated, colorless, and had a sunken chest. His fingernails had grown into inches-long corkscrews. His teeth were rotting, and all over his body were innumerable needle marks from his drug addiction. "Howard

Hughes died believing the myth of more. He died a billionaire junkie, insane by all reasonable standards."[3]

How many similar stories do we need to hear before we will understand that the more thrills we seek the more we will find that thrills pass away? How many disappointments do we need to experience before we realize that material things do not ultimately satisfy? How many over-rated invitations do we need to accept before we understand that the answer to our problems and the key to our meaning and fulfillment does not come from anything the world invites us to receive but can only come from the "One who created us for himself."

This is God's plea to us through Isaiah: "Why do you spend your money for that which is not bread, and your labor for that which does not satisfy?" (v. 2). "Why do you eat out of dumpsters when I have prepared for you a free banquet of Ritz Carlton proportions? Isn't it about time you listened to my invitation? Isn't it about time you inclined your ear in my direction? Isn't it about time you allowed the wise words of life I have shared to become flesh within you?"

Some listen; others don't. For there are those who would agree that more does not make people happier, but they don't need God to convince them. They can find the answers on their own. For them, God is a crutch. They believe with Jesse Ventura that "religion is for weak-minded people." When God is mentioned, they protest, "I don't need God. I am the master of my ship, the pilot of my plane. I am smart and resourceful enough to handle whatever comes my way." This philosophy of life sounds noble in our individualistic culture but nothing could be more foolish, for we are not as strong and resourceful as we would like to believe.

A groom found out how foolish he was when he and his new bride stayed at the Watergate Hotel on their wedding night. The concerned bride asked, "What if this place is still bugged?" The groom said confidently, "Don't worry, honey; I'll look for a bug." He looked everywhere: behind the drapes, behind the pictures, under the rug. Finally, he said, "Aha!" Under the rug was a disc with four screws. He took out his Swiss army knife, unscrewed the screws, and threw the screws and the disc out the window. The next morning, the hotel manager asked the newlyweds, "How was your room? How was the service? How was your stay at the Watergate Hotel?" The groom suspiciously asked, "Why are you asking me all of these questions?" The hotel manager replied, "Well, the couple in the room under you complained that their chandelier fell on them."[4]

We think we know, but we have no idea. We think we understand, but we don't. When we fail to understand the truth, it can have a damaging effect upon us. And, more importantly, when we fail to sense our true need and understand the real truth about God, it can be a detriment to our very lives. This is why God says to us: "My ways are not your ways. My thoughts are not your thoughts. My ways are higher than your ways, and my thoughts are higher than your thoughts" (v. 9). "I know you better than you know yourself. I created you and know every hair on your head and every intricate line on your fingers. I designed you for the purpose of being in relationship with me. If you only knew, if you only recognized what you are capable of accomplishing if you would allow me to empower you."

Some of us still won't listen. So in desperation, God says, "What must I do to convince you that I love you and want what is best for you?" Then God put skin on and came to earth and loved us, taught us, was mocked for us, ridiculed for us, pierced for us, crucified for us, and then rose from the dead for us. Now, with scars on his hands, God reaches out to us and pleads, "Now will you listen to me?"

Perhaps when the invitation is put in those terms, we are more curious about what The Invitation truly offers. The text says that God will have mercy on us, abundantly pardon us, give us guidance, and make us "go out in joy and be led back in peace" (v. 12). But listen closely, for God might have other words for us: "Put away all those things you don't need. Quit pretending to be strong. I love you. I forgive you. I want to live inside you. I have a purpose for you. I want the best for you, and only I can give it to you."

Some time ago I preached to a youth group. At the conclusion of my message, a young teenager approached me. She was on the verge of tears. She said, "I have to find out if something is true."

"What's that?" I asked. She said, "You mentioned in your talk that God loves me. Do you believe that? Because I don't believe anyone has ever loved me. My dad left me and my mother abused me, and I have gone from one institution to another. I've been sexually abused, neglected, and you are telling me that God loves me?" "That's right," I said. "God loves you!" She paused for a moment as tears began rolling down her cheeks. Then she said simply, "Well, if God loves me, then nothing else matters. If God loves me, that's all that matters."

Perhaps some of you reading this sermon feel like I am writing directly to you. Maybe you have accepted every invitation this world has to offer and it has been like salt water to your thirsty soul, making you thirstier than ever. Perhaps some of you have attended church your whole life yet never really have come to grips with the love of God. Oh, you have heard all about it before but never really allowed yourself to experience it. Perhaps some of you have accepted The Invitation before, but now your relationship with God is stale and you need to taste the fresh Bread of Life again. The good news is that God's banquet of blessings has been prepared, and you are invited! There is a place at God's table reserved for you. A special engraved invitation written by a pierced hand is yours. Isn't it time for you to accept it?

Come and receive God's forgiving grace. Come quench your thirst for forgiveness and acceptance. Come and feast on God's wisdom. Come and find nourishment for your soul, strength for your life, and purpose in living. Come! You're invited never to be the same again.

---

1. Information shared with me by Dr. William L. Self.

2. Poem by Laura Goethel.

3. Bill Hybels in *Leadership*, Vol. X, no. 3 (Summer, 1989), p. 38.

4. David O. Dykes, Pastor of Green Acres Baptist Church in Tyler, Texas, www.gabc.org.

A Happy Ending

A. A. Milne, the creator of Winnie the Pooh, wrote a simple, yet telling poem in his work, *Now We Are Six*:

> *When I was One, I had just begun.*
> *When I was Two, I was nearly new.*
> *When I was Three, I was hardly Me.*
> *When I was Four, I was not much more.*
> *When I was Five, I was just alive.*
> *But now I am Six, I'm as clever as ever.*
> *So I think I'll be six now for ever and ever.*[1]

This is a cute poem, but beneath its adorable rhyme lies a very sensitive issue for all of us: resistance to change. The truth is that most of us are creatures of habit, and once we get comfortable we like things to remain the same. If you don't believe me, look at where you are sitting now. Then look at those sitting around you. Next Sunday in worship, see if you experience a little déjà vu. See if you find yourself and most of those around you in the exact same seat each Sunday. We like for things to remain the same.

Resistance to change is not always bad. In fact, there are times when resistance to change is important. Some things should not change. Certain convictions should be kept, and certain principles need to be maintained. If not, our lives and the world as we know it would collapse. September 11 taught us that! Will we ever see the American Flag without upholding its principles?

However, when resisting change becomes a habit or a response from fear or laziness, it is tragic. It's tragic because we stop growing, stop maturing, and we betray our potential. We literally stop ourselves from becoming that which we are destined to become.

When resistance to change sneaks in to the realm of faith, it is doubly tragic. In fact, it is downright sinful. Our attitude is "I have been to Sunday school. I have read the Bible. I have learned all I need to know." And we foolishly believe that we have it all figured out. The result is that we are no longer open to God's guidance and wisdom. We are no longer open to the various ways God moves in and through us. Instead, we dig our feet in as if to say, "I will not be moved, not even by God." And then we languish in spiritual stagnation. This is a bad place to be, but it's so easy to get there. We have grown up. We have been educated. We have decided on a career. We have chosen the person with whom we intend to spend the rest of our lives. We buy a home where we want to live and raise a family, and we join a church we enjoy. Then life happens. And then the worst happens. We sit back, let down our guard, get comfortable, and proudly say, "I have arrived. I am as clever as ever. I am going to stay here forever and ever."

It is at these listless moments that we become the most vulnerable to temptation, sin, and failure. The exploits of King David are a testimony of this. When he was young and longing to please God, he was driven by God's dream for him. He went through all kinds of struggles in making himself ready to be king. He agonized night and day, day and night to make sure he was prepared for the future God had for him. Then he felt he had finally arrived. His major battles were completed. Jerusalem was secured as the eternal capital and he was crowned king. He had fulfilled his dreams. He had conquered all foes except one: himself. And basking in self-glory he failed to recognize his weakness. So he fell. And we all know the story of Bathsheba and the murder of Uriah.[2]

It is dangerous and foolish to drift into spiritual stagnation and complacency. John Wesley knew this danger. That is why he directed the small bands and classes to ask each other when they met, "How is your soul? Are you growing? Are you moving on towards perfection?"

The essence of Christianity is change. The outstanding preacher J. Wallace Hamilton makes this clear: "[Christianity] not only accepts change as part of God's purpose for life, it demands it. That's what it's here to do, to change things, to change the world. And the Christian, because he believes in a living God, faces not toward yesterday but toward tomorrow."[3] Our Christian history bears witness to this statement because Christian history is filled with stories of remarkable change. And not just change for the sake of change, but change for the sake of God's Kingdom. Hebrew prophets like Jeremiah and Amos called people to examine their hearts and move from empty worship to a deeper concern for the poor and needy who lived in the shadows of the Temple doors. Jesus called people to change their ideas about who were their brother and sister. Martin Luther called the Church to change its understanding of grace and salvation. Nineteenth-century abolitionists called people to change their hearts and express the change by giving up an economic system that depended on slave labor.[4]

Our scripture lesson symbolizes God's critical call for change. It teaches us that we as God's people are always being led from the wilderness of stagnation into new lands of growth and promise. We are always being pushed to move from where we are to where we need to be. God has rolled away the reproach of Egypt — the reproach of our past — and is leading us to new places, new understandings, new experiences, new ways of thinking about our faith, and new ways of living our faith.

So in the spirit of this text, I want us to look at the challenge of change and how we need to approach it.

The End Is The End

Some time ago, the Associated Press shared a story about a man who had entered the country illegally. The immigration authorities sought to deport him, to send him back to his homeland. But as they studied the case, they were confronted with a very unique international dilemma. The illegal alien stood there waving his arms, attempting to tell the authorities in broken English that they could not deport him since his homeland was no more.

197

He had come from a small country in Central Europe, and in the shifting of boundaries after World War I his country disappeared. It no longer existed.[5]

Is this not what has happened to many of us? The old and familiar world we were so comfortable with is gone. Old ways of thinking and understanding have changed. Life as we once knew it has disappeared, and we can't go home again. We are people without a familiar framework, and we long for that which once was.

I remember returning to the tennis courts of my childhood. It was the place where I had first learned to serve. It was where I first won a set against my dad. It was a place of happy memories. Yet when I returned to visit these nostalgic tennis courts, my heart broke. All over the courts were huge cracks with weeds growing out of them. The nets were torn and lying on the ground. The green surface was worn down to the hard gray concrete. And there was a sign in front of the courts that said, "Coming Soon: More Classroom space." They were turning my wonderful tennis courts into a classroom! An old, special place of my youth had died, and I grieved a loss that day.

All of us have difficulty accepting the end of something sacred. We want the old world to stay with us. We want old thinking, traditions, and customs to continue. We want to go back to the familiar and comfortable. In fact, some of us long for the old life to return so much that we resist change altogether. We refuse to accept it and continue living a fantasy of yesterday. Some of us are happy eating the stale manna of the past and are not willing to try the new cakes and grains of tomorrow. We are convinced that we are not going to like the way it tastes.

If we are ever going to be the people God calls us to be, we must "put away childish things" and move forward into change. We need to accept the end of one chapter of our lives and move into the next. We need to accept that our old life has died, and our new life needs to begin.

Perhaps I am speaking to you where you live? Maybe this year has been a challenging one and you want to move on to a better one, but cannot find the energy or courage to take that first step. Maybe someone has hurt you, and you feel it is time to forgive and move on, but resentment has become a good friend. Perhaps a loved one has died, but you can't seem to bring closure to your loss and get on with life. Maybe you are in an unhealthy relationship, but it's convenient and you fear being alone. Maybe you have grown out of your present job, but the routine of it is all you have ever known. Maybe you feel called into full-time ministry, but don't want to give up your lavish lifestyle. Perhaps your faith is growing into new ideas, concepts, and experiences, but the rigid beliefs of your past will not allow you to embrace growth. Do yourselves a favor. In the name of the God and the person God calls you to be, embrace the changes and growth God desires for you!

Did you know that lobsters must leave their shells in order to grow? Apparently, this is frightening for lobsters because the shell protects them from their predators who desire to tear them apart. Yet as they grow, the old shell must be abandoned. If they do not leave the old shell behind, it will soon become their prison and, finally, their tomb.[6]

Don't remain in your comfortable shell of the past or even the present. Get out of it. If you don't, you might get so comfortable that you'll never be able to get out. Then you will suffocate in the knowledge of what might have been.

The End Is The Beginning

One of the magnificent promises of our faith is the promise of new beginnings. Scripture and life affirm this promise. Whenever something ends, something new begins. And out of the negative comes the positive. So it does not matter how bad things have ended or how final circumstances appear. God always creates new beginnings. As God spoke through the prophet: "I am about to do something new" (Isaiah 43:19). God never permits failure to be final or the end to be the absolute end. By the power of God, when something ends, something new always begins. Natalie Sleeth eloquently expresses this truth in the "Hymn of Promise":

> In the bulb, there is a flower,
> In the seed, an apple tree;
> In cocoons, a hidden promise:

199

Butterflies will soon be free
In the cold and snow of winter
There's a spring that waits to be
Unrevealed until its season,
Something God alone can see

There's a song in every silence,
Seeking word and melody
There's a dawn in every darkness,
Bringing hope to you and me.
From the past will come the future;
What it holds, a mystery
Unrevealed until its season,
Something God alone can see

In our end is our beginning;
In our time, infinity
In our doubt there is believing;
In our life, eternity
In our death, a resurrection;
At the last, a victory
Unrevealed until its season,
Something God alone can see[7]

This is a profound hymn because it vividly describes God's promise of new beginnings. Yet the hymn confirms something even more important: God grows us through seasons, stages, and changes. God uses change to stretch and strengthen our souls. Therefore, change is an inevitable part of our faith journey. Remember what Paul said in 2 Corinthians: "All of us are ... being transformed into the same image [of Christ] from one degree of glory to another" (2 Corinthians 3:18).

We are invited to embrace this transformation. We are called to cooperate with God in these changes that move us through different degrees of glory. God encourages and empowers us to grow, but God will not do the growing for us. We must accept the end, move forward, and begin again with what God has in store for our lives. And as we move forward, we will experience a happy ending because we will feel the exhilaration of a new beginning.

I heard about a woman who felt the exhilaration of a new beginning. She was caught stealing and sentenced to prison. After serving time in prison, she sold everything she had, except for a few necessities, and gave it all away to the poor. Then she moved to the mountains and, as time passed, became an excellent painter. When she reflected on her transformation, she wrote, "When you have been caught, you have nothing to hide. And when you have nothing to hide, you have nothing to fear. And when you have nothing to fear, oh my, what you can become!"[8]

When we claim our new beginning, the winter of our life ends and spring begins. We realize there is a whole new world of possibilities — a promised life pregnant with potential. We realize there is so much more to life than the small circle we live in. We shake hands with a new purpose and destiny. We no longer keep God in a box. We understand God in new ways because we see the new and different ways God is working in and around us. We see ungodly things in the world we never saw before and are motivated to stand against them. We see Godlike things in the world and stand up for them. We grow in ways that we never thought we could grow. We live in ways that we never thought we would live. We arrive at a level of faith we never thought we could experience. We sense God's sanctifying and glorifying grace at work within us, all because we said, "Yes," to a new beginning!

I challenge you to claim the new beginning that God has in store for you. Don't stay in the wilderness of the end when a new beginning is calling you to "Go," as Kipling said, "Go and look behind the ranges. Something lost behind the ranges. Lost and waiting for you. Go!"[9] Mark Twain once said, "Twenty years from now you will be more disappointed by the things you didn't do than by the ones you did do. So throw off the bowlines. Sail away from the safe harbor. Catch the trade winds in your sails. Explore. Dream. Discover."[10]

The Beginning Is The End

When we embrace a new beginning, we are able to celebrate the end: the end of an old, worn-out life; the end of a life stuck in the wilderness of the past; the end of a life once stopped by stagnation; the end of a life stunted by fear. And as we look over the grave of our past and have the happiest funeral of our life, we will affirm with honorable pride, "The old has passed. The new has come. I am a new creation in Christ!" Then God just might say with a lump in his throat, "Finally, my child sees but a glimpse of what I see."

In *Waiting for Godot*, Vladimir asks Pozo: "Where are you going?" Pozo gives the Christian answer: "On."[11] As you look upon what needs to change in your life, God is asking you, "Where are you going?" May you respond:

> *[On as] you make me new*
> *With every season's change.*
> *[On] as you are recreating me:*
> *Summer, winter, autumn, spring.*[12]

1. "The End," from *Now We Are Six* by A. A. Milne. Copyright 1927 by E. P. Dutton, p. 102, renewed copyright 1955 by A. A. Milne. Used by permission of Dutton Children's Books, an imprint of Penguin Putnam Books for Young Readers, a division of Penguin Putnam Inc. All rights reserved.

2. Reginald Mallet, *Sermons by the Lake* (Franklin, Tennessee: Providence House Publishers, 2001), p. 26.

3. J. Wallace Hamilton, *What About Tommorow?* (Old Tappan, New Jersey: Fleming H. Revell Company, 1972), p. 42.

4. Barbara K. Lundblad, *Transforming the Stone: Preaching Through Resistance to Change* (Nashville: Abingdon Press, 2001), p. 125.

5. Hamilton, pp. 38-39.

6. Brent Mitchell, *Fresh Illustrations for Preaching and Teaching from Leadership Journal*, ed. by Edward K. Rowell (Grand Rapids, Michigan: Baker Book House and Christianity Today, Inc., 1997), p. 43.

7. Natalie Sleeth, "Hymn of Promise" copyright 1986 Hope Publishing Co., Carol Stream, IL 60188. All rights reserved. Used by permission. Hymn appears in

The United Methodist Hymnal: Book of United Methodist Worship (Nashville: The United Methodist Publishing House, 1989), #707.

8. Shared with me by Reverend Brad Dinsmore.

9. From Rudyard Kipling's, "The Explorer," www.poetryloverspage.com.

10. Quoted in David C. Cooper, *The Seven Spiritual Laws of Success* (Atlanta: Discover Life Ministries, 2000), p. 73. Used by permission.

11. William Sloane Coffin, *The Courage to Love* (San Francisco: Harper and Row Publishers, 1982), p. 90.

12. Nichole Nordeman, *Every Season*, copyright 2000 Ariose Music (adm. by EMI Christian Music Publishing). All rights reserved. Used by permission.

Dying To Live

In his book *The Mustard Seed Conspiracy*, Tom Sine shares the story of his parents' friends and their love for gathering wild mushrooms. One weekend this couple came home with several baskets of mushrooms. Realizing the impossibility of being able to consume all the mushrooms by themselves, they decided to invite others over to their house for a mushroom party. The turn-out was terrific, and they had a wonderful time eating mushroom crepes, omelets, and soufflés. They ate until they could not eat another bite and then scraped the leftover mushrooms into the cat's dish.

Around midnight, as the guests were getting ready to leave, someone went into the kitchen and noticed the cat sprawled out on the floor in convulsions. Next to the cat was an overturned dish of mushrooms. The guest screamed, "The cat!" Everyone ran into the kitchen to see what was causing all the commotion and, after seeing the cat, decided to call the doctor, fearing they would meet the same doom. The doctor informed them that they should not take any chances and should immediately drive to the hospital to get their stomachs pumped.

About 1:30 in the morning, they dragged back into the host's house to get their belongings. They were sick and exhausted. As they sarcastically thanked the hostess and made their way to the front door, someone asked, "What happened to the cat?" The group tip-toed to the kitchen, quietly opened the door, and found the cat asleep on the floor ... with eight kittens.[1]

At times, it is difficult to distinguish between dying and giving birth. You would think it would be easy to tell the difference.

205

However, experience shows us that the distance between death and birth is not very far. The unavoidable truth is that death must precede birth. Experiencing something new, even when it is positive, can be as painful as dying. Just listen to newborns scream as they make their miraculous move from the familiar womb into a foreign world. Ask a teenager how painful it is to move away and be separated from old friends. Ask a recent graduate how difficult it is to leave college and enter a new world of responsibility. Ask a couple how challenging it is to leave a self-centered life in order to raise a child. The truth is that all of us must die in order to give birth to something new. A bad habit must die to provide room for a good one. Certain ways of thinking must change in order to get the desired action. A place of comfort must be left in order to move to a healthier one. All such radical changes must occur in order for something new to be born.

Given the truth of death before birth, we should not be surprised by Isaiah's description of doom in the middle of chapter 43. For Second Isaiah describes a birthing process that begins with remarkable death and destruction. The sea is split in two. Armies, warriors, and the horses and chariots they came in on are disintegrated, and we are commanded to erase from our minds any memories of the past, killing any thoughts of the glory days. It appears that God is finally fed up with the world and is initiating some sort of holocaust to wipe everything out. But all of this death and destruction is prelude to God's creation of something new.

It would seem that destruction would defeat the virtue of creation. Perhaps we ask, "Is this the only way for God to create something new?" And Isaiah rises up from this text and shouts, "Yes!" For Isaiah vividly explains for us that what God is up against demands a permanent eradication. It was literally the sea, warriors, armies, chariots, and horses which had kept the people of God in bondage. But today these oppressive images represent all the things in our lives and in our world which keep us in bondage. The sea of indifference drowns much of the compassion in this world. The warriors of sin come and seize and destroy that which brings life. The chariots of evil trample over God-inspired dreams. Armies of

206

hate march right into our hearts and claim ownership of the deepest part of us. Memories, at times, are like an impenetrable wall towering between who we are and who God has called us to be. Therefore, when God creates change, it is more like surgery than a "Flintstone" band-aid. Tumors must be extracted before healing can take place. If left alone, they will grow, unchecked, to life-threatening proportions. The fatal nature of our bondage demands nothing less than divine surgery to make us whole.

However, God's revolution is not what most of us expect. For God's revolution does not involve weapons, a consuming fire, or even a rod of lightning. It does not involve divine wrath obliterating the wicked and lifting up the righteous. In fact, God's action against our chains of bondage involves no outward force whatsoever. God's force is symbolized with three things: a tree, some nails, and sacrifice. God used them to conquer sin, bondage, and death, because used together they epitomized sacrificial love. The incredible irony is that instead of allowing us to die in our sin, God in Christ lovingly decided to die on a tree with our sin. As the fatal bullet of sin raced towards us, God put skin on, and in sacrificial love jumped in front of us and took the blistering bullet for us.

God's one desire for us is that we allow our sins to die in him. Do you remember what Paul said? "How can we who died to sin go on living in it? Do you not know that all of us who have been baptized into Christ Jesus were baptized into his death?" (Romans 6:2-3). In short, Saint Paul is saying, "You must die in order to live!" For the cause of death, which is sin, must die in order for the source of life, who is God, to live within us. Just as Christ died to redeem the world, so we must die to our sins in Christ in order to become a new creation.

It is difficult to swallow such bitter-tasting truth. We live in a world that likes to be inclusive. We don't like to give up what we want in order to have what we need. After all, who says you cannot have your cake and eat it too? But bondage cannot co-exist with freedom, especially the freedom which God desires to initiate in our lives. The gifted writer Urban T. Holmes III makes this clear for us:

Any good gardener knows that beautiful roses require careful pruning. Pieces of living plant have to die. It cannot just grow wild. [Likewise] pieces of us ... need to die if we are to become the person that is in God's vision.[2]

If this is really what it takes to experience something new, most of us would rather settle for the way things are. We may be aware of our sinful habits and unhealthy lifestyle, but we are comfortable and don't want to give anything up. Therefore, we plant our feet against the threshold of death and go kicking and screaming into change, even when it is for our own good.

Barbara Brown Taylor remembers the time she witnessed a protest to death. She was attending an Easter Vigil at Christ Church in New Haven, Connecticut, and the time came for a three-year-old named Ellen to be baptized. Nothing unusual about it except that the three-year-old's parents wanted her to be baptized by immersion. This is a problem with a church which only has a bird-bath baptismal font. Still, the priest agreed and came up with a 36-gallon garbage can decorated with ivy. It was not pretty, but it suited the purpose. When the priest bent down to pick Ellen up, she screamed, "Don't do it!" She planted her feet against the garbage can, causing the water to spill on the floor. Again, she screamed, "Don't do it!" Taylor does not remember whether or not Ellen did it, but she can still hear that child's protest ringing through the rafters of the church. Though only three years old, Ellen believed she would die and wanted no part of it.[3]

All of us resonate with those three words: "Don't do it!" We express them in one way or another. When we feel God leading us to leave sin behind, we shout, "I don't want to do it!" When we hear God calling us out of our comfort zones, we scream, "I don't want to do it!" When we feel God pulling us away from our past, we hang on with tooth and nail and scream, "I won't do it!" Most of us go kicking and screaming into redemptive change. Ironically, we favor bondage over freedom. We feel more at home in Egypt than the Promised Land!

Yet every human being must choose between two deaths. We can die in our sin, or allow our sin to die. One is a horrific death, the other is a glorious one. If we are honest with ourselves and search the depths of our being, I believe we would all find a home-sickness which yearns for the glorious death which leads to genuine freedom. The poet Louisa Tarkington expresses this yearning:

> I wish there was some wonderful place;
> In the Land of beginning again;
> Where all our mistakes and all our heartaches;
> And all of our poor selfish grief;
> Could be dropped like a shabby old coat at the door;
> And never put on again![4]

There *is* a wonderful place to begin again: at the foot of the cross. Jesus says, "You can begin again. For I have died for all your shameful stuff. All you have to do is relinquish those seething and suffocating sins, and I will nail them to me on the cross and make sure they never have dominion over you again. Come and die to your old self and experience a new beginning. Come and die to sin and move from darkness to light. Come and die and receive the new life which only I can give to you."

When the Impressionist Movement emerged, the traditional artists were appalled. They were upset with how and where the Impressionists painted natural light. Until the Impressionist Movement, artists had painted indoors, never looking at an outside scene. But the Impressionists came along and began painting outside, and the result was a richer perspective of what they were painting. And so, because of people like Monet and Cezanne, who were willing to begin something new, to come out from the inside, to come out of the darkness and into the light, we are able to experience a beauty beyond words.

It is difficult for us to come out from the inside. We are more comfortable in the dark, in our sins, in our past. It is easier to stay inside our doors of shame and only daydream about what life would be like outside the door. But what would happen if we would open the door and experience the light of a new beginning? What would happen if we were willing to come out of the darkness and see the beauty of God's light reflecting on the canvas of our souls? What would happen? I know. God would come to us in Christ and gently take off our old, shabby, dirty, ugly coat and say, "Bring to me the family robe of righteousness, for my child has come home." All we have to do is shed our sin and claim our inheritance as children of God!

A beggar sat every day on a street corner across from an art studio. For days, an artist had seen him and decided to paint his portrait. When the artist completed the portrait, he invited the beggar into the studio. The artist said, "I've got something I want you to see."

Inside the studio, the artist unveiled the portrait. At first, the beggar did not recognize himself. He kept saying, "Who is it?" The artist just smiled and said nothing. Then suddenly the man saw himself in the portrait — not as he was in his dejected state, but as he could be. Then the beggar asked, "Is that me? Is that really me?" The artist replied, "That's who I see in you." Then the beggar said, "If that's who you see in me, then that's who I'll be."[5] Have you ever wondered who God sees in you?

God wants to do something new with you. Do you not perceive it? It springs forth, where the screaming jackals of your nature are silenced. Do you not perceive it? Your sins being forgiven. Do you not perceive it? A life free from bondage. Do you not perceive it? God's refreshing Spirit quenching every dry, deserted corner of your soul. Do you not perceive it? A beautiful death birthing a life of love, joy, peace, and hope. Do you not perceive it? Come and die an invigorating death. Your life is waiting.

---

1. Tom Sine, *The Mustard Seed Conspiracy* (Waco, Texas: Word Books, 1981), pp. 15-16.

2. Quoted in *A Guide to Prayer: For Ministers and Other Servants*, ed. by Rueben P. Job and Norman Shawchuck (Nashville: The Upper Room, 1983), p. 203.

3. Barbara Brown Taylor, *God in Pain: Teaching Sermons on Suffering* (Nashville: Abingdon Press, 1998), p. 49.

4. Exact source unknown.

5. David C. Cooper, *The Seven Spiritual Laws of Success* (Atlanta: Discover Life Ministries, 2000), pp. 102-103. Used by permission.

Can You Hear It?

There is a monastery in Europe which was built in a most difficult location. To get to it, you must climb into a basket that is connected to a long rope and be pulled up over 500 feet. It is a long way down, and the only thing that keeps you from falling is a rope. So if you are afraid of heights, it is not a very pleasant ride. Years ago, two women were making their first visit to the monastery, and while riding in the basket, they noticed the rope was frayed and torn in places. One of the women nervously asked the monk who was riding in the basket with them, "How often do you replace the rope here?" The monk replied, "After the old one breaks."[1]

Is this not a metaphor for our lives? The weight of sin and the gravity of pain and tragedy cause the fabric of our lives to fray and, at times, come apart. However, we believe we can hold ourselves together without any help. And even if we do fall apart, we think it is just a matter of picking up the pieces and starting all over again. But when the weight of life becomes too heavy and we snap into oblivion, putting the pieces back together becomes more difficult than we may have anticipated. Suddenly, we see the mess we have made of our lives. Yet all of it could have been prevented if we had recognized our weakness and asked for reinforcement.

Perhaps I just described you. Maybe you are frayed and on the verge of coming apart. Maybe you have been battered, beaten, and bruised and are hanging on to life by a thin, frayed rope. Maybe you have taken a frightful fall and are looking at the scattered pieces of your life asking, "How will I ever put myself back together?"

213

Perhaps you feel ill-equipped to face your challenges and are just plain terrified.

If any of this touches you where you live, Isaiah is chomping at the bit to speak to you. In fact, Isaiah is leaping off the page to tell all of us how he has handled life and won. Isaiah eagerly desires to tell anyone who will listen how he has been able to stand victoriously amidst the booming blows of life. Listen to Isaiah's insights:

> *The Lord God has given me the tongue of a teacher, that I may know how to sustain the weary with a word. Morning by morning he wakens — wakens my ear to listen to those who are taught. The Lord God has opened my ear, and I was not rebellious, I did not turn backward. I gave my back to those who struck me and my cheeks to those who pulled out the beard; I did not hide myself from insults and spitting. The Lord God helps me; therefore I have not been disgraced; therefore I have set my face like a flint, and I know that I shall not be put to shame; he who vindicated me is near. Who will contend with me? Let us stand up together. Who are my adversaries? Let them confront me. It is the Lord God who helps me; who will declare me guilty?*
> — Isaiah 50:4-9a

The first thing I was struck by when reading this text was Isaiah's wisdom: his wisdom in realizing he needed more wisdom; his wisdom in knowing he needed insight; his wisdom in knowing he needed God; his wisdom in knowing that without God his life was meaningless. Now, I am sure there were times when Isaiah was tempted to forget such wisdom. After all, he knew he had the tongue of a teacher and was smart and sharp enough to sustain the weary with a wise word. He knew he had the power to impact others. He was a gifted man — a great and mighty prophet who could inspire others to hear the word of God. But Isaiah was also wise enough to rely completely on the One who was the source of his gifts and graces. He was wise enough to listen to the One who gifted him with wisdom. For Isaiah says that when God opened his

214

ears he was no longer the teacher; he became the student. And he did not rebel against it. He welcomed it. He allowed God to open his ears and fill his mind and heart with things that he could not provide for himself. For Isaiah it did not matter how eloquent, smart, capable, sophisticated, mature, or wise he was, there was always a time to hush, be humble, and yield to the guidance of God.

Oh, how our world needs the wisdom of Isaiah. Oh, how *we* need the wisdom of Isaiah. Oh, how everyone needs to embrace the source of all wisdom. But the world thinks otherwise, and, sometimes, so do we. We have become so sophisticated, so modern, so advanced, so technologically oriented that we wonder if God's wisdom has kept up. We live in an incredible age. We have witnessed unthinkable discoveries in science, medicine, psychology, and biology. We are now equipped to do the unimaginable. We can turn on a computer and talk face to face with someone who is at the other end of the world. We can walk into a doctor's office looking as one person and come out looking as a different person. We have more information on more things than we could ever master. We have medicine that enables us to live longer. We are even able to play God by cloning life forms! But the question must be asked: Are we better as human beings? Are we happier? Are we more satisfied? Are we more loving? Are we more forgiving? Are we more patient? Are we more peaceful? Are we more whole? Have we become the world which God intended? Are we reaching our destiny as people of God? The answer is an emphatic "NO!" Despite better education, we still hate. Despite availability of information, we are still impatient. Despite our sophistication, we still sin. Despite cell phones and beepers, we still find it difficult to communicate with one another.

However, we go on believing that if we just have the right possessions, the right data, the right advancements, we will be happy. Will we ever learn that this thinking is just plain false? Remember what the experts said about space exploration? It was supposed to be the last great frontier. Later, we were told that the ocean was supposed to be the last great frontier. Yet now, more than ever, many people have realized that the last great frontier is not the outer space or under space but the inner-space. The last great frontier is our souls.

215

We discovered the last great frontier when 9/11 occurred. When the towers tumbled before our eyes and terror covered us like the night, what did our nation reach for? Not bank accounts! Not portfolios! Not fancy cars! They reached for God and each other. Suddenly, it was politically correct to cry out to God and acknowledge that we are unable to fix ourselves. Suddenly, it was politically correct to confess that we needed God. Suddenly, our smugness of believing that we had all the answers left us. Finally, only one word was adequate: "Help!" Oh, how September 11 taught us the wisdom of Isaiah — his wisdom in needing God.

Some time ago, I watched an executive of a major car company being interviewed on television. The interview focused on the advanced technology of modern automobiles. There was extensive conversation on computer chips, gadgets, and all the bells and whistles that accompany cars of today. At the conclusion of the interview, the car executive was asked, "Can you fix these cars?" He responded, "No. There was a time I could take a wrench and fix anything under the hood. Now, I don't even try. These cars are made in such a way that even I cannot fix them."

We like to believe we can tinker with ourselves and fix what's wrong. We like to believe that all we need is to find the right education, the right pill, the right position, the right relationship, and we will be satisfied. Yet the truth is that it does not matter how many degrees you have, how much money you possess, how much power you control, how much influence you express, how many cars you own, how many stock options you hold. If you don't have God, you possess nothing. We are created in God's image. Therefore, it is ludicrous to believe we can know meaning without a relationship with the "One who has made us for himself."

Remember the story of the agnostic who fell off a cliff? Halfway down, he caught hold of a bush. As he hung high above the ground, he shouted, "Is anybody up there?" Again, he shouted desperately, "Is anybody up there?" A voice answered, "Yes, this is the Lord." The man yelled frantically, "Help me!" There was a moment of silence. Then the Lord answered: "Let go of the bush and I will save you." There was another long silence as the man looked down at the ground far below. Finally, he yelled, "Is there anybody else up there?"[2]

216

How funny we must look to God, hanging on to what we believe will save us, searching for help outside of God. But there is no one else. There is only God — who knows us better than we know ourselves — who has made us for himself — who has designed us to communicate with him — who has called us to be in relationship with him. Anything else leaves us empty. As Billy Graham has said, "There is a God-shaped void in all of us that only God can fill."

Isaiah understood the God-shaped void completely. This is why, in verse 4, Isaiah says that he went to God each morning — not once a week, not once a month, not twice a year, but every morning. Every morning he knelt before the throne of God, knowing he could not face the day without God's leadership. He cocked his ear toward God and waited for guidance to face the day. No matter how important or mature he became, he knew that he needed God's grace like flowers need rain. He knew that he needed God's wisdom like he needed breath to live. He knew that he needed God as much as he needed the blood coursing through his veins. He knew that he needed God as much as a baby needs the security of a parent's arms. Oh, how we need the same kind of wisdom — the wisdom to recognize our need for God.

So why don't we recognize this crucial need more? Why don't we pay more attention to the vacuum within which yearns for the Spirit of God? The truth is that we drown it out. For some of us, this drowning out is innocent enough. We overbook our days and schedules with activities in order to satisfy a culture which rewards a breakneck pace. But we pay so great a price. For it is as Fosdick has written:

> *We hammer so busily that the architect cannot discuss the plans with us. We are so preoccupied with the activities of sailing, that we do not take our bearings from the sky. When the Spirit stands at the door and knocks, the bustle of the household drowns out the sound of his knocking.*[3]

How painfully true.

In addition to those whose chaotic schedules drown out God, there are some who *intentionally* drown out their need for God. They stay busy, knowing that if they are quiet too long, they may discover the existential pain within — the pain of being disconnected to God. They may discover a large gap between what they are and what God has created them to become. They may discover the discontent within their hearts. Their silence will be so deafening it may just be too much to bear. So you will witness people plugging their ears with the numbing sounds of television, cell phones, CDs, and mindless chatter in order to drown out their wounded cries for God. But we must come to terms with the fact that our need for God does not die nor does God die when we cease to believe in him or turn away from him. But *we* begin to die the very moment our lives cease to be illumined by the steady radiance of God.[4]

This is why we need Isaiah's experience. The text expresses it well for us, but our English language does not do it justice. When Isaiah says, "God wakens my ear," it literally means in the Hebrew, "God dug out my ear."[5] Imagine what would happen if we allowed God to dig out our ears! Bishop Richard Trench eloquently tells us what might happen, when he prays:

> *Lord, what a change within us one short hour*
> *Spent in thy presence will avail to make!*
> *What heavy burdens from our bosoms take!*
> *What parched grounds refresh, as with a shower!*
> *We kneel and all around us seems to lower;*
> *We rise, and all the distant and the near,*
> *Stands forth in sunny outline, brave and clear;*
> *We kneel, how weak! We rise, how full of power.*[6]

A tremendous transformation occurs when we spend time with God, when we are in tune with God, and when we are aligned with God. We find resources beyond ourselves. God receives us with love, wisdom, and courage. God breathes new life into our nostrils and we begin to breathe normally again. We begin to see, taste, feel, hear, and smell the world the way God desires for us to experience it. We begin to stand up to life because we intimately know

218

the one who is standing behind us. We have a peace that passes all understanding because we begin to recognize God's presence in the midst of our daily lives. We no longer see ourselves as victims but as victors. And we finally arrive at the place where we can say with Isaiah: "Who will contend with me? ... Who are my adversaries? Let them confront me. It is the Lord God who helps me" (vv. 8-9).

There is an old story about a Christian in ancient times who was standing charges before an angry Roman Emperor:

> *"I will banish you," raged the emperor. "You cannot," the Christian replied, "for the whole world is my Father's house." "Then I will slay you," said the emperor. "Neither can you do that, for my life is hid with Christ in God. I fear not them who have power only to destroy the body but have no power to destroy the soul." "Then," retorted the emperor, "I will take away your treasure." The Christian responded, "You cannot do that, for my treasure is in heaven where moth and rust do not corrupt." Frustrated, the emperor finally said, "I will drive you away from man, and you shall have not a friend left to be near you." The Christian quietly affirmed, "No, you cannot do that either; for I have a Friend from whom you cannot separate me. There is nothing you can do to harm me for neither life nor death nor things present nor things to come can separate me from his love."*[7]

This is the attitude we embrace. This is who we become when we allow God to saturate us with wisdom and love. So why don't we go to God more often? There is no good reason why we should neglect God. For God is closer to us than our very breath, always ready and willing to give us everything we need for life.

Wallace Chappell used to tell a story of a farmer who had two sons. His wife, who was a Christian, had died, and he was making every effort to guide his young sons to the Lord. Each morning, just before they started the morning chores, they noticed that their father disappeared. They always wondered where he went but never knew the secret of his disappearance. Months after his death, his two sons were working in the barn. Suddenly, one of them discovered a small room in the rear of the barn. They thought it was just filled with hay. But when they opened the door, they discovered a bale in the corner with an open Bible on it. In front of the bale were two worn out places on the ground, indentations which had taken a long time to depress. The two sons, caught by surprise, just stood there in reverent silence. Then one said, "So that's where he was and what he was doing." The other answered, "I am just wondering how many of those prayers were said for us." Then the first son knelt in one knee print and the second in the other. And a few minutes later when they got up, they rose with their father's Lord within their hearts.[8]

Where is your special place? Do you have one? If and when you do, you will be able to experience what Isaiah experienced. In fact, if you are quiet in your place, you will hear the steady beat of your heart beckoning you to kneel before God. You will hear God's heart beating faster as you come into his presence. You will hear the deep, mystic sigh coming from the depths of your soul as you commune with God. You will hear God's deafening cry of joy echoing through time saying, "My child has finally come!"

Do you hear God's call for you? Or maybe I should ask, "Will you hear it?"

---

1. Bill Floyd, *Stories I Love to Tell* (Decatur, Georgia: Looking Glass Books), pp. 100-101.

2. *Just for Laughs* (The Christian Communications Laboratory, 1982), p. 130.

3. Quoted in *Abingdon Preacher's Annual 1994,* ed. by John K. Bergland (Nashville: Abingdon Press, 1993), p. 371.

4. Based on a quote by Dag Hammarskjold quoted in John A. Stroman, *God's Downward Mobility* (Lima, Ohio: CSS Publishing Company, 1996), p. 13.

5. I am grateful to Dr. Fred B. Craddock for this insight.

6. Quoted in Benjamin P. Browne, *Illustrations for Preaching* (Nashville: Broadman Press, 1977), pp. 78-79. Used by permission.

7. Browne, pp. 22-23. Used by permission.

8. Wallace D. Chappell, *All for Jesus* (Nashville: Broadman Press, 1975), pp. 66-67.

Good Friday
Isaiah 52:13—53:12

Wounded Healers

I once watched a television show which scared the daylights out of me. I don't remember the name of the show, but the episode still haunts me. The story was about a self-sufficient man who experienced an auto accident and was left paralyzed. He could not speak. He could not move his body. Yet he discovered he was able to move his pinky finger. Tragically, the ambulance drivers who picked him up at the accident scene thought he was dead. So instead of taking him to the hospital, they drove him to the morgue. As the drivers were wheeling him into the morgue, his little finger began to tap on the gurney. The ambulance drivers at first did not hear the tapping because the gurney wheels were clicking and squeaking. It was then that the man on the gurney began to panic. But just as they started to place him in a refrigerated tray, one of the drivers's shouted, "Stop! He's alive!" The other driver responded, "How can you tell?" To which the other replied, "I see a tear in his eye."[1]

This captivating story demonstrates two eternal truths about life: first, even though we believe ourselves to be self-sufficient, we cannot avoid being painfully wounded at one time or another; second, just as the driver knew the man was alive by recognizing his tears, we should understand the authentic existence of others by recognizing their painful wounds.

The brutal truth of life is that we all are wounded by pain. For some, the wounds are physical, gnawing persistently each day. For others, the wounds are emotional, causing paralysis in living. And still, for some, the wounds are spiritual, aching and longing for healing. We do not have to look too deep within ourselves or others to understand that we are all wounded at one level or another.

Yet as Christians what should our response be to being wounded? How does God want us to handle our wounds? Is there hope for the wounded? I believe with all my heart that there is a salve for our wounds. There is hope for our scars. And this hope begins with our willingness to heal the wounds of others.

Using Our Wounds To Heal The Wounds Of Others

In his brilliant book *The Wounded Healer*, Henri Nouwen describes how we are able to use our wounds to heal others. He makes the profound claim that "in our own woundedness we can be a source of life for others"[2] or, to put it another way, we can become "wounded healers."

Now, the question is: As Christians, where does the process of becoming a wounded healer begin? One of the great privileges of my life was being able to help serve communion with Archbishop Desmond Tutu. As I stood next to him, holding the communion elements, I remember seeing his hands. They were not the soft hands you might expect of an important church dignitary; rather, they were the hands of a suffering servant of Christ. They were rough, callused, and scarred — hands not afraid to serve the one who also possessed wounded hands.

At the service of communion, Tutu said something which I will never forget. He remarked that it is truly awesome that people can come to the foot of the cross and be overcome and saved by the love and suffering of Christ — a love that truly died for our sins. Then Archbishop Tutu continued, "Some Christians stay at the foot of the cross and never climb up on the cross to see what Jesus sees."[3] This is where being a wounded healer begins — climbing up on the cross to see what Jesus sees and to feel what Jesus feels.

I need to warn you, however. What Jesus sees and feels on the cross is not pleasant. Isaiah 52 and 53 vividly describe the ugly and painful wounds Jesus suffers for us, reminding us of just how wounded we are. And as we hang on the cross with Christ, it does not take long to discover why he was willing to bear such wounds.

Right here in front of us, right in our churches, there are some who suffer the wounds of loneliness. Right now, in our churches, there are some who suffer the wounds of depression. Right now, in our churches, there are some who suffer the wounds of misuse and abuse. Right now, in our churches, there are some who suffer the wounds of a debilitating disease. Right now, in our churches, there are some who suffer the wounds of an unforgiven past.

Your response may be, "So, what can I do for these people? I am wounded too." My response to you would be, "Exactly. That is the point. That's the reason you are prepared to help!" Each one of us has the gift of being a wounded healer because we all have the "gift of understanding." This is what being a wounded healer is all about — being able to reach out and identify with the wounded and say, "I understand. I have been wounded too. How can I help?"

If and when you do reach out, you will find that people will eagerly receive you. I cannot tell you how many people come in to my office in tears and say to me, "I just want someone to listen to me. I just want someone to understand me. I just want someone to love me."

There is an old story about the great preacher Charles Allen. He says that, over the years, people jokingly have told him that he is the "world's greatest counselor." He explains: "Someone comes to me and I ask, 'How are you doing?' And they tell me. Then I ask, 'What do you think the problem is?' And they tell me. Then I ask, 'What do you think you ought to do about it?' And they tell me. And I say, 'Sounds good to me.' And then they say, 'Charles, you are the world's greatest counselor!' And I say, 'Ain't it the truth.' "[4] Actually, it is not that glib, but it is that simple. All Allen is doing is listening with an understanding ear, an attentive ear, a safe ear, a caring ear.

Some years ago, while serving my first pastorate, I remember going to visit the home of a member whose father had just died. I sat with him for about an hour and a half as he described the wounds he was suffering. I listened closely because my father had also died recently. What I remember most about this conversation is that I did not say more than a few words to him. I listened and listened. He did most of the talking. A few months later, I ran into him at a restaurant. He gave me a big hug and said, "I will always remember your visit with me after my dad died. I cannot thank you enough." I responded, "Of course, but I did not do much." He replied, "Yes, you did. You understood."

One of the most effective ways of demonstrating the love of Christ is being present with someone in their woundedness, listening to them, and allowing them to be sure they are understood. Christ is counting on us to be his listening ears, his loving heart, and his understanding presence. The Apostle Paul put it this way: "Bear one another's burdens, and in this way you will fulfill the law of Christ" (Galatians 6:2).

When We Become Wounded Healers, We Heal Our Own Wounds

My mother has created a profound ministry by being a wounded healer. When my dad died of cancer years ago, the wounds my mother felt were indescribable. It is one thing to lose your father, but those of you who know the experience know it is quite another thing to lose your spouse. My mother was left wondering, "What do I do with these wounds of mine? Will there ever be light in the midst of this darkness? Will there ever be hope in the midst of this hopelessness? Will I ever find healing?" I believe that the Spirit of God gathered up my mother and her wounds and provided a way for healing to occur. And her healing is now a powerful ministry to those suffering from cancer. Every month for many years now, my mother has surrounded herself with people struggling with cancer and has offered through her wounds understanding, comfort, and healing. She reaches out in love as she provides an all-inclusive way to treat cancer for those who have tried everything else medical science offers. With her capable staff, she provides physical, emotional, and spiritual support. By God's grace, some of the people my mother seeks to help are able to find a quality of life in the midst of their cancer they never believed possible. But the sweetest thing about this ministry is that it is through her ministry of healing others that her own wounds have been healed.

In his novel *A Farewell to Arms*, Ernest Hemingway offers these profound words: "The world breaks everyone and afterward many are strong at the broken places."[5] This is what happened to my

226

mother. She became strong at the broken places. And it is what happens when we become wounded healers, as well. We become strong at the broken places of our lives. Our wounds begin to heal because they are being used to give comfort and strength to others. Therefore, we can affirm, "My wounds were not the end of me. God took my wounds, my understanding, my empathy and has used them as a healing balm for the wounded." And we are able to say with the Apostle Paul, "Oh, yes, I am more than a conqueror!"

Being A Wounded Healer Means Healing The Wounds Of Christ

Some years ago, there was a very popular song sung by Bette Midler titled, "From A Distance."[6] The chorus said, "God is watching us from a distance." And though the song had a great message, which spoke of God seeing our troubled world, I always had difficulty with the song theologically, for the cross does not tell me that God watches us from a distance. The cross tells me that God in Christ is right here in the midst of us, carrying the burdens of the world. God in Christ suffers with us in the midst of our woundedness. Therefore, we do not worship or follow a God who does not understand what it's like to be wounded. The message of Good Friday and, more specifically, Isaiah 52 and 53, is that we have a God who is wounded for us and who is wounded with us, making him the ultimate wounded healer. So instead of singing, "God is Watching Us," it may be better to sing the song performed by Joan Osborne, "What If God Was One Of Us?"[7] For God became one of us in Jesus.

This great truth of God being one of us in Jesus clarifies the point of Christ when he says, "Truly I tell you, just as you did it to one of the least of these ... you did it to me" (Matthew 25:40). In Christ, God became one of us and became wounded like the rest of us. And it is through Christ that we understand that God Almighty is intimately connected to us and is deeply impacted by the care and compassion that we attempt to give even to the least among us.

Mother Teresa was the incarnation of this profound truth. When she heard that there were people in Calcutta dying in the streets because the religious culture said they were "untouchable," she said, "Not as long as I live and can help." So she went to Calcutta, built a hospital, and went out to the streets to find those who were dying of disease and malnutrition. She would bring them to the hospital where they could be held, rocked, prayed for, and loved. Then she told them about the love of Christ. Some got better, and some died in her arms.

Why did Mother Teresa do such a thing? She saw in those who were suffering and dying something that no one cared to see. She revealed what she saw when she was asked to speak to a group about what drove her to this kind of ministry. This little, frail woman with a big, strong spirit arose to the podium and said, "What you do for them, you also do for him."[8]

Look around you very carefully. You will see the wounded, the sick, the lonely, the hungry, the thirsty, and the depressed. And if you are willing to reach out with your wounds to heal their wounds, you may just see the face of Christ and realize you are healing the wounds of Christ. "What you do for them, you also do for him."

---

1. Exact source unknown.

2. Henri Nouwen, *The Wounded Healer* (New York: Doubleday, 1972), cover.

3. Spoken at a chapel service at Candler School of Theology.

4. Shared with me by Reverend Brad Dinsmore.

5. Ernest Hemingway, *A Farewell To Arms* (New York: Scribner, 1953 [1929]), p. 239.

6. Song written by Julie Gold.

7. Song written by Eric Bazilian.

8. Story told by Dr. J. Howard Edington, Senior Minister, The First Presbyterian Church of Orlando, Florida.

God Has The Last Word!

It is amazing how sounds will stir the mind and heart. For instance, music has a marvelous way of igniting an array of emotions. Someone can listen to a song, close their eyes, and feel once again the exhilaration of their first kiss or the bittersweet memory of love that was lost. A note or two of music can resonate a deep chord within. Movie makers know this well and use it to their advantage. Ever tried to watch a movie with your television muted? The drama of the movie is removed. The screeches, screams, and other spine-tingling sounds give the movie its impact.

There are two notes of music made for a particular movie which probably have caused more terror and fear than any notes ever created for the big screen. So effective was the creation that these notes have permeated the American psyche. They are the note "E" followed by the note "F." When they were first recorded for the score, the instrumentation was six cellos and three basses. Do you now remember? You don't! Then let me remind you that those two notes came from John William's score for the movie *Jaws*. When Williams was asked why he chose those two notes, he replied, "I was looking for something that would describe the shark to the listener in an unconscious way. The music [needed] to be very, very primal and unstoppable."[1]

If you have seen *Jaws*, you remember how primal and unstoppable was the shark. Perhaps after seeing the movie, you were one of many who thought twice before wading into the ocean. Williams took two simple notes and struck at the depths of people's emotions. In fact, I would venture to say that for most of us these

229

two notes translate into two words: (E) NO (F) HOPE! (E) NO (F) HOPE! (E) NO (F) HOPE! (E) NO (F) HOPE!

What are the sounds which evoke hopelessness within you? Perhaps it is the sound of a certain song that spurs a haunting memory. Maybe it is the sound of a door slamming shut. Maybe it is the sound of a particular person's voice. Maybe it is the sound of footsteps coming down the darkened hall. Maybe it is a nurse's voice calling your name in an emergency room waiting area. Maybe it is the sound of beeping next to a hospital bed. Or maybe it is the sound of silence, reminding you of your aloneness. Whatever your particular sound is, you know when you hear it, for it sounds like a shark is coming after you with all its primal and unstoppable power. And as it gets closer to you, instinctively, you feel like saying, "No hope! No hope! No hope!" The tragedy is that when we allow the shark's jaws around us, something within us begins to die.

Do you ever feel as if you're dead inside? Have you ever felt the attack of hopelessness and lost your vitality? Have you ever been swallowed up in disappointment and can no longer see the light of a new tomorrow? Have you ever looked into the menacing eyes of depression? Have you ever felt as if your spirit is locked away inside a musty tomb?

There is good news! The good news is that there are two Easter words which ring like the "A" and "D" notes of the Hallelujah Chorus. These words ring out so bright, so vibrant, so loud, and so strong that they drown out any "E" and "F" notes within you. It matters not whether you have a debilitating disease, a drowning depression, a dooming despair, or a defeating doubt, for if the power of these two words find their way into your soul, your hopelessness will be overcome. What are these two words? **He Lives!**

This is the penetrating meaning of Easter which Peter was commanded to proclaim in the tenth chapter of Acts. Peter was explaining to Cornelius and the others the revealed truth about Jesus Christ. Peter, an eyewitness to the resurrection power of Jesus Christ, shared his testimony. As he was preaching, the Holy Spirit fell upon those who heard him!

I am not an eyewitness as Peter was, but I am a witness nonetheless. And there is no other time this is more clear than Easter

Sunday. I, like Peter, have been commanded by my Lord to proclaim the Good News of Jesus Christ. And my fervent prayer is that as I lift high the message of Easter, God's Spirit will fall upon you, and you will come to experience God's amazing power of creating new life. Today we celebrate the truth that what has been dead will be made alive in Christ!

During the volcanic eruption of Mount Saint Helens, within certain areas the intense heat melted away the soil, leaving only bare rock coated with a thick mantle of ash. The result was the destruction of all living things in that area of the volcano. Forest Service naturalists wondered how long it would be before life would return to these barren areas. Then one day a park employee discovered a lush patch of wildflowers and ferns in the midst of the desolation. He wondered why and how. It took him a few seconds to notice that the patch of vegetation was formed in the shape of an elk. Plants had sprouted from the organic material that lay where an elk had died and been buried by ash. From that moment on, the naturalists looked for patches of beautiful flowers and grass as a clear indicator in calculating the loss of wildlife.[2]

The resurrection is God's way of revealing to us that nothing which belongs to God will ever go to waste — not even mortal bodies. It is God's way of revealing to us that nothing in life is so dead and hopeless that it cannot be transformed and resurrected.

Perhaps you are wondering if this is really possible. Maybe you are trying to crawl your way out of life's jarring jaws, and you really want to know if it is possible to experience the recycling grace of resurrection. Perhaps you feel like your life has been one funeral after another, one disappointment after another, one loss after another, and you desperately want to know if it is possible to experience a transformation of all the lifeless, hopeless, and useless parts of your life. Well, yes, it is possible! It's possible if you are willing to open your deepest and darkest tombs and pray, "Lord, here is all the junk, the pain, and the despair that is decomposing within me. Take it, transform it, and breathe into me new life!"

As pastor of a certain church, I once conducted a healing service. I arrived at the service with the anointing oil, the elements of communion, and the book of worship. I watched as people entered the chapel, most of whom were lost in despair and darkness. A woman came forward and placed a card on the altar. It read, "I have been fighting depression for ten years." I anointed her with oil and prayed out loud that God's light would pierce her darkness. The service soon ended, and we went home.

A week passed, and I was preparing for the Sunday service. Suddenly, this woman entered the sacristy and wrapped her arms around my neck. When she finally let go of me, I saw tears streaming down her face. She said, "I haven't felt this way in ten years. My life has been changed. It's no longer dark. I can see the light. I see things in a new way! I can't thank you enough." I replied, "It wasn't me. I didn't do anything ... It wasn't me!" You see, the resurrection had occurred in her life. How do I know? You should have seen the radiance of her face.

This is why we celebrate Easter. This is why the trumpet sounds. This is why the sanctuary is overflowing with lilies. This is why there is a liturgy of pageantry. The same power that raised Jesus from the dead will raise us from the dead! The same power that gave Jesus life will give us life! The same power that breathed into Jesus' tomb will breathe into our tombs!

Tony Campolo tells of the time he attended his first African-American funeral. A friend of his named Clarence had died. Campolo said that the pastor who led the service was incredible. He spoke about the resurrection in beautiful terms. The congregation was lifted and thrilled. The pastor also comforted the people by reciting words from the fourteenth chapter of John: "Let not your hearts be troubled. You believe in God. Believe also in me. Because I live you shall live also...." Finally, as the service came to its end, the preacher did the most notable thing of all. Campolo said that for the last twenty minutes of the service the pastor preached to an open casket. A few minutes into the eulogy, the preacher began yelling at the corpse saying, "Clarence, Clarence!" Campolo said that the preacher yelled at the corpse so loud that he would not have been surprised if Clarence had answered. The pastor continued, "Clarence, there were a lot of things we should have said to you that we never said to you. You got away too fast,

Clarence. You got away too fast." Then Campolo said the preacher began a litany of beautiful things — things which Clarence had done for people throughout his life. He lifted up Clarence's enormous faith and how that faith influenced others. When he finished, he said, "That's it, Clarence. There is nothing more to say. And when there is nothing more to say, there is only one thing left to say: Goodnight, Clarence. Goodnight!" With that, the preacher grabbed the lid of the casket and slammed it shut. Boom! Shock waves went through the congregation. Then the preacher lifted his head slowly, wearing a huge smile on his face, and said, "Goodnight, Clarence, because *I know, I know, I know* that God is going to give you a good morning!" Then the choir stood up and began singing, "On that great gettin-up morning we shall rise, we shall rise!" And everybody was dancing, hugging, and celebrating.[3]

Easter gives us permission to dance in the face of death and say, "Death has been swallowed up in victory. Where, O death, is your victory? Where, O death, is your sting?" (1 Corinthians 15:54-55). For God in Christ has put everything under his feet and is the judge of all things, living and dead. And as judge, the Lord has conquered our sin, has overcome our despair, and defeated everything which is an enemy of life.

We pray and God responds:

> *Lord, they have conspired against you ... Yes*
> *Lord, they have ridiculed you and mocked you ... Yes*
> *Lord, they have spat upon you and whipped you ... Yes*
> *Lord, they have driven nails into you and pierced your*
>   *side ... Yes*
> *Lord, they have hung you on a cross and put you in a*
>   *tomb ... Yes*
>
> *Lord, is it dawn? ... Yes*
> *Is your tomb empty? ... Yes*
> *Is that you? ... Yes*
> *Are you telling me that you're alive? ... Yes*
> *Does this mean that everything you said is true? ... Yes*
> *Does this mean that since you have conquered death, I*
>   *too will conquer death? ... Yes*

Does it mean that because you live, I will live? ... Yes
Are you telling me that you have the last word? ... YES![4]

---

1. Quoted in Joseph Novenson, "Decreation and Recreation" (*Preaching Today*, tape 212).

2. Philip Yancey, *What's So Amazing About Grace* (Grand Rapids, Michigan: Zondervan, 1997), p. 253.

3. Tony Campolo, "The Jubilee of God" (*Preaching Today*, tape 212).

4. Written by Charles D. Reeb.

The Life You've Always Wanted

The other day I came across some interesting epitaphs. There is one in Nevada which reads: "Here lays Butch, we planted him raw. He was quick on the trigger, but slow on the draw." This one is in Georgia: "I told you I was sick!" What about the one in Maryland: "Here lies an atheist, all dressed up and no place to go." There are two worth noting in South Carolina: "He fought a good fight, but his knife was dull"; "Where she is, is better than where she was." But there is one in England that hits too close to home: "Dead at 30; buried at 60."[1]

Epitaphs reveal a truth that we all must face. This truth is that all of us will leave a legacy. When we die, we will leave some kind of lasting mark which will reflect what we did with our precious time on earth. This comes as a sobering truth to many (perhaps even for you), for if you look around your neighborhood, workplace, and community you will find those who fulfill the English epitaph. They have already died and are just waiting for burial. Their life is without meaning, purpose, or direction. They live paycheck to paycheck, Friday to Friday, or vacation to vacation. They are like the man who wrote:

> *I get up each morning, dust off my wits*
> *Pick up the paper, and read the obits.*
> *If my name is missing, I know I'm not dead*
> *So I eat a good breakfast — and go back to bed.*[2]

The Apostle Paul would describe this person as the "living dead."

235

And the legacy he would leave behind would be sad, indeed — the talents wasted, a destiny wasted, a life wasted. Dead at 30, buried at 60.

Let me ask you a pointed question: "What will be said about you when your life is ended? What will be said about you at your funeral?" Or perhaps a better question is: "How would you like to be remembered?" Maybe you would like to be remembered as a nice person. That's not bad. Or maybe you would like to be remembered as a success — a person who excelled at a particular skill or profession. Or perhaps you want to be remembered as a wonderful father, a good mother, a great sister, or supportive brother. Our culture would certainly have no problems with these legacies. For, in proper perspective, they are noble.

However, our faith calls us to be more than just nice, good, and successful persons. As worthy as these qualities are, we are called to be more. Unfortunately, "more," for many, means more pleasure, more position, more power, and more prestige. But more of only these things leads to less, and less usually leads to empty. I believe the examples below prove my point:

> *In 1923, eight of the world's most successful financiers sat down at a business meeting. Present were the president of the largest independent steel company, the president of the largest utility company, the greatest wheat speculator, the president of the New York Stock Exchange, a member of the President's cabinet, the greatest "bear" on Wall Street, the president of The Bank of International Settlements, and the head of the world's greatest monopoly.*
>
> *These men controlled more wealth than [was] in the U.S. Treasury. Newspapers and magazines printed their success stories and urged the youth of the nation to follow their examples. Yet 25 years later, this is what happened to them:*
>
> *The president of the steel company — Charles Schwab — lived on borrowed money for five years before he died bankrupt.*

*The president of the greatest utility empire —
Samuel Insull — fled the country in disgrace to avoid
prosecution.*

*The greatest wheat speculator — Arthur Cutter —
died abroad insolvent.*

*The president of the NYSE — Richard Whitney —
was sentenced to Sing Sing prison for larceny.*

*The member of the President's cabinet — Albert
Fall — was pardoned from prison so he could die at
home.*

*The greatest "bear" on Wall Street — Jesse Liver-
more — died a suicide.*

*The president of the International Bank — Leon
Frazer — died a suicide.*

*The head of the greatest monopoly — Ivar Krueger
— died a suicide.*

*All of these men learned well the art of making
money, but not one of them learned how to really live.*[3]

Perhaps some of you have made the same discovery. Maybe
you have discovered that not all the things you believe are so worth-
while are of the same worth. Maybe you realize that so-called success is not as meaningful as the world makes it out to be. Maybe
you find yourself behind your desk at work or in your bed awake at
night looking for something deeper, something more, something
beyond this world. Maybe the "good life" and the evaporating fun
of party and play is just not cutting it anymore. Could it be that
your life has become meaningless and empty and you desire something more? If this is true, maybe you are ready now to make the
move from success to significance.

Peter and the other apostles made this significant move. In our
scripture lesson, we find Peter and the rest of the apostles taking a
courageous stand for Christ. They were told repeatedly by the
Sadducees to stop preaching the Good News, or they would suffer.
But the apostles were not initimidated. They were so compelled
and consumed by the power and purpose of the gospel that they
considered it a privilege to suffer for the sake of Jesus. They were
determined to proclaim the Good News of Jesus Christ until their
dying day.

237

However, Peter and the apostles had not always lived such significant lives. Let's rewind at bit and see where it all started. In the Gospel of Mark, we read that Simon (who would later be called Peter), and Andrew, James, and John were fishing on the Sea of Galilee. They apparently were very successful in their profession because Mark points out that James and John had hired servants. They were successful enough to pay workers to help them. Life was good! They were growing a company. Yet Jesus came along and said, "Drop your nets. You were made for more than this. There is a bigger enterprise to be part of than fishing for fish. I am going to make you a fisher of people. Follow me and you will be part of the divine enterprise which is bigger than any of you can imagine. You are going to help me transform the world!" This call was so powerfully potent that Peter and the others walked away from their thriving business and comfortable lifestyle to follow Jesus. They left the ordinary in order to do the extraordinary. They said goodbye to mediocrity and said hello to God's mission. They could not resist the pull of ultimate meaning, purpose, and adventure. Surely, it was scary, but they were willing to take the leap of faith in order to be more than just average people, living an average life, achieving average goals. So in our text for today, we find Peter and the apostles boldly living out the adventurous call of Christ which had captured them.

Sir Frances Drake's sailors used to sit on the coasts of England and share stories of the sea with young men. But the sailors did not talk about the pleasures of the sea. They proudly spoke of the sea's dangers. They shared tales of high waves and stout winds and gallant ships riding out the storms. The young men were so compelled by the thought of such adventure that many of them ran away from home to become a part of it.[4]

Jesus walks on the shores of our lives today and tempts us with the experience of his impossible grace. He calls us just as he called the disciples of old: "You want adventure? Follow me. You want challenge? Follow me. You want excitement? Follow me. You want to fulfill your destiny? Follow me. You want to experience transformation in yourself and in others? Follow me. Follow me into the high waves of world changing, hate breaking, sin binding, love finding ministry!"

Sounds pretty good, doesn't it? Then why don't more follow this call? For there is a difference between being saved by Christ and being a disciple for Christ. What is the difference? The difference is found in living a committed, sold-out life for Christ and discovering that it requires one dirty, scary four-letter word: *risk!* You see, the way of Christ is the way of risk. To be a Christian is to risk. One of the things we must understand is that Christ is not looking for those who play it safe. He questions those who only pray for comfort, ease, and security. Why do we fool ourselves into believing that when we became Christians life would become easier? Where is that idea found in the Gospels? Nowhere! Instead, we read about a Savior who says, "Sell all that you have and follow me. Drop your nets and follow me. Deny self, take up a cross, and follow me."

One of the risks we have to take in order to follow Christ is to do what Simon, Andrew, James, and John did: Change priorities! We have to come to the moment of truth where we confront those sins which keep us from living for God and depart from our old life. We have to look deeply within ourselves and be honest about what we love more than God. Then we must take the idol off our shrine, put it on the altar of God, and pray, "Lord, do with it what you will. For your love, ministry, plan, and purpose for my life come first!"

This kind of sacrifice is very difficult for us. For some carry the attitude of, "Yes, Lord, I want you to save me from my sins, but I don't want to give them over to you. Yes, Lord, I want to be with you one day in the everlasting Kingdom, but I do not want to help build your Kingdom here on earth. Yes, Lord, I want to receive your unconditional love, but I don't want to share it with others."

During the Revolutionary War, George Washington had many soldiers volunteer to fight during the summer months. Yet as winter approached, with rations in short supply and blankets scarce, they began to slip silently away from camp and return to the warmth of their homes. After experiencing this, General Washington publicly declared that he could not win a war with "summer soldiers."[5]

239

If we are just sitting around being "summer Christians," nothing gets accomplished. When we choose comfort over the cross, barriers don't get removed, people go unloved, the gospel does not get proclaimed, and lives are not changed. They hymn writer was not keeping this in mind when he wrote:

> Hide me, O my Savior, hide,
> Till the storm of life is past;
> Safe into the haven guide;
> O receive my soul at last.[6]

It's important, at times, to hide in the presence of God, and relish what God has done for us. But God desires us to move out and beyond. God needs us to leap out of our comfort zones, take a risk, make a sacrifice, and move to the heartbeat of the gospel. In short, we need to let go of our fears and live dangerously in the hands of God. No, it won't always be easy. For as we open ourselves and love others, we risk getting hurt. When we take a stand for Christ, we risk not being popular. When we step out in faith with our gifts, we risk failure. But the greater the risk, the greater the reward. The bigger the challenge, the more exciting the adventure. The more we lose ourselves for the gospel, the more we find ourselves. This is precisely what Jesus meant when he said, "Those who lose their life for my sake will find it" (Matthew 10:39). When we lose ourselves, risk ourselves, give freely of ourselves for the gospel, we connect with the life for which we were created. We come face to face with our destiny. We discover a life of meaning for which we have been desperately searching.

So instead of praying, "Lord, make things easier, safer, more comfortable," we should pray, "Lord, give me the biggest, toughest, riskiest task ever. I believe, with your help, I can make a difference!" This is the attitude of a determined disciple for Jesus Christ!

For many of us, attitude is the problem. Sometimes we have less than desirable attitudes about our ability to be disciples for Jesus Christ. We complain about our busy schedules. We moan about being tired. We can't participate in a church event because that's the weekend we planned to go to the beach. We are good at making excuses. However, one thing I have learned is that we make time for what is important. For instance, I never say, "I just don't have time to eat today," or "I am too tired to pay my bills." And you never hear a mother say, "My baby is crying and hungry, but I am just too tired to feed him." We make time for these activities because they are important. Yet when it comes to serving Jesus Christ, we make all kinds of excuses.

Some believe they are too young and don't have enough experience to serve Jesus Christ. But that's not a good excuse. "Raphael painted his works at a very young age and died at 37. Alfred Tennyson wrote his first work at eighteen. Victor Hugo was only seventeen when he received prizes at a poetry competition, and he earned the title 'master' before he was twenty. John Calvin joined the reformation at 21 and at 27 wrote *The Institutes of the Christian Religion.* Isaac Newton was 24 when he formulated the laws of gravity. Charles Dickens wrote *Pickwick Papers* at 24 and *Oliver Twist* at 25. Charles Spurgeon was a powerful preacher in his early twenties and by age 25, pastored the largest church in London. Martin Luther King, Jr., shook the nation with his call for civil rights when he was still a young man before being cut down in the prime of his life. And don't forget that Jesus himself had transformed the course of human history by the time he was 33."[7]

Some believe they are too old to serve Jesus Christ. But that's not a good excuse, either. "Moses was eighty when God called him to lead Israel out of Egypt. Michelangelo was writing poetry and designing architecture until the time he died at 89. Goethe wrote a part of *Faust* at age sixty and finished it at 82. Daniel Webster wrote his monumental dictionary when he was seventy. Verdi produced the famous piece, 'Ave Maria,' at 85. John Wesley preached for forty years, produced 400 books, knew ten languages, and at age 86 complained that he was unable to preach more than twice a day."[8]

We may not have the gifts of a John Calvin or John Wesley, but all of us have been given gifts, talents, and skills to be used to change our world with the gospel of Jesus Christ. If you don't know what your gifts are, ask God to reveal them to you, and he will, with great delight.

It is important that you discover your spiritual gifts. For I believe one day we will all give an account of the gifts we used and the gifts we refused to use for the glory of God. That is what the parable of the talents is all about. Remember what happened to the man who buried his talent in the ground? Well, let's just say that the person who gave him the talent was very disappointed. There is nothing more tragic than a buried talent.

What are you doing with the gifts God has given you? Are your mother, father, sister or brother, even the cat and dog better and different because you are a Christian? Are your co-workers, neighbors, friends, and even enemies better and different because you are a Christian? Are the people with whom you spend a significant amount of time better and different because of your witness to them? Have you made a difference in people's lives by sharing with them the unbelievable love that has been lavished upon you? You see, the essence of risking and sacrificing, the essence of all this adventure and challenge for Christ is to witness change — change in ourselves, change in others, change in institutions, and change in the world through the saving love and power of Jesus Christ!

One of the first Bibles I ever received had this message written on the cover: "Expect great things from God; Attempt great things for God."[9] This is a motto I have tried to live by since I was a child. How about you? "What are you doing with your life today to give it back to God as a gift? Are you preparing yourself spiritually, emotionally, mentally, physically, financially, and relationally to meet the next opportunity? Are you fully motivated [to serve God] in every area of your life? Or have your lost your zeal and enthusiasm? Do you need to fan into flame the gift of God that is in you? Are you sitting on the sideline [or are you immersed in ministry]? Now is the time to take action!"[10]

There is a poignant story about the great artist Leonardo da Vinci. One day, he was in his studio finishing a magnificent painting. As he gazed over what was soon to be another masterpiece, he called a student over, handed him the paintbrush and said, "Here, you finish it." The student protested, "What do you mean? I am not worthy to touch one of your paintings. I am not able to complete so beautiful a work." Da Vinci replied, "Will not what I have done inspire you to do your best?"[11]

Consider what Christ has done in your life. Reflect on what Christ has blessed you with. Recall all the gifts Christ has given you. Does that not inspire you to do your best? It should! So may you go back to your homes, workplaces, and communities and pray, "Lord, you can count on me! Put me to work. I promise to give you my best." If you live up to those words, your legacy will be eternal.

---

1. Linda Schiphorst McCoy, *It's News To Me!: Messages Of Hope for Those Who Haven't Heard* (Lima, Ohio: CSS Publishing Company, 2001), p. 11.

2. Quoted in David C. Cooper, *The Seven Spiritual Laws of Success* (Atlanta: Discover Life Ministries, 2000), p. 19. Exact author and source of poem unknown.

3. *Ibid.*, pp. 5-7.

4. J. Wallace Hamilton, *Ride the Wild Horses: The Christian Use of Our Untamed Impulses* (Old Tappan, New Jersey: Fleming H. Revell Company, 1952), pp. 50-51.

5. William L. Self, *Defining Moments* (Lima, Ohio: CSS Publishing Company, 1999), p. 119.

6. Charles Wesley, "Jesus, Lover of My Soul," *The United Methodist Hymnal: Book of United Methodist Worship* (Nashville: The United Methodist Publishing House, 1989), #479.

7. Cooper, p. 18. Used by permission.

8. *Ibid.*, p. 19. Used by permission.

9. Attributed to William Carey.

10. Cooper, pp. 75-76. Used by permission.

11. Ben Patterson, *The Grand Essentials* (Waco, Texas: Word Books, 1987), p. 26.

A Vexing Vision

Have you have heard the expression, "Something got lost in the translation?" On the Internet there are programs which will translate an English document into several different languages. All you do is type in a phrase or a word and the program translates it into French, Spanish, German, or whatever language you desire. Sound helpful? It is, especially if you are learning a foreign language. But how do you know if these programs create an accurate translation? A linguist had the same question and decided to test the accuracy of the translation. He typed in the lyrics to the nostalgic tune, "Take Me Out to the Ball Game":

> *Take me out to the ball game.*
> *Take me out with the crowd.*
> *Buy me some peanuts and Cracker Jack.*
> *I don't care if I never get back.*
>
> *Let me root, root, root for the home team.*
> *If they don't win, it's a shame.*
> *For it's one, two, three strikes, you're out,*
> *At the old ball game.*[1]

He then ran the program in his computer to translate the song into German and then back into English. When he read what the program gave back to him, he was convinced that something got lost in the translation. The song went from a celebratory chant to something that looked like a harsh war cry:

Execute me to the ball play.
Execute me with the masses.
Buy me certain groundnuts and crackerstackfusig.
I'm not interested if I never receive back.

Let me root, root, root for the main team.
If they don't win, it is dishonor.
For there are one, two, three impacts on you.
At the old ball play.[2]

The essence of the song was lost.

Something similar can happen to the words found in the ninth chapter of Acts. Whenever we read the dynamic account of Paul's conversion and call, we are so awestruck by the drama of the text that something very important gets lost in its translation into our lives. After the blinding light and booming voice from above, there is a radical message for us that is often overlooked. This oversight is understandable because the message lost in this text confirms our fears about what it means for us to be followers of Christ. It reminds us of the level of discipleship to which we are called.

What is this radical message? It is found in the vexing vision from God to Ananias. That's right, Ananias. We sometimes forget that he is in this passage, too! He often gets ignored or pushed aside, but Ananias is the authentic hero of this story. He has fallen into a deep, comfortable sleep, and all of a sudden he sees a vision and hears a voice say, "Ananias, I want you to go to Saul of Tarsus and lay your hands on him so that he can regain his sight." Maybe Ananias thought, "Jesus wants me to do what? Please tell me this is a nightmare and not a vision." But after Ananias complains and questions, Jesus simply says, "Go! Just go. This man Saul is to be one of my most powerful instruments."

Now, put yourself in Ananias' shoes. Imagine the shock, confusion, and anger of finding out that Jesus wants to use you to recruit a future missionary who presently takes great pride in torturing and murdering Christians. It is not so difficult for me to imagine. Whenever I turn on the television and watch documentaries on the Crusades or the Holocaust and see and hear the horrible and heinous ways that people were tortured and killed, I ask myself, "What kind of human could do that to another human?" Then I read the ninth chapter of Acts and meet the kind of person who could do such a thing — a person being called by God to be a missionary of Jesus Christ.[3] This vision is vexing indeed.

What is so miraculous about this scriptural passage is not the blinding light that stopped Saul in his tracks, no matter how dramatic. The incredible miracle is that Ananias ended up following what appeared to be a ridiculous and outlandish command. And in following the command, he answered a call that was less flashy, but more risky. He trusted in the Lord's wisdom, not in his own logic. He turned away from what was reasonable to follow the irrational love of Jesus Christ.

So as this vision and action of Ananias stare us in the face, the penetrating question arises: Are we willing to do the same? Are we willing to follow Jesus with the same kind of trust and commitment? Do we dare follow Jesus in ways considered illogical, unreasonable, and irrational? Is there enough courage within us to follow Jesus into the face of our enemy and discover what change really looks like?

Ananias' vision is vexing because it confirms that if we genuinely worship and follow Jesus Christ, we are going to be called to think outside the box and go places we probably would never want to go. We will be asked to go to great depths and heights that may be unreasonable, according to society's standards. The Spirit of Christ will quicken us to grow and change in ways that may be painful, but always adventurous.

I remember teaching a Sunday school class years ago. One of the verses of scripture we were studying was Jesus' plea, "Love your enemies; do good to those who persecute you." As we began our discussion of the verse, a lady in the back of the room stood up and exclaimed, "That's stupid! I think that is just stupid!" Then she bent down, grabbed her black, leather-bound King James Bible, stormed out of the room, slammed the door behind her, and sat in the sanctuary and waited for worship to begin.

Many of us are prepared to love the lovable, but we are not prepared to love the unlovable. We are willing to receive the unconditional love of Christ but not willing to give the same love to

247

others. We want justice to be served but do not want the unjust to be called to serve Jesus Christ. We are bold enough to claim Jesus Christ as our Savior and Lord but not always bold enough to go to the places where that claim may take us.

Yet just when we think there are no more heroes willing to take a risk — to go beyond the reasonable in the name of Jesus Christ, we read about Ananias who did exactly that. He went, despite the fact that probably every fiber of his being was against it. He went, despite the risk of appearing foolish. He went, despite the risk of losing his life. He went and paid a visit to his worst nightmare, Saul of Tarsus. And we are left asking, "How was Ananias able to do such a thing?"

The answer to that question is found in verse 18. When Ananias entered the house of Judas and saw Paul, the first word he said to him was, "Brother." Can you believe it? He called a man he certainly feared and most likely hated, "Brother!" This could be compared to a Jew in Auschwitz walking up to a Nazi guard and saying, "Brother," or an African-American attending a KKK march and saying to the white hoods, "You are my brothers!" What possessed Ananias to say such a word? My hunch is that when Ananias looked upon Saul, he saw him the way Christ saw him — as Paul.

Picasso painted a portrait of Gertrude Stein in 1906, which is now on display in the Metropolitan Museum of Art in New York City. What is so interesting about this painting is how long Picasso toiled with it before its completion. It is said that Stein sat for Picasso more than ninety separate times. However, what was even worse was that when his friends looked at the finished portrait, they complained that it looked nothing like Gertrude Stein. Picasso responded to the criticism by saying, "Everybody thinks she is not at all like her portrait, but never mind; in the end she will manage to look just like it." Picasso, with his uncanny ability, had portrayed Stein's inner essence, not her facial characteristics. More importantly, he portrayed Stein, not as she had been, or as others saw her in the present, but as she would become in the future.[4]

Dostoyevsky once said, "To love a person means to see him as God intended him to be." I believe that was what Ananias was able to do when he looked upon Paul. God in Christ gave Ananias the gift of seeing Paul the way he was intended to be. I wonder what would happen if we could do that. I wonder what would happen if we looked upon our adversaries or enemies with the eyes of Christ. Consider, for a moment, the awesome change that could occur if some of us prayed for the wisdom and courage to see that boss who insulted us, that friend who betrayed us, or that sibling who wounded us as they were intended to be. Could it be that our hearts would be transformed as radically as Paul's was on the Damascus road?

It is my conviction that if we looked at others through the eyes of Christ we would understand anew that Jesus died for the whole world, not just for people we think he should have died for. We would see that even our most evil enemy was destined to be a child of the King. Then the power of reconciliation would be a totally new experience for us. Suddenly, we would come to the refreshing realization that love is stronger than hate, reconciliation is more powerful than resentment, and acceptance is more transforming than prejudice.

There is a wonderful old film called *The Defiant Ones*, that portrays this truth. The movie is about two convicts who escape from a chain gang. They are shackled together — one man is black and the other man is white. In a moving scene, they both fall into a deep ditch with muddy sides. As he tries to claw his way out of the ditch, one convict discovers that he cannot make it because he is shackled to his mate, who has been left at the bottom of the ditch. Soon both convicts realize that the only way to make it out of the ditch is by climbing together.[5]

What is often lost in the translation of Paul's conversion story is the understanding that two people were changed, not just one. Yes, Paul was changed, but Ananias was too. Ananias saw his enemy as a brother, as an equal, as a co-worker for Jesus Christ. As a result, scales fell from Ananias's eyes, hate dissolved into love, walls came tumbling down, and the gospel prevailed and was proclaimed like never before.

The same vision and opportunity that was given to Ananias is given to us today. Jesus has given his Church the power to break down the walls that exist between our enemies and us. We have been given love to tear down the walls of hatred and build a pathway to our enemies. We have been given a voice to tear down the walls of injustice and build a pathway to peace. We have been given hands to tear down the walls of suffering and build a pathway to joy. Most of all, we have been given the Holy Spirit to tear down the walls of bitterness and brokenness and build a pathway to wholeness. So what are we waiting for? We have work to do.

---

1. Song written by Jack Norworth.

2. Lee Strobel, "Meet the Jesus I Know" (*Preaching Today*, tape 211).

3. Philip Yancey, *What's So Amazing About Grace?* (Grand Rapids, Michigan: Zondervan, 1997), p. 70.

4. William H. Willimon, *Pulpit Resource*, 29.2, p. 25.

5. Desmond Tutu, *No Future Without Forgiveness* (New York: Doubleday, 1999), p. 8.

Need A Lift?

Journalist Bob Garfield researched health articles in *The Washington Post*, *USA Today*, and *The New York Times*. His research showed that, according to so-called experts,

- 59 million Americans have heart disease
- 53 million suffer migraines
- 25 million people have osteoporosis
- 16 million struggle with obesity
- 3 million have cancer
- 12 million have severe disorders such as brain disease.[1]

The results are that 543 million Americans are seriously ill, which is shocking in a country whose population is only 266 million people. Garfield's response to this was, "Either as a society we are doomed, or someone is seriously double-dipping."[2]

I don't know the answer to this discrepancy, but it appears that our whole country is weighted down by personal challenges. For some, it is one or more of those illnesses which we are forced to deal with day in and day out. For others, it is a deep sadness or depression. And for most, it is the nagging stress of life which leads to illness or depression. It seems that everyone is a statistic. Everyone has some personal problem or challenge with which they have to cope. Therefore, most of us don't run the race of life, we crawl it, and we consider ourselves successful if we just survive to see another day.

Perhaps in our more courageous moments we question in protest: "Is there more to life than just trips to the doctor and avoiding as much pain as possible? Is not life more than just eating, drinking, sleeping, and trying to stay healthy? Is not life more than survival? Is it possible to lift myself above the day-to-day grind? Is it possible to elevate myself beyond mere existence?"

Our text gives us some clues about being elevated above the stress pool of life. At a glance, this text is exactly what we want. An outer-circle disciple of Jesus named Tabitha had become ill and died unexpectedly, and the Apostle Peter arrives with a big *S* on his chest and rescues Tabitha by bringing her back to life. Sounds good, doesn't it? It would be so nice to have someone like Peter who would come and rescue us from our problems. But the text reveals more than a miracle of resuscitation. If we look closer, we can see that we too can be lifted up by following the examples of the characters in this text.

I am sure Peter had his own challenges, but they did not stop him from seeking to reach out and help, heal, and bring someone back to life. In fact, when Peter was called to revive Tabitha, he was literally healing a man in another city. He could have claimed his good deed for the day or the week and explained, "I can't be everywhere all the time or everything to everyone. I need some personal time." Who would have blamed him for that? Yet the text clarifies that when Peter was asked to help Tabitha, he did not hesitate; he went "without delay." Peter must have received joy from lifting up others.

I would venture to say that all of us would be a great deal happier if we would not dwell on our problems. For when we dwell on our problems, they become much bigger than they are in reality. As a result, we don't have challenges; our challenges have us. The best way to rise above this self-defeating behavior is to move our attention away from ourselves and onto others. For when we focus our attention upon others, we remove ourselves from our problems and gain perspective. We discover that our problems are not as overwhelming as we first believed them to be. And it is in this discovery that we find strength because we realize that we can do more than just exist, we can make a difference in people's lives.

However, there is a deeper discovery to be found in helping others. When we are generous, we understand in a profound way that we were not made to live only for ourselves. We were made by a loving God for the purpose of loving others. Once we come to this realization, we become in tune with the very spirit of our existence. For when we give ourselves away, we find our ultimate fulfillment because we are living the gracious life for which we were destined. Jesus said it this way, "Those who lose their life for my sake will find it" (Matthew 10:39).

Miss Thompson found her life. She was a teacher who had a poor student in her class named Ted. He was very sloppy in appearance — expressionless — unattractive. All of his classmates did not hesitate to remind him of his eccentricities. Miss Thompson did not either as she took her red pen and placed *X*s beside his many wrong answers. But Miss Thompson did not fully appreciate the kind of world in which Ted was living. All she had to do was read his records:

> *1st grade: Ted shows promise with his work and attitude, but (has) poor home situation.*
> *2nd grade: Ted could do better. Mother seriously ill. Receives little help from home.*
> *3rd grade: Ted is a good boy but too serious. He is a slow learner. His mother died this year.*
> *4th grade: Ted is very slow, but well-behaved. His father shows no interest whatsoever.*

Christmas arrived. The children piled beautifully-wrapped gifts on Miss Thompson's desk. Ted brought one too. It was wrapped in brown paper and held together with Scotch tape. Miss Thompson opened each gift, as the children crowded around to watch. Out of Ted's package fell a gaudy rhinestone bracelet, with half of the stones missing, and a half-filled bottle of cheap perfume. The children began to snicker, but Miss Thompson silenced them by splashing a droplet of the perfume on her wrist and letting each one smell it. She also put the bracelet on.

At day's end, after the other children had left, Ted came up to her desk and said, "Miss Thompson, you smell just like my mother.

And the bracelet looks very pretty on you. I'm glad you like my gifts." As soon as Ted left the room, Miss Thompson began to cry and asked God to forgive her and change her attitude.

The next day the children were greeted by a new Miss Thompson, a teacher reformed and committed to loving each of her students, especially the slow ones, especially the Ted's of the world. As a result of Miss Thompson's loving care, Ted began to show great improvement. By the end of the year, he actually caught up with many of his classmates and even moved ahead of some.

Time passed and Miss Thompson had heard nothing from Ted. Then, one day, she received the following note:

> *Dear Miss Thompson:*
> *I wanted you to be the first to know. I will be graduating second in my class.*
>
> *Love, Ted*

Four years later, another note arrived:

> *Dear Miss Thompson:*
> *They just told me I will be graduating first in my class. I wanted you to be the first to know. The university has not been easy, but I liked it.*
>
> *Love, Ted*

And four years later:

> *Dear Miss Thompson:*
> *As of today, I am Theodore Stallard, M.D. How about that? I wanted you to be the first to know. I am getting married next month, the 27th to be exact. I want you to come and sit where my mother would sit if she were alive. You are the only family I have now; Dad died last year.*
>
> *Love, Ted*

Miss Thompson attended that wedding and sat where Ted's mother would have sat. The love and generosity she had shown that young man entitled her to such an honor.[3]

It is amazing what can happen when a little love and encouragement are shared. It can literally elevate a life far beyond its potential.

Do you know anyone who is dead? Oh, they may still be breathing, but they have no life. Perhaps it is someone like Ted, a person who has been beaten and bruised by life and is only a kind word away from succeeding. Maybe it is someone like Tabitha, who has worked herself to death, and all she needs is someone to watch her children for a little while so she can get some rest. Maybe it is a neighbor who lives alone and doesn't receive any phone calls or visits anymore, and his/her life is as empty as his/her home. Maybe it is that youth in your neighborhood or school who gets bullied all the time. Maybe it is that discouraged employee who is only one compliment away from elevating his/her attitude and turning his/her performance around. Maybe it is your spouse who longs to hear the words, "I love you," or "You look very nice today." Maybe it is a recent graduate who had big dreams, but he/she was shot down by a cynic. It does not take much to bring them back to life: just a little love and encouragement, just a touch of generosity will do.

What does this encouragement and love look like? Children are the best teachers in this realm. They are wiser than we realize. A group of four- to eight-year-olds were asked the question: "What does love mean?"

> Rebecca, age eight, said, "When my grandmother got arthritis, she could not bend over and paint her toenails anymore, so my grandfather does it for her all the time, even when his hands got arthritis too. That's love."
>
> Billy, age four, said, "When someone loves you, the way they say your name is different. You know that your name is safe in their mouth."
>
> Chrissy, age six, said, "Love is when you go out to eat and give somebody most of your French fries without making them give you any of theirs."
>
> Terri, age four, said, "Love is what makes you smile when you are tired."

Danny, age seven, said, "Love is when Mommy makes coffee for Daddy and she takes a sip before giving it to him, to make sure the taste is okay."

Bobby, age five, said, "Love is what's in the room with you at Christmas if you stop opening presents and listen."

Nikka, age six, said, "If you want to learn how to love, you should start with a friend you hate."

Jenny, age four, said, "There are two kinds of love. Our love and God's love. But God makes both kinds of them."

Noelle, age seven, said, "Love is when you tell a guy you like his shirt, then he wears it every day."

Tommy, age six, said, "Love is like a little old woman and a little old man who are still friends even after they know each other so well."

Jessica, age six, said, "You really should not say, 'I love you,' unless you mean it. But if you mean it, you should say it a lot. People forget."[4]

Yes, we do forget. But my hope is that from this day forward we will remember. To help you remember, think of one person you could love this week — one person you could encourage this week — one person you could take to lunch and really listen to them because no one else does — one person you could write a note to and tell them how wonderful you know they are — one person you could encourage with the words of Peter: "Get up! I want you to know you are worth something to me, and you are worth everything to God." This person may be your spouse. This person may be your child. This person may be the neighbor you see at the mailbox every day. This person may be your employee. This person may be the waiter or waitress at a restaurant. Whoever and wherever they are, let them see the love of God reflected in you!

I read of a father who often reminds his children: "Your life is God's gift to you. What you do with your life is your gift back to God. So do something great for God with your life."[5] That's good advice. So do something great for God. Make a difference to others by lifting them into life. For when you do, you too will be lifted

256

up from your problems and brought back to life. You will experience the ecstasy of generosity because you will feel a little like how God feels when we allow him to love us. And when these sacred moments of generosity occur, I believe God smiles, for he sees the world the way he created it to be.

Years ago, a new breed of horse was tested in Canada. Researchers discovered that one horse could pull an eight-ton load. When they teamed two horses together, they anticipated that the horses would pull sixteen or eighteen tons. To their great surprise, the team pulled thirty tons! It is the principle called synergism. "The law of synergism states that two or more objects working together can produce a greater effect than the objects working independently of each other."[6]

Our text reveals to us the law of synergism, which is how God planned for human beings to live. Everyone in the text is helping one another. The disciples call for help. The widows show their love and appreciation for Tabitha as they present the tunics she had made for them. Peter arrives and with loving, healing hands revives her. Then Tabitha returns to her work of charity with greater passion and love than ever before. Peter receives hospitality from a leather worker named Simon and stays and rests there for a little while. Soon he leaves in order to help the next person in need. The people in the text were all working together, helping each other. This is a beautiful picture of the way life ought to be. This is the picture of the way your community should be. This is the picture of the way the Church ought to be. This is the true picture of the way God created the world to be.

A few years ago, an unusual event occurred at the Special Olympics in Seattle. Nine mentally and physically challenged Olympians assembled at the starting line of the 400-meter race. The gun went off, and they ran as hard as they could. About half-way through the race, one boy stumbled and fell, hurt his knee, and began to cry. The other eight runners heard the boy crying, and one by one they stopped running and went back to help him. They picked him up and gave him reassuring hugs. Then they linked arms and finished the race together. The judges were confused about who was the winner. But after some discussion they decided to award all nine runners a gold medal. For, truly, they were all winners.[7]

Imagine what we would accomplish if we were willing to help one another up. Imagine the lives which could be changed if every member of the church was willing to allow the love of God to flow through them in order to bring the dead to life. Imagine how different the world would be if we became concerned not about winning the race, but helping others to finish it. Imagine, imagine, just imagine how it feels to run hand in hand toward the finish line, knowing no one is left behind.

---

1. Quoted in John Ortberg, *If You Want to Walk on Water, You've Got to Get Out of the Boat* (Grand Rapids, Michigan: Zondervan, 2001), p. 132.

2. *Ibid.*

3. Charles R. Swindoll, *The Quest For Character*, pp. 178-181. Copyright 1982 by Charles R. Swindoll, Inc. Used by permission of Zondervan.

4. From Internet for Christians Newsletter, January 28, 2002, www.gospelcom.net.

5. David C. Cooper, *The Seven Spiritual Laws of Success* (Atlanta: Discover Life Ministries, 2000), p. 75. Used by permission.

6. *Ibid.*, pp. 9-10.

7. *Ibid.*, p. 10.

Easter 5
Acts 11:1-18

Love Without Limits

The eloquent preacher Tom Long tells the story of a small church-related college that held an annual event called Christian Emphasis Week. It was the task of the Christian club on campus to invite a speaker who would come and lead a college revival. This particular year they invited a preacher who had come highly recommended. They were told of his dynamism and his unique way of communicating the gospel.

The first night of the revival the chapel was filled with the faithful. There were no "animal house" type fraternity characters in attendance, just the faithful. The speaker began the service the way most preachers would: he read a passage of scripture. But when he finished reading, he did something which shocked the audience. He closed the Bible, threw it across the stage and out an open window and said, "There goes your God." Then he proceeded to preach a sermon on the difference between worshiping the Bible and worshiping the God of the Bible.[1] Imagine the surprise those students had when the preacher turned their bibliolatrous religion upside down.

I am sure the "circumcised believers" were no less surprised when Peter threw their understanding of the Law out the window. Peter's adversaries stated that the Law was the only way to be saved. Peter responded, "I used to believe that way too until God got a hold of me and showed me that his love was not limited to a set of rules or laws." Peter continued with a compelling testimony of how God had stretched his boundaries and threw out his understanding of what was clean and not clean, dissolving his pre-conceived notions about who could be saved. What's more is that God not only revealed this radical truth to Peter through a vision, but God wanted Peter to experience its reality. So God created an opportunity for Peter to experience the boundless love of God. Peter became a vessel of the Holy Spirit, and a household of Gentiles were converted! After sharing this incredible story, I suspect Peter was prepared to run for the hills to avoid being stoned to death. But he did not have to run for the hills. After Peter's compelling testimony, the critics were speechless and had a change of heart. They all agreed that God's saving love and power is intended for the Gentiles, as well as God's chosen people.

I imagine Jesus had wished it to have been as easy to convince people of God's boundless love. Unfortunately, Jesus was unable to avoid the wrath of those who felt that they and they alone were the exclusive recipients of God's love. It all began when Jesus returned to his hometown of Nazareth. It appeared to be a regular Sabbath service. Jesus opened up the scriptures and read these liberating words from the prophet Isaiah:

> *The Spirit of the Lord is upon me, because he has anointed me to bring good news to the poor. He has sent me to proclaim release to the captives and recovery of sight to the blind, to let the oppressed go free, to proclaim the year of the Lord's favor.*
>
> — Luke 4:18-19

Then Jesus preached. And it must have been a very good sermon because the people were proud of their local boy's eloquence. They were proud until Jesus began explaining the implication of Isaiah's words being fulfilled in him. They were proud until he threw their nostalgic understanding of the scripture out the window.

What Jesus did that remarkable day in Nazareth was tell his hometown crowd that Isaiah's words, which they had heard a hundred times, were now finally coming alive for them and everyone. He told them that he was the manifestation of God's radical love to all, the outsiders, the poor, the least, last and lost, and even to those not part of the in-crowd. Jesus told them he had come to challenge their privileged theology by erasing any lines of distinctions. How did they respond? These hometown friends of Jesus drove him out of the synagogue and attempted to throw him off a cliff!

This atmosphere of anger toward "outsiders" still exists today. Everyone has their "Gentiles"! Everyone discriminates against and draws lines of self-righteous distinction. You would think, by now, our world should have moved passed such archaic and cruel ways of thinking. But even after Martin Luther King's prophetic call for equal rights and all those years of many singing, "Red and yellow, black and white, they are precious in his sight," racism still runs rampant, and hate crimes are on the rise. And as outrageous as it may seem, some extremist groups discriminate in the name of God and Holy Scripture! People continue to make distinctions between who does and does not count.

I once went into a barber shop on a Saturday afternoon. The people in the shop were pleasant enough. I sat down in the chair to get a haircut and join in the conversation. We talked about sports and favorite restaurants. Then the conversation turned sour. I'm unsure how it began, but all kinds of racial slurs spewed out of the barber's mouth. He said, "Don't you know, they are all animals." I was silent. And my thunderous silence was heard. The barber said, "You sure got quiet all of a sudden." And I nodded my head. "Am I offending you?" he asked. And before I could respond, one of the patrons who knew me said, "He is a minister." Suddenly, there was an awkward pause, and the conversation shifted to a different subject. As I left the shop, I kept asking myself, "How could a person be so obtuse and cruel?"

Lest I become too self-righteous, I want to take a scalpel to my own heart. You may want to be included. Think of the person you cannot stand to be around. If you are poor, maybe it is the rich man who drives down the road in a shiny sports car. If you are rich, maybe it is the unrefined person who drives a clunker with the radio blaring. Perhaps it is the sloppy neighbor down the street who never cleans up his/her yard. Perhaps it is the eccentric co-worker whom everyone loves to ridicule. Maybe it is the foreigner who cannot speak very good English. Maybe it is the teenager who has tattoos and piercings all over his body. Try to feel your irritation when you are around those kind of people. Now, as you have them in your mind, hear these words of our Lord: "I choose to give to [them] the same as I give to you ... are you envious because I am generous?" (Matthew 20:14-15).

How does that make you feel? — Like telling Jesus to go jump off a cliff? Like telling Jesus he's crazy? You're not alone. In fact, you are in a lot of good company. The Bible is filled with people who thought our Lord was crazy. In the Old Testament, Jonah thought God was crazy. Interestingly, God gave Jonah a similar vision to Peter's, but Jonah was more stubborn than Peter.

Jonah was the man who wanted to do God's will until God told him to go to Nineveh — wicked, wicked Nineveh! What was he supposed to do there? Persuade the Ninevites to turn from their evil ways and be saved by God. Jonah responded, "You want me to do what? Go to where? Go to whom? Those awful, evil Ninevites who live across the tracks? And I am to save them for you? Lord, you must be crazy or kidding! Tell me you're kidding. Obviously, you have mistaken me for someone who cares about those kind of people. This is where I came in, and this is where I get off!"

So Jonah thought that if he left Israel he would be free of Israel's God. He got as far as the shore of the Mediterranean, hopped on a ship, and said, "I am free at last! For I am free of God!" But soon Jonah found himself turned upside down and inside out in the belly of a large fish. And, to his surprise, he found the God of Israel there, as well. So Jonah repented and decided not to run from God anymore. God led Jonah into Nineveh and did a mighty work, through Jonah, in the hearts of the Ninevites. Jonah's boundaries and barriers were obliterated.

What God did for Jonah and what Jesus commanded Peter to do in Joppa, our Lord now commands us to do in our world today. God commands us to erase any lines of negative distinction between human beings and destroy our exclusive boundaries and barriers which we have helped to maintain. God commands us to turn our institutions, ideas, and paradigms upside down and inside out by reminding our world that every human being, red, yellow, black, and white, is a child of God. For when we are cut, we all bleed.

When we are tickled, we all laugh. And when we hurt, we all cry. We are all God's children.

Years ago, a newspaper carried a story of a reporter who was covering the war in Sarejevo. The reporter noticed a little girl walking slowly in front of him. He was surprised to discover she had been severely wounded by sniper fire. Before the reporter could react, a man rushed over and scooped up the little girl and pleaded with the reporter to drive him to the hospital. Without hesitating, they loaded her into the back seat and took off for medical help.

After a minute or two, the man said urgently, "Please hurry; she is dying!" The reporter drove faster. A few minutes later, the man in the back seat said, "Hurry, please, my little girl is still breathing!" The reporter sped on. A minute or two later the man said, "Hurry, please, my little girl is still warm." Soon they pulled up to the hospital, but it was too late. The girl had died in the man's arms.

The man and the reporter walked somberly to the restroom to wash the little girl's blood from their hands. As they were washing, the man said, "Now comes the hardest part." "What is that?" asked the reporter. The man said, "Now, I have to go find that little girl's father and tell him she is gone." The reporter was stunned and said, "But I thought you were the father! I thought she was your child!" The man replied, "Aren't they all our children?"[2] Aren't they? Aren't we all God's children?

God never intended God's boundaries to be less than the whole world. Therefore, none of us have a monopoly on God's love. We may feel like we do when we look down on someone different than we are, or when we snicker at someone's misfortune, or when we say, "Thank you, Lord, that I am not like them," or when we say, "It's too bad they do not believe as we believe." But woe be unto us whenever we reek of such arrogance! For when we try to restrict God's grace to ourselves, we cut ourselves off from that very grace. Why? Pierre Teilhard de Chardin may have said it best, "It is impossible to love Christ without loving others, and it is impossible to love others without moving nearer to Christ."[3]

I first learned about God's limitless love through a man named Walter. I met Walter while serving as a hospital chaplain during seminary days. Walter was a patient on the floor to which I was assigned. One day a nurse approached me and said, "Excuse me, Chaplain, but you see the man in the room across the hall?" I said, "Yes." She said, "His name is Walter and he has been in the hospital for two weeks. He is dying of cancer, and no one ever comes to see him." I responded, "No one?" She said, "No one." She continued, "I don't normally do this, but would you mind going in to see him?" I said, "Sure." As I approached Walter's room, the nurse said, "And, Chaplain, Walter is a very bitter man."

When I entered his room, I said, "Hello, Walter, my name is Charley, and I am one of the chaplains of the hospital." He said, "You are, are you? Well, I don't need a chaplain, and I certainly don't need God! Can't you see I'm dying?" I replied, "Well, you don't need God, and you don't need a chaplain. Do you need a friend? Because I can be a friend." He retorted, "Charley, I don't need anyone. Just leave me alone!" So I proceeded to the door with my tail tucked between my legs. Yet before I could leave the room, Walter said, "I have not always been this way, you know. There was a time when I grabbed hold of life with both hands and could do anything. I was good at my job. I was good at my marriage...." It was obvious that Walter wanted to talk, but, truthfully, I had such disdain for him that I did not want to listen. However, like Jonah and Peter, God had something different in mind for me. So for the next thirty minutes Walter talked about the joy of his life before cancer and the anger and bitterness he felt toward God because of his cancer.

After we talked, I asked if I could have a prayer. He said, "I don't think it will do any good, but if you want to, go ahead." So I took his fragile hand and began to pray. At the conclusion of my prayer, I said, "Lord, wrap your arms around Walter like a warm blanket. Amen." When I opened my eyes, I could not believe what I saw. There were tears streaming down Walter's face, and his hands were up in the air, waiting for a hug. I leaned over and hugged him, and he began to rock me back and forth. As he rocked me, he kept repeating, "Yes, Lord, cover me like a blanket ...Yes, Lord, cover me like a blanket ...Yes, Lord, cover me like a blanket."

I had no control over what happened that day. But God moved through me and into Walter, making that day an event I will never forget. As I embraced Walter, I felt so intimately connected to Christ, for my eyes were opened once again to the fact that all of us are God's children; and all of us need prayer; and all of us need each other; and all of us need the radical, life changing, world changing, barrier breaking, boundary busting love of Jesus Christ! I left Walter's room saying with Peter, "Who was I to hinder God?"

> The world says, "No!"
> Jesus says, **"YES!"**
> The world says, "Not yet."
> Jesus says, **"Right now!"**
> The world says, "Shorter."
> Jesus says, **"Longer!"**
> The world says, "Narrower."
> Jesus says, **"Wider!"**
> The world says, "Smaller."
> Jesus says, **"Bigger!"**
> The world says, "Shallower."
> Jesus says, **"Deeper!"**
> The world says, "Punish."
> Jesus says, **"Mercy!"**
> The world says, "Hate."
> Jesus says, **"Love!"**
> The world says, "Just a few."
> Jesus says, **"Everyone!"**

> The world says, "Threaten him!"
> Jesus says, **"That won't stop me!"**
> The world says, "Arrest him!"
> Jesus says, **"That won't stop me!"**
> The world says, "Ridicule him!"
> Jesus says, **"That won't stop me!"**
> The world says, "Wound him!"
> Jesus says, **"That won't stop me!"**
> The world says, "Crucify him!"
> Jesus says, **"That won't stop me!"**
> The world says, "Shut him up in a tomb!"
> Jesus says, **"That won't stop me!"**

Jesus is relentlessly in love with the world. And thank God for such love. Where would we be without such love? For if the truth be known, all of us, to one degree or another, are on the outside, where it's cold and lonely, yearning for Christ to pull us inside and wrap his warm arms around us. And would you believe there is enough room in his arms for everyone? There is room. There is plenty of room.

---

1. Thomas G. Long, *Pulpit Resource*, ed. by William H. Willimon, 29.1, p. 16.

2. *Ibid.*, p. 18.

3. Quoted in Long, p. 18.

Easter 6
Acts 16:9-15

When All Is Said And Done

Life has a way of presenting us with defining moments. I remember facing a defining moment in my ministry. I went to see a man in the hospital who was dying. He was not active in the church I pastored, but I knew who he was. When I entered his hospital room, his whole family was standing in a semi-circle around his bed. They greeted me, and then the man told his family that he wanted a moment alone with me. So they left us alone.

As soon as his family had left, he began to cry. I sat by his bed and began to stroke his hand while he expressed his grief. After a few minutes, I asked him, "Are you afraid?" He said, "No. I feel sure that death will not separate me from Christ." Then I said, "Then you must be sad about leaving your family." He replied, "Yeah, but that's not what is bothering me." "Then what exactly is it?" I asked. He turned his head away from me, lifted his eyes to hold back the tears, and said four words that still haunt me to this day: "I wasted my life." Then he began to tell me how he did not do the things he should have done — how he squandered his gifts on possessions, drugs, and alcohol — how he could have done so much more with the life God had given him — how he did not follow the path God had for him. I told him that the grace of God was big enough to forgive a wasted life. Yet as I left the hospital room, I thought how tragic it would be to come to the end of your life and realize you have wasted it.

Would you do an exercise for me? Don't worry, it is a mental exercise and won't tax you physically. However, the exercise is designed to give your mind and soul a workout! Imagine for a moment that your life is over, and you are led into a small room. In this room there are two chairs; one for you and one for God (guess who gets the larger chair?). In front of these two chairs are a television and a DVD player. Imagine God coming into the room with a DVD labeled with your name and the title, "What Might Have Been." Imagine sitting in that room with God and watching the DVD share all that God might have done with your life if you had let him. Imagine seeing what God might have done with your financial resources if you had generously trusted him. Imagine seeing what God might have done with your talents and gifts if you had stepped out in faith and used them. Imagine seeing what God might have done with your relationships if you had given him room to work. Imagine seeing what God might have done with *you* if you had confronted sin and yielded to God's empowering grace.[1]

Now, I don't know if God will make us watch a video titled "What Might Have Been." I hope not. It would be rather cruel. And I am not asking you to do this exercise so you will wallow in self-defeat. But I have asked you to do this because we have only one chance to fulfill God's dream for us. So let me get straight to the point: What have you done with your life up to this point? Do you feel like you have not taken advantage of the life God has given you? Well, take heart, because as long as you have breath, it is not too late. At this very moment, you can make things better!

To help motivate us to take advantage of God's gifts to us, I would like to lift up a very familiar, yet inspiring biblical character. In fact, he is such a household name that we sometimes gloss over his remarkable accomplishments. His name is Saul, but the Lord called him Paul. If there ever was a person who took advantage of the gifts, talents, and resources God has given, it was Paul.

Paul Decided
Our scripture lesson is a vivid example of Paul taking advantage of his gifts and deciding to live out God's purpose and plan for him. After a very difficult and disappointing beginning to what was supposed to be a "Great Missionary Journey," Paul was called in a vision to go to Macedonia and share the Good News. At this point

in the journey, Paul had every alibi and excuse in the world not to obey God: it's too dangerous; it's too long of a trip; I don't want to fail again; I am not competent enough to handle it. But when faced with the decision of destiny or defeat, Paul chose his destiny.

We all face the same decision. All human beings will choose between destiny or defeat. Between today and your last day, you will make critical decisions based upon the kind of person you want to be and the life you want to live. The only question is: Will your decisions be worthy of the gifts God has given to you? Hopefully, whatever decisions you make, they will not be as shameful as these decisions:

> An Illinois man pretending to have a gun kidnapped a motorist and forced him to drive to two different ATM's. The kidnapper then proceeded to withdraw money from his own bank accounts.
> A man walked into a Topeka, Kansas, Kwik Stop and asked for all the money in the cash drawer. Apparently, the take was too small, so he tied up the store clerk and worked the counter himself for 3 hours until the police showed up and grabbed him.
> Police in LA had good luck with a suspect who just could not control himself during a lineup. When detectives asked each man in the lineup to repeat the words, "Give me all your money or I'll shoot," the man shouted, "That's not what I said!"[2]

Bad decisions!

We are the persons we are today because of the decisions we have made. However, what is equally true is that all of us are the persons we are today because of the decisions we have not made. Not to decide is to decide. If we don't decide, someone or something will decide for us. When we fail to decide, we miss opportunities and are faced with less options. The longer we wait to make a decision, the easier it becomes for bad habits to creep in and cause us to make the wrong decision. Helen Keller once said, "Science may have found a cure for most evils, but it has found no remedy for the worst evil of all — the apathy of human beings."[3]

269

However, many of us don't see our apathy; we just see our excuses. We say, "I would develop my gifts more thoroughly, but my friends and family don't support me. I would pursue a healthier job but I need the money and security of my present one. I would grow in my relationship with my spouse, but my spouse is not interested. I would devote myself more fully to spiritual growth, but I can't find the time. I would realize more of my potential, but no one will help me."

Then some of us are masters at the "When/then game"[4]: *When* I find the time, *then* I will figure out what I want to do with my life. *When* I feel confidant, *then* I'll try using my gifts. *When* my boss is more supportive, *then* I'll perform better. *When* my spouse is more affirming, *then* I'll work on our marriage. But the truth is, "If you are not actively pursuing the person you want to be, then you are pursuing the person you don't want to be."[5] Not to decide is to decide!

So are you ready to make a decision about the kind of life you want to live? Let me ask you some questions which may help: What do you enjoy doing more than anything in this world? What keeps you up at night (besides indigestion)? A conviction, a worthy wish, or driving dream? What is your greatest passion, and does it intersect at the Church's greatest need? And my final encouragement is found in the words of Howard Thurman: "Ask yourself what makes you come alive, and then go do that. Because what the world needs is people who have come alive."[6]

Paul Was Determined

We cannot overstate Paul's determination. For it was not always easy for Paul to live up to his name and live out God's plan for him. When Paul, Silas, and Timothy had reached Troas, Paul's "Great Missionary Journey" had been anything but great. Paul and Barnabas got into a squabble and parted ways. Paul's ambitious plan to go to Bithynia was thwarted by Jesus. And, worst of all, they had not converted a soul! It would have been enough to make any one of us give up and go home. But Paul was determined to finish what God started in him and "pressed on." As he set sail to Macedonia, little did Paul know that he was headed for the greatest

270

missionary adventure of his life — one that began with the founding of his most beloved church: the church in Philippi.

As you reflect on Paul's determined spirit, perhaps you say with admiration, "I would love to have that kind of determination, but whenever I get ambitious, it does not take long for laziness and discouragement to squelch my drive." Well, it may comfort you to know that Paul was no Superman. He was human and had the same weaknesses as the rest of us. I am certain there were days when Paul felt like quitting. Yet Paul knew that God had given him all the resources he needed to succeed.

You are no different from Paul. God has given you all the resources you need: a mind, a dream, and, most of all, the Holy Spirit. You have the resources and ability to be as determined as Paul. Perhaps you just need to remember the determination you had before you knew what it meant to give up. For instance, when you were a baby, you did not know what it meant to quit. When you were one year old and trying to walk, you did not say, "Well, that was stupid of me! I am such an idiot! I guess I was not destined to be a walker. It was so embarrassing to fall in front of those people. I don't want that to happen again. I am just going to crawl the rest of my life instead of risking the humiliation of falling."[7] We never did that! But as we grew older and began to hear, process, and speak language, those dirty, four-letter words started to creep into our vocabulary. Dare I print them in this book of sermons? Words like "can't," "quit," "won't," and "don't."

As a teenager, I had a tennis coach who had played basketball for the L.A. Lakers. He was a tremendous athlete. He taught me many lessons about tennis, the most important of which was determination. For instance, he would make me do a dreaded exercise which involved bending my knees and getting lower and lower to the ground. I loathed this exercise and whenever he asked me to do it I would protest, "I can't! I can't!" One day I said that word one time too many. He jumped over the net, ran up to me, put his face in mine, and said, "Son, get that word out of your vocabulary because *can't never could!*" He was right. We are our own worst enemies. We tell ourselves we "can't" and it becomes a self-fulfilling prophecy.

Paul must have known the defeating power of the word "can't." Paul must have known that even the Holy Spirit cannot do much with a person who is convinced that he/she *can't*. Why else would he have proclaimed to the Philippian church, "I *can* do all things through Christ who strengthens me" (3:14). Paul was confident that no matter what life threw at him, the power of Christ would be there to shield him. You see, God never quits on us. Why should we quit on God? Yet whenever we do quit, God says to us, "Get up! Get up! Get ready to go again. For you don't want to miss the best part of your life!"

Whenever Paul felt like quitting, he must have sensed this kind of encouragement from God. What else would have enabled him to write and, most of all, live out these words:

> *... As servants of God we have commended ourselves in every way: through great endurance, in afflictions, hardships, calamities, beatings, imprisonments, riots, labors, sleepless nights, hunger; by purity, knowledge, patience, kindness, holiness of spirit, genuine love, truthful speech, and the power of God; with the weapons of righteousness for the right hand and for the left; in honor and dishonor, in ill repute and good repute. We are treated as impostors, and yet are true; as unknown, and yet we are well known; as dying, and see — we are alive; as punished, and yet not killed; as sorrowful, yet always rejoicing; as poor, yet making many rich; as having nothing, and yet possessing everything.*
> — 2 Corinthians 6:4-10

Paul Deflected

As you can readily see from Paul's testimony to the Corinthians, Paul had enemies who did everything they could to intimidate him. His critics within the Church insulted him. The Jewish leaders slandered him. The government authorities threatened and physically tortured him. But Paul was not buying. He deflected all such intimidations like waving gnats from his face and said with righteous arrogance, "Should a person like me flee? If God be for me, who can be against me?"

There will always be critics when you are attempting something, noble, taking the high road, or living out what you understand to be God's purpose for you. There will always be jealous or insecure people desiring to foil your plans. There will always be backbiters who will try to intimidate you. There will always be critics affirming your failures. Yet when you do fail, and you are down in the dirt of self-pity, and your critics continue to shake their fingers at you saying, "I told you so," just remember:

> The victim says, "I can't";
> > the victor says, "I can do all things through Christ who strengthens me."
> The victim says, "It's not my fault!"
> > the victor says, "I am responsible for my actions."
> The victim says, "We never did it that way before";
> > the victor says, "Nothing venture, nothing gained."
> The victim lives in fear;
> > the victor walks by faith.
> The victim sees problems;
> > the victor sees opportunities.
> The victim strikes back;
> > the victor turns the other cheek.
> The victim harbors resentment;
> > the victor forgives even as God has forgiven him.
> The victim gives up;
> > the victor presses on.
> The victim explains why it can't be done;
> > the victor believes it can be done.
> The victim offers excuses;
> > the victor sets an example.
> The victim is reactive;
> > the victor is proactive.
> The victim says, "With man this is impossible";
> > the victor says, "With God all things are possible."
> The victim says, "The odds are against us";
> > the victor says, "If God be for us, who can be against us?"[8]

273

Sir Edmund Hillary made several unsuccessful attempts at scaling Mount Everest. After those failures, he finally succeeded. But he learned from his failures. For instance, one time he stood at the mountain's base and shook his fist towards it and said, "I'll beat you yet because you are as big as you are going to get — but I'm still growing." Every time Hillary climbed and failed, something inside of him grew and grew and grew. Then there came that special day when all of his growth made a difference, and he did not fail.[9]

Perhaps you are on the cusp of a great decision for your life. Perhaps you are ready to move beyond your mediocrity. Maybe you are deciding to be the person that God has called you to be. Maybe you are willing to take advantage of all those situations of your life that have caused you to grow. Maybe you are just about ready, and all you need is one slight push. I believe I have just the right motivator:

> *I read of a reverend who stood to speak at the funeral of a friend.*
> *He referred to the dates on her tombstone from the beginning ... to the end.*
> *He noted that first came the date of her birth and spoke of the following date with tears,*
> *But he said what mattered most of all was the dash between those years.*
> *For that dash represents all the time that she spent alive on earth,*
> *And now only those who loved her know what that little line is worth.*
> *For it matters not how much we own, the cars, the house, the cash.*
> *What matters is how we live and love and how we spend our dash.*
> *So think about this long and hard. Are there things you'd like to change?*
> *For you never know how much time is left. You could be at dash mid-range.*
> *If we could just slow down enough to consider what's true and real*

274

And always try to understand the way other people feel.
And be less quick to anger and show appreciation more
And love the people in our lives like we've never loved
before.
If we treat each other with respect and more often wear
a smile,
Remembering that this special dash might only last a
little while.
So when your eulogy is being read with your life's ac-
tions to rehash,
Would you be proud of the things they say about how
you spent your dash?[10]

When all is said and done in your life, will there be more said than done, or done than said? You decide! The clock is ticking, and God's adventure for your dash is waiting.

---

1. John Ortberg, *If You Want to Walk on Water, You've Got to Get Out of the Boat* (Grand Rapids, Michigan: Zondervan, 2001), pp. 47-48.

2. Taken from an e-mail titled "Today's Humor."

3. Quoted in David C. Cooper, *The Seven Spiritual Laws of Success* (Atlanta: Discover Life Ministries, 2000), pp. 29-30. Used by permission.

4. Phrase coined by Susan Jeffers.

5. Attributed to Theodore Roosevelt.

6. Quoted in "The Candler Connection."

7. Ortberg, p. 136.

8. Cooper, pp. 47-48. Used by permission.

9. Ortberg, p. 24.

10. "The Dash," by Linda Ellis, copyright 1996 by Linda Ellis, www.lindaslyrics.com. Used by permission.

Ascension Of The Lord
Acts 1:1-11

In The Event Of Power Failure

A friend of mine once shared a story about his first visit to Niagara Falls. He said it was magnificent — the rush and roar of the water — the display of raw power. But as he looked upon the water gushing forth, he remembered a picture in a textbook. It showed Niagara Falls in the middle of winter, and much of the water was frozen. Big lightning-shaped forms of water were at a standstill. There was no movement, no action, no power. As my friend reflected on the picture, he thought how disappointing it would be to go to Niagara Falls and not hear the roar and feel the power of the water, but only see the great Niagara frozen.

Can you relate to that image? Frozen power. Maybe you have felt like that after a full day of pressure at the office. Maybe you see it on the face of your child after she has been hurt at school. Maybe you sense it as the winter of illness sets in. Suddenly, you are frozen and powerless, and there seems to be nothing encouraging you, motivating you, or inspiring you.

In fact, do you remember the last time you possessed power over your life? Well, do I have good news for you! You don't need to be powerless anymore. You *can* experience a God-given power over your life. Jesus promised it to us: But you will receive power when the Holy Spirit has come upon you (Acts 1:8).

Jesus gave us a beautiful promise, a promise that his powerful Spirit would come to dwell within those who believe in him. The apostles who originally heard this promise were so unsure of what Jesus meant and when this power would be received that Pentecost came as a surprise. Yet when they were filled with the power of the

Spirit, they could not contain it. The Spirit motivated and empowered them to become witnesses "to the ends of the earth," and Christianity spread like a rushing flood of water throughout the world.[1]

The good news is that this power that was given to the disciples and the early Christians is available to us. When we surrender our lives to Jesus Christ, we are given a powerful resource from which to draw. The Holy Spirit, the very Spirit of Christ, will live inside of us and give us power for living. The whole Bible bears witness to this incredible truth. In the New Testament there are numerous references that specifically mention the power of Christ. Just take your pick. Here are some of my favorites:

> *"I am sending upon you what my Father promised; so stay here in the city until you are clothed with **power** from on high."* — Luke 24:49

> *"Be strong in the Lord and in the strength of his **power**."* — Ephesians 6:10

> *"Now to him who by the **power** at work within us is able to accomplish abundantly far more than all we can ask or imagine."* — Ephesians 3:20

> *"For God did not give us a spirit of cowardice, but rather a spirit of **power** and of love."* — 2 Timothy 1:7

> *"His divine **power** has given us everything needed for life."* — 2 Peter 1:3

But could it be that these verses hold no power for you? Could it be that even though you are a Christian you have never known the power that Jesus promised? Or maybe you have a faint memory of the power but have not experienced it in quite some time. Whatever the case, do you wonder why Jesus' promise of power has not manifested itself in your life? There may be several reasons for this lack or loss of power. However, it is usually because of the reasons listed below. See if you find yourself in these hindrances to power.

We Feel Powerless Because We Don't Expect The Power

Bishop Noah Moore told the wonderful old story of a crowd that went to the hilltop to pray for rain. Drought had devastated the area. Crops and cattle had died, and the land was parched. As the desperate crowd went up the hill, an African-American woman joined them. She had a raincoat, rain hat, rain boots, and an umbrella. She looked silly, so someone asked her, "What are you doing with all this stuff? Don't you know it has not rained in weeks?" Her response was priceless: "Why are you climbing up this hill, anyway? If I ask God for rain, I expect a downpour!"[2]

The key to manifesting the power of Christ in your life is to expect something to happen. Unfortunately, many of us miss the power of Christ in our lives because our spiritual imaginations are closed, and we do not expect anything to happen. This is not some principle of positive thinking; it is a simple spiritual truth. The power of Christ will not move within us unless we awaken and earnestly desire to be moved by it. Christ will not force his power on us anymore than he will force his will on us. Christ loves us above all, and there is no such thing as forced love. Therefore, because Christ does not force his power on us, it often lies dormant under a thick, dark cloud of low expectations. The mundane mess of a mediocre life has allowed cobwebs to develop over our souls, keeping the lifeless air in and the refreshingly powerful breath of Christ's Spirit out. This is why we should treat Jesus' promise of power as a clarion call for a divine explosion in our lives and pray this prayer:

> *I have tried to open the door but, Lord, there is the rust,*
> *the accumulated rust of years upon the bolts. You must*
> *do it for me, Lord; break through! Smash that rusty*
> *lock; batter my heart, three-personed God.*[3]

We Feel Powerless Because We Neglect The Power

One New Year's Day, during the Tournament of Roses Parade, a beautiful float suddenly stopped. It was out of gas. The entire parade was held up until someone brought a can of gas. The amusing thing was that the float represented the Standard Oil Company. Standard Oil's truck was out of gas, even with all its oil resources.[4]

We laugh, but that is a living parable for many in the Church. There are Christians who sputter through life with no spiritual power because they have run out of gas. Oh, they have a deep reservoir of power at their disposal, but they fail to use it.

Is this you? Do you find yourself trying to run on empty? Do you find yourself trying to run on fumes? Have you been giving and giving and giving and do not have much left to give and wonder why? Probably, it is because you have neglected the power of the One who lives within you.

Whenever someone drags into my office feeling burned out, I ask, "When was the last time you spent ten minutes alone with God?" Often I get the reply, "It's been awhile," or "I can't remember the last time," or "I have never been able to find time." Then I sit quietly, and soon it begins to sink in that in order to receive power we must be plugged in to the power source.

I know this is true in my own life. Whenever I become tired, irritable, or impatient, I ask myself, "Have I been neglecting those quiet, sacred moments with God?" Nine out of ten times I have. It is then that I remember the healing truth of Henri Nouwen's words:

> *Without silence the Spirit will die in us and the creative energy of our life will float away and leave us alone, cold, and tired. Without silence we will lose our center and become victims of the many who constantly demand our attention.*[5]

Author Jamie Buckingham once visited a dam on the Columbia River. He had always believed that the water spilling over the top provided the power, not realizing that it was just froth. Later, he learned that under the froth there were turbines and generators, quietly transforming the power of tons and tons of water into electricity.[6]

Are you trying to get by with froth? Do you start your day with a cup of coffee, an insincere grin, and a "fake it till I make it" attitude, only to see it dissolve by noon? Look deep within. You possess a generator, a power source. It is Christ. And if you had ears to hear, you would hear him say, "Don't you think you have ignored me long enough? Why don't you pay attention to me? You don't have to face life powerless. I am here to sustain you. I am here to guide you. I am here to empower you."

The old Celtic Christians talked about a "thin place." By that, they meant a sacred space where the wall separating you from God is so thin that the love and power of God flows through and envelops you. When was the last time you were at the "thin place"? When was the last time you gave Christ ten minutes of silence? When was the last time you placed your ear to that thin wall and listened for the voice of Christ? When was the last time you waited quietly and expectantly for Christ to penetrate the "thinness" and fill you with power?[7]

If the power of Christ seems unreal to you, could it be because you have not set aside some quiet time which allows him to embrace you with his love and power? Some feel powerless because they have neglected the power.

We Feel Powerless Because We Are Afraid Of The Power

It may be surprising, but it's true. There are many people in the Church who resist the power of Christ because they are afraid of what it might compel them to do. They resist because it might cause them to say things they normally would not say, feel things they normally would not feel, or be led to places they normally would not go. I meet people all the time who, I believe, are at the edge of an incredible God-driven destiny; they feel the conviction, the fire, the power. Yet something hinders them. Usually, it is that consuming adversary we call *fear*: "I am afraid of what my friends might think. I am afraid of failure. I am afraid it might be different than I expected. I am afraid that I will lose my comfortable lifestyle. I am simply afraid."

I am continually amazed at the number of people I run into who feel they are called to be more, to do more, but they are terrified ever to attempt to live out their calling. They have incredible gifts and graces aching to be used, but they stop short because their fears paralyze them. They do not step out in faith because they fear the risk. They do not move with the heartbeat of their passion because they fear the transformation. They do not listen to the voice of Christ telling them who they can be because they fear change.

281

Does that describe you? Do you feel the power of Christ pulling you towards something incredible but fear the consequences of going through with it? Do you feel the power of Christ moving you to change something in your world but fear the risk of being involved? Do you feel the power of Christ compelling you to become the person you know deep inside you were created to be but fear leaving your comfort zone?

Remember what scripture says, "Perfect love casts out fear" (1 John 4:18). And I will add, "Perfect power casts out fear." You need not be afraid. If the power of Christ is inspiring you to move, to act, you can be sure that the power of Christ will give you everything you need to see it through. Paul put it this way to the Philippians: "I am confident of this, that the one who began a good work among you will bring it to completion by the day of Christ Jesus" (Philippians 1:6).

The migratory plover is a marvelous bird. It spends its summers in the far arctic regions of the north and its winters in South America. When migrating, it makes a non-stop flight that covers a distance of 10,000 to 12,000 miles. Included in the long journey is a 2,500-mile flight over nothing but ocean. As the plover flies, it never veers from its course more than a half mile unless driven by the wind or interrupted by some lurking danger. If, by chance, it is sidetracked, there is a powerful radar system built within its organism that brings it back on course. If God does that for a bird, what do you believe God will do for you?[8]

> *He who, from zone to zone,*
> *Guides through the boundless sky thy certain flight,*
> *In the long way that I must tread alone*
> *Will lead my steps aright.*[9]

Don't be afraid of releasing the power that lives within you. Don't run from it. Surrender and embrace it. It is your destiny. For it will lead you to that magnificent place where you can honestly say, "It is not I who live, but Christ who lives in me." And when you get to arrive there, watch out. When you unleash the power of Christ dwelling in you, watch out. For amazing things will happen.

You will begin to do things you never thought you had the courage to do. You will begin to influence people you never thought you could influence. You will be driven by a purpose larger than yourself. You will begin to become the person that you and God dreamed you could become.

A story is told about a saint named Abbot Joseph, who was one of the of the desert fathers who lived during the fourth century C.E. Abbot Joseph was in charge of a large community of monks living in the desert, and he spent most of his time offering spiritual wisdom and guidance. One day a disappointed monk came to see him. This monk had done everything he was told, had followed all the rules of his order, but still felt there was something missing. He said to the Abbot, "Father, according as I am able, I keep my little rule, and my little fast, my prayer, meditation, and contemplative silence; and according as I am able I strive to cleanse my heart of thoughts. Now what more should I do?" The desert father rose up in reply and lifted his hands to heaven, and his fingers became like ten lamps of fire. As the young monk looked on with amazement, the Abbot said, "Why not be totally changed into fire?"[10]

I dare you to let the power of Christ inspire you. I dare you to let the power of Christ lead you. I dare you to let the power of Christ transform you into a ball of fire and set ablaze your world with the love of Jesus Christ. I dare you!

1. Adapted from *Circuit Rider* © copyright The United Methodist Publishing House, Charles D. Reeb — January/February, 2002.

2. Audio recording of a sermon by the late Bishop Noah Moore.

3. Prayer by James Stewart, quoted in *Abingdon Preacher's Annual 1994*, ed. by John K. Bergland (Nashville: Abingdon Press, 1993), p. 118.

4. www.sermonillustrations.com.

5. Henri J. M. Nouwen, *The Only Necessary Thing: Living a Prayerful Life* (New York: The Crossroad Publishing Company, 1999), p. 49.

6. www.sermonillustrations.com.

7. Tony Campolo, *Let Me Tell You a Story* (Nashville: Word Publishing, 2000), p. 95.

8. Moore, audio recording.

9. William Cullen Bryant, "To a Waterfowl," quoted in James Earl Massey, *Sundays in the Tuskegee Chapel* (Nashville: Abingdon Press, 2000), p. 70.

10. Barbara Brown Taylor, *Gospel Medicine* (Boston: Cowley Publications, 1995), pp. 131-132. Originally referenced in *Circuit Rider* © copyright The United Methodist Publishing House, Charles D. Reeb — January/February, 2002.

More Beyond

Centuries ago, Portugal adopted a national motto. The motto read: "No More Beyond." It was an appropriate statement since Portugal, at the time, was the end of the world. But later some adventurous persons sailed beyond Portugal and discovered a whole new world. So the question arose: "What do we do with our national motto?" After much debate, one person simply scratched out a word, and the new motto became: "More Beyond."

Whenever life tumbles in upon us, it is easy to have a "No more beyond" attitude. While facing what appear to be insurmountable challenges, we say to ourselves, "Certainly there is no life beyond this one." Before long, we convince ourselves that there is no more light beyond our darkness. Then the mental bars of defeat and discouragement appear, and we begin to lock ourselves up in our self-made prisons.

I am sure Paul and Silas were tempted to wallow in this attitude when they were locked up in a dark, dingy prison cell, facing the grim reality that they might not see another tomorrow. But Paul and Silas reflected a spirit far beyond their circumstance. The hymns they sang while shackled in chains testified to their inner assurance that God was bigger than the challenge they faced. As they winked at their adversity, God shook the foundations of the prison, tore apart their shackles, and flung wide the prison doors. They were free!

Use your spiritual imagination and see Paul and Silas running from their destroyed prison into our twenty-first-century lives. They appear lifting high torches of light and shouting, "Whatever challenge you face, it is not the end! There is something more beyond it! We have experienced it. For we know a God who is greater than pain, greater than tragedy, and greater than death. We know a God who frees those who are in bondage. Come to know this God and you too will find more beyond whatever challenges you encounter!"

As you continue to imagine the powerful witness of Paul and Silas, my hope is that your spirit will be saturated with undaunted courage, and your once-defeated life will, through faith, come to embody the attitude and spirit of a determined disciple of Jesus Christ. To encourage you, I want to highlight certain truths which appear in this magnificent passage of scripture. As you begin to understand these truths, you will be better equipped to live a victorious life. Let's take a look.

There Will Be Opposition

Contrary to popular opinion and certain television preachers, Christians are not immune from pain and disappointment. The notion of a cotton-candy theology that promises all health and wealth and no turmoil or tribulation is melting away with every tragedy that befalls our world. The reality of this sobering truth hit home in a cartoon that appeared in *The Atlanta Constitution* after a man named Mark Barton walked into an Atlanta business office and shot and killed several people. In the cartoon, a small boy is sitting next to his mother, and a newspaper is lying on the table. The headline reads, "Atlanta Murderer: Mark Barton." Confused, the boy is looking up at his mother saying, "You said monsters don't exist."[1]

Unfortunately, there are Christians who are like that little boy in the cartoon. When the monsters of life appear and begin to pounce on them, they do not understand why. The evil and pain they experience confuses their distorted view of Christianity. Eventually, they blame their suffering on lack of faith. Some may even give up all together on God. As a result, they become spiritually bankrupt and are left with no inner resources with which to battle the trials of life.

Scripture does not teach that Christians will escape the tragedies and turmoil of life. In fact, scripture teaches that opposition is inevitable. For example, we read that before Paul and Silas were thrown into jail, they were stripped of their clothing and beaten with rods (v. 22). Sounds awful, doesn't it? Yet when we read the New Testament, we notice that such treatment was routine. Paul confirms this in 2 Corinthians when he gives a litany of trials and tribulations that he and others of the faith had to endure. Take a look at the list: "afflictions, hardships, calamities, beatings, imprisonments, riots, labors, sleepless nights, and hunger" (2 Corinthians 6:4-5). After reading this litany you must conclude that if Paul were alive today he would be nauseated by those who tout a prosperity gospel.

Paul knew that he would face opposition. However, what is important to remember is that he did not cower from this fact. His resolve remained strong. In fact, later in the aforementioned passage Paul's rhetoric is on the offensive:

> We are treated as impostors, and yet are true; as unknown, and yet are well known; as dying, and see — we are alive; as punished, and yet not killed; as sorrowful, yet always rejoicing; as poor, yet making many rich; as having nothing, and yet possessing everything.
> — 2 Corinthians 6:8-10

For Paul, it was unimportant how badly Christians were treated, for he believed they were empowered by a towering faith that enabled them to endure and rise victoriously above any opposition.

We Do Not Face Opposition Alone

In the beautiful mountains of North Carolina, there are many stories about the Native Americans. I like the one about the ritual of initiation for Cherokee boys entering manhood. Near age eleven, the young Indian travels deep into the Pisgah forest, armed only with a bow and arrow. This ritual is intended to prove his bravery, yet the entire night he is terrified. Every hoot of an owl sounds like a menacing monster. Every cracking twig sounds like a bear or bobcat. Every rush of wind sounds like whispers of the demonic. But when morning finally comes, the young brave sees another Cherokee hiding behind a tree. It is his father, who has been lovingly watching all night long, making certain that his child did not have to face the darkness alone.[2]

This story reflects a powerful truth that should anchor us when we face opposition. This truth certainly anchored Paul. As he sat in that dark prison cell with Silas, I am confident he was comforted by the promise which he wrote about in his letter to his friends in Rome: "I am convinced that neither death, nor life, nor angels, nor rulers, nor things present, nor things to come, nor powers, nor height, nor depth, nor anything else in all creation, will be able to separate us from the love of God in Christ Jesus our Lord" (Romans 8:38-39). This is the promise which gave Paul the capability to survive and overcome opposition. He knew that he had a source of strength that could sustain and empower him. As he faced the dark hours of persecution, he was certain that God was with him, giving him the courage to face the ugliest of terrors. He had the confidence that the same power which was with him in darkness would lead him into the light. Paul was absolutely persuaded that with God there was nothing strong enough, evil enough, or powerful enough that could defeat him, not even death. And so it is with us. When the storms of life rage and roar, God is near, caring and encouraging, making sure we do not face the darkness alone. But most importantly, God gives us the gift of light which pierces our darkness and liberates us to bloom again.

As I reflect on the witness of Paul and Silas, one of the images that keeps coming into my mind is one of violets cracking rocks. Have you ever seen it? It is inspiring. You hike up a mountain or walk down a sidewalk and find a huge rock with beautiful violets growing right through it! Incredible! Tiny, yet determined, violets with so much desire for sunlight that they literally crack the rock so they can bask in the sunlight and finally bloom victoriously.[3] I believe Paul and Silas were given the same type of strength to break out of jail. The hymns of faith and praise that they sang penetrated the walls of their cell. Even other prisoners heard the healing notes that were exploding with the power of the gospel. No cold, hard, rock-like prison could squelch the joyful notes of two men who were confident that they were in the hands of Almighty God. Their songs of faith burst forth in glory, and the foundation of the prison shook.

As Christians, we are like the violets that have the power to crack the rocks of opposition. We have the power to crack rocks of suffering. We have the power to crack rocks of tragedy. We have the power to crack rocks of doom and death. And that power is the Spirit of Almighty God revealed in Jesus Christ!

Opposition Can Be Turned Into Opportunity

The biblical scholar William Barclay wrote, "Endurance is not just bearing rough times, but turning rough times into glory!" I believe this was what Paul was declaring when he wrote, "We are more than conquerors" (Romans 8:37). Not only can we overcome the tragedies of life, but with the help of God, we can turn trouble into triumph! In Romans 8, Paul declared it another way: "All things work together for good for those who love God, who are called according to his purpose." When we put these inspired thoughts of Paul together, we should become aware that evil and tragedy are never the will of God, but God majors in taking the evil that ensnares us and turning it into good. Over and over again in scripture and history we see this. Over and over again in life we see this. When evil attacks with pain, God uses it to build character. When evil shows resistance, God uses it to build strength. When evil cripples with tragedy, God finds a way to victory. When evil destroys with death, God restores life. When the momentum of evil rolls our way, God takes that momentum, transforms it, and rolls it back into evil's way.

Wendell Wilkie was right when he said, "What a person needs to get ahead is a powerful enemy." The Chinese language affirms a similar principle. The word "crisis" in Chinese has two characters: one represents "danger" and the other "opportunity."[4] When we are faced with opposition, the same truth applies. God can take the worst evil and transform it into an opportunity for victorious change.

A friend of mine experienced such a change. She lives in New York City and was in Times Square on the morning of September

289

11, 2001, when terrorists turned the World Trade Center into rubble. A few days after the attack, still dazed and upset, she got on the subway for the first time since the attack. It was packed, and not a word was spoken. She looked around for a place to hold on as the train moved, but all the poles and seats were covered with hands. There must have been a sense of deep disappointment on her face because a huge, muscular, African-American man looked down at her, stuck out his bulging arm, and said, "Hold on to me. We have got to hold on to each other." As she wrapped her small hands around his rock solid arm, she tried to remember when she had felt something so strong and so secure. Soon tears began to run down her cheek. Seeing her tears, the man decided to hold her until she got off the train.[5]

Healing events like this have occurred all over New York in the wake of the terrorist attacks: strangers hugging strangers, black people hugging white people, Hispanic people hugging Asian people. Hate and prejudice have given way to love and compassion. What was once considered a tough city, where you never talked to a stranger, let alone embraced one, is now a city known for its unity, compassion, love, and faith! You see, God takes opposition and creates an overwhelming opportunity!

Jesus' work on the cross is the ultimate example of opposition being transformed into opportunity. Before Jesus, the cross represented suffering, shame, punishment, and death. But he came and transformed it into the symbol of forgiveness, victory, love, and life! So whenever we gaze upon the cross, we are reinforced by the reality that God in Christ takes what is ugly and makes it beautiful.

The great preacher Harry Emerson Fosdick once told a true story about the transforming love of Jesus Christ. A young woman lived in war-torn Armenia in the early 1900s. A Turkish soldier chased her and her brother down a dead-end alley. The soldier killed her brother, but she escaped. Later she was captured and put to work in a military hospital as a nurse.

One day the man who had murdered her brother was a patient in the hospital and assigned to her ward. When she recognized him, she was horrified. But he had been critically wounded and she knew that the slightest neglect would cause his death. Suddenly, a very different battle waged within her. One side of her wanted vengeance. She thought, "Here's my chance. No one will ever know." But Christ's Spirit reigned victorious inside her. She nursed him back to health and prayed for him daily.

When the soldier fully recovered, he asked the nurse in amazement, "Why? You recognized me. Why did you care for me so faithfully?" She replied, "Because I serve him who said, 'Love your enemies and do them good.' That is my faith." The soldier was silent as he reflected on such foreign words. Then he replied, "Tell me more of your religion. Tell me more of your Lord. I would give anything to have a faith like yours!"[6]

Isn't that what happened in that infamous jail so many years ago? Paul and Silas were faced with opposition and, yet, with God's help were able to seize an opportunity. They transformed their cell into a sanctuary, and their jailer came to the altar. They did not fight evil with evil but overcame evil with good.

Paul and Silas had a choice, and now we have a choice. We can stay locked up in our own prison, or we can seize the opportunity that God has created out of opposition. Let us pray that God will help each of us look opposition in the face and say with unwavering courage:

> *I will be untouched in the midst of fire*
> *I will stand firm in the midst of a storm*
> *I will not crack in the midst of chaos*
> *I will not lose heart when the world is torn*
>
> *I will not fear when heat blazes*
> *I will not fret when drought comes*
> *I will bear fruit in the midst of all of it*
> *I will march to a different drum*
>
> *I will discover victory in tragedy*
> *I will trust in El Shaddai*
> *I will laugh in the face of death*
> *I will wave evil and pain good-bye*[7]

1. Cartoon by Mike Luckovich of *The Atlanta Constitution*. The cartoon appeared in newspapers in August of 1999.

2. *Abingdon Preacher's Annual 1994*, ed. by John K. Bergland (Nashville: Abingdon Press, 1993), p. 31.

3. I am grateful to Maxie Dunnam for giving me this image of the violet.

4. Attributed to John F. Kennedy.

5. True story shared with me by the very woman who was embraced by this stranger: Lindsey Alley.

6. James W. Moore, *Yes, Lord, I Have Sinned But I Have Several Excellent Excuses* (Nashville: Abingdon Press, 1991), pp. 26-27.

7. Poem by Charles D. Reeb.

Sermons On The First Readings

For Sundays
After Pentecost
(First Third)

Calling Others In God's Name

Richard E. Gribble, csc

The realization that God calls all people of faith to service and discipleship, and thereby to be a prophetic voice in the contemporary world, is manifest most strongly through the multiple ways God speaks to us. Reading the scriptures, personal meditation and reflection, and the experiences of daily life show God's face to us. For me, however, the hope and the challenge of God's message to be prophetic is found most in the observation of one who is prophetic and staunchly defends one's beliefs and calls others to a similar degree of faith. It is appropriate, therefore, that this book of sermons on the prophetic life be dedicated to two men who have been significant prophets to me: my friends, Joe Ross and Joe Carey.

Introduction

British poet Francis Thompson's epic work, "The Hound of Heaven," is in many ways an autobiographical poem that speaks of the never-ending search that God conducts in the quest of our souls. Thompson, a drug addict whose great talent was only discovered later in life, was called by God, but it took some time for the message to penetrate through the facade of his significant problems that wrapped his potential in a blanket of ignorance and fear. Once the call was heard and the message received, this great poet began to call others in God's name.

Prophecy is a concept that is ordinarily associated with figures we meet in the Hebrew Scriptures, what Christians call the Old Testament. Certainly the great prophets of this era of salvation history, men like Elijah, Isaiah, Jeremiah, Micah, and Amos, to name just a few, spoke God's word to ofttimes rebellious people and helped initiate a change in heart, what the Greeks call *metanoia*. But if this is where our idea of prophecy ends, then we have truly missed a great deal of beauty. Prophets who call us to greatness in God's name are all about us; we simply need to recognize their words and heed their message. God calls all men and women in varied ways to lives of service and discipleship. Similarly, we are asked to be prophetic and to proclaim God's message to others. Made in the image and likeness of God, as the book of Genesis clearly states, we are the presence of God to others. This awesome responsibility and privilege beckons us to hear God's call and then to pass the call along to others. We act as prophets and call others to faith in God's name, through our words and actions. We must be mindful, therefore, of what we say and do, for such actions communicate who we are and what we believe.

The first third of the Pentecost or Proper cycle reminds us of our need to take the Resurrection message and proclaim it to all

295

peoples as contemporary prophets. It is appropriate, therefore, that the First Lesson scripture passages for this season concentrate on the ministry of the prophets. Scripture calls us never to limit our potential, to work together as a Christian family of faith, to learn to appreciate and gain strength through diversity in society, to speak and spread the truth, and never to block our sense to the needs and cries of the poor, as we do our little bit each day to complete our Master's work on earth.

These sermons are the reflections of one person of faith on the Hebrew Scriptures and what they can and must mean for us today. We cannot shirk our responsibilities as followers of Christ and the consequent challenge to live active lives as contemporary prophets. We have the common vocation to holiness that is manifest each day through the ways we call others in the name of Christ to achieve their great potential. It is my hope that those who read and hear these sermons may be inspired to be prophetic in all that they say and do, carrying forth God's message and doing their share day-by-day to build God's kingdom in our world.

Richard Gribble, CSC

Never Limit Others, Ourselves, Or God

Once upon a time a badly deformed little girl was born to a very wealthy family. The parents, who were ashamed and humiliated, wanted no one to know about their child. It so happened that in a nearby village there was a poor couple who very much wanted to have children, but none had been sent their way by God. Thus, the rich family, hearing about the poor family, sent an emissary to ask if they wanted their child, realizing that the little girl was badly deformed. The poor family was overjoyed and said, "The child's condition makes no difference to us. It is still one of God's children and we can love and care for the little girl. We will be happy to take the child." The emissary delivered the message to the rich couple who, in turn, had their little girl delivered to the poor parents who were thrilled to have the child.

The poor family loved and cared for the little girl with extraordinary tenderness and kindness. They taught her to read and to develop her mind. Each day they spent several hours reading to her and teaching her everything they knew. As the child was unable to walk or to use her hands in the normal fashion, she overcame these handicaps through the development of her mind. Her memory was extraordinary; when she learned something she never forgot it. Her ability to understand people and events and her insight into people's lives was uncanny; no one in the village had ever experienced someone like her before. Word of this little girl's ability and her brilliant mind came to the attention of the king, who lived in a great city that was not too far from the village. The king sent messengers to the small village to ask the girl's adopted parents if the child could be brought to the palace so he could meet her. The parents were most happy to oblige and thus they brought their foster-daughter to visit the monarch. When the king met the child he was extremely impressed and asked if she might stay in the palace as a trusted advisor. The parents were concerned about who might look after the child, but the king allayed their fears by inviting them to come and live at the palace as well. All were happy with the king's proposal and readily agreed.

For many years thereafter the young girl, who had grown into a young woman, served as the king's trusted counselor. When the birth parents of the woman heard what had transpired, they were beside themselves with envy and bitterness because their daughter and the poor stepparents were surrounded by honor, while they lived in obscurity. They failed to see the potential in their daughter and lost the opportunity of a lifetime in the process.[1]

This little story, told by the priest author Joseph Girzone, speaks of how people many times limit the potential of others. In a more generic sense we often, consciously or unconsciously, limit ourselves and even God, and we do so to the detriment of all. Today on this festival day of Pentecost, when the Christian Church throughout the world celebrates its birth through the coming of the Holy Spirit upon the apostles and representatives of people throughout the world, we are challenged to see how we can exercise our full potential and that of others. The Church is the people of God and thus finite in its membership, but it is guided by the Spirit of God who is infinite. Thus, we must allow the Spirit to dispel our doubts and to expand our horizons to see the potential that exists in ourselves and others.

Today's familiar reading from the Acts of the Apostles describes what happened that first Pentecost, fifty days after the Lord's Resurrection. The apostles and other disciples of Jesus most assuredly lived in fear after the ascension. Recent events had created a roller coaster of up and down emotions for these first followers of Christ. The people experienced the heights of ecstasy on Palm Sunday and moved to the depths of despair on Good Friday. The pattern was repeated with the great joy of the resurrection that was followed by the reality of Jesus' return to the Father in his ascension. Jesus had promised the apostles that he would send the Spirit, but like many of his words the disciples probably did not fully understand what the Lord meant and what the manifestation and ramifications of his words might be. Thus, the Spirit comes in the form of flaming tongues of fire giving the apostles the ability to speak foreign languages so all assembled might know and experience the amazing power of God. Yes, God allowed poorly-educated Galilean fisherman and Christ's other followers to do what they were not able to do, namely to speak in foreign tongues. God thus demonstrated in a very concrete, audible, and significant way that one should never limit the potential and possibilities that God can provide.

This great lesson is made crystal clear in the person of Peter. We recall how both the Synoptic evangelists and Saint John portray Peter as not only the chosen leader of the apostles but the one apostle during Jesus' earthly life who often does not understand or fails the Lord most grievously. We remember that immediately after Jesus designates Peter as "the rock" upon which the Church will be built, the Lord predicts his own death. The apostle cannot understand Christ's need to die for his people. The events of Good Friday morning are etched in our minds when Peter denied Jesus three times, just as the Lord had predicted. After the descent of the Spirit on Pentecost, however, Peter is a completely new man. He speaks clearly, boldly, and continuously about Jesus, his message, and the need for people to give their lives to the service of the Lord by following the Gospel message as it was then understood in the oral tradition. Peter, a man of faith but one who was weak and broken as well, was transformed by the power of God into a well-versed spokesman for the Lord. As we hear in today's reading, he echoes the words of the Prophet Joel who spoke to the Hebrews in Judah.

On Pentecost the Holy Spirit came to a diverse crowd assembled in Jerusalem. Why did the Spirit manifest himself in this way? Certainly one of the primary answers is that God wished all to know that the salvific message of Jesus is universal. God became incarnate not only to be present to the Jewish people, but also so that all might hear the message and believe. God, the creator of all, sent his Son, to bring salvation to all of God's children, from every people and nation, language and way of life. God is able to see the potential in every one of his creations and thus none are excluded. God manifests his desire to be present to and to assist all people, for no one is a stranger to God. Today we are challenged to seek a similar attitude in our relations with others, ourself, and God.

What lessons can we learn from this great event of Christian history that occurred so long ago? What relevance can we derive from the great Pentecost event? The answers can be succinctly given in not limiting the possibilities that we, our neighbor, and even God can achieve in this life. The Spirit allowed the apostles to do what they and others must have thought impossible. Similarly, God can produce in us and others results that we might think impossible. We only have to believe and allow God to act to experience such outcomes.

Many times we limit the possibilities that a situation can provide. Life at times places us in situations and asks us to do things we would rather not do. We are instantly and almost naturally placed on the defensive when we encounter unpleasant, stressful, or even problematic situations. Most people see unpleasant situations or periods of personal or communal crisis as events or periods of time that we simply "must get through." We sometimes hunker down and accept the difficulty; other times we take the stoic approach and get mentally and physically tough so we can maintain our sanity and composure during this period. These methods of self-preservation can be useful, but all events provide opportunities to grow and learn. It is rather easy for people to encounter events that bring joy and happiness because the challenge is less. When tragedy, problems, unexpected difficulties, and painful situations arise, we are more wary and often place guards in front of us to fend off the blows of various kinds that we know are coming. Yet, the placement of barriers between ourselves and the situation prevents us from gaining any important lessons from the encounter. Thus, we must ask what we can gain from a personal illness or the infirmity or death of a family member or close friend. What lessons can be learned from walking the road of addiction with an important person in our life? How can the loss of our job bring about some good in our life? How in general can we allow the events of life, both those we enjoy and long to experience and those filled with pain which we would rather avoid, to become sources of grace and opportunities for growth?

It is unfortunate but we are far too adept at limiting others. Like the birth parents in the story, we are often too rash in making judgments on the merits and potential of others. Without a full hearing and often without sufficient forethought, we sometimes systematically dismiss others and, thus, limit the potential they can provide for ourselves and others. Because of her physical deformity the parents thought their child had no potential and, thus, to rid themselves of their burden they sought foster parents. The poor family, on the other hand accepted the little girl for who she was and celebrated and promoted what she could do, the exercise of her mind. About fifteen years ago a film titled *My Left Foot* told the true story of the Irish-born writer, Christy Brown, who because he was born with a severe case of muscular dystrophy was considered a burden by all. Only with time and his own determination did Christy's potential as a writer surface. We are often like the rich parents in the story and like those who refused to see any potential in Christy Brown. We see only what we wish to see and hear only what we want to hear. We are open only to what is obvious to the senses, and make our decisions on a person's potential based on these observations. The miracle of the Pentecost event tells us, however, that such an attitude is not that of the Spirit and must be exorcized from our person. We simply cannot limit the potential of others.

One of the great tragedies, especially of the fast-paced contemporary world in which we live, is the tendency for many people to limit themselves. We often say to ourselves we are not intelligent enough, attractive enough, athletic enough, or even at times religious enough to do a particular task or engage a new job. We limit our own potential to what we have done in the past and, therefore, know is possible, rather than allowing ourselves to move forward, engage new challenges, and grow in unexpected and wonderful ways through the gifts of God's Spirit. It is true that we often hear of egocentric individuals who believe that the whole world revolves about them and that nothing is too good or impossible for them. Yet, the reverse scenario, namely how people denigrate themselves and do not allow their potential to shine, while not generally a public issue, is all too prevalent in our world. We lower ourselves and, thereby, lessen our potential for achievement. Our self-esteem is damaged and we find it difficult to extricate ourselves from the rut in which we live. But we must recall the wonderful expression often seen on car bumpers, "God doesn't make any junk." We must believe in our own potential as assuredly as we believe in the possibilities of situations and people.

Our inability at times to seek and appreciate the potential in situations, others, and ourselves leads us to place limits on God. How many times have we prayed for someone or some thing and the response we receive is not what we expected or obtained in the timely manner we desire? We might think God doesn't care or that the task or need is even too difficult for God to handle. Sometimes we might even tend to believe that God is not present when we observe bad things that happen, seemingly without reason, to good people. There are times in our lives when we don't trust God sufficiently to seek answers from him to our difficulties and problematic situations. Instead of seeking the assistance of God, we look to other things — people, ideas, the material world — for the solutions and/or consolation we seek. There are times as well when things are going so well in life that we barely give God a thought. Possibly without knowing it, we place God in a small bottle with a cork in it and set him on a mantle in our homes where the divine presence gets as dusty as books on a shelf. When we need God, then we go, dust off the bottle, and open the cork, with the expectation that God will act precisely as we wish. How would any of us feel if we were so treated by a member of our family or a close friend? God will never treat us like that; the miracle of Pentecost as related in today's reading and our overall knowledge of the gospel message tells us this is true.

On the day of Pentecost the Holy Spirit came to the apostles in a very special way. This event transformed timid and even frightened disciples into men of action. The apostles no longer lived in fear, but rather, buoyed by the power of the Spirit in their lives, were energized to go forward and preach the universal message of salvation which Christ brought to our world. On Pentecost the universal Church was born as people from all nations heard the message and were enlightened by the Spirit. Our listening once more to this great event of Christian history must spur us on to realize that the message of Christ will only be proclaimed fully when we cease to limit situations, others, ourselves, and most especially God. The little girl in Joseph Girzone's story had great potential, but it was masked by a physical deformity. Once the potential was discovered by those with patience and foresight, many people of the land benefited from her wisdom. Let us in a similar way not limit the potential before us. God can and will act. May we, in turn, trust God, demonstrate our faith, and exercise our potential today and each day of our lives.

---

1. Joseph Girzone, *The Parables of Joshua* (New York: Doubleday, 2001), pp. 66-67.

Holy Trinity
Proverbs 8:1-4, 22-31

Working Together As One

Nature is filled with examples of how the world functions better when things come together and act as one. Ancient philosophers understood this need for unity quite well. In their efforts to explain the world which they observed, they postulated, without the advantage of modern science, that all things were composed of four basic elements: earth, water, air, and fire. Everything that existed was a measured combination of these four elements and could exist in no other way. Earth was the "stuff" of the object observed. Water was added to the stuff to form it into various objects, be it a rock, tree, or human being; air was what filled the stuff. Fire was the glue which solidified the earth, air, and water combination. All things existed as a combination where four became one.

Ancient civilizations also discovered, I am sure quite by accident, the value of alloy metals. Probably around some evening fire two dissimilar metals were melted, mixed, and then when cooled formed a third metal which was stronger, longer-lasting, and more durable than either of its constituent elements. Brass and bronze are good examples. Brass is made from a combination of copper and zinc; bronze is created from a fusion of copper and tin. The copper, zinc, and tin each contribute in important and unique ways to create the third metal. Brass and bronze can exist only in these ways.

A river system is another example of nature's desire for unity. The Mississippi River system is a good example. The Mississippi itself is formed in the northern regions of Minnesota from a combination of several tributaries. As it flows south it combines with

305

additional rivers, two of which, the Ohio and the Missouri, are mighty in their own right. When the Mississippi flows into the Gulf of Mexico it is a unity of many which act as one.

Nature in seeking unity imitates in a very real way the oneness that is God. This is an appropriate image as we celebrate the Holy Trinity and our belief in God as Father, Son, and Holy Spirit. Throughout the Christian era, theologians have made attempts by use of models or other analogies to understand the Trinity. Augustine analogized the Trinity to the processes of the brain — memory, intelligence, and will. A person's mind could only exist if these three constitutive parts were present. Thomas Aquinas, the great scholastic theologian and philosopher, and even the twentieth-century German Jesuit, Karl Rahner, wrote extensively on the Trinity. After 2,000 years, however, the Trinity is and will remain a mystery of the faith. Along the road as well several infamous heresies have arisen in attempts to explain God's action in the world, including Modalism, a fourth-century concept which said that God has acted in history at different times in different modes, initially as Creator, later as Redeemer, and later still as Sanctifier, but not as a unity.

Despite all the intellectual attempts to understand this fundamental mystery of our faith we are no closer to perfect knowledge, but as our reading from the book of Proverbs indicates, we do know that the way God exists is how it was ordained by God. God's first great action was to create all that we have. We hear that wisdom is the great creation of God, existing before the physical and material world. Wisdom was present with God at the creation of the world, rejoicing with the Lord in what God created. Wisdom is seen to be preeminent. If God's wisdom preceded creation, then God is the one who created all. God created the world, but God did not stop. Rather, our world is recreated each day through the dynamic forces present and the miracle of life which produces all sorts of new forms, both plant and animal throughout the centuries.

God's second action in the world is redemption in the person of Jesus Christ. Saint Paul tells us in his letters that it is through the faith given us by Jesus that we have the ability to boast, not only of our ecstacies, but of our afflictions as well, with the certainty that through faith we can persevere.

Sanctification in the person of the Holy Spirit is God's third action in our world. It is the Holy Spirit, God's Spirit, who came in a special way on Pentecost Sunday to dispel fear and doubt, to enlighten, and as Jesus says in the Gospels to guide us. It is God's Spirit active in the world which guides all creation and gives all men and women the opportunity to exercise faith in order to build the Kingdom of God in our world.

God has acted in history in different ways, but always as a unity of one. God can only be God in this one way, a unity, a community enveloped in love which is the Creator, Redeemer, and Sanctifier — Father, Son, and Spirit. The most fundamental revelatory characteristic of the Trinity is that the unity of God is lived as a community of love. Salvation history demonstrates this through the mighty acts of Yahweh recorded in the Hebrew Scriptures, the miracles and message of Jesus of Nazareth as recorded by the Gospel evangelists, and the action of the Spirit who descended upon the Apostles at Pentecost. Besides Salvation History the communitarian nature of God has been expressed through the human understanding of the mutual indwelling of the Godhead. In the Orthodox tradition we are told that the divine persons within God draw life from each other. The divine persons in God sustain each other through a community of mutual love.

As nature seeks to imitate the unity of God, so must we, God's greatest creation, search for greater unity in our lives. We have some good examples of human solidarity with which we are all familiar. How is it that peoples from many lands, every continent, and numerous tongues could come together in what was described in the early part of our century as the "melting pot" and be as one nation? Why would fifty independent and sovereign governments choose to forego their autonomy and form one United States of America? More fundamentally, how is it that two people, sometimes very different, can through the magic of love and lots of hard work come together as one through marriage?

We must seek unity in every aspect of our lives. In the work place, if we can form one unit and work together then the tasks we undertake become easier and are completed more swiftly, the product we produce is of better quality, and the possibility for future work becomes greater. In our neighborhoods if we come together we can celebrate who we are as a community. Using the Saul Alinksky approach of organizing, we can find methods which will allow us come together to accomplish important tasks of advocacy or the important business of political action. We can celebrate as one in block parties and we can watch over each other through Neighborhood Watch programs. In our families we most especially need to come together. Families, especially with the hectic pace of life today that often forces both parents to work and the demands of time and energy, must, despite the challenge, come together as one. Families must not only eat together, they must pray together as well. Families must make decisions and they need to do it together. Families need to experience both the agonies and the ecstacies, as the famous novelist Irving Stone would say, and they must do it together. Whether it is the company, the neighborhood, or the family, each person contributes in a unique and important way.

Humankind lives Trinitarian faith, the unity of God, by our common response to the generic call to holiness and by the relationships we enjoy. The closer we come to imitating Christ and living his message of love, the more developed our relations with others will become. We must live for others and by this example of discipleship experience more fully the triune life of God. Our life in Christ must be one that imitates the co-equality of God; oppression, domination, and the objectification of others are incompatible with Trinitarian faith. As Saint Paul writes, "There is no longer Jew or Greek, there is no longer slave or free, there is no longer male or female, for all of you are one in Christ Jesus" (Galatians 3:28). Living as Christ lived gives us the perfect model for a community of faith. Since through Jesus we have the revelation of the triune God, and with the triune God community, it follows that in order to live Trinitarian faith we must be people who live for others. We do so in the ordinary and the great things of our daily lives. If our attitude ever centered on ourselves, today's celebration of the Trinity must tell us that we need to live more fully for others, in imitation of Jesus, who lived totally for others.

Living for others and seeking to be united, as God Incarnate, Jesus Christ, lived for others and is united with the Father and the Spirit, must be our goal. Jesus himself prayed for this very thing. John the Evangelist (17:21) records Jesus' prayer before he died in this way: "That they may all be one. As you, Father, are in me and I am in you, may they also be in us, so that the world may believe that you have sent me." My friends, may we act and believe the same.

Contemporary Prophets

On March 24, 1980, Oscar Romero, Archbishop of San Salvador, was saying Mass at a cancer hospital operated by a group of religious sisters. Midway through the service, gunmen entered the rear of the chapel, a hail of bullets rang out, and in another moment the archbishop lay dying in a pool of his own blood. Oscar Romero was a man who spoke for his people. He spoke for human rights; he spoke out against those in the government who made decisions that favored the rich and elite at the expense of the poor. He spoke for land reform; he spoke out against injustice. Oscar Romero spoke with authority; he spoke the truth; he spoke with love. Oscar Romero was a prophet.

It seemed from his earliest days that Romero was destined to be a priest. He was born in 1917 in an eastern mountain village of El Salvador and at age thirteen entered the minor seminary. A brilliant student, he was assigned to Rome for his theological training and was ordained there in 1947. He returned to his native land and was an instant success in ministry, first in parochial work and later in higher education. In fact, he was so successful that he was raised to the position of auxiliary bishop after completing work in education and parishes.

The 1960s was a difficult time for many and so too for Oscar Romero. His rather traditional and conservative theological perspective was tested when many changes came to the Catholic Church in the wake of the Second Vatican Council. But he negotiated the changes well so that by the early 1970s he was a strong advocate for many groups who found themselves on the fringes of the Church and society. In 1977 he was appointed Archbishop of San Salvador, the primatial see of the country. Romero was a man who truly heard the cry of the poor and acted upon his conviction that the Church must serve all people. He promoted land reform for peasants, spoke against government death squads, and in general advocated Christian principles of social justice. He was severely critical of decisions that failed to meet the needs of the masses, but benefited the wealthy. Romero was fearless in his proclamation despite threats against his life, shortened through the hate of others. His courageous actions and words demonstrate how God's word continues to be voiced in contemporary society.

Elijah, like Oscar Romero, was a prophet, one of the first great prophets who preached God's message to the Northern Kingdom of Israel after the split between North and South that occurred shortly following the death of King Solomon. Elijah spoke boldly against Ahab, King of Israel, who compromised his faith through his marriage to Jezebel, a worshiper of Baal, the god of the local pagan peoples. Elijah, like Oscar Romero, was not a popular person with the hierarchy in his land, but he knew that he was right and he understood the responsibility he incurred from God's call to be a prophet. The task would not be easy, but Elijah was ready for his encounter with the prophets of Baal and was totally confident that he would prevail.

The prophet uses this confrontation with the priests of Baal to demonstrate without a shred of doubt the emptiness of their message and the foolishness of their worship. Elijah knows Baal is a false god and, thus, he uses tactics that ridicule those who find any merit in such misguided worship. He taunts the priests of Baal, causing them to slash themselves and to dance about the altar they constructed. He asks if their god is asleep or on a journey, chiding the priests to call out louder. Elijah knows the emptiness of the priests' efforts and, thus, he intentionally ridicules the actions of these false prophets. Elijah took a great chance, however. Yes, he fully believed that the priests of Baal were in error and he knew in his mind and heart for certain that Yahweh was the one and only God. Nonetheless, Elijah took the chance that God would not allow him to be embarrassed before his adversaries, that the Lord would answer as the prophet asked and send fire to consume the holocaust. The confidence he held in God was fully rewarded.

Elijah was a prophet who was not afraid to confront adversity, to speak out with full confidence that God was with him every step of the way. Similarly, Oscar Romero many centuries later was uninhibited in speaking against those, even in his own faith community, who refused to listen to the cry of the poor. Both men were prophets who spoke God's word and courageously acted without counting the cost of their discipleship. Countless others over the Christian era have continued this tradition of boldly proclaiming God's message to peoples who many times are not receptive to the challenge that is presented. We in a similar way are called to be contemporary prophets, to go forward as God's messengers into an often hostile environment and speak against the great fascinations of our world, today's false gods — power, wealth, and prestige — the three great sins of the human condition. We have been commissioned through our baptism to demonstrate to our world, by word and deed, that there is something much more important than the fascinations of this world which tend to dominate the thoughts and actions of people today.

We must recall that this fascination with the world and its allurements is nothing new, but rather, has been the situation faced by humanity almost from the outset. In order to demonstrate the proper way to negotiate through the mine field of the three great temptations of life, Jesus, before he began his public ministry, allowed himself to be tempted by Satan in the desert, as reported by all three Synoptic evangelists. First, Satan tempts Jesus with the false god of power. He tells Jesus to command these stones to turn to bread. After forty days in the desert Jesus was obviously hungry, but the Lord does not need such demonstrations of power. He realizes that humans do not live on bread alone, but are nourished more importantly through God's word. Next Satan entices Jesus with the sin of great wealth. He displays all the kingdoms of the earth before him, saying it could all be his if he would simply bow down and worship Satan. But Jesus is above all this and says only God will be so worshiped. Lastly, Satan baits Jesus to demonstrate the great prestige that is his by taking him to the parapet of the Temple and challenging him to throw himself down, realizing that angels will come, because of his stature, to rescue him. But Jesus again resists the empty promises and false gods of Satan with the rejoinder that God is not to be put to such a test. Jesus does not need the false promises of Satan. He is confident that the power, wealth, and prestige granted him by the Father is to be used not for his exaltation only, but rather for the good of those to whom Jesus was sent.

We live in a world which, unfortunately, is more and more dominated by false gods who are promoted by equally fraudulent prophets. As with Jesus, Elijah, and Oscar Romero, we must make a stand against this raging tide and the emptiness of the message that is presented. We simply cannot allow ourselves to de drawn in, let alone dominated by the things of this world, especially when materialism is used to oppress others.

Power is a gift that is given in some measure to everyone of God's children. If we use the gift judiciously to assist others, to organize our affairs and those of society so that decisions, laws, and policies can support the common good, then we have used the gift of power wisely. Unfortunately, people who possess significant amounts of power often use it as a club to beat people into submission. In such cases those with power lord it over others and will not let up until they have attained precisely the goal they seek, the outcome they expect, or the rise or fall of the person whom they seek to dominate. Jesus warned against this problem when he instructed his apostles that they were not to seek the places of power, but rather to be servants of all (Luke 14:7-14).

Wealth is a second false god that challenges our contemporary society. A television commercial that was popular a few years back aptly described this false worship, "Who says you can't have it all?" We are almost brainwashed from our earliest days into the belief that the more we obtain of the goods of this life, the more acceptable we will be in society. We are told that wealth is the ticket to high society and success, but we all know the adage, "Money doesn't buy happiness." Many very generous people give freely of their resources to charitable causes, educational institutions, and churches, making possible numerous wonderful and significant projects. Yet, too many people today gather wealth simply to be gathering it. Money and the material world become false gods to which many bow. Jesus warned us against this problem as well when he told the parable of the wealthy man and the grain bins, asking his disciples where all his great wealth was to go when God calls (Luke 12:16-21). Those who promote the necessity of wealth as a ticket to acceptance in society are as misguided in their advocacy as the priests of Baal whom Elijah encountered so long ago, and the rich and powerful whom Oscar Romero confronted in recent memory.

Prestige is a third false god of today's world. All people rightly enjoy the opportunity to be recognized for a job well done, for a task successfully completed, or a significant accomplishment in life. There is certainly nothing wrong in being so praised. However, there are people who live simply to have others recognize who they are and the things that they do. For these people, status and being well-known are the things for which they live. People who worship the false god of prestige must associate only with the "correct" people — those who are intelligent enough, attractive enough, athletic enough, and influential enough so others stop and take notice. These are the ones with whom people of status will associate; others who don't "measure up" are of no consequence. Some people, as tragic as it is, consider it a waste of time to spend their time, talent, and treasure with an individual or group who cannot advance their cause with others or promote their person in society.

False gods and their prophets abound in our world, but, fortunately, there are many counter examples of people, who when tempted to go the way of the world choose to be contemporary prophets, like Elijah, and speak God's truth by denouncing false prophets and the gods they worship. Oscar Romeo stood against the tide of a ruling military dictatorship and the opinion of many of his fellow bishops to preach the message which he knew to be true, namely God's care, love, and peace to the poor and ill-educated who stood on the fringes of society. He stood proudly with those to whom God sent him as their servant. He was never cowed by threats and he became a martyr through his courage to speak the truth, knowing as scripture states, "You will know the truth and the truth will make you free" (John 8:32). Let us in a similar way be prophetic in what we do and say and by such means be evangelists, bringing others closer to God and thereby to eternal life.

Living For Others

Harriet Tubman was born into slavery in Dorchester County, Maryland, in 1821. Like all slaves in that time period Harriet, together with her ten sisters and brothers and her mother and father, worked the fields, in this case a large tobacco plantation. Day after day, week by week over many years, slaves did the same thing. At sunrise work began and at sundown it ended; the monotony of existence was severe. Certainly slavery was an ignoble existence, not only because of the menial and backbreaking work, but more importantly because it was a life which degraded human dignity. Slaves were not only perceived as unimportant humans, they were considered as non-persons. Harriet Tubman never received a word of encouragement, welcome, or invitation in her early life, either from her white slave master or her fellow black slaves, who had been beaten down so severely by life that they no longer possessed any self-respect.

This was the life of Harriet in her early days, but in 1849 she managed to escape to the North and freedom. These were the high days of the American abolition movement, led by William Lloyd Garrison and Frederick Douglass. Harriet quickly joined this movement and soon thereafter became a "conductor" on what was known as the Underground Railroad — a secret organization which smuggled slaves to freedom in the North. In the ten years prior to the commencement of the Civil War, Harriet Tubman made at least fifteen expeditions into the southern regions of Maryland and in the process rescued over 200 slaves. She continued her work even when a large reward was put forward for her capture and arrest.

317

Harriet Tubman had never been given a word of kindness, welcome, or invitation in her days as a slave, but her life as a "conductor" with the Underground Railroad exemplified these important qualities. Slaves called her Moses, not only because she was their deliverer, but more importantly because she cared about them. John Brown, the one whose failed raid at Harper's Ferry focused the nation's attention on the issue of slavery, called her General Tubman.

Harriet Tubman risked her life on numerous occasions to bring to freedom those who were oppressed. She was a deliverer, as Moses was to the Israelites when they were in bondage in Egypt. She serves as a good example of a person who lived for others by her courageous life.

How can one define the divinity of God? Many of us might respond by saying God is omniscient, omnipotent, full of love and compassion. These are certainly attributes of God, but the question needs to be repeated — how do we define the divinity of God? One possible answer to this seemingly simple but actually quite difficult question would be this: The degree that we live for others is the degree to which we become God-like. Since God always has and always will live totally for others, namely for us, it makes sense to say that to the extent we live for others we live like God. Thus, to define the divinity of God, in a way, is to live for others.

Today's powerful reading from First Kings demonstrates how people lived for others. Elijah, whom we encountered last week and will see again in the coming Sundays, has just predicted a great drought that will strike the land of Israel. God will take care of Elijah, his chosen prophet; God will live for him. First, Elijah is sent to the Wadi Cherith where he is fed by wild ravens who bring bread and meat, both morning and evening. Then God sends the prophet to the widow of Zarephath about whom we hear today. This woman has nothing, barely the basics to live for one day. Besides lack of food I suspect she possessed little hope as well. Yet, despite her desperate condition, she assists Elijah when he calls upon her. She goes out of her way to meet the prophet's needs, even when she has nothing to give. She meets his needs before her own and those of her son, the one who probably should have been first on the priority list. Because the woman in a very real way gives her life for Elijah, she, in turn, is rewarded by God, just as the prophet predicted. The jug of oil does not go dry nor the jar of flour meal go empty. Because she took care of God's messenger, God, through the prophet, takes care of her.

The second half of the story shows how Elijah goes out of his way, in a special manner lives for the widow. Elijah was the "man of God," the one recognized as a prophet who had a special relationship with God. We recall how he called upon God to ridicule the false prophets of Baal and to expose their misguided message and their ill-founded allegiance to their deity. Now Elijah calls upon God to restore the life of the widow's son. His faith is rewarded as he provides for the woman's needs. In a special way, Elijah lived for the woman, but God lives for all for all time.

The common Christian vocation to holiness demands that we respond to the needs of those around us; we are to live for others. We are called to be present to others' needs, to assist them in their burdens, and to love people as we love God. We must never lose sight of Jesus' response when asked how to live. His answer was clear in articulating the Golden Rule: Love God with your whole being and love your neighbor as yourself (Mark 12:28-34). This rule of life seems so simple, because the words are few and un- complicated, but we all know that as complex as the idea of love can be so too can be the difficulty in loving God and our neighbor as ourself.

The great trial we have on earth, the test that comes to us from God, can be well-illustrated by an Asian tale. The contrast between heaven and hell can be described in this way. The image of hell, so says the tale, begins with the description of a long banquet table around which many are seated preparing to eat. The meal is ready, abundant, and has been prepared by the finest chefs in the world. The plates, cups, and saucers are made from the finest china and the glassware is Waterford crystal. The scene seems normal except the silverware is unusual; each utensil is three feet long. In the scene nothing is happening; nobody is eating. Instead of eating, all of those at table are bumping into and hitting each other with their silverware. The guests almost come to blows from their anger with each other. The utensils are so big that one cannot feed him or

319

herself and, thus, nobody gets anything to eat. Chaos is the result. The image of heaven begins with the same banquet table. The meal is prepared; the people are present. Again the plates and glassware are the best money can buy and the silverware utensils are three feet long. All in heaven are eating, however. These people have learned that the only way they can eat is by feeding each other. Mutual cooperation allows all to be fed.

This Asian tale says something very powerfully, I think, about our need to live more fully for others. Those who live in hell never come to the knowledge that the only way to exist and live fully is by living for others, by meeting their needs and assisting them with their burdens. Those who live in heaven, in contrast, have discovered what is truly important — namely, that to live for others is the one and only way we can find life and most especially the eternal salvation which is our goal.

We are all called to live for others in the various ways we lead the life God gave us. Parents probably demonstrate the concept of living for others best. Parents sacrifice for their children, often denying themselves some of the goods of this world — their precious time or even opportunity — so that their children can have more. Loving and understanding parents work hard so that their children can become more productive members of society. This task becomes increasingly more difficult with time as the demands of this life never seem to become less but only grow greater and more complex. The human drama of a father living for his son was played out many years ago in the annual Iron Man competition held on the island of Oahu in Hawaii. One man entered the contest with his crippled son. During the 2.5-mile ocean swim, the man towed his son behind him on a rubber raft holding a tow rope in his mouth. From the ocean the competition switched to a 125-mile bike ride over the lava beds of the island. The man placed his son in a specially designed basket on the handle bars. Then, after all this, the man ran a 26.2-mile marathon with his son strapped to his back. When he finished the grueling race, reporters gathered around and asked, "Why did you do it?" The man answered, "I did it for my son who will never be able to do it." The man's heroic and herculean effort was for him an act of love, a way of living for his son, which he felt privileged to complete.

Living for others can and must also be part of our daily work routine. A good employer or supervisor is one who encourages, nourishes, and assists junior personnel so they can learn and have full and productive careers with the company. Mentoring is important. We can all remember that special teacher or coach in school who went out of his or her way to assist us, whether it was with a concept we could not understand or the encouragement necessary to continue to persevere on the field of play. Sharing our lives, expertise, and experience with others is critically important and is the way we live for others.

We must never forget our duty to live for one another in the civic community that we share as citizens of this great land. Fraternal groups such as the Lions, Kiwanis, Rotary, and a host of others get involved to make things better for others, especially those who might benefit most from some extra assistance. All of us must get involved to assist the stranger, the outcast, and in general those who live on the margins of society, not by their own choice most times, but rather, because we have placed them there. Meals on Wheels, volunteering at a local soup kitchen, participating in a neighborhood clean-up project are all ways we can live for others in our local community.

We certainly cannot forget our responsibility to live for our brothers and sisters in the Church. The ways one can assist are innumerable as are the opportunities, but we must first take the initiative. Local churches and parishes have many programs and groups that reach out to our brothers and sisters and serve them, but the greatest way we can help might simply be the attitude we bring to any endeavor we engage. If we are committed and enter our varied apostolic works with a welcoming and friendly attitude, then most assuredly, this will be communicated to those we serve. Sometimes living for others can be done on a grand scale and other times it is simple and almost effortless, if we only think about what we are doing and the one for whom we live. We must realize that since all is gift from God, all must be shared — time, talent, and treasure — but most especially our lives. Living for others is not easy and, if done well, will certainly cost us a great deal. In fact, if we live for others fully, it will cost us our lives. Jesus makes this absolutely clear: "For those who want to save their life will lose it, and those who lose their life for my sake will save it" (Luke 9:24). Harriet Tubman was only one woman but through her sacrifice, her ability to live for others, many of her sisters and brothers in the bondage of slavery experienced a new beginning. May we who seek to follow the Master always give our lives for others and in the process find the eternal reward which only God can give.

Proper 6
Pentecost 4
Ordinary Time 11
1 Kings 21:1-21a

Living The Life God Gives Us

There once was a businessman who, after a long hard day at the office, cried out loudly to God with his complaint, "O Lord," he began, "I am so tired and want something new in my life. Each day I get up at the crack of dawn and go to the gym to get in some exercise. Then I come home and get a quick breakfast, throw down a final cup of coffee, and then I am off to fight the traffic on the expressway to work. I work like a slave for eight, ten, sometimes even twelve hours, associating with people who are often exasperating, uncooperative, or short-sighted in their outlook. Then after all this I get in the car again, fight the traffic on the way home, and arrive exhausted. After a quick dinner, the kids want to play and so I make time for them. Finally, it is off to bed after an hour of television, and the whole process begins again. O Lord, is it possible for my wife and I to change places so she knows how hard I work and my daily frustrations?"

God listened to the man's plea and told him, "No problem." Thus, the next day when the man arose he was his wife and she was her husband. The man, who was now the mother and wife, arose at the same time as before, only now (s)he was preparing breakfast and making lunches for the children and her husband. Then she had to get the children up and ready for school. After everyone was off to their places, it was now time to wash the dishes, clean the kitchen, make the beds and straighten up the house. After this there was wash to do, groceries to be purchased, and several errands to be run. Then she took in the mail and paid all the bills. By this time it was 3 p.m. and the children were returning from school. She prepared a snack for each, plus their classmates, and helped each with their homework. By this time it was time to begin dinner which was ready just when her husband arrived home. They ate together and then it was necessary to wash the dishes again, and then attend the local PTA meeting. She returned home for a half hour of relaxation before going to bed. In order to satisfy her husband, she managed to mount sufficient energy to make love. After all this the man, who was a woman for the day, said to God: "O Lord, I learned my lesson well. I now know how hard my wife works and I will be content with the role I have. Can I return to my real state in life?"

God replied, "There is no problem, but you will have to wait nine months. You just got pregnant!" This humorous story presents many important ideas that we see in today's powerful reading from First Kings. Things might seem to be difficult or incomplete, but we must learn to be satisfied with who we are and what we have, including the life God has given us.

Ahab had everything a person could possibly need, at least it appears this way from what we are told about him. He had all the power, wealth, and prestige to satisfy anyone, save himself. He wasn't content with what he had, nor it seems with who he was; he wanted more. He, like the businessman, figured that things would be better it he had something that he did not need. Thus, he went and asked Naboth for his vineyard. He must have figured that this would be a simple deal, that Naboth would certainly not challenge his request, especially since Ahab was the king and he was willing to give Naboth a better vineyard or its value in money. But Naboth would not agree to the king's offer. He could not give up his ancestral inheritance which for the Hebrews was almost sacred. To sell or trade one's ancestral inheritance was a sign of disowning the past and one's forebears.

Thus, Ahab returned home disappointed and, again like the businessman, complained that he could not have things his way. He voiced his discontent to his wife Jezebel who was cunning and deceitful. She had no concern for God nor the people of the land and, thus, she concocted a plan to get her husband what he wanted. Jezebel and Ahab were both greedy; they were not satisfied with what God had given them. She also seemed totally unconcerned with the possible consequences of her actions. Jezebel believed she was without peer and needed to answer to no one, not even God. Ahab was a coward, but Jezebel was forceful and placed her plan into action with great delight.

Once Naboth had been killed and the vineyard taken by Ahab, the time of reckoning came. Elijah, the great prophet who speaks God's message fearlessly, told Ahab that his actions would lead to disaster for him. Like the businessman who wanted things his way, got what he wished for, but then discovered the consequences of his request, so too did Ahab learn of his impending doom at the hand of God. Ahab's inability to find ways to accept his life, in this case, his failure to understand Naboth, cost him his position and eventually his life.

In varied ways, sometimes small and other times rather grand, we at times act like the businessman and Ahab. We are not content with who we are, what we have, or the situation in which we find ourselves. We always believe that, as the saying goes, the grass will be greener on the other side, but this is not always the case. Our perceptions are limited; we see only one side of the story, one face of the multi-faceted lives of others and conclude that what they have or do must be best. Thus, envy and greed enter our hearts and we seek to satisfy our need. Often we are impatient with our current status and want something different, simply because it is different. We make conclusions, often based on very sketchy evidence, that what others have is better. The need to "keep up with the Joneses" captures our attention and we seek fulfilment in the things of the material world.

Our inability to appreciate who we are, what we have, and the life we lead is manifest in many ways. Our daily relationships are, unfortunately, often tainted with this lack of appreciation for what we presently have. There are times when we will only associate with those who will advance our cause, our ability to move forward in society. We migrate toward those who are bright and intelligent, attractive and athletic, powerful and influential, wealthy and talented. At the same time, possibly without realizing it, we push to the side those who are not what we "need" so as to "know" those who will make a difference. Sometimes we are highly impatient in our relationships. We want people to act in a certain fashion and in accordance with the timetable we have generated. Giving people space and allowing them to operate in a manner and time they believe to be correct is unacceptable; we will not give people the benefit of the doubt. In these cases we often toss our relationships aside without giving these people our best and complete effort.

Often our lack of appreciation applies to ourselves. Many people do not love nor appreciate themselves; their self-esteem is very low. Some of us consider ourselves inadequate in many ways. We want to be the "other person," the one who is all that society says is important, the one who possesses the things that the world now worships as false gods. Certainly any of us would be foolish not to make the most of who we are and what we have by improving our native skills, appearance, and potential. There are many positive aspects to self-improvement, but sometimes we become fanatical about change because we dislike ourselves so much. We must learn to appreciate the person God created in us. As the little bumper sticker says, "God didn't make any junk." What God has created in us is unique, special, and wonderful for as the book of Genesis says, we are made in the image and likeness of God.

Problematic family situations today create an environment that leads people to escape reality. It is a rare family today which does not experience several trials along the way. Rather than finding ways to negotiate these crises, some people choose another way. Some lose themselves in alcohol, drugs, or abberant behavior. We are often not up to the challenge of a problem child, a family member in failing health, or an economic crisis that threatens our family's livelihood. When we are not willing to meet these challenges, we abdicate our responsibilities. Parents give up on their children, and children, in turn, give up on their parents. Couples give up on each other. We throw up our hands in frustration and "throw in the towel" on life.

For many people today, especially in the first world environment of the United States, our lack of appreciation is centered on the material world. We are not satisfied with what we have; we always want more and better in everything. We want the designer

326

dress, suit, or pair of shoes when an equally good quality brand, but without the special name, is more than adequate. We become dissatisfied with the ordinary and believe that only the extraordinary will satisfy us. We have become greedy, like Ahab and Jezebel, with our time, talent, and most especially our treasure. This problem exists in individuals and our society. We want more and will not be satisfied until we obtain what we "need."

A story about those who are greedy and not satisfied with what they have demonstrates the dangers and consequences of such an attitude. Three sisters, who were kind and generous and possessed great faith, lived in a cabin in the hills. One day when working in the backyard garden, the sisters unearthed a large box. When they removed the top they saw it was filled with gold coins. They all shrieked loudly, "Beware of the soul-taker!" They were uncertain what to do — should they cover the box up and pretend like nothing had happened or should they flee from the house?

It so happened that four men had recently moved into the cabin next door. They heard the commotion at the sisters' home and went to investigate. The sisters informed their neighbors, "We are trying to flee from the soul-taker." "What is a soul-taker?" one of the men responded. "Please show us." The sisters took the men into the backyard and then, pointing at the box of gold coins, said, "That is the soul-taker!" The men laughed under their breath and said to one another, "They think the money is a soul-taker." One of the men said to the women, "If you sisters are so frightened, please go to town for a few hours and we will take care of the problem for you." The women agreed and left immediately.

The men made their plans. First, they decided to split the money four ways. Then they determined that two men would stay and completely unearth the box of gold while the other two went to town, bought some food, and made plans for a quick get-away. The two who stayed began to think, "It would be better to split the money two ways; we will receive more." Thus, they decided to ambush their friends when they returned and kill them. The two who went to town had similar thoughts. They decided to poison the food and feed it to their compatriots. Then they would bury their bodies in the hole where the box had been and split the money between them.

When the two men from town returned, they were abused and killed by their friends. But before the bodies were buried, the two murderers decided to eat the food provided since it was fresh. They soon became sick and died. When the sisters returned they found the four men dead and the box of gold still there. "We told them it was a soul-taker, but they refused to believe." The women immediately made plans to leave their home.

Let us, my friends, learn a lesson from the businessman, the story of Naboth's vineyard, and the "soul-taker." Let us be satisfied with who we are, what we have, and the life God has given us. Let us not run away from, but rather, engage our lives and in the end discover our true purpose and home in God, the source of all we need, the source of all that is good.

God Has Plans For Us

The name Robert Stroud is not one commonly heard in ordinary conversation, but this man's contribution to humanity will live on in the minds of many under a different title, "The Birdman of Alcatraz." By nature Robert Stroud was not a congenial man. As a youth he was always getting into fights, disagreements, and various altercations. When he was only nineteen he killed a man in a barroom brawl, was convicted of second-degree murder, and sentenced to the federal penitentiary at Leavenworth, Kansas, since the crime was committed on federal land.

One might think that incarceration in a federal prison would lead Robert Stroud to reform and get his life in order, but he continued his former ways, being even more disruptive and troublesome. One day a fight broke out in the prison among the inmates which brought guards from throughout the compound to the site in an attempt to restore order. In the melee Stroud killed one of the guards using a little wooden knife he had crafted in his cell. The warden at Leavenworth thought the attack so onerous that he recommended Stroud be executed for his offense; the jury at his trial agreed. Robert Stroud was scheduled to die in the electric chair.

Although it seemed Robert Stroud's fate was sealed, God had a plan for this man which necessitated that he be alive and, thus, an intercessor arose in the form of Stroud's mother. Like any loving parent, Mrs. Stroud did not want to see her son die, especially such an ignoble death as execution in the electric chair. Since the only person who could commute Stroud's sentence was the President of the United States, Mrs. Stroud journeyed to Washington, D.C., to

329

see President Woodrow Wilson. She was not able to see the President, but she did have an interview with the First Lady who, in turn, spoke to her husband on Stroud's behalf. Woodrow Wilson commuted Stroud's sentence to life in prison in solitary confinement. Robert Stroud was, thus, sentenced to spend the rest of this life without seeing any human beings, except the guard once per week when he was allowed the privilege of a shower. Even his meals were slipped through a special opening in his cell door.

God had a plan for Robert Stroud; God had not given up on him. The manifestation of God's plan began quite innocently one day when a small bird came and perched on the windowsill of Stroud's cell which looked out onto the Kansas countryside. Over time the bird came back, and with more time still one bird turned into many birds. Stroud received permission to house these birds in his small cell. He read voraciously all the material he could obtain on birds and their care, especially diseases to which these animals were susceptible, and he conducted numerous experiments over several years. His study, research, and findings were collected into a book published in 1939, *Stroud's Digest on the Diseases of Birds*. At the time it was the most comprehensive and authoritative study ever done on bird diseases and their cures.

Robert Stroud was a troublemaker who was twice convicted of murder and he was slated to be executed, but God rescued him from the jaws of death and provided him with the opportunity to make something special out of his life. He made the most of his opportunity through a significant contribution to the study of birds. God took care of Robert Stroud, and like this convicted murderer, God will take care of us.

The life and work of Robert Stroud provide some interesting parallels to what we hear about Elijah in today's First Lesson from First Kings. We have encountered this prophet the past three weeks and will hear about him again next week as well. Today's passage is situated after Elijah's triumph over the false prophets of Baal. The heavens have just opened and the drought which the prophet predicted has ended. Ahab and his wife Jezebel are incensed with Elijah's actions with the prophets of Baal and, thus, in response make plans to end his life. Like Robert Stroud, Elijah was slated for death and waited for his fate under the broom tree, but God had other plans for him. God sent an angel not once but twice to provide Elijah with food and drink. God had more for Elijah to do and, thus, the means to escape death was provided.

God's plan for Elijah, to walk forty days and forty nights to Mount Horeb, was a monumental task, but he was given what he needed to complete the task. Then God revealed himself, not in the power of the wind or earthquake, nor the strength of the fire, but rather in the gentleness of a soft breeze, what some biblical translations call a "sheer silence." God wanted Elijah to know that he would be present not only in the obvious and magnificent happenings of life, but also in the everyday and routine. God is ever present and will reveal the plan he has for our life, if we will only be open and receptive to the opportunities provided.

God had a plan for Robert Stroud and God had one for Elijah. God also has a plan for us, and when it is revealed it will come with what we need to discover the plan and the strength and courage to carry it out. How many times have any of us wondered why things have worked out the way they did? Why did we meet a certain person? Why did events follow one course and not another? Why did sickness, tragedy, or death cross our path at a particular time in life? Some may answer that with the gift of free will we can determine many of the paths we trod by the decisions we make. This is certainly true. Yet, through the wisdom and guiding hand of God, the great conductor of life, we are given special opportunities, usually in a situation unique to us, that determine how our life will proceed. God has a plan for our life of discipleship and provides the path and the tools to get us where he wants us to be. Robert Stroud and Elijah had no hope; both were slated for death. But God interceded in each case, for the Lord had a plan that was not to be frustrated.

God has plans for us that are revealed in many ways. How often have we been saved from serious problems in our lives and we wondered why? When we were spared the pain, difficulty, or tragedy what have we done in response to God? Do we realize that events transpired in a certain way because God desires something from us, that the Lord had some purpose in directing events as they happened? We periodically read or hear about near-death experiences that provide the catalyst for the transformation of a person's life. Does God have to go this far with any of us so that we will get the message? We may not have a near-death experience, but we have all been given various warnings. In some cases we have had brushes with death through a car accident, serious injury of another sort, or disease, or have been a victim of violence. Why were we saved? We often hear people ask after some natural disaster — why did I survive and my neighbor did not? The answers can only be given by God, but succinctly it is because God is not finished with us. God is still honing and refining us, for the Lord still has work for us to do. When God saves us in any way, we are also provided the tools and opportunity needed to do something positive with the life we have. God does not force us; we are never placed in handcuffs and enslaved to do God's work.

There are times in life when certain people are chosen and others are not, and again we generally ask, "Why?" We might be chosen to do something that appeals to us, but there are times as well when we are asked to do what is distasteful or even repugnant. We can attempt to shy away or we can go forward in faith, confident that all we need for the task at hand will be provided, and more besides. There are times as well when we wish we could just fade away, not be present, even die. Life for some becomes so painful and is filled with such drudgery and frustration that we want to opt out. Adversity gets the best of us and we choose not to continue. Such an attitude is inconsistent with the call of the Lord. Yes, when problems mount and we are proverbially knocked to our knees by life, we can sit in the dirt, if we wish, throw in the towel, and say, "I quit. I am defeated." On the other hand, Christians are called to rise from adversity, shake off the dust created by the problems of life, and move forward to claim the new day that can and must be theirs. God will provide what is necessary, but we must respond.

Numerous stories exist of people who have been slated for death or have overcome great obstacles and in the process have taught others magnificent lessons. The recent popular book, *Tuesdays with Morrie*, touched our hearts in showing how a man with ALS (Lou

332

Gehrig's disease) could, through his courage and strength, teach a former student and young reporter all about living and dying.

Another remarkable story is one I heard several years ago. On the morning of June 19, 1971, Bill Mitchell was on top of the world. Riding his brand new motorcycle to a job he loved, gripman on a San Francisco cable car, Bill seemed on cloud nine. Earlier that day he had soloed in an airplane for the first time, the fulfillment of one his fondest dreams. Twenty-eight — handsome, healthy, and popular — Bill was in his element.

In the flash of an eye Bill's whole world changed. Rounding a corner as he neared the cable car barn, Bill collided with a laundry truck. Gas from the motorcycle poured out and ignited through the heat of the engine. Bill emerged from the accident with a broken pelvis and elbow and burns over 65 percent of his body.

The next six months were a period of great trial for Bill. After several blood transfusions, numerous operations, and many skin grafts, Bill was released from the hospital. Walking down the street, he passed a school playground where the children stared at his face. "Look at the monster!" they exclaimed. Although he was deeply hurt by the thoughtlessness of the children, he still had the love and compassion of friends and family, and the grace of a good personal philosophy on life. Bill realized that he did not have to be handsome to make a contribution to society. Success was in his hands if he chose to begin again.

Within a year of the accident Bill was moving again toward the success he had enjoyed earlier. He began to fly planes. He moved to Colorado and founded a company that built wood stoves. Within a short time, Bill was a millionaire with a Victorian home, his own plane, and significant real estate holdings.

In November 1975, however, the bottom again fell out of Bill Mitchell's world. Piloting a turbocharged Cessna with four passengers on board, Bill was forced to abort a take-off, causing the plane to drop like a rock about 75 feet back to the runway. Smoke filled the plane and, fearing that he would again be burned, Bill attempted to escape. Pain in his back and the inability to move his legs thwarted his efforts.

In the hospital again, Bill was informed that his thoracic vertebrae were crushed and the spinal cord was beyond repair. He would spend the rest of his life as a paraplegic. Although doubt began to invade his generally optimistic mind, Bill began to focus on the cans and not the cannots of his life. He decided to follow the advice of the German philosopher Goethe: "Whatever you can do, or dream you can do, begin it. Boldness has genius, power, and magic in it." Before his accidents there were many things Bill could do. Now he could spend his time dwelling on what was lost or focus on what was left.

Since that 1975 plane accident Bill Mitchell has twice been elected mayor of his town, earned recognition as an environmental activist, and run for Congress. He has hosted his own television show and travels the nation speaking to groups about his message of proper attitude, service, and transformation. Bill's message is to show people that it isn't what happens to you that is important, but what you do about it that makes all the difference.

Bill Mitchell's experience is not typical, but it does present an example of one who triumphed over the greatest of adversities. It was his attitude of perseverance and positive outlook that kept him going, even in the darkest nights of his life.

Robert Stroud was slated to die for the murder of a guard in Leavenworth Federal Penitentiary, but God rescued him and because of the Lord's action, science and the study of bird diseases was significantly advanced. Similarly, Elijah was saved by God to continue his ministry with the Hebrew people. In various ways and at different times in our lives, God rescues us and provides the opportunity and tools to use our new lease on life to build the Kingdom of God. Let us, therefore, learn from today's scripture lesson and be open to God who might be found in the powerful and majestic, but will always be found in the silent and the routine happenings of our daily lives.

Completing The Master's Work

Classical music provides some significant examples of great musical compositions that were never finished by their creators. A perennial favorite with many, Wolfgang Amadeus Mozart never completed his magnificent *Requiem* mass. Franz Schubert, who like Mozart lived only a short life, but produced over 600 works of music, wrote only two movements of his Eighth Symphony. Orchestras today still play this great composition, known appropriately as the "Unfinished Symphony." Living in the latter nineteenth and early twentieth century, the Italian opera composer Giacomo Puccini also left a master creation unfinished, but thanks to his students, Puccini's last and greatest composition, *Turandot*, is performed many times each year throughout the world, because his disciples completed their master's work.

Giacomo Puccini was one of the greatest composers of opera who ever lived. His great and glorious music, written for and performed in the great opera houses of the world, has delighted people for more than a century. It was quite common to hear people along the streets of any great city whistling or humming one of the many popular melodies from such great works as *Tosca*, *La Boheme*, *Madama Butterfly*, *Manon Lescaut*, and *Gianni Schicchi*. Toward the end of his life Puccini took on a significant challenge, the composition of another great opera. Using a libretto written by fellow Italian Renato Simoni, who adapted a work of the eighteenth-century Venetian playwright Carlo Gozzi, Puccini tackled the composition of an opera that told the story of a gallant young man, Calaf, in his efforts to win the hand in marriage of the stern, mysterious, and seemingly cold Chinese Princess Turandot. Puccini was in his sixties when he began the opera's composition. For four years he labored long and hard, but Puccini was a very sick man and he knew he was running out of time. God would soon call him home.

Puccini returned home to God before his master work was completed. Because he was a famous man, Puccini had many friends, including a cadre of loyal students who were known as his disciples. These young men and women would not allow their master's great work, his *magnum opus* to lie unfinished. Thus, they gathered together, studied the text of the opera, and then when ready began the difficult task of finishing their master's work. In 1926, two years after his death, Puccini's greatest work, *Turandot*, was performed for the first time, appropriately enough at Milan's La Scala Opera House with Arturo Toscanni, the most famous conductor of the day, at the podium. When the opera reached the middle of the third and final act, the music abruptly stopped. Toscanni paused, set down his baton, and said, "Thus far the master wrote, but he died." After a moment of silence the great conductor again picked up his baton, turned to the audience, and with tears in his eyes said, "But his disciples finished his work." Thunderous applause was heard as the opera continued; the work of the master had been completed.

Giacomo Puccini was a master composer who created many delightful and significant operas and in the process gained many disciples and thrilled millions of music patrons. His life and work are emblematic of the life and prophetic ministry of Elijah about whose exploits we have heard the past four weeks. Today we gain more insight into this great figure of the Hebrew Scriptures and salvation history by learning about his relationship with his student and successor, Elisha.

Elijah was a fearless prophet who courageously did what God asked of him. We remember how he was asked to go to the widow of Zarephath to encourage her and demonstrate that charity and goodness are rewarded by God. We saw him summarily defeat the 400 prophets of Baal by exposing their message and god to be false. He next took on Ahab and his wife Jezebel after their wicked

336

deeds led to the death of Naboth and the confiscation of his vineyard. Last week we learned how Elijah was saved from death and then strengthened in body and spirit by God in order to continue his ministry among the Hebrew people. Elijah did many great things and influenced several significant people, but the ministry that God gave him was a task that was much greater than one man's efforts; the ministry required another to carry on when God's plan for Elijah's life called him home. As the students of Puccini learned much at their master's feet, so Elisha was trained for the ministry of prophet by observing what Elijah said and did.

Like Puccini's student disciples, Elisha was loyal to his mentor; he would not leave his side. Today's reading omits a portion of the whole story, but if we had heard the full account we would have noticed that on three occasions Elijah tells his young protégé to leave and three times Elisha refuses to abandon him. The younger man realizes he needs to be with his mentor in order to receive the great gift, namely a double portion of his spirit. Elisha was picked by God to continue the great work of Elijah because there was more that needed to be done. God, however, did not send Elisha on mission without the requisite tools and skills for the job. No, on the contrary, Elisha had witnessed the great works of his mentor, he was given the double portion of his spirit, and he inherited Elijah's mantle which fell as the chariot took him to heaven. In a very real way Elisha became the new Elijah.

The stories of Puccini and his students and that of Elijah and Elisha illustrate the responsibility we have to continue the work of our Master, Jesus of Nazareth. The relationship that bonded Puccini to his students was the same that united Elijah and Elisha. The younger and less experienced learned from the older and wiser. Society tells us that the student is understudy to the teacher, and Jesus agrees, but the Lord goes on to say that once a student has completed the course of study the teacher and student are on a par (Luke 6:40). Jesus was the most important teacher of all time, for he demonstrated in word and action the pattern and method of life that will bring us home to the Father. Jesus came into our world, as one like us in all things but sin, to initiate a mission. He came to

337

preach the Good News to all, to teach, and to set the perfect example. In short, Jesus came to inaugurate the reign of God in our world. But we know that despite his efforts, Jesus' work remained unfinished at the time of his passion, death, and resurrection. Jesus knew this would be the case and he spent the bulk of his time preparing his chosen disciples to continue his work. Thus, the Lord commissioned the apostles to continue his work on earth: "All authority in heaven and on earth has been given to me. Go therefore and make disciples of all nations, baptizing them in the name of the Father and of the Son and of the Holy Spirit, and teaching them to obey everything that I have commanded you. And remember, I am with you always, to the end of the age" (Matthew 28:19-20).

As Elisha was given the proper tools to conduct his ministry, so Jesus provided the apostles with all they would need to continue their Master's work. After the Resurrection, when the apostles were gathered in the Upper Room, Jesus came to them and said, "Peace be with you. As the Father has sent me, so I send you." He then breathed on them and continued, "Receive the Holy Spirit" (John 20:21, 22b). On the great day of Pentecost, as recorded by Saint Luke, the Holy Spirit was sent upon the apostles in such a powerful way that they were able to speak to all the assembled people, even though they came from all parts of the then known world (Acts 2:1-13). The apostles had Jesus' message, his example, and his special blessing. They were ready to do their share to complete the Master's work.

We can look at our world and state without reservation that the apostles and the countless disciples of Jesus who have followed have done a great job in spreading the message and building the kingdom, but the work still is not completed. Therefore, we, the contemporary disciples of Jesus, must take our responsibility seriously and do our share to further Jesus' ministry in our world. Our task is to work ourselves out of a job, to complete the Master's work. But we would all agree that is a tall order. The world needs our efforts, but we must realize it will not be easy. G. K. Chesterton, the famous British essayist, wrote back in 1910, "Christianity has not been tried and found wanting. It has been found difficult and left untried." We have a mission that is clear and we possess the tools to carry it out, but we must apply our skills, use the gifts, and commit ourselves to the task.

The Master's work is seen in every aspect of our lives. In our families and with friends we are called to demonstrate peace and love, especially when we don't feel like loving. At our place of work the mission of Christ is certainly ours, especially today when unethical work practices and the drive to obtain as much power, wealth, and prestige as possible can easily push us off the correct road. We need to apply what Jesus said and taught in the way we do business. In our local communities we continue Jesus' mission through our assistance in local government and participation in community activities, including the right and privilege to voice our opinion at the ballot box. In our Church we help build God's kingdom with our service to brothers and sisters, especially those who have most need of our assistance — the stranger, the elderly, the sick of body or mind, the handicapped, the criminal, and those whom society has placed on the margins for a host of unjust reasons.

The students who followed Giacomo Puccini knew enough that when his *magnum opus* was not finished at the time of his death, they could do their best to complete their master's work. Elisha prepared himself and then received the tools necessary to continue the work of his mentor, the great prophet Elijah. In a similar way we, the Church, the Body of Christ as Saint Paul calls us, must continue our Master's work. As Elisha became in a special way the new Elijah, so must we become the Christ in our world. As disciples we will never be the Christ in reality, but in his physical absence we become the presence of Christ to others. We must now do our level best to continue his work. Saint Teresa of Avila, the sixteenth-century religious reformer and spiritual mystic, expressed our mission in a prayer popularized by the contemporary Christian musician and singer John Michael Talbot: "Christ has no hands on earth but yours. No hands no feet, but yours. Yours are the eyes through which Christ sees with compassion for the world. Christ has no hands or feet but yours." May we who seek to complete our Master's work believe and profess the same.

Proper 9
Pentecost 7
Ordinary Time 14
2 Kings 5:1-14

Strength Through Diversity

A wealthy businessman decided to take a walk and eat his lunch at the same time. He strolled by a park. There he purchased a hot dog and a soft drink. As he walked through the park two different "street people" approached him one by one. Each asked, "Can you help me? I am hungry." Each time the businessman looked straight ahead and kept walking. After finishing his lunch, he stopped and bought a chocolate eclair for dessert. As he was about to take the first bite, he was forced to jump out of the way as a young boy raced by on his skateboard. The eclair went flying and landed on the ground. The man picked it up and tried to clean it off, but it was no use. It was now a muddy eclair. Before discarding it, however, he had an idea. He strolled over to one of the beggars who had approached him and handing the man the eclair said, "Here you are, my good man. This is something for your hunger." The businessman walked away smiling and returned to his office.

That night the man had a dream. He was sitting in a large and crowded cafe. Waitresses were scurrying about bringing customers delicious cakes and tortes. All the waitresses ignored the businessman, even though he was waving his hands at them continually. Finally he caught the eye of a young woman and asked for something to eat. She returned a few minutes later with a dirty piece of pastry. The man was outraged. "You can't treat me this way. I have a right to be served like all the others. I expect good service and food for my money." "You don't seem to understand," the waitress responded kindly. "You can't buy anything here. We don't accept money. You have just arrived in heaven and all you

341

can order here is what you sent ahead while on earth. The only thing we have in your record is this dirty eclair."

How do we treat people? Are all people our brothers and sisters or only a select few? Do we believe in strength through diversity or is diversity an obstacle that hinders our progress? The story of the businessman and the chocolate eclair illustrates the message that today's lesson from Second Kings describes, namely the need to reach out to those who are different and in the process show them the face of God.

Hanson's disease, commonly known as leprosy, is very rare today, but in biblical times it was common and unquestionably a scourge to its victims. People with leprosy were ostracized from society for several reasons, at least one of which was proper. Leprosy is highly contagious and, in biblical times, there was no known cure. Thus, it certainly made sense to keep those afflicted away from others. However, victims of leprosy were treated in a prejudicial way. The unsightliness of their decaying flesh made them unclean, as stated in Jewish law. Anyone who came in contact with a victim of leprosy, even if it was to touch something that a person with leprosy had previously touched, was rendered a person unclean as well and ritually impure. An elaborate ritual was required to be made pure again and re-enter everyday Jewish society. From this background one can see that even though Naaman was a powerful and possibly even famous man, his leprosy placed him on the outside. He was different and unacceptable in the minds of many because of his affliction.

How did Elisha react when he was told about Naaman's condition? The normal reaction would have been to do nothing or even flee the area, for not only was Naaman a leper, but he was also a foreigner and a pagan. Thus, under the conditions of the day, the prophet or any practicing Jew most probably would not have been concerned. Yet, as we hear, Elisha does what is completely contrary to what would be expected. He did not hesitate to assist Naaman. The prophet did not care that the man was not a Jew nor that he was a leper. Who he was and his affliction were inconsequential to Elisha; all that concerned him was that a person in need sought his assistance.

342

How did Naaman react to the response of the prophet? We hear that he was sincerely disappointed, as he wanted to see the prophet work some miracle in his presence. The instruction to go and wash in the Jordan seemed too simple. Possibly Naaman did not believe Elisha could effect a cure unless it was some spectacular and highly visible action. Naaman, in the end however, is convinced by his attendants that he should do what the prophet suggests. Elisha's actions demonstrate to Naaman and all who witness this event that God is not only present in the great and magnificent, but also in the simple and ordinary, such as the action of bathing. Naaman also learns that there is a need to trust. He has in his head a certain image of what the prophet must do in order to cure him, but he comes to realize that he must place his faith in the actions of another. Although Naaman and Elisha are different in many ways — they come from different nations, have different religious backgrounds and beliefs, and live in different stations in life — they each come to understand and appreciate the reality that knowing and working with people who are different brings great strength to those open to the possibility.

The story of the businessman and the chocolate eclair and the lesson learned in the encounter between Elisha and Naaman are clear illustrations of our need to appreciate diversity and to reach out to those who are different. We, through these lessons, have the opportunity to discover the reality of strength through diversity. For most people it is not much of a chore to do something extra for someone we know — a family member, close friend, neighbor, or even colleague at work. We hardly think twice about such assistance because we are confident that should the tables be turned and we be the person in need, those we have helped will assist us. In general we have no problem reaching out to people who are of the same ilk as ourselves, those with the same educational level, same economic prosperity, same political and religious views, those with the same ethnic and racial identity and social background. We must recall, however, Jesus' words, "Beware of practicing your piety before others in order to be seen by them; for then you have no reward from your Father in heaven. So whenever you give alms, do not sound a trumpet before you, as the hypocrites do in the synagogues and in the streets, so that they may be praised by others. Truly I tell you, they have received their reward. But when you give alms, do not let your left hand know what your right hand is doing, so that your alms may be done in secret; and your Father who sees in secret will reward you" (Matthew 6:1-4).

Elisha's action in reaching out to Naaman, a leper and a foreigner, was simply a precursor to how Jesus continually reached out to those who were different. He assisted the Syro-Phoenician woman, a foreigner, cured the ten lepers who were outcasts, aided the woman with the hemorrhage, cured the blind Bartimaeus, and forgave the sins of Mary Magdalene and the woman caught in adultery. Jesus indiscriminately reached out to all. He believed that diversity would enhance the world and thus did what he could to demonstrate strength through diversity.

Our challenge is to avoid the errors of the businessman and to imitate the actions of Christ in reaching out to those who are different than we are, seeing in such encounters the possibilities that exist. Can we reach out to the homeless by our assistance in some community program that shelters those who normally go without? Is there a way we can assist the mentally or physically challenged to assist their struggle for acceptance and dignity in our world which reacts so negatively to those who are not like everyone else? Can we in some way assist those who have not had the great opportunity of education which most of us take for granted? Have we thought of ways to promote ecumenical dialogue with other Christians and even non-Christians in the same spirit that Jesus sought out and helped those who needed him most?

Today's reading asks another important question — what is our reaction when someone different than us reaches out to give us assistance? Naaman was hesitant, somewhat fearful, and certainly distrustful of Elisha when he did not respond in a manner the foreigner believed to be appropriate. What happens when someone who is different reaches out to us? Do we hesitate because we believe people have ulterior motives? Do we go further and run away because we are fearful of those who are different? Can we see the need to be transformed from such attitudes to the certain belief, even the conviction, that diversity can assist us?

Social service agencies and civil rights groups often use the term "strength through diversity" to promote the unity of the human family. The expression means that people can find greater communal and personal strength, not so much physical strength, but psychological and moral strength, by associating with others and treating them as equals. This is the goal, but we must admit that we are a long way from achieving this utopian ideal. Rather than being one as Jesus suggests in John's Gospel, "That they all may be one. As you, Father, are in me and I am in you, may they also be one in us, so that the world may believe that you have sent me" (John 17:21), we are separate, fractured, and divided. Some are acceptable and others receive from us the proverbial "dirty eclair."

If we are a true Christian community, then we must learn to live as one. We will always have different opinions, different strengths and weaknesses, different ideas and methods to resolve problems. But our vision and attitude must be common; we must work to build the Kingdom of God in our lifetime into a community of love, peace, and reconciliation. This can never be done if we differentiate between peoples allowing some to receive our attention, expertise, and effort, while others only receive an afterthought. When the businessman neglected the beggars, he instantly differentiated between himself and these two men. When he offered the dirty eclair to one man, he instantly differentiated and placed himself above that person. Such actions are incompatible with Jesus' prayer, "That all may be one." We are called to move beyond prejudice, ignorance, insensitivity, and lack of compassion to an inclusive attitude which seeks to find the good and strength in all people. Then strength through diversity is possible.

One simple story demonstrates the need for diversity. A young pastor was asked to entertain some very energetic youngsters. He decided to play a game called Giants, Wizards, and Dwarfs. He told the children, "You must decide now if you will be a giant, wizard, or dwarf." One little girl came up, pulled the pastor's pants leg and said, "Where do the mermaids stand?" "There are no mermaids," the pastor countered. "Oh, yes, there are," she responded. "I am one of them." This little girl was not to be denied her identity. She knew who she was and was proud of it. So, my friends, where do the mermaids in our life stand — those who do not fit neatly into our boxes and pigeonholes? God challenges us; our response is awaited.

Love Means Speaking The Truth

"When Christ calls a man, he bids that man to come and die." These words were written by Dietrich Bonhoeffer, a well-known Lutheran pastor and theologian, in a book influential to many, *The Cost of Discipleship*, first published in 1937. Bonhoeffer lived his Christian call to holiness and spoke the truth; he did so without counting the cost. He did what God asked of him without qualification, reservation, or question. He did not look over his shoulder and wonder why, but rather, lived what he wrote. His life of discipleship and words of truth cost him his life.

Bonhoeffer was born in the state of Prussia in 1906. He grew up in an academic environment near the University of Berlin where his father was a professor of neurology and psychiatry. Later in his own study of theology he became interested in the historical-critical method of Adolph von Harnack and was a disciple of Swiss theologian Karl Barth who promoted the new "theology of revelation." After completing his doctorate, Bonhoeffer spent 1931 at New York's Union Theological Seminary in a post-doctorate fellowship and exchange program. Returning to Germany he resumed duties which he had earlier begun as a pastor and writer.

In 1933, however, things changed for Bonhoeffer, the German people, and ultimately the world, with the rise of the Nazi regime and Adolf Hitler. Bonhoeffer was one of the first and certainly the most vocal opponent of the Nazi ideology of anti-Semitism. He knew the truth of the Nazi's plan and he refused to keep quiet. Between 1935-1940 he headed an underground seminary for Germany's "Confessing Church," (even though it was proscribed in 1937) which led the German-Protestant resistance to Hitler. He was able to continue his work as pastor and theologian in the early war years under cover as a member of the military intelligence community. Bonhoeffer believed that the root evil for many of society's problems was a lax attitude toward morality which he said was fostered by the ready distribution of "cheap grace" to members of the Church. He was an ecumenist and promoted this belief in his speeches and writings.

In April 1943 Bonhoeffer, as a result of his books, essays, and talks that challenged the Nazi regime, was arrested for insurrection. He was ordered to be imprisoned, but this only strengthened his beliefs. It was at this time that he wrote his most famous work, *Prisoner of God: Letters and Papers from Prison.* Implicated in the failed July 1944 plot to assassinate Hitler, Bonhoeffer was transferred to a concentration camp in Flossenburg, Bavaria, where on April 9, 1945, only days before the Allied liberation of the facility, he was executed. Dietrich Bonhoeffer died for the Christian beliefs which formed his life; he was a martyr who never counted the cost.

Christianity is a commitment that requires us as disciples to speak the truth and not count the cost. If we have the eyes to see and the ears to hear, we can recognize the truth as articulated by prophets in our midst today. When we hear the word prophet what images and names come to mind? Possibly some think of great evangelists, such as Sinclair Lewis' protagonist Elmer Gantry, who stand on street corners with the Bible in hand and preach hellfire and damnation to those who refuse to reform their lives. Others may think of the door-to-door sale of religion. Some may not agree with the theological perspective of many of these groups, but we certainly must respect the courage and zeal manifest in their efforts to proselytize. The names of prophets that come to mind are familiar to all: Isaiah, Jeremiah, Ezekiel, or possibly one of the so-called minor prophets — Amos, Zephaniah, or Jonah. What is a prophet? A prophet is one with the rare privilege to speak God's word with great authority. But the privilege of the prophetic voice incurs significant responsibility as well.

Scripture describes the office and mission of the prophet in Hebrew society. Moses, the great liberator of the Israelites and their first prophet, heard the cries of the people for a representative to speak God's word: "The Lord your God will raise up for you prophets like me from among your own people; you shall heed such prophets" (Deuteronomy 18:15). Prophets are tasked to speak the truth, that is God's word, and to do so fearlessly. They speak with authority, proclaiming God's word as it is revealed to them, but they do so knowing of the responsibility that comes with their office: "Anyone who does not heed the words that the prophet shall speak in my name, I myself will hold accountable. But any prophet who speaks in the name of other gods, or who presumes to speak in my name a word that I have not commanded the prophet to speak — that prophet shall die" (Deuteronomy 18:19-20).

Amos, from whom we hear this morning, prophesied to the Northern Kingdom of Israel. Like Bonhoeffer and many other prophets, past and present, Amos did not want the job. As he says, "I am no prophet, nor a prophet's son; but I am a herdsman, and a dresser of sycamore trees, and the Lord took me from following the flock, and the Lord said to me, 'Go, prophesy to my people Israel.' " Amos did as the Lord commanded, even though it was difficult; he spoke the truth to a hostile group of people. He may have doubted his ability, but he did not question the authority of God's call nor its reality. His message was strong and forthright, telling King Jeroboam that his reign will end with the sword and predicting that the Northern Kingdom of Israel will be lost. Amos must have been afraid to proclaim such a hard message, but he had the courage which only God can give and, therefore, fearlessly stated what needed to be said. Dietrich Bonhoeffer followed in the line of Amos and proclaimed a hard message to the Nazi elite, but it was a missive they needed to hear.

Jesus was the preeminent prophet for as the Son of God. He spoke from personal knowledge of the Father. The Gospel evangelists describe Jesus' teaching and how the people were spellbound by what they heard. Jesus' teaching was new and different; it was authoritative (Mark 1:21-22). Jesus' message was challenging, yet he proclaimed it, as Saint Paul suggests, when it was convenient and inconvenient (2 Timothy 4:2). He was courageous because he spoke God's word not when it seemed to be acceptable or appropriate in the ears of the hearers or when he would receive a favorable hearing. Rather, often Jesus' message raised conflict; it shook people up. Jesus' message was challenging to the people's sensibilities because their zone of comfortableness was rocked severely. Some heeded Jesus' message and became his followers. Others disregarded or were indifferent to the message and others still were violently opposed to what they heard and orchestrated his death.

Amos was one of the great prophets of the Old Testament who proclaimed the truth of God's word as it was presented to him. He spoke with authority and did what God asked of him, but Jesus was the preeminent prophet because he knew the Father. Lest, however, we think that prophecy ended with Jesus, we can look at people like Dietrich Bonhoeffer, Oscar Romero, the assassinated Archbishop of San Salvador, or the retired Anglican archbishop of South Africa, Desmond Tutu, to see that contemporary prophets are in our midst. In the church there are courageous people who today challenge us and serve as prophets. Some speak out on behalf of the mentally and physically challenged and others proclaim the rights of the elderly. Some are advocates for the rights of prisoners and others speak for the poor, the homeless, the destitute, and those who have little or no voice in our society. Are we listening to these voices, or is the message we hear too harsh or do we feel it is not applicable to us? Do we listen and accept reality when people speak the truth, or do we cover our ears and run from the message because it is too challenging?

There are many others in our contemporary society who speak the truth as prophets and, as a means of responding in love to God's call, probably don't even realize it. Parents have been given special authority by God to proclaim the Lord's word in speech and action to their children and, thus, serve as prophets. Mothers and fathers must take responsibility in proclaiming God's word, whether it is a word of discipline, praise, or love to their children. Parents perform a prophetic role by steering their children along the correct path of life. This task is often quite difficult, especially when it is necessary to guide children away from things they enjoy or people they consider their friends. God's word is proclaimed so that people can fulfill their potential, using wisely and completely the gifts God has given them. Parents may, therefore, have to practice tough love in their words and actions, but we must remember that the scriptures are filled with examples of how God, in the words of the prophets, excoriated the Hebrews in an effort to bring them to the correct road. Similarly, Jesus, chastised many in his day in an effort to get them on the right road. Parents also serve as prophets when they provide advice and encouragement when their children make the fundamental decisions in life — where to go to school or to live, what occupation or career to choose, whether one should marry. The prophetic role of parents should never be underestimated.

Teachers, coaches, and mentors also have the rare privilege and the significant responsibility to act as prophets through the instruction, encouragement, guidance, and admonition they give to those placed in their charge. All of us have experienced the benefit of well-trained, disciplined, and encouraging teachers and coaches. Teachers proclaim God's word and, thus, serve as prophets by sharing the knowledge they have with inquisitive minds in a way that is inviting and engaging. Many people find their life's work through the positive influence of some great teacher in their youth. Coaches are prophets by the challenge they present to work harder, be competitive, play fair, learn teamwork, and above all win and lose with grace and class.

Ministers, priests, and other parish leaders have a special call to echo God's word and exercise the role of prophet. These people, possibly to a greater extent than most, have the opportunity to walk with people in the highs and lows, the agonies and ecstasies of life. These ministers to God's people have a rare privilege to bring God's word in a very concrete way to all who hunger for God in their lives. Whether it is preaching, teaching, counseling, listening, or being an advocate, those in public ministry are charged to bring God's word to the situation at hand. Like parents, teachers, and coaches, pastors, priests, religious, and parish leaders will often find the proclamation of God's word to be difficult, but true prophets, people like Bonhoeffer, Amos, and Jesus of Nazareth, were not

351

concerned with difficulty; they fulfilled the Lord's commission to echo his words and manifest his actions in their lives.

All under the tutelage of parents, teachers, coaches, and mentors must listen to the voice of God that comes to them from these contemporary prophets. I suspect most people would agree, after some reflection, that many of the greatest lessons in life have been gained when a prophetic voice spoke God's word to us. It might have been a gentle reminder of something that needs attention, the encouragement never to give up, or a significant challenge to correct something that is askew or out of balance in our lives. The well-lived Christian life is filled with challenges and we must not shy from them. Rather we must meet the challenges and obstacles head on, negotiate over them, and continue moving forward despite the difficulty and pain.

Contemporary prophets who respond in love to God's call abound in our society. Some may be archbishops, some may be pastors, but most are everyday people we know, love, and encounter. Let us, therefore, consider our call to speak God's word; let us be prophets. May we be Christ to one another today and to eternal life.

Proper 11
Pentecost 9
Ordinary Time 16
Amos 8:1-12

The Lord Hears
The Cry Of The Poor

The year 1992 marked the quincentenary of the arrival of Christopher Columbus in the New World, an event which initiated the greatest transformation of life in the common era of human history. Columbus' great discovery is remembered for what the age of exploration brought to human society through the expansion of the world — geographically, culturally, religiously, and economically. The quincentenary, however, was also marked by major protests that attempted to focus world attention on the significant errors made by the conquistadors, some out of zeal, others from ignorance, and far too many out of a lust for power and possessions. The rape of the lands of the New World and the destruction of peoples and their cultures were realities that cannot be side-stepped nor denied.

Columbus' discovery set in motion the age of exploration that did many good things for many peoples. Both Europe and the New World benefited greatly from the agricultural exchange with each land receiving new and important products from the other. Both regions also eventually benefited from the broadening of learning that came about from the cross study of cultures.

When the Spanish came to the New World their purposes were twofold: to bring the message of Christ to the pagan peoples of the New World and to achieve economic gain. In their zeal to achieve both ends, the people whom they encountered, namely the native peoples of the region, suffered greatly. The assumption was made by Church and State officials that the Indians were by nature inferior to the Spanish. Few if any gave credence to the highly-developed cultures present in the Aztec and Inca civilizations of contemporary Mexico and Peru. No appreciation was given to native religion. On the contrary, zealous Franciscan, Dominican, and Jesuit missionaries treated the native peoples as children and believed fervently that unless these people were converted to Spanish Catholicism they had no chance for salvation and eternal life. Thus, these zealous churchmen sought conversions at almost any cost, often coercing the Indians into acceptance of the faith.

The desire for economic profit directly affected the manner in which Indians were treated as well. Sugar quickly arose as a cash crop on the Caribbean islands and in Brazil and Indians were almost immediately pressed into service on the sugar plantations. In western South America and New Spain (Mexico), Indians were sent to the silver and gold mines. Labor was necessary for these operations and Indians were readily available and abundant. The Encomienda System was initiated, a program that placed Indians in camps where their basic needs were provided while they worked for Spanish profit. This system of virtual slavery, in different forms, lasted until the middle of the sixteenth century.

There were prophetic voices who spoke out against the injustices present and who were advocates for the Indians, but they were in many ways a lone cry in the desert. Antonio Montesinos and Bartolome de Las Casas, two Dominican friars (priests) were advocates for the Indians. Their polemics, raised to both State and Church officials, led to changes and some alleviation of the suffering of the native peoples. Yet, the suffering and abuses continued.

It has taken the world too long to acknowledge the errors, even though many were not intended, of many who were pioneers in the age of discovery. Peoples were oppressed and the earth was raped in order to line the pockets of nations and individuals with monies that came from the riches of the land. The situation of the discovery of the New World demonstrates, unfortunately, that human civilization continues to struggle with oppression of the poor and personal greed, problems against which Amos prophesied to the Northern Kingdom of Israel many centuries before Christ.

354

Amos presents a hard and profound message to the ruling classes of Israel for their failures to lead properly and care for those whom God had placed in their charge. In today's lesson the prophet uses the image of summer fruit to tell the Hebrews that the time of their judgment is near; God will bring ruin to the people of Israel and will never pass by again. Why has God made such a harsh sentence upon the nation of Israel? Amos enumerates for the people and for us the many transgressions of abuse of power and greed that have placed the ruling classes at odds with God. The rich and powerful in Jewish society have abused the people by trampling on the needs of the less fortunate and bringing to ruin the poor of the land. Amos charges the merchants with cheating their customers. They fix scales and balances to their own favor. They measure out less than a full ephah in produce when sold, but use more than a shekel of weight to determine the price. The rich mix the refuse of the wheat with the good grain to stretch their profits even more. Finally, Amos accuses the rich and ruling classes of selling the poor for silver and the needy for a pair of sandals.

Amos has not finished his polemic, however, as he aims to show why these people oppress the poor so badly. He cries out against the greed of the rich and shows how it is manifest in their manner of life. These people cannot wait until the new moon feast, a day that allowed no work by Hebrew law, is over so they can continue their sordid business dealings. In a similar way, the merchants want the Sabbath to pass quickly so they can again sell their wheat.

The prophet holds no punches in his accusations nor in his prophetic prediction of what these practices will gain for the nation of Israel. He forcefully proclaims that God will punish the people for their improper treatment of the poor and the greed that motivates their action and pervades their attitude. The sun will go down at noon, great feasts will be turned into occasions of mourning, and songs will be transformed into lamentations in punishment for the peoples' actions. Even worse Amos predicts how God will abandon the people. A famine will come upon the land, not a lack of food and drink, but more importantly the dearth of God's word. The people will look high and low, east and west for God, but the Lord will not be found. Amos' words, as we know, came true for the entire nation of Israel, as the ten northern tribes were conquered by the Assyrians more than 700 years before Christ.

The problem of greed and how it manifests itself in the oppression of the poor, experienced by the rich Hebrews in Israel and the conquistadores in the New World of the sixteenth century, is, unfortunately, present in our contemporary society as well. Society today in different ways is constantly subjugating and suppressing the poor in all their cases — the economically poor, the intellectually less gifted, the socially and culturally backward, the physically or mentally challenged, the religiously ignorant. Society wants and is friendly to winners and we are told in many ways that the poor are losers. Thus, we shy away from those who will not advance our cause. The poor do not possess sufficient money, intellect, influence, class, or physical prowess to meet our needs. We, therefore, possibly unconsciously, do precisely what the priest and the Levite in the familiar "Parable of the Good Samaritan" did; we simply pass them by. One cannot possess such an attitude and be a true Christian. We must not hold an attitude that estranges or keeps at a distance others who through possibly no fault or action of their own are poor. Rather, we must draw people closer, take the attitude of the despised Samaritan, and make sufficient time to meet the needs of the poor. The Lord hears the cry of the poor and so must we!

Contemporary business surely needs to hear the message of Amos. Understandably profit is the bottom line in business, but in the drive to achieve economic success in the dog-eat-dog world in which we live, there is a tendency to cut corners or do things in ways that often shortchange others. In order to get ahead financially, we may fix the scales or intentionally measure inaccurately at the expense of another. Too often today the daily newspapers report instances of companies that have conducted business in an unethical manner and those on the bottom of the ladder are the ones who suffer most.

Amos speaks of how people in his day could not wait until the Sabbath ended so they could continue to practice their business.

Civil law today has no restrictions on the days we conduct business, but we, like our ancestors in the faith, do not consider the meaning and value of the Lord's Day and the need to do something different than our usual work on this special day given us by God. Yes, it is true, as Jesus says, "The Sabbath is made for man, not man for the Sabbath," but we must seriously consider our need to spend more time with God and a bit less with our day-to-day work.

Contemporary society is also plagued with the sin of greed. We never seem to have enough of anything or the right type of the things we actually possess. We are not content with that which will suffice; we want more and better of all things. There are times when the length we will go in order to obtain what we want is truly remarkable. Sometimes we are so greedy, especially in business, that we place others, but seldom ourselves, in jeopardy. Having sufficient economic resources is important in today's world, but when business goes bad who suffers? We seldom hear of high management or stockholders taking cuts or losing their positions. On the contrary, the owners and managers maintain their livelihood and the workers, those who can least afford to compromise what they have, lose everything.

Greed in all its manifestations leads only to doom as it leads only to the detriment of others and eventually to the loss of our souls. Russian novelist Fydor Dostoyevsky's tale "The Onion" expresses succinctly but clearly where greed leads: Once upon a time there was a peasant woman, and a very wicked woman she was. One day she died leaving not a single good deed behind. The devils caught hold of her and plunged her into the Lake of Hades. Her guardian angel stood by and wondered what good deed of hers he could remember to inform God. The angel told God, "Once she pulled up an onion from her garden and gave it to a beggar woman." God replied, "Take that onion and hold it out to her in the lake and let her take hold of it and be pulled out by it. If you can pull her out of the Lake of Hades, she may enter paradise. But if the onion breaks, she must stay where she is." The angel ran to the woman and held out the onion to her. "Come and catch hold," cried the angel, "and I will pull you out." And the angel began cautiously to pull the woman out. He had almost pulled her out when other sinners in the lake, seeing how she was being saved, began clutching hold of her legs so they too could be pulled out. However, the woman was wicked and began to kick at them saying, "I'm to be pulled out, not you. It's my onion, not yours. Let go." As soon as she uttered these words, the onion broke. The woman fell back into the Lake of Hades where she remains to this day. And the guardian angel wept as he went away.

The Hebrews were given the Law and the land and they failed to use them wisely by using them for all. Their greed and oppression of the poor led them into exile. The Spanish had good intentions, but they too allowed greed and poor choices to throw them off stride. One Spanish traveler, Cabeza de Vaca, after an eight-year sojourn from Florida to Mexico City, wrote to the King of Spain about his experience. He concluded his letter in an apologetic tone for the failures of his contemporaries:

> We had come to conquer, to enslave, and to use the people and the land and all therein, yet I learned so profoundly while barefoot and possessing nothing that it is not ours to own, that it is all the land of the Lord alone, and we are simply given it as caretakers. How much suffering will come from our greed and selfishness I cannot tell. Among the Christians there was very little desire to even assist one another, yet we called ourselves gentlemen. What kind of world will come from this I do not know, but this I can say: That greed and possession is not the way; that enslavement and destruction of the land will bring nothing but great sufferings and that in creating a new world all things are possible but these things must be done from the spirit of the Christian heart. In no other way can we honor Christ on this earth.

My friends, let us listen to the words of Amos, heed the lessons of history, hear the cry of the poor, and respond in love!

Sermons On The First Readings

For Sundays
After Pentecost
(Middle Third)

The Justice Of God

Richard E. Gribble, csc

Saint Paul wrote to the Corinthians (1 Corinthians 13:13), "And now faith, hope, and love abide, these three; and the greatest of these is love." Love of family and good friends sustains us through good times and bad; it is the sustenance that together with God's love gives life the enduring quality it possesses. This book is dedicated to my good friends, Andy, Jan, Chris, Jeff, and Bethany, whose unwavering support and great love is a constant reminder to me of Paul's words and love of God for all people.

Introduction

"Taxation without representation is tyranny" is an expression we all learned in elementary or high school history class as one of the great battle cries of the American Revolution. Patrick Henry, Samuel Adams, Benjamin Franklin, and a host of other patriots used these words to express what they perceived to be an injustice perpetrated by the British against its vassal citizens in the American colonies. In order to promote justice and secure liberty, the Fathers of this nation spoke out against the actions and attitudes of a ruling nation whose ideals and actions had become corrupt in the treatment of its citizens.

The justice sought by Americans against a domineering state has been pursued by God for his people for many centuries. The challenging message of the prophets who spoke against the religious leaders of Israel and Judah was timely in its warning for the peoples of the day, but it was also timeless as today many of the same failures by people in positions of authority continue to be perpetrated. God, through the voice of the prophets, such as Hosea, Isaiah, and Jeremiah, demanded that justice, that is righteousness, fair treatment, and conformance to the truth, be heralded throughout the land. God's sense of justice in punishing acts contrary to God's desires is fair, but the Lord always stands ready to welcome back the person who is willing to be transformed. God punished the Hebrews for their idolatry and the behavior of their religious leaders toward the poor, but God was always ready to renew his relationship with Israel. God will always be faithful to the covenant with his people.

The First Lessons in this middle third of the Pentecost or Ordinary Time season describe the up and down nature of the Hebrew's relationship with God. The message of the prophets was both timely and timeless. The failures of the religious leaders to serve the poor and marginalized in society, the very people who were their charge, is described fully by Hosea and Isaiah. Additionally, the sin of idolatry, seeking consolation and truth in other nations and their gods, is condemned by the prophets. God had provided the Hebrews all they could possibly need and still, as Isaiah (5:4) says, "the nation produced wild grapes." The message of the prophets was not heeded in Israel or Judah, and thus, God's justice was served through the loss to the Assyrians of the Northern Kingdom in 722 B.C.E. and the infamous Babylonian Captivity of Judah between 587 and 539 B.C.E.

The message of the prophets, spoken to the Hebrews, must also be applied today. God continues to shower upon the world multiple and varied gifts, but the problems described by the prophets continue to exist — the poor are continually oppressed and the false gods of power, wealth, and prestige are worshiped. The prophetic voice continues to be heard in the words and actions of South African freedom fighter Nelson Mandela, social activist Dorothy Day, and internationally-acclaimed evangelist Billy Graham. Are we listening to these prophetic voices or is God's warning once again being ignored?

Christianity professes the goodness and justice of God for all people. The Lord listens to our pleas and answers our prayers in order to bring about a more just and God-centered society. As followers of Christ we have an obligation to continue to speak and act in God's name, to exercise our voice as prophets, and through our efforts to bring the justice of God to our world.

These sermons describe God's disappointment in the actions of his people, but regardless of his displeasure God's benevolence and goodness prevailed. Consequences did arise for the failures of the religious leaders of the Hebrews, but God always stood ready to welcome home the lost and to create an environment for a new beginning. It is hoped that readers will be able to see and understand their role as proclaimers of the word and contemporary prophets, doing their share to create a more just and humane society where the proclamation of God's word is heard, the world is transformed, and the glory and praise of God is triumphant.

Richard E. Gribble, CSC

Knowing What Is
Truly Important In Life

When she was a little girl her parents bought a cottage by the lake. It was a small and humble place, but it soon would be filled with many memories. Each summer the family would go to the lake. She and her brother and sisters went swimming almost every day. On special occasions her father would rent a boat and the whole family would paddle around the lake. She learned how to fish and even tried her hand at water skiing. Vacations were a constant source of joy because of the little cottage by the lake.

When she grew a little older and entered high school, other interests were found besides the cottage by the lake. Clothes, parties, and especially boys occupied the majority of her time. She went to summer school to improve her mind but also to enhance her social life. The few times that she did go to the lake were with her friends. Horseplay, long walks along the shore of the lake, and roasting marshmallows over a dying camp fire were memories which she collected.

As time passed she graduated from high school, went to college, and got a job. She became successful and married the man of her dreams. She was far too busy to go to the little cottage by the lake. Even when her parents died and left the house to her, she could not muster the energy or resolve to go to the lake; it no longer seemed to fit her taste. After all it was small and inconvenient due to its location; it would take lots of remodeling to satisfy her tastes. The lake was more like a big pond; it was hardly something of which to be proud. When she had children, they convinced her to go to the lake a couple of times, but her attitude rubbed off on them

363

and no one had a good time. In the end she abandoned the cottage completely. She was a successful business woman who lectured and traveled widely and thus did not have any time for the cottage. Besides, she had all that was needed, a fancy car, designer clothes, and a palatial home.

One day while at work she received a message from her secretary. Vandals had broken into the little cottage by the lake and burned it to the ground. It didn't matter to her, but for some strange reason she felt compelled to go to the lake. When she arrived she stood in the ashes of what once was the little cottage by the lake. Surrounded by the charred rubble she remembered and began to cry uncontrollably; she couldn't stop. At that moment she came to a stunning revelation. If all the fancy things she had — the car, designer clothes, and palatial home — were lost she would not cry as hard as she was now for the little cottage by the lake. The place had become part of her and she never realized it. That day when she left, the lake looked bigger than it ever had before. Her tears had made it so.[1]

What is truly important in life? What has meaning and value beyond all other things? The woman in the story only came to realize the importance of the little cottage after it was gone and it was too late to show her appreciation. Today our reading from the prophet Hosea challenges us to ponder what is important in our lives. The metaphorical language of the future destruction of the nation of Israel cautions us to make certain we have placed our priorities in order, with the full realization that nothing is more important than our relationship with God.

Hosea preached God's message and warning to the Northern Kingdom of Israel, as did Amos from whom we have heard the past few Sundays. The symbolism of the passage we heard today is significant. God asks Hosea to take a harlot for a wife, a gesture that signifies how the nation of Israel has consorted with harlots, namely the gods of peoples in the surrounding area. Israel has been unfaithful to God in its failure to abide by the most basic precept of the law, the abolition of false gods. They have broken the covenant and strayed far from the course they were asked to follow as people unique and special to Yahweh. Hosea's metaphorical relationship with the harlot Gomer produces three offspring, each of which is symbolic of the punishment God plans to inflict upon Israel for its faithlessness. The firstborn, Jezreel, signifies that God will bring an end to the kingdom of Israel. The independence the nation has enjoyed since its split from Judah in the time of King Rehoboam (1 Kings 12) will soon end. We know historically that what Hosea predicted happened when the Assyrians conquered Israel and dispersed its people in 722 B.C.E. Hosea's secondborn, a daughter named Lo-ruhamah, symbolizes that God will no longer have pity on Israel nor forgive the sins of the people. God, however, will remain faithful to the nation and people of Judah. Thus, God distinguishes between the sins of Israel and the faithfulness (at least at the time) of Judah. The third child, a second boy named Lo-ammi, testifies to God's proclamation that Israel is no longer God's people nor is the Lord the people's God. Israel has been disowned by God and will now suffer the cruelties of the world as an orphan.

We might wonder *why* God abandoned his people. What did the Hebrews do that brought Yahweh's wrath, especially after many previous offenses seemingly did nothing to jeopardize God's faithfulness to the covenant, namely to be the God of Abraham, Isaac, and Jacob forever? The answer is that the people totally lost their way and placed their attention on things that were not important. Like the business woman in the story, everything save what was truly important became the focus for the people of Israel. Not only did they forget God, but they placed the customs and ways of the pagan peoples in the region above those of the Hebrews. The people allowed their prosperity and assets to blind them. God was ever patient and sent numerous prophets who issued many warnings, but now the time of reckoning has arrived. The people must be punished for their idolatry.

People in contemporary society, as in all human history, must battle against the great forces of power, wealth, and prestige that vie for our attention and often sidetrack us from concentrating on what is most important: our relationship with God. Jesus also had to contend with the great temptations of the world, but he managed to overcome the enticements of Satan and continue his ministry to initiate the Kingdom of God in our world. Matthew's Gospel (4:1-11) is the classic New Testament text that demonstrates how Jesus handled the three great temptations, the same allures that led the Hebrews of Israel into disfavor with God and brought destruction to the nation. After Jesus had spent forty days in the desert preparing himself for his public life in Galilee and Judea, he was tempted by Satan. First the devil enticed Jesus with the allure of power by commanding him, because he was a powerful person, to change stones into bread. Jesus responded that there was something more important than power and bread, namely the word of God. Next, Satan tried to convince Jesus of the need for great prestige. He took the Lord to the pinnacle of the Temple and suggested that he cast himself off. Satan said that because the Lord was an important man, his angels would certainly not allow anything bad to happen to him and, thus, would break his fall. But Jesus replied that he did not need such attention and told Satan that one should not put the Lord God to such a test. Lastly, Jesus was tempted with wealth, an attraction we find so common in our consumer-driven first world existence. Satan displayed before Jesus all the kingdoms of the world, telling him it could all be his if he would prostrate himself in homage before the devil. Again, Jesus was up to the test, saying one must never worship the material world, but rather God and God alone is to be so honored. God alone is the one whom we must serve.

Contemporary society, increasingly so it seems, concentrates its efforts in accumulating as much power, wealth, and prestige as possible, under the misguided notion that these are the things that will get us where we need and want to be. We become possessive and fail to see that if we can release ourselves from such fascinations and desires we will receive all we could possibly need. A little story demonstrates how misguided at times we can be.

Once upon a time there was an old man from the lovely island of Crete. He loved his land with such great intensity that when he perceived his death was near, he asked his sons to take him outside and lay him on the beloved earth. As he was about to expire he reached out and grabbed in each hand some soil. Then he died a happy man. When he arrived at the gates of heaven, God, dressed as an old man with a long white beard, welcomed him and told him that he had been a good person. "Please," said God, "come into the joys of heaven, but you must drop that soil." "Never," responded the man. Thus, God departed sadly, leaving the man outside the gates.

A few eons passed and God again came to the man, this time appearing as an old crony and drinking buddy of the man. After a few drinks and stories of the past, God said, "Now it's time to enter heaven, but you must drop that soil." Again the man refused. Many more eons passed and God returned a third time to the man, this time appearing as his beloved granddaughter. God, in the voice of the girl, said, "Oh, Grandpa, we all miss you so much. Please come inside with all of us." The man agreed, but by this time he was very old and arthritis has attacked his hands so severely that his gnarled fingers could no longer form a clenched fist and in his efforts to raise himself the soil sifted between his fingers and his hands were once again empty. He then entered heaven and the first thing he saw was his beloved island.

Success and possessions in the things of the world — power, wealth, and prestige — may aid us in ways on this earth, but it is the things that we often feel are unimportant or give little credence that can really make the difference in life. The woman with the cottage by the lake discovered this reality. The Hebrews to whom Hosea prophesied never listened and God's judgment upon them was severe. Their flawed understanding of wealth cost them everything. Another story can show us who is truly wealthy and knows the important things in life.

Once upon a time there was a very rich and proud man named Carl who loved to ride his horse through his vast estate as a way to congratulate himself for his great wealth. One day he came upon Hans, an old tenant farmer, who had sat down to eat his lunch in the shade of a great oak tree. Hans' head was bowed in prayer, but when he looked up he saw Carl and said, "Oh, excuse me, I didn't see you. I was giving thanks for my food." The rich man was indignant at the coarse dark bread and cheese Hans ate. "I don't think I would feel much like giving thanks if that is all I had to eat." The poor man replied that he felt it was sufficient. He continued telling the rich man of a dream he had the previous evening, feeling it important that he know. In the dream a voice called out to him and said, "The richest man in the valley will die tonight." Carl, the rich man, only replied, "Ah dreams, nonsense."

The man rode away thinking that the poor man's dream was amusing and decided to forget it, but the thought would not leave his mind. He had felt fine all day until the poor man had recalled his dream. Now he was not sure how he felt, so he called his doctor that evening and the physician came over promptly. Carl told the doctor the dream and although the physician thought the whole incident to be poppycock, he agreed to examine the rich man. The doctor reported, "You are strong as a horse. There is no way that you will die tonight." The doctor was just closing his bag when a messenger arrived out of breath at the manor door. "Doctor," he cried, "come quickly. Old Hans just died in his sleep!"[2] Let us, my friends, learn a lesson and know that God and God alone is the one who is truly important in life!

---

1. Paraphrased from "The Lady of the Lake," in John R. Aurelio, *Colors! Stories of the Kingdom* (New York: Crossroads, 1993), pp. 40-41.

2. Paraphrased from "The Isle of Crete," and "Hans and Carl" in William J. Bausch, *A World Of Stories for Preachers and Teachers* (Mystic, Connecticut: Twenty-Third Publications, 1998), pp. 236-237, 245-246.

Know Yourself And Know God

Is the life you lead one for which you want to be remembered? That very challenging and thought-provoking question must have come to the famous Swedish scientist Alfred Nobel when in the common everyday exercise of reading the morning paper he discovered the challenge of God before his very eyes.

Nobel, who was born in 1833, was gifted intellectually. He read voraciously every book he could find, but he especially loved literary classics. By the time he was fifteen he could read, write, and speak four languages besides his native Swedish. Although he showed promise in the "humanities" area, it was his love of science and his desire to be an inventor like his father that most excited him. When Nobel was sixteen he had exhausted the educational possibilities of his native district in Sweden and, thus, decided to go abroad for more training. He first went to Paris and then across the Atlantic to the United States where he spent four years studying science and engineering principles, ideas that had become much more important after the onset of the Industrial Revolution in the latter decades of the eighteenth century.

With his education complete, Nobel returned to his native land and began to tinker around in his laboratory, creating an invention or two, but nothing of any significance. In the 1860s, however, he began to conduct experiments with nitroglycerin, a highly volatile and unstable substance. An explosion during one experiment killed Alfred's younger brother. The experience crushed Nobel in one way, but in another it became the catalyst to find a way to harness the energy of this substance and make it useful to the world.

Nobel discovered a functional use of nitroglycerin, but it came about quite by accident. One day in his workshop, he noticed that some of the nitroglycerin, which is a liquid above 55 degrees Fahrenheit, had leeched into some packing material which surrounded the many bottles of chemicals sent him for his various experiments. Nobel found that this third substance, made from the initial two, had all the energy capacity and blasting potential of nitroglycerin, but was stable and, thus, could be better controlled. Without knowing it, Alfred Nobel had invented dynamite.

The uses of dynamite throughout the world made Nobel a rich and famous man overnight. Mountains could be blasted away to make room for railroads, but it could also be placed in bombs, projectiles, and other weapons of war. With patents received in 1867 and 1868, first in the United States and later in Great Britain, for dynamite and blasting caps, Nobel gained great notoriety. With the discovery of oil on land he owned in the state of Russia, Nobel became one of the richest men in the world. He could sit back, relax, and enjoy life.

Alfred's serenity came to an abrupt halt one day when he picked up the morning paper and read the headline, "Dynamite King Dies." The story and obituary in the paper were erroneous, for he was very much alive and well. Nobel decided to read the article, however, in order to know what people would think of him after his death. Besides all the normal facts and dates of an obituary, he read a description which labeled him "the merchant of death." The expression disturbed the scientist greatly. Certainly the comment came in reference to his association with dynamite, but this did not lighten the blow. Nobel realized at that moment that the life he had led was not one for which he wanted to be remembered.

Something needed to be done to correct how people perceived him. The past was history and its record was etched in stone, but the future was something over which Nobel had some control. A rich man, he pondered how he could use his money for others. He decided to change his will, leaving his vast fortune in trust to a committee which each year would select people who, in theory and practice, had made positive contributions to the furthering of humankind. Thus, in 1901, five years after his death, the first Nobel

370

Prizes were awarded, initially in five areas, physics, chemistry, literature, medicine, and the famous Nobel Peace Prize. Later, in 1968 and thereafter, a prize in economics was added. Alfred Nobel had experienced conversion. God had been challenging him in many ways, but he never took the time, nor realized the significance of God's presence; he never understood himself and how others saw him. He was determined to change and not allow the presence of God to pass him by again!

Is the life you lead one for which you want to be remembered? Do you know who you are, or is life more a masquerade? Do you understand how much you have, or are you never satisfied with what life provides? The life of Alfred Nobel and the surprise yet inaccurate announcement of his death in the daily newspaper raised these questions for him. In a similar way these important questions were raised for the Hebrews by Hosea in his ministry as prophet. Unfortunately, despite the gifts they were given, the challenge was too much and their response too late, insufficient, and weak for God and they lost everything.

The image we receive in today's lesson from Hosea is much different than last week. We recall how the idolatry of the Hebrews, manifest through their worship of alien gods, was analogized to the prophet's relations with a harlot, with the offspring of their union symbolic for failures of Israel and God's rejection of the people. Today, on the other hand, we hear about a more sensitive, yet nonetheless definitive action by Yahweh against the nation of Israel.

Our reading is broken down into four parts, which taken together speak of how God, who was faithful to Israel despite the nation's failures, chastised the people and brought destruction, in order to bring them salvation. The first section of the passage speaks of God's fatherly care for Israel. The Hebrews as a collective people were the child that was unique and special to God, the nation loved by God and called forth in the great exodus from Egypt. God taught the people and led them as a father leads an infant child, cared for them, and fed them in the desert. Yet, the more God called them and met their needs, the further the people drifted from Yahweh and toward Baal. The second section of the reading speaks of how

371

God plans to punish the Hebrews for their indiscrete behavior, as a loving parent punishes an errant child. Because the people have refused to return to God, Assyria will overrun the nation and its leader will become ruler in Israel. The people will call upon the most high God, but the Lord will not raise them up any more. The prophet, however, is not through proclaiming God's word and goes on to tell the people that the very act of disobedience and the wrath of God that it provokes are the very elements that call forth a renewal of God's love for his own people. As a loving parent pardons the child who has gone astray, so the parent's love increases, knowing at times it is the path of "tough love" through chastisement that may be the proper road to take. God acts as a parent and renews his love, and it is this love for the wayward child that will bring salvation. As God says in the words of the prophet, "I will return them to their homes."

Why does Hosea speak to the people in this way? Why did God present the prophet such a difficult message? The basic reason is that the people have lost their way; they do not know who they are and where they are going. They have lost perspective in life. They claim they are God's people, but they serve and worship Baal! They, like Alfred Nobel, have coasted along and things seem to be fine. The rich have abused the poor; the privileged have oppressed the lowly. The Hebrews were seemingly never content with what they had or who they were. But when the day of reckoning came and God asked for an accounting of their lives, they were not ready. Yet, despite all their apostasy, idolatry, and many other offenses against Yahweh, the Creator of all things could never abandon them fully. God gave them life and wishes them to return one day to their land and regain their lives, which had been stripped away because of their faithlessness.

In life we, like Alfred Nobel and the Hebrews, forget who we are. Some of us gain great prestige in life and forget our origins, that is the people and the life circumstances in which we were raised. Some of us get so caught up in who we are and what we do that we forget those whom we are asked to serve, namely those entrusted to our care and the people who have helped us achieve our present state in life. A short but important story captures our need always to keep the proper perspective on who we are in this life.

On two special days every year a physician goes to a special place in his closet and takes out a coat that is out of style, patched in one arm, and rather tawdry, stringy, and dirty. It is his coat for the day. Years ago, it seems, when he was an intern in the lower Manhattan section of New York, he received a call on a blustery and cold winter evening. A little girl had come to his apartment, banging on the door, asking his assistance. He threw on a jacket and followed the child to a stinking one-room tenement apartment, where a little boy, the girl's brother, lay terribly sick. His parents were hovering over him. Despite the doctor's well-intentioned efforts, the boy died before his very eyes. The doctor was shivering, not only because of the death of the child, but because there was no heat in the apartment. The boy's father took off his coat and gave it to him, saying, "Here, you are cold. Thank you for trying to save my boy." The doctor realized immediately that this was the only means the family had to say thank you, and thus he did not have the heart to refuse the gift. Now that he is a prominent physician and quite wealthy, he still wears the coat the family gave him on two special days, the anniversary of the boy's death and the day he graduated from medical school. He wears the coat to remind himself what life is all about.

Besides our periodic failure to know ourself, we sometimes fail to reflect sufficiently how our lives affect others. Again, like Nobel and the Hebrews, we are rich in possessions, prestige, and power. We might need to be chopped down a bit, pruned back, and honed in the crucible of life to round off the sharp edges, cut down the mountains, and fill in the valleys of our lives. What will it take for us to look seriously at who we are? If we are not careful we will become like Dorian Gray, the protagonist in Oscar Wilde's macabre novelette, and see only the beauty and seldom, if ever, the bumps, bruises, and shortcomings in our lives as well.

There are times in life that we, like the Hebrews, Nobel, and unfortunately countless others, are never content with what we have and who we are. We want to be more than we are and have more than we presently possess. We fail to see how truly rich we are.

Again, however, a little story can possibly bring us down to the reality of life.

One cold winter day a lady heard a knock on her front door. She went to the door, peered through the window, and saw two children huddled inside the storm door in ragged third-hand coats. "Any old papers, lady?" they inquired. The woman was about to say no when she looked down and noticed the children's shoes, thin sandals sopping wet from the snow and slush. "Come in," said the woman, "and I will make you a cup of hot cocoa." There was no conversation, but soggy sandals left muddy footprints on the hearthstone. The woman provided toast and jam with the cocoa to fortify the children against the severe elements outside. One of the children, a little girl, held the cup of cocoa in her hands, admiring it from all sides. Her companion, a little boy, asked, "Lady, are you rich?" The woman, looking at the shabby slipcovers on the couch where the children were seated near the fire, responded, "Mercy, no, child." The little girl, however, rejoined, "But your saucers match the cups." Her words struck the woman powerfully. They were plain blue pottery, but the cups and saucers did match. After a half-hour the children thanked the woman and returned to their task of collecting old newspapers. The woman returned to her chores. She tested the potatoes for dinner and stirred the gravy. Potatoes and gravy, a roof over her head, a husband with a good and steady job: these things matched as well. The woman tidied up a bit and noticed that the muddy footprints of the small sandals were still wet upon the hearth. She decided she would leave the marks when they dried in case she ever forgot how rich she was.

Self-understanding and realization are true gifts, but they cannot be discovered without some significant inward searching and evaluation. For most people this is a rather perilous journey to look inside and to discover the person we truly are. We will find much good. Made in the image and likeness of God, we are God-like in our being and, thus, naturally good. Along the path of life, however, we sometimes deviate from our proper course, causing us to experience the bumps and bruises that are the reality of every human life. We seek to be perfect, as Christ commands, but we will never find this ideal. However, if we know ourselves and can accept who we are and what God created in us, we have come a great distance toward gaining the insight we need to find life. For Alfred Nobel it was the warning of an erroneous obituary that caused him to re-evaluate his life; for the Hebrews it was the hard words of the prophet's proclamation. What will it take for us? Let us look inside, discover ourselves, and then use the life God gave us — our talents, strengths, and weaknesses — to build the kingdom today and each day of our lives.

Conversion To The Lord

"I'd sell my soul to play for the Washington Senators." Joe Hardy, the protagonist in the popular Broadway musical *Damn Yankees*, says these words in a fit of frustration. Joe is what we call today your average middle-aged couch potato. He sits in front of his television and watches baseball, and most of the time his beloved team, the Senators, are defeated by "those damn New York Yankees." Joe always wanted to play ball, but things just did not work out that way. Marriage, children, and work occupied the life of Joe Hardy. Thus, one day in frustration he says he would sell his soul to play for the Senators. It just so happens that the devil is listening to Joe and appears quite suddenly in his living room. Satan will make a deal with the middle-aged man. The devil will transform Joe into a young, strapping athlete, as he once was, and he can play for the Senators, but when the season is over Joe's soul belongs to him. After a moment of thought, Joe agrees and he is instantly transformed into a young man again.

Joe manages to get a try-out with the Senators and the manager is quite impressed. Soon Joe is making newspaper headlines as a star, and the Senators begin to move up in the standings. As the season begins to draw to a close, the Yankees and Senators are neck and neck for the pennant and a chance to go to the World Series. Joe has made a great contribution, but in most respects his heart misses his old existence, especially his family and friends at work. He begins to think how he might get out of his pact with the devil.

377

The whole season comes down to one final game: whoever wins goes to the Series. The last game between the Senators and Yankees comes down to the last inning and ultimately the last out. Joe is playing center field for the home team Senators who are ahead by one run. A crack of the bat sends Joe racing toward the fence. As he runs back he is transformed into the middle-aged couch potato he really is. The devil is upset that Joe has broken his pact and wants to return to his old existence. Now a middle-aged man again, Joe still manages to run and make the catch, crashing through the center field fence in the process. He runs for fear that others will discover who he truly is; Joe Hardy was transformed in body, but he was not converted in his heart.

Joe Hardy wanted to play ball for the Senators so badly that he was ready and seemingly willing to put everything on the line and make a pact with Satan. He was transformed on the outside, but he was never converted on the inside. His heart and his mind were always the middle-aged couch potato he really was. Joe was actually fortunate that he was not converted, for he would have lost everything he truly was and wanted to be. In a similar, yet contrasting way, we are challenged by today's reading from the prophet Isaiah to be transformed — truly converted — to a new, deeper, and more committed relationship to God. We seek transformation, not on the outside like Joe Hardy, but rather, a true and permanent conversion on the inside, a conversion of mind and heart.

We are all familiar, at least by name and reputation, with the great prophet Isaiah and his book of prophecy, the longest in the Hebrew Scriptures. Written over a long period of time and, thus, addressing many different issues present in the Hebrew community, the words of God as proclaimed by the prophet have served to challenge people of faith throughout the centuries. As with the whole of scripture the demands and the promises of Isaiah are timeless and require our attention. In this first section of the book, chapters 1-35, Isaiah addresses the people of Judah before their exile to Babylon, warning them what will occur should they not heed the cautions and challenges he presents.

We hear in today's reading about God's challenge to the Hebrew community to move beyond their rather staid understanding of sacrifice to a new and deeper level of relationship with God. Yahweh, the prophet says, has had enough of burnt offerings; the Lord is no longer delighted with the blood of bulls, lambs, or goats. Isaiah is not saying that God does not appreciate the sacrifice, but Yahweh realizes that for many people the offering is hollow. The external sign of a sacrifice is worthless without the proper interior conversion, and God knows that for many in the community of Judah their hearts are far from his. Isaiah wants the people to know that external worship alone, that is action without an interior conversion, is sheer hypocrisy. It means nothing to act without an interior desire to worship God. Thus, the Lord provides the prophet with the words that will challenge the people to move beyond action to a true transformation of self, a conversion to a oneness with the Lord. What does God want to see? Isaiah is very clear and specific: cease doing evil and learn to do good; seek justice and rescue the oppressed; defend the orphan and plead for the widow.

If the people wondered how they were to achieve this interior conversion, Isaiah provides a method that comes from God. It will not be as easy as Joe Hardy's external transformation, but then Joe's change was not only abrupt, it did not last. The permanent transformation, that is the conversion that the Hebrews seek, must come from God. Yahweh can transform their lives of sin and make them more whole. However, Isaiah is also very clear that the people must be willing to achieve such a change; they must be open and obedient to God's message and challenge. Then and only then will the people experience the true transformation that they need, the true conversion God seeks in them. Yes, God is disappointed with the renegade actions of the people of Judah, but Yahweh never abandons his people completely and, thus, always provides a way out, a promise of renewal to Judah, if the people will be converted.

The prophet continues, saying it is only by repentance that disaster will be averted. If the people rebel, they will be devoured by the sword of their enemies. We all know very well from salvation history that God was not pleased with the lack of effort shown by the people of Judah. Their inability to be converted to a new and stronger commitment to the Lord cost them greatly — fifty years of exile in Babylon.

We, like the Hebrews, need to be transformed, converted on the inside, to a richer relationship with God. We need to look into our hearts and ask the ofttimes difficult question — what must I do in order to be more like the person God wants me to be, the person who God created in me? This is the conversion we need, but many of us, like Joe Hardy, in our efforts to seek renewal, experience only an external transformation, one that looks good but is as hollow as the ritual sacrifice the Hebrews offered to God without the interior desire for renewal. We transform our appearance in the hope that we will be a new person, that others will sense something different about who we are. We change our actions in different ways. We may eat better, exercise more, and even eliminate a bad habit or two. These are obviously good ideas, so long as they are accompanied with an interior conversion of heart and mind. Too often, however, the external and internal do not coincide; there is a disconnect between what people see and what God knows to be true. We might lose lots of weight and get into excellent condition for some period of time, but if our attitude and approach to life is not converted, we will generally fall back into our former overweight and out-of-shape existence. We can be transformed rather easily, but it takes much more work to be converted.

The conversion that many seek in our physical appearance is often the desire of our spiritual lives as well, but the same problem of external transformation and internal conversion applies. Unfortunately, many times our spiritual lives are rather hollow. When we pray, are we merely going through the motions, or do we truly wish to give praise and thanksgiving to God? Do we petition the Lord with a true faith, or are we skeptical in our pleas and hold back? When we come to church on Sunday or if we make a visit during the week, is it with the intent of showing up in order to impress others? Are we afraid of what others might think of us if we do not attend, or are we doing our best to seek a new and deeper commitment to God? Do our external actions and our internal desire match?

Life is in many ways a continual experience of transformation. Each and every day opportunities come our way that provide both challenge and the opportunity to grow. It might be painful, but if we have courage and hold out, we might be amazed at what God can do with us. A little story demonstrates the struggles we find in seeking conversion and the pain that it entails, but also the great reward for those who have the courage to seek transformation in the Lord.

Once upon a time two grandparents were in a curiosity shop seeking to buy something special for their granddaughter for her birthday. At almost the same time they both spied a teacup that was beautifully decorated. They said together, "We must buy this cup, for it is the most beautiful we have ever seen." At that very moment the grandparents were startled when the teacup responded, "Thank you for that compliment, but I was not always so beautiful." The teacup proceeded to tell the grandparents its story. "Once," said the teacup "I was simply a soggy lump of clay. But then one day a man with dirty and wet hands threw me onto a wheel and started turning me around and around, and I became so dizzy that I cried out, 'Stop, stop!' 'Not yet,' said the man. He began to poke and punch me until I hurt all over. 'Stop, stop!' I cried. 'Not yet,' he answered and continued to shape me. Finally he did stop, but then something worse happened. He put me into a furnace until I got hotter and hotter and screamed, 'Stop, stop!' 'Not yet,' again the man responded. Finally, when I thought I was going to burn up, he took me from the furnace and a lady began to paint me. The fumes were so bad that I thought I would become sick to my stomach, and thus I exclaimed, 'Stop, stop!' 'Not yet,' said the woman. Finally she did stop, but then she gave me back to the man who again placed me in that horrible furnace. Again after much time in the furnace I pleaded, 'Stop, stop.' 'Not yet,' came the reply. Finally the man took me out of the furnace and allowed me to cool. And when I was cool, a nice lady placed me on the shelf right next to a mirror. When I saw myself in that mirror, I was amazed. I could not believe how I had been transformed from an ugly and soggy piece of clay into a beautiful teacup. And I cried for joy."[1]

Let us be like the teacup and seek the conversion which may be painful but, coming from God, will bring us great beauty. Our reward in heaven will be great!

1. Paraphrased from "The Teapot," in William J. Bausch, *A World of Stories for Preachers and Teachers* (Mystic, Connecticut: Twenty-Third Publications, 1999), pp. 276-277.

Maximizing Your Potential

Once upon a time two beautiful flowers lived side-by-side in a magnificent garden. One was bright yellow and the other was bright blue. From the first moments of their existence these two flowers received profuse praise from the world for their vigor and beauty. "I love your face," said the sun to the yellow flower. "I love your eyes," said the sky to the blue flower. "I love your overall beauty," said the butterfly. "I love your pollen," said the bee. "And I your nectar," said an ant. "I love the shade that you provide," said the grasshopper. The two flowers basked in their glory and all the accolades they received. "Never stop," they said to the world.

One day the yellow flower began to do some work. "What are you doing?" asked the blue flower. "I am making pollen," she answered. "You shouldn't be doing that. It will make you old before your time." The yellow flower did not heed the warning but continued to make her pollen. The next day the blue flower was complimented by the sky, but the sun said nothing to the yellow flower, which seemed a bit withered and worn. "What did I tell you?" said the blue flower. "You must spend all your time making yourself beautiful or no one in the future will care about you." The blue flower primped her petals and primed her color. The yellow flower was content to make pollen.

Several days later a young man was strolling through the garden. He spied the blue flower and picked it. "This must come to my house," he said. "What did I tell you?" said the blue flower to the yellow. "Now I will adorn this man's house while you will sit in the hot sun and wilt." In time when the man was finished with

383

the blue flower he discarded it into the fire. In time when nature had finished with the yellow flower, there was a whole field of yellow blossoms.[1]

This delightful but very challenging story contrasts what happens to those who are prepared and those who are complacent. It is also a tale which demonstrates how different people respond to the gifts given to them by God. Some use gifts wisely and produce an abundance, while others pass up opportunity or use very minimally or unwisely the gifts and possibilities God sends our way. Today's reading from the prophet Isaiah, known as the "Song of the Vineyard," illustrates the failure of the people of Judah to use wisely what God had given them and the consequent result that comes from such an abuse of God's gifts.

In metaphorical language Isaiah summarizes all that God had done to date in salvation history to make the land of Judah a fruitful place and a great nation. Using the image of the people of Judah as a vineyard, the prophet says that God did everything possible for the people. God placed the people in a very fertile land, a place as scripture says, that flowed with milk and honey. God cleared away all the stones from his land, that is the peoples of the region who would not allow the Israelites to grow and flourish. God gave the people the law to show them how to live their lives by loving God and neighbor. The people were special, even unique to Yahweh; they were a singular group, a chosen vine, that God planned to nourish to produce a rich harvest. In order to accomplish this, God sent judges, kings, and finally prophets to govern and assist the people, and to proclaim God's word to them. Even with all this, however, the fruits of the vineyard, that is the works of the Hebrews, were not good. On the contrary, the vineyard produced wild grapes. God expected more from his chosen people. What more could the Lord have done?

The Hebrews did not use the gifts they had been given wisely. They had the land, the law, and the special protection of God. They were given all they could possibly need. Although the people were special to God and were granted opportunities, gifts, and talents, the people made poor choices. They chose other gods; their religious leaders exercised their worldly power and authority wrongly

384

and abused the people, especially the poor. The Hebrews showed little appreciation for all God had done for them; they squandered the opportunities that came their way.

In some important ways the blue and yellow flower in the story were very much like the people of Judah. Both were given equal gifts; they were radiantly beautiful. Both as well were provided the opportunity to do something today to prepare for tomorrow. The blue flower was complacent and missed the occasion to work now in order to prepare for the future. Destruction was the result. The yellow flower, on the other hand, exercised her gifts wisely and fully and in the process created a whole sea of yellow blossoms. The people of Judah, unfortunately, acted more like the blue flower; they were complacent. Even more than complacent, however, they misused the gifts God provided them.

Because the people did not produce good fruit, God's judgment is proclaimed on the nation. The hedge and the wall, symbolic of God's protection for the nation and its people, will be removed. God will allow briars and thorns to overrun the vineyard, a symbol that the nation of Judah will be conquered by pagan peoples. God's sustenance will also be removed; no rain will come to the vineyard. God expected justice but received bloodshed; Yahweh sought righteousness, but obtained only a cry!

Lest we think that the story of the flowers and the Song of the Vineyard are not applicable to our contemporary situation, we must examine our own lives and see how we have used the many and wonderful gifts God has given us. God does not ask too much from us, but the Lord does command that we exercise our potential, be prepared for what may come, and use our gifts wisely. We have all received many wonderful gifts, but have we exercised our potential with what we have been given? We have all been given the gift of faith. This great gift from God is well-defined in the letter to the Hebrews (11:1) as "the assurance of things hoped for, the conviction of things not seen." We have been given the gift of faith, but have we used it to its full potential? When our faith is tested do we give into temptation; do we give up when the situation looks bleak, such as in sickness, unemployment, or problems at home, work, or school? Or do we demonstrate our faith and trust God, as did

Abraham, Moses, Isaiah, and the other great biblical figures of faith? Do we share our great gifts of faith with those not as privileged as ourselves? We have all been given many talents — in the classroom as students and teachers, on the athletic field as players and coaches, in the arts as musicians or painters, in the professional world as physicians, engineers, or architects. How would we answer Jesus when he says, "From everyone to whom much has been given, much will be required; and from the one to whom much has been entrusted, even more will be demanded" (Luke 12:48b). Does the world, whether that be our family, place of business, or the Church, receive some compensation and benefit from all we have been given? Do we show gratitude to God by giving back some of what we have been given?

So often we squander all we have been given or we use poorly or unwisely the manifold gifts of God. The Lord's gifts are bestowed upon us for our benefit and the good of all. We should not seek some compensation or reward for what we do, but rather be content to do what God asks of us, realizing that the gifts we truly seek are not of this world. As Jesus says, "When you have done all that you have been ordered to do, say, 'We are worthless slaves; we have done only what we ought to have done'" (Luke 17:10).

The misuse of God's gifts is illustrated in a little story. Jake was one of the most colorful and well-known people in a small town. Everyone knew him, liked him personally, and appreciated his work as an artist. One day Jake went to the local general store to pick up a few items. He paid for his purchases with a twenty-dollar bill. Everything was normal until the sales clerk noticed after Jake had left that she had ink smudges on her sweaty palms and there was a similar smudge on the twenty-dollar bill. She went to the store owner, who in turn called the police. The bill was counterfeit. When the police went to Jake's home, they noticed that a real twenty-dollar bill was taped to his easel. It seems that Jake had meticulously painted very detail of that bill. A more thorough search of the apartment revealed several beautiful portraits and country scenes that Jake had painted. When sold at auction, some went for $10,000. It seems Jake spent as much, if not more, time creating one twenty-dollar bill as he did painting the expensive canvases. In essence Jake not only tried to steal from the store, he stole from himself in wasting the potential he had been given.

Let us be wise and exercise properly, fully, and for the betterment of God's people the great gifts we have received. May we reject complacency and the temptation to abuse others with the gifts we have. Let us follow the example of Christ who came not to be served, but to serve and give his life as a ransom for the many (Matthew 20:28). Our reward in heaven will be great!

---

1. Paraphrased from "A Tale of Two Flowers," in John Aurelio, *Colors! Stories of the Kingdom* (New York: Crossroad, 1993), pp. 79-80.

**Proper 16
Pentecost 14
Ordinary Time 21
Jeremiah 1:4-10**

Answering The Call Of The Lord

He was born to a pious German woman and her Lutheran pastor husband in 1875. With parents of erudition and raised in a Christian environment, it was not unexpected that he studied at the university. He was a brilliant student and achieved doctorates in both philosophy and theology by the time he had reached his early twenties. As an academic he was well-known, especially in his immediate purview of colleagues. In 1910, however, he wrote a book, *The Quest for the Historical Jesus*, a monograph that used historical criticism to analyze the Gospel narratives and made him an international celebrity in theology almost overnight.

At the top of his field, one might think it odd to change direction in life, but God was calling him to do something different, to dedicate himself to music. As a young man he had toyed with the idea of being a professional musician. Now, as he approached the age of forty, he began to tour the major European cities as a concert organist. His interpretation of the music of Johann Sebastian Bach, both on the concert stage and on some of the first phonographic recordings, was praised by critics.

After conquering two different disciplines, theology and musical performance, God called him to change directions in his life again. This time the shift was a radical step — he was invited to become a medical missionary in Africa. The challenge would be great, but he went with confidence that all would be provided. French Equatorial Africa had only been "opened" by Christian missionaries a few decades previously. In the 1920s he established a hospital on the Gonge River in the nation of Gabon. The facility served two functions: as a hospital, meeting the immediate needs of the local area, and as a leper sanitarium for the greater geographic region.

After laboring for more than thirty years in Africa as a doctor, the world officially recognized the contribution of Albert Schweitzer. In 1952 he was awarded the Nobel Peace Prize. The inscription read, "Granted on behalf of the brotherhood of nations."

Albert Schweitzer accepted several different calls from God and he did so without hesitation and with complete commitment to the task. He did not question the nature of the call, its perceived difficulty, nor his suitability for the task. He placed trust in God that what he needed would be provided. His confidence was not misguided, for the world has been made a better place because one man took the call from God seriously and answered using the gifts and talents he possessed.

Albert Schweitzer is an excellent example of how one man answered the call of the Lord. In a similar way we are encouraged by today's reading to contemplate our call from God. God will call, but the manner and the timing may not be as we expect. Therefore, it is necessary to have sufficient faith to follow, as did Dr. Schweitzer, the call of the Lord.

Like all the prophets we read in the Hebrew Scriptures, Jeremiah was called to answer God's call in his life by proclaiming God's message. However, as we hear in today's reading, Jeremiah, one of the so-called three "major" prophets, was called from the moment of his conception. As the prophet writes (1:5) God's words to him, "Before I formed you in the womb I knew you, and before you were born I consecrated you; I appointed you a prophet to the nations." Jeremiah did not think himself qualified for this great task. Possibly he declined the invitation because he felt he did not possess sufficient talent. He probably knew the task would be great and did not feel up to such an arduous and possibly dangerous role in God's plan. It could also be the case that Jeremiah realized that his role might make him very unpopular with certain segments of Hebrew society. He may have come to the conclusion that the role of prophet would cost him greatly and that he did not have sufficient strength to answer God's call in this way. Jeremiah complained to God that he was a mere youth, but Yahweh answered that he was to go where God sent him and he was to speak God's word to the people. God touched the prophet and placed on his lips the words he needed to complete his task. The Lord gave Jeremiah the ability and the authority to destroy the enemies of God and overthrow the forces that were allied against God's plans. He was to plant new beginnings for Judah, a new crop that would bear good fruit.

God calls us at numerous times in our life and in a multitude of ways. We always have the chance to respond. Jeremiah was called to be a prophet while still in the womb, but most of us will grow into an understanding and knowledge of God's call in our lives more gradually. The important thing is to be open to the call and the many possibilities and opportunities it brings. This need for openness is well-illustrated by the famous parable of the workers in the vineyard (Matthew 20:1-16). We remember that the owner of the vineyard, who represents God, invites those who seek work to come to the vineyard at different times. As God called the workers, so the Lord may call us in the morning, mid-day, afternoon, or twilight of our life. We, therefore, must be ready to hear God's call and respond. We should be content when and how God calls and not be envious of others, who may respond late in life or in a manner that we would have liked but never followed, yet receive the same attention and compensation as ourselves. The point of the parable is, of course, that God's mercy is abundant. We seem to think if we respond early to God's call we may miss out on something, but the reality is that an early response translates into the opportunity to enjoy all that God provides for a longer period of time. The ability and courage to answer God's call should always be paramount in our lives.

God calls, but as with Albert Schweitzer, neither the timing of the call nor its nature can be known in advance. We do know, however, that all people are called to the common vocation of holiness and, therefore, the common response of discipleship must be ours. How we live our lives of holiness and the method of discipleship that we choose will vary with individuals. Many people are called to marriage and family. This specialized vocation of sharing completely two lives and making them one in heart and mind, together

391

with the all-important responsibility of assisting children to discover the call of the Lord in their lives, is certainly highly valued by God and our society. Jesus obviously respected the institution of marriage from his presence at Cana at the outset of his public ministry (John 2:1-12), and God from the very outset commanded men and women, "Be fruitful and multiply" (Genesis 1:28). Some people are called to the special witness value associated with the single life, a sign that is especially important in a society which often labels the solitary life as odd or even abnormal. Many people who are never called nor possess the gifts that the commitment of marriage requires nevertheless seek to "be normal" and in the process create great consternation for themselves and much pain for many. The vocation of the single life should be highly valued. All of us are called to varied professional vocations as teachers, physicians, engineers, clerical workers, civil servants, and a host of other day-to-day occupations. We, like Albert Schweitzer, may change our work vocations, with the belief that the Lord and/or opportunity calls us to do something new and different.

There are times as well when many people are called to do something that they did not choose nor desire. Like Jeremiah and many other leading figures in the scriptures, life may necessitate a change in plans. From all we can tell from his writing, Jeremiah did not care to be a prophet, nor for that matter did Jonah, who ran away, and Amos, who did not feel qualified for the job. Nevertheless, all of these prophets in the end answered God's call as it was spoken to them. In the opinion of many, the premier example of one who answered the Lord's call is Mary of Nazareth, the Mother of God. Engaged to Joseph at a young age, she probably expected to live a rather ordinary life as a Jewish wife and possibly mother. Then, without warning and with almost no time even to think about the opportunity, Mary's whole future was transformed by the visit of the Angel Gabriel and the invitation extended for her to become the Mother of God. Unhesitatingly, she responded with her famous *fiat*, "Here am I, the servant of the Lord; let it be with me according to your word" (Luke 1:38).

Like the great figures of scripture, we may be asked to walk a road less traveled, more treacherous, and not one we choose. We may have the difficult task of walking the road of ill-health with a loved one. It is not what we expect nor choose, but this may for a time, long or short, be the vocation that God asks of us. Are we ready to answer the call? We may be asked to follow a route we did not plan for the betterment of others — the needs of children, people in the community who ask our service, fellow workers who require our assistance. It may not be what we expected, but it is the call of the Lord and we need to respond. Too often we take short-cuts and do not allow the opportunities of God's call to grab us; we allow them to pass by and they are lost, possibly forever. Abraham Maslow, the famous psychologist, often challenged his students by asking, "Who among you will be the next Einstein, the next Roosevelt, or the next Schweitzer?" When the students squirmed uneasily in hearing the challenge, he would respond, "If not you, then who?"

Yes, God will call in many ways and at different times. The call may not be what we expected or want, but the task is to have sufficient faith to know that the vocation to which we are drawn is God's call and, therefore, pregnant with possibilities. A well-known story helps us to understand the need for faith in following the call of the Lord.

Long ago on a high mountaintop three trees were speaking about their future dreams. The first tree said, "I would really like to made into a cradle, so that a newborn baby might rest comfortably and I could support that new life." The second tree looked down at a small stream that was flowing into a big river and said, "I want to be made into a great ship, so I can carry useful cargo to all corners of the world." The third tree viewed the valley from its mountaintop and said, "I don't want to be made into anything. I just want to remain here and grow tall, so I can remind people to raise their eyes and think of God in heaven who loves them so much."

Years passed and the trees grew tall and mighty. Then one day three woodcutters climbed the mountain in order to harvest some trees. As they cut down the first tree, one of the men said, "We will make this one into a manger." The tree shook its branches in protest; it did not want to become a feed box for animals. It had grander ideas for its beauty. But the woodcutters made it into a manger and sold it to an innkeeper in a small town called Bethlehem. And when the Lord Jesus was born, he was placed in that manger. Suddenly the first tree realized it was cradling the greatest treasure the world had ever seen. As the woodcutters cut down the second tree, they said, "We will make this into a fishing boat." The tree protested, but the woodcutters did as they planned and a man named Simon Peter bought it. And when the Lord Jesus needed a place from which to address the crowds that were pressing upon him, he got into that little fishing boat and proclaimed the Good News. And the second tree suddenly realized it was carrying a most precious cargo, the King of heaven and earth. The woodcutters then came to the third tree and said, "The Romans are paying good money these days for wooden beams for their crosses. We will cut this tree into beams for a cross." The tree protested so hard that its leaves began to shake and then fall onto the ground, but it was cut down, none-theless, and made into beams.

One Friday morning the third tree was startled when its beams were taken from a woodpile and shoved onto the shoulders of a man. The tree flinched when soldiers nailed the man's hands to the wood; the tree felt shamed and humiliated. But early on Sunday morning, as the dawn appeared, the earth trembled with joy beneath the tree. The tree knew that the Lord of all the earth had been crucified on the cross it made, but now God's love had changed everything. And the cross from that third tree stands tall to remind people to raise their eyes and think of the God in heaven who loves them. And did you notice, how in each case, being cut down was the price that was paid for entering into God's glory?

Let us be more like Albert Schweitzer and Jeremiah and answer God's call. The journey we will take may be long and possibly circuitous, but in the end the goal we seek, salvation with God, the source of all good things, is worth our best effort. Let us answer God's call; our reward in heaven will be great!

Be Thankful For What You Have

Once upon a time there was a fisherman who lived with his wife in a tiny hut by the sea. One day as the man was fishing, his line jerked violently, and when he pulled it in he found a huge fish which spoke to him, "Fisherman, I beg you to let me live, for I am a prince turned into a fish." The man said, "Why not? Any fish that can talk deserves to be thrown back." Thus, the man went home that evening with nothing for dinner. He told his wife the story and she berated him, "Why did you not make a wish before you let him go?" But he replied, "What would I ask for? I am happy." Then his wife said, "Go back and tell the fish we want a cottage; I am tired of living in this little hut." So he went back and said, "Fish of the sea, listen to me. My wife has a wish to make of thee." And the fish came swimming to shore and asked what she wanted. The fisherman replied, "A cottage." When the man returned home, his wife was in a lovely cottage with flowers outside and a bench on the front porch. He said to her, "Now you will be happy in this beautiful cottage." She only replied, "We will see!"

One week later the woman said to the fisherman, "Husband, this cottage is getting too small for us. Go tell the fish that I want a mansion." The man protested saying, "The cottage is fine; I can't go ask for something else." But the woman prevailed and the man returned with a heavy heart and called out to the fish, in a sea which was now rougher: "Fish of the sea, listen to me. My wife has a wish to make of thee." The fish came to the shore and asked, "What does she want this time?" "She wants to live in a mansion," replied the fisherman. The fish replied, "All right, you shall have a mansion." When he returned home, he beheld a lovely mansion with magnificent fireplaces and gorgeous furniture and rugs. "Now you will certainly be happy," the man said to his wife. Again she replied, "We will see."

Two weeks later the woman again came to her husband and said the mansion was not adequate. "Go back and tell the fish," she ordered, "that I want to be a queen and live in a castle." But the fisherman was again horrified and protested, "I can't do that. He has already given us so much." But the woman insisted and, thus, again the man went to the sea, that was now churning with white caps and dark green water, and made his usual cry, "Fish of the sea, listen to me. My wife has a wish to make of thee." The fish again appeared and asked, "What does she want now?" "Alas," said the fisherman, "she wants to be a queen and live in a castle." "All right," said the fish, "she can be a queen and you can both live in a castle." When the man returned home, he saw a giant stone castle with servants and trumpeters to announce the arrival of important guests. His wife was seated on a throne of gold inlaid with precious stones. The man remarked, "Oh, this is magnificent. Now you can be a queen and we will live in a castle. You will be happy now." "We will see," was the woman's only response.

Three weeks later the woman again came to her husband and said, "Go tell the fish that I want to be the pope." The man was thunderstruck and speechless. When he gathered himself, he told his wife, "I cannot ask for this favor. It is beyond reason." But she replied, "You must ask, for I am the queen and you must obey." Thus, the fisherman again returned to the sea which by this time was dark and nasty and a fierce wind was blowing. He called out as before, "Fish of the sea, listen to me. My wife has a wish to make of thee." The fish came to the shore and said, "Now, what does she want?" "She wants to be the pope," the fisherman responded. "All right, go home. She now is the pope." When the man returned home, he saw the castle had been turned into a huge cathedral and he saw hundreds of bishops walking the grounds. Many were kissing the hem of his wife's robe, for she was now the pope. The man told his wife, "Now you are the pope; you can't ask for anything more. Now you will be happy." "We will see," came the response.

Four weeks later the woman again said to the fisherman, "Husband, go back to the fish and tell him I want to be the ruler of the world and the sun and the moon and the stars. I want to be empress of the universe!" The man pleaded, "No, I cannot do this. It is impossible. I can't." But his wife badgered him day and night and drove him to agree finally to her demands. Thus, he once again went to the sea which was a cauldron of wild waves, with thunder and lightning overhead and rain pounding the surf. He again called out, "Fish of the sea, listen to me. My wife has a wish to make of thee." The fish again came to shore and asked, "Well, what does she want this time?" The fisherman shouted over the storm, "She wants to be ruler of the heavens and the sun and the moon and the stars. She wants to be empress of the whole universe." "No!" shouted the fish. "Go back home and you will find your wife in a tiny hut by the sea, and it is there that you will live hand-to-mouth until you die." And when the fisherman returned home, he saw his wife in the hut just as the fish had predicted.[1]

The woman in the story was never satisfied with what she had. From rather humble beginnings, her requests for material possessions and then power and prestige only became greater until at last the fish said, "No," and she and her husband returned to the humble hut where they began. The Hebrew people had been given much by Yahweh. They received their special status as a people unique and special to God; they were God's holy people. They were given the Law to serve as a guide to living their lives. They were given great leaders such as Moses, who challenged Pharaoh, executed the Israelites' release from bondage, and then led the people through the desert to the door of the promised land. Joshua followed Moses and directed the conquest and settlement of the land. Judges, kings, and prophets were sent to rule, guide, and exhort, but even with all that God had provided, the people were not satisfied. Their failure to show gratitude properly and to respond rightly to the graciousness of God cost them dearly; they were exiled to Babylon. Today the prophet Jeremiah summarizes Israel's failures and predicts that they, like the fisherman and his wife, will eventually lose all they had gained because of their greed and lack of gratitude.

The whole of chapter 2 of Jeremiah's long book of prophecy is his first oracle against Israel. Jeremiah wrote to the people of Judah just prior to their exile. His was one of the last warnings and, thus, he became the bearer of woe, a condition created by the unfaithfulness of the people. The prophet stigmatizes Judah's religious leaders' desertion of Yahweh through their worship of pagan idols and cults. The people have entered into alliances with those who will draw them away from God and the Law. Thus, the central charge the prophet makes against the people is idolatry — an accusation that is made against all of Israel's religious leaders.

God is mystified by the attitude and actions of the Hebrew people. In the voice of the prophet, God asks, "What wrong did your ancestors find in me that they went far from me, and went after worthless things and became worthless themselves?" (2:5). Jeremiah tells the people that it was God who brought the people into a plentiful land "to eat its fruits and its good things" (2:7b). But instead of responding in thankfulness and praise to God, the people defiled the land and made the heritage of God an abomination. Even priests, who were responsible for the law, did not know Yahweh; rulers transgressed God's will by oppressing the people, and many prophesied by Baal.

The prophet goes on to speak of Israel's folly in transferring loyalty to an unknown god. This is especially tragic because no nation of that day with a god changed deities, and Israel should know after all that has happened that there are no other gods but Yahweh. Israel has transferred its loyalty from Yahweh to something that brings them nothing. The prophet claims that the heavens should be appalled and shocked at Israel's actions, for the people have committed two evils: they have forsaken Yahweh, the fountain of living water, and they have created for themselves new gods. But these new gods are like cracked cisterns that can hold no water; they are useless, empty, and void. Ironically, Jeremiah tells the people that all this tragedy could have been avoided if the people had listened to the prophets and been faithful to their covenantal ties with God.

We have all been blessed by the abundance of God. These blessings come in material things, opportunities that come our way, the faith we share, the talents we have been given, and even the responsibilities that life demands. In our consumer-driven society we all, at times, tend to be like the fisherman's wife. We want more and more and are never quite satisfied with what we have. We wish to move to the next level of materialism, power, and opportunity. In our greed, which may be unrealized, we fail on a few fronts. Often we fail to be thankful to God for what we have been given. Most of us know that there are three basic forms of prayer — praise, petition, and thanksgiving. All of us are very good at payers of petition. When we need or want something, we immediately make the connection with God through prayer and voice our request. Sometimes we are rather demanding in our request. We want what we perceive we need and we want it immediately. Many are good at prayer of praise, knowing that God must always be praised as the Creator, Redeemer, and Sanctifier of the world. Often, however, we fail to acknowledge the good things we have and our prayers of thanksgiving are few. Rather than thanking God we almost "assume" that we deserve what we have and simply want more. We make the mistake of the fisherman's wife and the Hebrew people. If we are not careful, we too will lose all we have.

Our society often fails to give thanks to others. Many take what others do as an expectation and rarely, if ever, say thanks. It may be part of a youngster's regular routine to be dropped off at school by a parent, but before exiting the car should not the child say, "Thank you"? In most families the lady of the house prepares the meals, generally working very hard in the process. But do family members acknowledge her work by stating and meaning, "Thank you"? At our 8 to 5 jobs it is most assuredly the task of clerical people to keep their supervisors on schedule and to assure that their paperwork is complete and accurate, but how often are these hardworking employees given a heart-felt "thank you" for what they do? Too often people simply assume that this is their job and, therefore, no thanks is given.

On a more general level, are we as a people thankful to God and others for the opportunities, talents, and responsibilities we have? We can certainly thank God for our talents by exercising them well, fully, and wisely, and not allowing them to stagnate nor hurt others. We can be grateful for opportunities by doing our best to fulfill what these occasions bring. We cannot participate in every plan or possibility that comes our way, but we often ignore and pass by opportunities out of laziness, selfishness, or lack of interest. Such actions express an attitude that says, "I am not grateful." We must be thankful as well for the responsibilities that life presents to us. Often these responsibilities, such as caring for an elderly parent, the need to attend to a wayward teenager, or answering the call of the community or church to service, may not be the easy route nor what we expected. Yet, even in the darkest hours, we must be grateful. Jesus showed us the perfect example, for when he knew that death was imminent, he asked God, "My Father, if it is possible, let this cup pass from me; yet not what I want but what you want" (Matthew 26:39b). Jesus accepted his fate and was grateful to God for what he was asked to do. Our attitude must be the same.

The fisherman's wife was never satisfied with what she had and her lack of gratitude cost her and her husband all that they had gained. The Hebrews, in a similar way, failed to demonstrate their gratitude to God for the multiple gifts showered upon them. Their failure led to exile in Babylon. Let us, therefore, not follow this same path, but rather be grateful for all that God has given us, in time, talent, and treasure. Let us use these gifts wisely for the betterment of all. If we can, our reward in heaven will be great!

---

1. Paraphrased from "The Fisherman and His Wife," in William J. Bausch, *A World Of Stories for Preachers and Teachers* (Mystic, Connecticut: Twenty-Third Publications, 1998), pp. 73-75.

Proper 18
Pentecost 16
Ordinary Time 23
Jeremiah 18:1-11

Salvation — It's Up To Us

Once upon a time there was a piece of a jigsaw puzzle. It did not know it was a piece of a jigsaw puzzle; it only knew that it was there and it was pretty nice to be there. There were many other pieces which also knew little of themselves or their whereabouts. The pieces lived together, jumbled up in a big box. This first puzzle piece seemed to live quite well on its own. It ate its own food, drank its own drink, did its own work, and enjoyed its own peace. Seldom did the puzzle piece consider why it was different than all the other pieces. It rarely wondered, for example, why it ate and drank things that others would not try or why it felt quite comfortable next to some pieces and very uncomfortable next to others. These questions rarely came; they certainly did not affect how the puzzle piece lived its life.

One day, for some inexplicable reason, the first puzzle piece felt drawn, as if by a large magnet, to another piece. Maybe it was their common green color, maybe it was not. It only knew that the two fit perfectly together. It was as if it had been ordained to be that way from the beginning. When some other pieces saw that the two pieces had come together on their own, they also began to pair up — reds with reds, blues with blues, square pieces with square pieces. Some pieces could not find a proper fit; others did not want to try. Those, however, that did find a match felt more fulfilled.

A little later two pairs found that they could become one group of four. In a flurry of activity, two pieces became three, two pairs became a quartet, and two quartets an octet. In the midst of all the activity, the original puzzle piece yelled out, "Where will it all end?"

401

The question stunned the pieces; all was quiet. No one had ever thought of this before. One piece offered an answer, a second another response. The way was not clear, the future was uncertain. Without clear vision the pieces began to separate and for the first time in their lives they felt loneliness. The confusion that had been caused was worse than their original state. Something had to be done; it was simply intolerable to live without an answer. Then all of a sudden, miraculously or mercifully, someone or something dropped a picture in front of them. All the pieces stopped and stared. "It is us," they all shouted in unison. "At last, we know exactly how we fit and where we go!" In the end all the pieces reunited, the puzzle was solved, the picture was completed, and everyone lived happily ever after.[1]

The puzzle pieces were composed of all sizes, shapes, and colors. On the surface they did not seem to belong together at all, but once they realized that their unity and ability to complete the picture was up to them, they began to work as a team, in unison. Yes, they needed some assistance from above, someone or something to show them the "big picture" and how they fit together, but they had to be willing and ready to come and act as one. Their unity was a question of free will, the ability to say yes or no to any and all questions, opportunities, and possibilities.

In some important ways the story of the puzzle pieces closely illustrates the life and opportunities that the Hebrew people had. Unfortunately, unlike the puzzle pieces, who upon seeing the big picture were able to come together and find unity, the Hebrews were too independent and distrustful of each other to bring unity to the southern Kingdom of Judah and its people. God, the potter, was molding them, but as a result of the poor use of their free will, they failed to form themselves into a cohesive unit. They had the opportunity to grow toward God, but they wasted their chance. If we are not careful, the same fate may happen to us.

We hear in today's First Lesson the famous tale in Jeremiah of his visit to the potter's house. The prophet is told to go to the potter and observe his work so that the word of God can be proclaimed to him there. The potter is working hard at his trade, molding and shaping his clay pots as he wishes. God, of course, is the potter and the people of Judah the clay in his hands. God can mold the people of Judah to his own wishes. God can shape and control, but he does so in response to the people. God wishes the nation, the people of Judah, to be vibrant and pro-active. If the potter creates a beautiful pot, a unique people special to God, and the people, through their own free will, wander away in order to do evil, then God will re-mold the pot into another form that is not as worthy as the first. If, however, an inferior pot is made first and the people, again through their own free will, transform their lives and choose righteousness, God will refashion the first pot and create a new one that is far superior. God can create goodness and beauty from what appears to be evil and ugly. But God can also transform attitudes of superiority and cries of victory into a great defeat. God warns the Hebrews, as we hear at the end of today's lesson, "Look, I am a potter shaping evil against you and devising a plan against you. Turn now all of you from your evil way and amend your ways and your doings" (18:11c).

The people are like the puzzle pieces; they are of all types and are all jumbled up in the box. They have the overall picture provided by the Law and the prophets who speak God's word, but they have chosen to ignore the picture, God's plan for them. The leaders of the Hebrews have been derelict in their responsibilities, especially toward the poor. Power and prestige have corrupted the leaders so that individual pursuit and need have come ahead of the community's necessities. God is greatly disappointed in the actions of his chosen people and will now act to punish those responsible for the nation's failures.

We believe that God is all-loving, omniscient, omnipotent, and filled with compassion. Knowing this reality, we might legitimately ask why the world suffers. Why do pain, problems, and suffering exist in such abundance? If the Hebrews were God's chosen, holy, and special people, why does God, as we just heard, threaten evil against them? Why do people in positions of public trust commit acts that cause others not only to lose faith in the individual, but in the system as well? Why do people fight one another and the only question between them is the color of their skin, their political preference, or religious belief?

403

The basic answer to these challenging questions is personal choice, our free will to say yes or no to God at any time in any way. Soren Kierkegaard, the famous nineteenth century existentialist philosopher and theologian, once wrote, "Faith is a matter of choice, our personal decision in finding God." This personal decision, our free will, is why the world suffers. It is free will that allows the drunk to drive and kill others. It is free will that allows people in public service to break the law and thus lower the integrity of the system. It is free will that places certain members and groups in society on the fringe and does not allow them to participate. Free will moves us closer to or further from God. As Kierkegaard wrote, it is our decision; faith is our choice. We must, therefore, judiciously guard and rightly use this most precious gift.

God is the one in control and we, God's greatest creation, have absolute dependence upon God. The Lord does not act arbitrarily, but rather, responds by taking human free will into consideration. God reacts to our words and actions. God most assuredly wishes good to prevail and desires conversion of hearts and minds; the Lord will always be faithful to his commitment to us. We are reminded by the Pauline author in 2 Timothy: "If we have died with him, we will also live with him; if we endure, we will also reign with him; if we deny him, he will also deny us; if we are faithless, he will remain faithful for he cannot deny himself" (2:11-13). God, like any loving parent, waits for us, his sometimes prodigal children, to return home. Like the father in the famous parable of the prodigal son (Luke 15:11-32), God waits for us; all we need do is to make the first step.

We must make a commitment to use our free will wisely. In our homes and in our relationships with family members and close friends, we must use our free will to foster and build up relationships and to promote love and harmony in the home. Too many times today people use their free will to be confrontational, offering their own opinion as the only valid one. We assert our power to the detriment of others. But we can, if we choose, seek unity, like the puzzle pieces, to see how we can fit and work together in God's overall picture for our world. A commitment to the proper use of free will must also be made in our daily lives in society and in the decisions we make regularly. Too often today we hear of political and business decisions that are made to benefit an individual or a select group of people. The basic Christian concept of working for the promotion of the common good seems to fade from our minds, and, therefore, our actions. Contemporary society, especially here in the United States, is plagued with what people call "random acts of violence." The exaltation of the individual, so much promoted by people today, is antithetical to the development of unity and community. The picture we desire will never be complete if we choose to "go it alone" or "do our own thing," as contemporary parlance puts it. In place of individualism, we must offer to be remolded by God into a united and whole people. In place of random acts of violence, we must substitute random acts of kindness. In place of exercising power, we must offer humility. We must be willing as individuals to sit at the lowest end of the table, as Jesus tells us, so that we can be asked one day to come up higher (Luke 14:7-11).

Free will, one of the two great gifts that separates us from the rest of God's creation, is a powerful tool that can be used for good or evil; the choice is *always* ours! God will never place any of us in handcuffs and demand compliance to a certain response or set way of doing things. Let us, therefore, this day recommit ourselves to the wise and proper use of this great gift. May we seek to be remolded by God, the great potter, into the image of Christ, so that we can be a people unique and special, a community that others would be inspired to follow. Let us set our goal to find our way to the loving embrace of God, the source of all that is good.

---

1. Paraphrased from "The Jigsaw Puzzle," in John Aurelio, *Colors! Stories of the Kingdom* (Mystic, Connecticut: Twenty-Third Publications), pp. 19-20.

Actions Bring Consequences

Once upon a time an otter rushed before the king and cried out, "My lord, you are a king who loves justice and rules fairly. You have established peace among your kingdom, yet now there is no peace." "Who has broken the peace?" inquired the king. "The weasel," answered the otter. "I dove into the lake to hunt for food for my children, leaving them in the care of the weasel. While I was gone, my children were killed. 'An eye for an eye,' the Good Book says. I demand vengeance!" The king thus sent for the weasel, who soon appeared before the monarch. "You have been charged with the death of the otter's children. How do you plead?" demanded the king. The weasel began to weep and said, "Alas, my Lord, I am responsible for the death of the otter's children, though it was clearly an accident. As I heard the woodpecker sound the danger alarm, I rushed to defend my land and in so doing trampled the otter's children by accident."

Hearing this the king summoned the woodpecker and asked, "Is it true that you sounded the alarm with your mighty beak?" "It is true, my Lord," replied the woodpecker. "I began the alarm when I spied the scorpion sharpening his dagger." Then the scorpion appeared before the king and was asked if he had sharpened his dagger. When the scorpion stated it was true, the king responded, "Do you understand that such an action is a declaration of war?" "I understand," replied the scorpion, "but I prepared myself only because I observed the turtle polishing his armor." But the turtle, when summoned by the king, said in his defense, "I would not have polished my armor had I not observed the crab preparing its sword."

The king thus asked the crab, "Were you preparing your sword?" The crab declared in his own defense, "I saw the lobster swinging its javelin and thus I readied my sword." But the lobster, when he appeared before the king, explained, "I began to swing my javelin when I saw the otter swimming toward my children, preparing to devour them." Thus, the king turned to the otter and said, "You, not the weasel, are the guilty party. The blood of your children is upon your head. Whoever sows death shall reap it."

The otter never considered that its action against the lobster would have such consequences. It never thought beyond its limited purview; it could not possibly fathom that it had done anything wrong. The story of the otter's children provides an important illustration of what a thoughtless act can produce. It also serves to warn us that we must seriously consider the consequences and ramifications of our actions. It was true for the Hebrews during the time of the prophet Jeremiah and it is true today as well.

God's frustration over the Hebrews' apparent disregard for their actions brims over into a powerful indictment against the nation of Judah. The people, especially the religious leaders, have been warned for centuries by the Judges, the Kings, and most recently the Prophets that God is displeased with the faithlessness of the people. Idolatry is rampant as people worship Baal, the god of their pagan neighbors, and set up shrines to false gods on the high places. Religious leaders and others in positions of power, wealth, and authority, regularly oppress the poor which places them even further on the margins of society. People have transgressed the law and made no effort to seek reconciliation with God. Thus, the Lord speaks an oracle against Judah, stating that it will be a doomed nation upon which God's wrath and judgment will fall.

The prophet forecasts a future of great gloom for Judah and its people. He says the Hebrews in Judah have been foolish, not knowing God, and demonstrating how skilled they are in perpetuating evil. God will abandon the people and the manifestations of this reality will be many. The birds will leave the land and with them their joyful song. The rich and fruitful land, once flowing with milk and honey, will become an empty waste and a desert. Cities which once flourished will be laid in ruin. The hills will quake and the earth will be made a waste and a void.

God's promised response to the actions of the people should have been no surprise. The on-again off-again relationship the Hebrews experienced with Yahweh led to punishment along the way. More than once during the period of the Judges, the people had fallen victim to the power of outsiders because Israel was unfaithful. Only when a Judge arose did the people begin to conform once again to God's law. The nation of Judah had seen the consequences of a nation's lack of faithfulness to God when the Northern Kingdom of Israel was conquered by the Assyrians. Yet it seems that the message of the loss of the ten northern tribes played no significant role in the conversion of the people of Judah. They never considered that a similar fate could be their lot if they failed to follow God's plan. They seemingly could not understand that there are consequences for their actions.

We live in a world of great beauty and opportunity, but a world which at times can be filled with fear, problems, and many challenges. Too often we go about our business with no thought of the source of both the beauty and the pain. God, the giver of all good gifts, provides us with the opportunity, talents, and time to do our small part to build God's kingdom in our world. Too often we feel, however, that all has been provided for us, and we come to believe that we are in control. We fail to consider how the things we do may affect others. Our attitude of superiority sometimes gets in the way. There is, however, a Hasidic tale that demonstrates the folly of such an understanding of life: Late one evening Rabbi Naftali was out for a walk. As he strolled the neighborhood, he met a watchman walking back and forth at his post. The rabbi asked, "For whom do you work?" The man told the rabbi the name of his employer, but then he continued. "And, Rabbi, for whom do you work?" The watchman's words struck at the heart of the rabbi, who replied, "I am not sure whether I work for anyone or not." Rabbi Naftali walked in silence with the watchman for some time. He then asked the watchman, "Will you come and work for me?" "Oh, Rabbi, I would be honored to be your servant," said the watchman, "but what would be my duties?" The rabbi answered softly, "You must keep reminding me of your question, for I have come to know now that I, like all people, must work for God."

Since we have been given so much we must never forget the reality that God's gifts are given to be used properly. Consequences certainly exist for ourselves based on our actions and work. Right and proper use of God's gifts and effective management of our responsibilities will please God and lead to a pleasant future. If, on the other hand, we squander God's gifts and/or abuse the responsibilities we have been given, the consequences may be devastating. In a similar way, our actions that affect others will also be placed in the crucible of God's judgment and we must be ready. A popular short story by the famous nineteenth-century American writer O. Henry illustrates God's judgment and the consequences for our actions.

Once there was a little girl whose mother had died. Each day the child waited for her father to arrive home from work, for the one thing she desired most was to sit in her father's lap and cuddle up to him. She was emotionally starved and desperate for affection. Each night, however, her father followed the same routine. He prepared dinner, ate with his daughter, washed the dishes, and then plopped into his favorite chair and read until bedtime. When his daughter came to sit in his lap, he would always give the same reply, "Honey, Daddy is too tired. I have worked hard all day. Why don't you go outside and play with your friends?" The girl went outside and amused herself as best she could. As one might expect, the inevitable happened. As the girl grew older she accepted expressions of affection from anyone and everyone who offered them. Finally, instead of playing in the street, she became a prostitute. One day the girl died from an overdose. She approached the gates of heaven and Saint Peter said to Jesus, "She's a bad one, Lord. You know she was a prostitute and died of a drug overdose. I guess that leaves only one place for her." Jesus, however, surprised Peter in saying, "Let her into heaven, but when her father's time for judgment comes hold him responsible for what happened in her life."

God's message of severe displeasure with Judah and the Lord's prediction of doom came about because the Hebrews were too "blind" to see the consequences of their actions. In our Teflon-coated society, in which we often hear people say, "It's her fault not mine," we often fail to take responsibility for and consider the ramifications of our actions. We are like the otter and in a knee-jerk reaction too often blame others and ask for restitution for problems of our own creation. Let us, therefore, learn a lesson and never forget the consequences of our actions. God can punish, but God always loves. Let us love God in return by loving others and taking responsibility for our actions, today and each day of our lives.

Be Compassionate
As God Is Compassionate

Once upon a time there was a great teacher, a guru, who had many followers. People came from far and wide to listen, learn, and be enlightened by this man. There were one-on-one classes and apprenticeships for those who came to learn. When the students had finished with their lessons, the guru sent them into the world to share their knowledge with others as masters in their own right. Just before each student left, the guru would give each a special gift — the teacher taught each student the mantra of life and death. Phrase by phrase the guru taught them until they had memorized it by heart. Then he gave them a warning that as long as they said this mantra faithfully, they would be blessed. Its power would give them insight and clarity of thought and allow them to discern the truth when surrounded by lies. Its power as well would keep them from despair and give them hope in the midst of misery and hopelessness. Their faith would be strengthened and one day their souls would find everlasting life. The disciples were grateful and humbled by this great gift. They were warned, however, that they were never to teach the mantra to anyone; it was for them alone, the enlightened of the world.

For many years students finished their studies with the guru, were taught the mantra, and then went into the world to share their wisdom and to pray the mantra in secret. One day a young man, who had been taught the mantra and was humbled by the gift, came to the master guru ready to enter the world. However, when the teacher warned him not to share the mantra with anyone, he asked why. The master responded, "If you share this mantra with others,

413

then what it was to do for you will be handed over to them, and you will live in darkness, even when the light is all around you. You will know only despair and misery of body and soul for the rest of your life. You will stumble over the truth and be endlessly confused. But worst of all, you will lose your faith and your soul. You will be damned forever."

The disciple turned white and was visibly shaken by the master's words. Nevertheless, he decided that he must do what he must do. He went to the nearest city and gathered multitudes around him. He taught them all many things and the people were enthralled with his stories and wisdom. Then he taught them the mantra line by line, just as the master had taught him. The people left muttering the mantra to themselves.

A number of the master's disciples were in the crowd and they were horrified at the man's actions. He had disobeyed the master and betrayed his community by giving away the wisdom of the mantra to unenlightened people. These disciples immediately went back to the master and told him what had happened. They asked the guru, "Are you going to punish the student for what he has done?" The master looked at them sadly and said, "I do not have to, for he will be punished terribly. He knew what his fate would be if he shared the mantra of life with those who were unenlightened. For him it has become the mantra of death. He will live in darkness and despair, without hope or knowledge of the truth. He will live isolated and alone, without the comfort of faith, and he will even lose his soul. How could I punish him further?" And with these words the old master gathered his few belongings, looked at his students sadly, and said, "I am going to that man who gave away my gift of the mantra of life and death." "Why?" they asked in unison. "Because," he said, "out of all my students he alone learned wisdom and compassion. Now that man is my master." And he left them to follow the man who walked now in darkness and despair, the one who had chosen compassion over wisdom and knowledge.

The story of the master and his disciple provides us with the opportunity to reflect upon how we approach the activities of our life. Do we do things for ourselves principally, or are we more concerned about the needs of others. The guru knew the power of

414

the mantra, but only realized later that in limiting its use he was being selfish and failing to show compassion. When he observed the compassionate act of his disciple, the one who had shared the mantra so all would be enlightened at the cost of his own darkness and despair, he knew that this man was the true teacher, and the one he must follow. God calls us, whatever our status in life, to be compassionate, even when hard words may be necessary. We are to be compassionate as God is compassionate.

Jeremiah had a very difficult mission in proclaiming the judgment of God against the nation of Judah. As we have heard for the past few weeks, the prophet proclaims the words which the Hebrews must have found very hard to hear. Some may have written off his message as the ravings of a madman; others may have believed that he was a voice crying in the desert and ignored what he proclaimed. There must have been others who believed that the warning was not directed toward them. Jeremiah, however, was crystal clear that God had made a judgment against the land and people of Judah. God would not forget their transgressions.

The harsh message which Jeremiah proclaimed could not possibly have been the words he wished to proclaim, but as a prophet he spoke God's message as it was revealed to him, with the hope that the people would reform. As a Hebrew himself, Jeremiah assuredly did not wish the fate that God planned. Thus, as we hear in today's reading, he proclaims a message of compassion as he mourns the loss of the nation. The prophet laments the fact that his people will suffer, but the message is clear — God has abandoned Judah. As the prophet proclaims, the harvest is past, the summer is past, and the people are lost. He mourns for the people and feels their pain. He weeps day and night over the people.

Jeremiah's message against Israel was indeed harsh and difficult to proclaim, but it was God's word and thus necessary. In a similar way, we at times experience the need to speak the difficult word, but we do so in a message that is proclaimed to bring health, wholeness, reconciliation, and possibly conversion and/or transformation to individuals and groups. Parents may find the need to warn their children against the multiple and varied vices which enslave many. The message is difficult to proclaim, but if done in a spirit of compassion, it becomes a message of peace and salvation.

Words of tough love may be necessary to those who are in the grip of an addiction. We would rather not challenge the person, but often it is only by such means that the message of transformation and conversion can be heard. Employers certainly do not like to tell their employees that one's work is unsatisfactory or that the company has made some personnel decisions and, therefore, their jobs will be lost, but this may be the only way for a person to see their inabilities, inadequacies, and possibly the need to move on in life to new ventures and challenges.

It is a much easier road to avoid conflict, to say nothing, or speak only those words that others want to hear. However, in many ways this may be the least compassionate way to assist people. We do nobody a favor by lying; the world is not enriched if we hold all the information we possess for ourselves. The compassionate and progressive thing to do is to follow what is often the difficult, obstacle-laden, and more restricted road. Jesus presents the challenge in this way in the Sermon on the Mount: "Enter through the narrow gate; for the gate is wide and the road is easy that leads to destruction and there are many who take it. For the gate is narrow and the road is hard that leads to life, and there are few who find it" (Matthew 7:13-14).Only by the more difficult path, the narrow gate of compassion, can we place ourselves and others on the correct path that leads to life.

Compassion is a virtue that many experience and exercise through giving. We give of our time, talent, and treasure to meet the needs of others. Certainly Jeremiah gave his life as a prophet to proclaim a hard and difficult message so that his people, the Hebrews, could once again find favor with God. In a similar way Jesus demonstrated compassion by curing the sick, teaching the people, searching for the lost, and ultimately dying to set us free from condemnation. All of us in our varied vocations in life are called to be compassionate through the common vocation of holiness. We may give many things to a variety of peoples and groups, but the most precious gift and the one that shows the greatest compassion and total union with others is our presence. The prophets and Jesus ultimately gave their presence as a compassionate action in the service of others. We must do likewise. A little story illustrates my point.

There once was a wise and much beloved king who cared greatly for his people and only wanted the best for them. The king took a personal interest in people's lives, often disguising himself and wandering about the streets in order see life from the perspective of his people. One day he disguised himself as a poor villager and went to visit the public bath. Many were enjoying fellowship and recreation. The water in the baths was heated, especially in the winter months, by a furnace in a dingy basement underneath the facility. One man was responsible for maintaining the water at the correct temperature. One day the king made his way to the basement to visit with the man who tirelessly tended the fire. The two men shared a meal together and got to know each other. Day after day and week after week the king came to the basement and visited with the man. No one else ever showed any concern for the man. One day the king revealed his true identity to the man. This was a risky move, for the monarch feared that the man might ask for some special royal favor. Instead, the king's new friend looked into his eyes and said, "You left your comfortable palace to sit with me in this hot and dingy cellar. You ate my meager food and showed that you cared about me. You could have bestowed upon me great gifts, but you have given me the greatest gift of all. You gave me the gift of yourself."

Let us demonstrate our compassion. Let us not hold things for ourselves only, but rather, let us, in imitation of the master's disciple, the prophet Jeremiah, and Jesus of Nazareth give away our life. Let us be compassionate as God is compassionate. The reward is eternal life.

Proper 21
Pentecost 19
Ordinary Time 26
Jeremiah 32:1-3a, 6-15

Compassion: Returning Home To God

During the reconstruction period following the great American Civil War, John Sommersby returned to his small Southern town, at least it seemed to be him. Everyone thought that Sommersby had died in the great war between the Union and the Confederacy; all the other soldiers had returned home some time before. He appeared to be different, but then people said that such a war changed a person in more than mind and spirit. He recognized his friends, however, and they recognized him; the whole town celebrated.

Still, despite the celebration there was some doubt as to the identity of the man who had returned. The family dog did not recognize him, and pets never forget the scent of their masters. When Sommersby went to have a new pair of shoes made for himself, the cobbler noticed that the pattern of his foot made before the war no longer fit. It would be John's wife, however, who would be the critical judge. Was this rather gentle and kind man the same person who had gone to war six years previously, a man who had many times been harsh and cruel to her?

Sommersby's home town had been devastated by the Union army during the war, creating an economic crisis. A leader, one who could come forward to take charge and restore the town to greatness once again, was necessary. That person would be John Sommersby. He had a plan to grow tobacco, but capital was necessary for the initial investment of buying the precious and expensive tobacco seed. Confederate money was good no longer and, thus, the people brought what valuables the Yankees had not taken —

rings, bracelets, a silver tea service — and placed it in the trust of John Sommersby, who gathered the valuables and went to buy seed. Although it took longer than expected, he returned with the tobacco seed which the people planted and nurtured to maturity. The yield was great and the price per unit of measure was even greater than Sommersby himself thought possible. The town and its people survived; they experienced redemption.

John Sommersby, however, would not be able to taste the sweetness of victory. Accused of wrongdoing during the war, he was tried and convicted. His punishment was to be hanged until dead. But was this man John Sommersby or someone who looked a great deal like him? The world would never know. The people in Sommersby's town had placed their trust in him, taken responsibility, and been restored. John Sommersby, or whoever this man was, had shown compassion and brought about the redemption of himself and his town through his courage and efforts.

The movie *Sommersby*, produced and released in 1993, depicts the redemption of a man and the community he loves. History is replete with examples of nations, institutions, and individuals who have sought and achieved redemption and the restoration of life to a new and fuller existence. The story of the Hebrews is one of the best examples of a people whose relationship with God was characterized by sin leading to its downfall. But God never forgot his chosen people, those who were "peculiarly his own," and thus, as today's First Lesson metaphorically describes, God will bring redemption to the Hebrews in exile in Babylon; the nation will be restored and the people returned to their homes.

For the past several weeks our scripture passages have concentrated on the many sins of the religious leaders, both in Israel (the Northern Kingdom) and Judah (the Southern Kingdom). We recall that Hosea prophesied doom for Israel because of the idolatrous practices that were so prominent and widespread in the Hebrew community. The first and most basic commandment of God's law was continually violated. Isaiah, writing to the Kingdom of Judah, told the religious leaders of the nation that God was not pleased with their treatment of the people (5:1-7). God had provided the nation with everything it could possibly need — rich land, God's

420

protection, prophets, monarchs — and still the nation produced a poor harvest. God's disappointment was great. Thus, for both Israel and Judah a common fate occurred, namely punishment at God's hand. For Israel this meant loss of their nation; for Judah exile to Babylon.

Jeremiah, from whom we hear in today's First Lesson, was present during the deportation of the Hebrews from Jerusalem, beginning in 588 B.C.E. Thus, he writes to his fellow Hebrews now in exile and presents them with a message of hope, stating that God will restore the nation; redemption is possible. Using metaphorical language, the prophet uses the purchase of a field as a symbol of restoration that God will bring to the land. Moreover, fields and vineyards will once again be bought and sold, prosperity will return to the land, and God's favor will once more shine upon his chosen people.

Jeremiah's message of redemption and restoration was, at it roots, a missive of hope. God, acting like a loving parent, had chastised Judah for its many sins of omission and commission, but now it is time to forgive and rebuild the Hebrew's nation and society. The process can only begin, however, after the people know and believe that God is with them in their endeavor. Thus, Jeremiah, speaking God's word, preaches to the people a message of hope, confident that God is with them.

The restoration and redemption effected by John Sommersby and that experienced by the Hebrews in exile in Babylon must be our hope as well. Throughout life, even on a daily basis, Christians seek to navigate the road that leads back to God, the source of our existence. The road home to God has some detours, potholes, and obstacles, and we will encounter some closures and stop signs along the way. The human condition of incompleteness means that at times along the road all of us will take the wrong turn, be stymied in our progress, or possibly even intentionally take an alternative route. When these times occur, and they most assuredly will happen, we must trust that our knowledge of God will provide the opportunity and avenues to get back on the correct road. God, Francis Thompson's metaphorical "Hound of Heaven," will leave no stone unturned or pathway not taken in a diligent search for us.

God will never tire nor give up in his quest to bring us home. The redemption and restoration that only God can provide for our hearts, minds, and souls is ours for the asking; we must simply respond to the initial invitation of God.

The Parable of the Prodigal Son (Luke 15:11-32) provides an excellent example of the compassion that God has for us on our return home to the Lord. We recall the dissolute life the young son, the so-called prodigal, had lived. When he determined the need to return, his road home, this is his restoration, had begun. It culminated when the boy's father, symbolic of God, provided the forgiveness and redemption he needed. The son never had to say one word; all that was necessary was that he be open to his father's love.

The timelessness of the scriptures tells us that the message of Jeremiah and the Parable of the Prodigal Son are illustrative of how God treats us today and always. God is filled with compassion and only wants what is best for his children. Thus, the Lord provides the means for us to navigate though the ofttimes dangerous and obstacle-ridden waters of life. Our effort is required as well, but with God we most assuredly will find the road home.

The compassion that God showed the Hebrews of old and all of us today must be a virtue which we also demonstrate in our relationships with others. We must remember Christ's exhortation to his disciples: "Be merciful as your Father is merciful ... For the measure you give will be the measure you get back" (Luke 6:36, 38b). Our need to be more God-like in our approach to others is best illustrated in a story.

A young man excitedly told his spiritual director about a dream he had the night before. "I dreamed that I had fallen into a deep pit from which I could not get out. A Confuscist approached and said, 'Let me give you some advice, my friend. If you ever get out of trouble, never get into it again.' A Buddhist came along and said, 'If you can climb up to where I can reach you, I will help you.' A Christian Scientist came along and said, 'You only think you are in a pit.' A self-righteous person said, 'Only bad people fall into pits.' An IRS agent asked, 'Are you paying taxes on this pit?' An optimist came along and said, 'Things could be worse.' A pessimist said, 'Things *will* get worse!' Then along came Jesus who, seeing my situation, jumped into the pit with me. He had me climb up on this shoulders and thus helped me out of the pit."

The story tells us that compassion is endemic to the life of Christian discipleship. We need to jump into the pit and not stand on the sidelines as a spectator or overseer. Let us be grateful for the great love and compassion that others provide and let us reciprocate in word and action, as we collectively travel the path to God and eternal life.

The Justice Of God

During the dark and sullen of days of the Great Depression in New York City there was one man who brought light and joy to an otherwise dreary and hopeless environment, the city's popular and charismatic mayor, Fiorello LaGuardia. The mayor was a favorite of all and was called by devoted New Yorkers "the Little Flower," for the five-foot four-inch mayor always wore a carnation in his lapel. LaGuardia was known for his flashy and colorful personality and the flare with which he did all things. He rode New York City's fire trucks, raided speakeasies with the police, and took whole orphanages to Yankee Stadium to watch the Bronx Bombers generally defeat their opponents. When the New York papers went on strike, he went on radio each Sunday and read the "funnies" to the children.

One bitterly cold winter night in January 1935, the mayor showed up at the night court which served the poorest ward in the city. LaGuardia dismissed the judge that evening and took the bench himself. In short order a woman in tattered clothing was paraded before him, charged with stealing a loaf of bread. She told the mayor that her daughter's husband had deserted her, her daughter was sick, and her grandchildren were starving. The shopkeeper from which the loaf of bread was stolen was insistent upon his revenge, however, and refused to drop the charges. "It's a bad neighborhood," the man said to the mayor. "She has to be punished to teach others a lesson."

LaGuardia heaved a great sigh, turned to the woman, and said, "I've got to punish you. The law makes no excuses. Ten dollars or

425

ten days in jail," he ordered. As he pronounced the sentence, LaGuardia was already reaching into his pocket. He extracted a ten-dollar note and gave it to the bailiff. "Here is the ten-dollar fine, which I now remit. Furthermore, I am going to fine everyone in this courtroom fifty cents for living in a city where a person has to steal a loaf of bread in order to survive and to allow her grandchildren to eat. Mr. Bailiff, collect the fines and give them to the defendant."

The following day the New York papers reported that $47.50 was turned over to a bewildered old woman who had stolen a loaf of bread to feed her starving grandchildren, fifty cents of which was contributed by the red-faced store owner, while some ninety petty criminals, people with traffic violations, and New York City policemen, each of which had paid fifty cents for the privilege of doing so, gave the mayor a standing ovation.

This true story in the life of one of New York City's most beloved personalities, Fiorello LaGuardia, is a good example of how justice can be properly administered. The mayor knew by the strict legal code the woman was guilty and, therefore, must be punished, but he also was wise enough to know that the restitution should be supplied by the very people in society who had created an environment that forced the original situation to develop. Thus, all who were responsible should pay. In a similar way, God was disappointed with the crimes, the sins, of the people of Judah, and thus punishment, namely exile to Babylon, was necessary. But the Lord also realized that the conditions which led to this eventuality were not created by all, but rather came as a result of the greed and indifference of the powerful and elite in society. Thus, it would be the rich who would pay the price for the exile of all.

Biblical scholars tell us that the book of Lamentations was most probably written by one individual who witnessed the first deportation of the Hebrews to exile in Babylon. The author speaks in a metaphorical way of Jerusalem as the lonely widow, bereft of its king and leading citizens. Jerusalem, a city which was once great, has now been humbled to a vassal status under the mighty arm of Babylon. The lot of Jerusalem and its people is bitter, for no one comes to the festivals, her gates are desolate, her priests cry out, and her youth grieve the loss of their futures. Judah will be cast into hard servitude and will pay a heavy price because the religious leaders of the day have created an environment that has caused people to sin. God is not pleased and must exact punishment; but the Lord judges rightly and, thus, those most guilty will pay the greatest fee.

The woe and lamentation that today's First Lesson describes became the historical reality for the people of Judah. The religious leaders were exiled and the nation placed under a vassal status to Nebuchadnezzar. Some people of the day may have thought that these events indicated that the God of the Hebrews had been defeated, but the author of Lamentations says this is not the case. Rather Judah's God does not rise and fall; the God of the Hebrews is universal and has himself caused this calamity. Judah rises and falls depending on the people's ethical and theological response to Yahweh. It is Judah's sin that has led the community into exile.

The images of God's justice that are depicted in the Hebrew Scriptures are found in the life and ministry of Jesus of Nazareth as well. Christ's attitude, like that of his Father, was one that differentiated between the good and the bad, the innocent and the guilty. Jesus was able to look beyond the letter of the law to the more fundamental and important spirit of the law. We recall Jesus' words, "Do not think that I have come to abolish the law of the prophets; I have come not to abolish but to fulfill" (Matthew 5:17). Jesus, as a practicing Jew, appreciated his ancestral heritage and kept the law, thus promoting the kingdom he inaugurated with his earthly ministry, but the Lord was able to know when and when not to apply the law. Maintenance of the Sabbath was fundamental to Hebrew society, as dictated by the third commandment of the Decalogue: "Remember the Sabbath day, and keep it holy" (Exodus 20:8). Yet, Jesus understood that slavish and unthinking adherence to the Sabbath proscriptions was not consistent with the spirit that the Father had intended. God's justice was able to differentiate and to know who had held the Sabbath in their heart and who had not. When the disciples were hungry, they ate heads of grain on the Sabbath; Jesus cured on this sacred day of rest. The Lord made his teaching and the justice of God quite clear, "The Sabbath was made for human beings, not humankind for the Sabbath" (Mark 2:27).

Another example of Jesus' justice in action is his encounter with the woman caught in the act of adultery (John 8:1-11). The religious authorities paraded the woman in front of Jesus to see how he would handle the situation, in hopes that he would do something contradictory to the tradition or law, and thus, add to the mounting evidence in the case they were building against him. The Lord is unconcerned about what the authorities think; his sole interest is the needs of the woman and her future. Yes, punishment must be given; justice must be satisfied, but Jesus will start with those who stand in accusation against the woman. When they all drift off one-by-one, Jesus is left alone with the woman. He asks, "Woman, where are they? Has no one condemned you?" She responds, "No one, sir." Then Jesus gave her the exhortation and challenge, "Neither do I condemn you. Go your way, and from now on do not sin again" (John 8:10-11). Like Mayor LaGuardia, Jesus stood ready to pay the price of the woman's fine, her punishment, but he wanted others to know that the environment of accusation and fear created by the religious leaders of the day had led to the woman's crime.

God's justice is exacted in our time as well. Like the religious leaders of Judah, we make many mistakes and sometimes, possibly unknowingly, create an environment that leads others astray as well. There are times in our lives when we feel as desolate and widowed as Jerusalem at the time of the exile. However, like the Hebrews who after their sojourn in Babylon ended were ready to be embraced by God, so we must stand ready to accept again God's forgiveness and love. There is no situation that is hopeless and no sin that God cannot heal, save that for which we never ask forgiveness. God stands ready to shower his love upon us, but we must be ready to accept. Also, we must be ready to go forward with our newfound reconciliation and love and make a new beginning in our lives. When we are saved, when we experience God's justice, we must make our renewed lives count. A little story illustrates this point.

428

One day a man dove into a raging swollen river to rescue a boy who had fallen in and was being pulled under. It was a tough struggle, but the man succeeded in grabbing an overhanging branch while clinging to the boy with the other hand. The man brought the boy to safety, none the worse for his brush with death. The boy was returned to his mother. As the man was leaving the house, the boy said, "Thank you very much, sir, for saving my life." The man, in turn put one hand under the boy's chin, looked him in the eye, and said, "That's okay, son. Just make sure your life was worth saving."

Fiorello LaGuardia exacted justice on a system that had precipitated a horrible situation, and God, in a similar way, brought justice to the Hebrews for their many sins and transgressions. God's justice will be done in our time, and thus we must be ready to accept what God asks and move forward renewed and prepared to start afresh. Let us be grateful for the presence of God in our lives and make God's justice, his rescue of us, fruitful. Let our lives be worthy of God's justice and love. The price we pay is worth the reward — our eternal happiness with God.

Sermons On The First Readings

For Sundays
After Pentecost
(Last Third)

Conversion To Christ

Richard E. Gribble, CSC

Contemporary life provides almost endless opportunities and possibilities that allow us to maximize our potential. The complexities of today's world, however, create many difficulties and hardships that can either defeat us or strengthen our resolve and faith. I have been privileged to witness and been greatly inspired by how people of great faith negotiate the hurdles of life and come out on top. This collection of sermons, which speaks of conversion, is thus dedicated to one of the champions, my friend Nancy, who has struggled but persevered, never losing hope and always bringing the face of Christ to those she meets each day.

Introduction

In his famous autobiography *The Confessions*, Saint Augustine wrote, "Late have I loved you, O Beauty ever ancient, ever new, late have I loved you." History reveals that Augustine, while now acknowledged to be one of the greatest saints, did not discover the Lord until he had wandered for many years and tried many different religions. Finally, as he says in his book, it was through the prayers of his mother that he was converted to Christianity and went on to become the great bishop, theologian, and defender of the Faith. Augustine experienced conversion in this life, a change that came about over time as he grew in the realization of God's call in his life.

When most people think of conversion, certain images and ideas come to mind. Most, I suspect, associate conversion with the transformation many experience in finding God. There was the dramatic conversion of Saint Paul on the road to Damascus (Acts 9:1-19), an event which many cite as the essence of religious conversion. However, conversion is a much broader concept than simply its application to religion, and most times it is a process that is ongoing, rather than one dramatic experience. We must apply the need and methods of conversion to the multiple aspects of our daily lives.

What in our lives needs to be converted? First and foremost the attitudes and opinions we possess and express in word and action need conversion. Life experience and numerous influences train us to think in specified ways, but we all must admit that our attitudes toward ideas, institutions, and most importantly people are not always God-centered. We sometimes are selfish and hold attitudes and express opinions that benefit ourselves and those special to us, often to the detriment of others. We act in an exclusive manner, dividing those we know into essentially two categories, those who are in and those who are out. Such attitudes are inconsistent

433

with Christ's example, which was always inclusive, calling all to himself and excluding no one. Jesus reached out to all, showing no partiality. We must do the same.

Relationships are another important common area of life that need our conversion. Often people carry old hurts and grudges, thinking that holding onto this pain will in some way punish those who inflicted it. The reality, however, is that we need to release ourselves from these past hurts. If we cannot, these grudges will act like a ball and chain attached to our ankle that weighs us down and does not allow us to move freely. It will probably take time, but we need to be converted to the sure belief that the only way to progress in the Christian life is to let go of the past and move forward. We must recall Jesus' words to the woman caught in the act of adultery and apply them to our relationships with others: "Neither do I condemn you. Go your way, and from now on do not sin again" (John 8:11b). The Lord gave release to the woman; we must do the same with one another.

Habits are a third area that might need conversion in our life. Whether we do something that is personally harmful, such as smoking, excessive drinking, or other addictive behavior, or participate in patterns of life that annoy or are distasteful to others, we need to be converted. As with most conversions, change of this nature will not be effected overnight, but the process of change is itself part of the benefit of conversion. We must start at some place and time; why not start today?

Conversion must be a daily event in which we participate. We need to be converted in heart, mind, and spirit to a greater understanding of our role in God's master plan, but we cannot gain insight without seeking daily conversion. We are provided numerous opportunities to be converted, to the Lord, toward more Christ-like attitudes and opinions, and away from the vices in which we all, to a certain extent, participate. Sometimes we ignore the opportunity, even when it is placed directly before us. Other times we actively run away, too fearful of what the opportunity to change may require of us. There are times as well when the opportunity arrives that we tell ourselves, "I don't need to change. Everything is fine

434

with me." The blindness of our head and heart will bring stagnation in the Christian journey and can, if we are not careful, lead to personal destruction.

These sermons are centered about the reality of our need to be converted to a broader and deeper understanding of our role in Christ's master plan. We must see the need to make the most of life, despite the hurtful and problematic situations that sometimes arise. We need to re-commit ourselves to Christ, confident that the Lord knows what he is doing and will provide the path and sustenance we need for the journey. We must learn that conversion will not be easy, but rather is a process filled with many obstacles and road blocks. The person who endures and stays the course will be the one who finds eternal life with the Lord.

Sermons are by nature personal, but I hope that these reflections present themes and messages that can be applied by all in our daily struggle to follow the Lord. If these essays provide some assistance along that sacred path, then these pages will be worth the effort made in their composition.

Richard E. Gribble, CSC

Proper 23
Pentecost 21
Ordinary Time 28
Jeremiah 29:1, 4-7

Make The Most Of Your Life

Once there was a wise king who died. His son, who was young and rather brash, came to the throne and after only two months ordered a review all of his father's appointments. He called in the royal secretary, the royal treasurer, and the viceroy for interviews. He found them all to be unworthy and sent them into exile with only the shirts on their backs. Next he decided to interview the local bishop. A courier was sent to the bishop's residence with this message: "You are to report to the palace and answer the following three questions: 1) What direction does God face? 2) What am I worth? and 3) What am I thinking? If you fail to answer all these questions correctly you will be banished from the kingdom."

The bishop, in total frustration, threw his hands in the air and exclaimed to his wife, "I have no idea how to answer these questions. I am doomed to spend the rest of my days as a pauper and a beggar." His wife responded, "No, I will go to the king and answer the questions for you." "The king will know you are not the bishop," he responded. "He has never met you," said his wife. "If I wrap myself in your cloak, cover my head with the hood, and lower my voice, he will never know." The bishop was desperate and, thus, he allowed his wife to go is his place.

When the bishop's wife arrived at the palace, she was ushered into the king's throne room. He began his interrogation immediately and in a brusque manner. "Which direction does God face?" She picked up a lighted candle and asked the king, "What direction does the light of this candle point?" "All directions," responded the king. "Thus, it is with the direction that God faces. God is the light

437

of the world and faces in all directions." An astute answer, thought the king, but he continued, "What am I worth?" "Twenty-nine pieces of silver," came the immediate response. The king began to laugh: "I have houses full of silver and gold and thousands of acres of fertile fields." The bishop's wife responded, "The Gospels tell us that Jesus was sold for thirty pieces of silver. Certainly you do not think that you are more important than our Lord. Since you are Christ's regent here on earth, I subtracted one piece of silver to determine your worth." The king was amazed at the response and accepted it. Nevertheless, he pressed on with the third question: "What am I thinking?" "You are thinking that I am the bishop, but in fact I am not. I am his wife." She then removed the hood and her long hair fell past her shoulders. The king was shocked and then he began to laugh. "You are truly a wise and intelligent woman," said the king. "Tell your husband that he will remain the bishop but then return to the palace. We can use a person of your intelligence and wisdom in the government."[1]

This Irish folktale shows how a clever woman outsmarted a brash and immature king, but it also demonstrates how one person made the most of a difficult situation. The king placed the bishop in what he perceived to be a "no win" situation. The prelate's solution to the dilemma was to "throw in the towel," surrender, and give up. He figured he had been defeated, so why continue the struggle. But the bishop's wife held a very different attitude, for she saw the possibilities that the challenge presented, and not only did she make the most of the situation for her disheartened husband, but she won the esteem of the king for herself as well. This story illustrates an important message, both in today's First Lesson and life in general, namely that we need to make the most of life, whatever God sends our way today.

Jeremiah, as we heard in today's reading, wrote to the Hebrew exiles in Babylon, informing them of the Lord's message. God, through the prophet, tells the people to build homes and live in them, to plant gardens, and to eat the produce from them. The people are told to marry and raise families. In short, the Hebrews are instructed to seek the welfare of the city where they presently live; they are to make the most of a difficult situation.

438

The prophet's words are both hopeful and pragmatic. The situation for the Hebrews was not the best, at least this is what might be the view from an external perspective. The people, for the most part, had been physically moved from their homeland, creating a sense of loss and uncertainty. Having observed the destruction of their northern neighbor, Israel, some 150 years earlier, many may have thought that this present situation was the end for Judah and, therefore, the Hebrews. One too many transgressions had led God finally to destroy the people, as the Lord had threatened since the time of the exodus, when the people fell into idol worship of the golden calf (Exodus 32:1-35). With such thoughts prominent in the minds of many, Jeremiah's words proclaiming God's message to live today, to build, plant, harvest, and raise families, had to be received with joy and generate a sense of hope. The people must have concluded that their relationship with God, although severely damaged, had not ended. God had not abandoned the people, but rather, had sent a message of hope to encourage the Hebrews to make the most of a less than desirable situation.

Jeremiah's message was also practical, telling the people the need to take advantage of the opportunities that the exilic situation provided. The tendency of the Hebrews in the past was to hang their heads, beat their breasts, and seek forgiveness from God, with the hope that the Lord would once again take them back, rebellious people that they were. But Jeremiah's message suggests that people must hold their heads high and not wring their hands, and proceed to live full lives under the conditions in which they now find themselves. God, through the prophet, is saying in essence, "This is the life I have given you *today*; make the most of it. Do not waste time; do not give up. Rather, be profitable for a brighter day will come."

Adversity, the unexpected, obstacles, and detours are all endemic parts of the human condition and form part of the lived experience of every human person. These less-than-ideal conditions may come to pass because of our own laziness, inadequate effort, refusal to cooperate, or sinfulness. Like the Hebrews, many of the conditions or situations of our lives come to pass because of what we have done or failed to do. We must be honest and accept the incompleteness of our own life, not in resignation, but with an eye to making the most of the situation. There are numerous circumstances in life, however, that come to pass through no omission or commission on our part, but rather, become reality through the actions or inactions of others or occurrences beyond human control, such as natural disasters which happen through the dynamism of our world. When adverse conditions strike us, we have two basic options. We can, if we wish, be like the bishop in the story, concede defeat, throw in the towel, and retire to our bed, figuring that the situation is too extreme or obstacles too high to negotiate. The Christian, however, must not follow this route, for the acceptance of defeat is truly inconsistent with Jesus' message: "Very truly, I tell you, unless a grain of wheat falls into the earth and dies, it remains just a single grain, but if it dies, it bears much fruit. Those who love their life lose it, and those who hate their life in this world will keep it for eternal life" (John 12:24-25). Hardship, pain, and difficulty are certainly not to be sought, but they cannot be avoided as well. We recall the popular line by British essayist G. K. Chesterton, who wrote in 1910, "The Christian ideal has not been tried and found wanting; it has been found difficult and left untried." Yes, it is true, there will be much dying on the way to the Father.

The true Christian is the person who, when given the opportunity to make the most of a given situation, takes up the challenge and produces good and abundant fruit. In sports this message was dramatically demonstrated in the 1964 Summer Olympics in Tokyo, Japan.

Billy Mills, a second lieutenant in the United States Marine Corps, was a good runner, but he wasn't a world class runner — at least that is what everyone thought. In 1964 the United States Olympic track and field team was selected through a series of trials with three athletes chosen for each event. Originally Billy Mills was not a member of the team, but an injury to one member of the 10,000 meter squad gave Lieutenant Mills a chance for glory.

Atypical to most Olympic track events, the 10,000 meters in 1964 did not require a qualifying race to narrow the field. Thirty-eight runners entered the grueling 6.2 miles, 25 laps around the newly-constructed red clay track in the Olympic stadium. All would run together, the world class and the unknown.

The race, run on October 14, 1964, had some of the best runners in the world entered, including the 1960 Olympic champion Peter Bolotnikov of the Soviet Union, Ron Clarke, the world record holder from New Zealand, and Gerry Lindgren, the American hopeful, who was a student at Washington State University. After fifteen laps of the race only four of the 38 competitors had any chance of winning. A little known Tunisian runner, Mohammed Gamudi, Clarke, Bolotnikov, and Billy Mills were ahead of the field running in a tight pack. As an unknown in the sports world, no one ever gave Mills a thought in this race, yet there he was in a position possibly to win the coveted gold medal. The four lead runners jockeyed for position on the track, still damp from an early morning rain. The final lap of the race approached, the gun was sounded indicating the stretch run, and the leaders began an all-out sprint. Bolotnikov, whose energy was spent, fell back. With 300 meters to go, Gamudi forged ahead of Clarke and Mills. As the final straight approached Billy Mills was ten meters behind, but somehow his adrenalin kicked in and he surged ahead, crossed the finish line, and eclipsed the Olympic record by eight seconds, in one of the most stunning upsets in track and field history. Billy Mills was given a chance; he made good on the opportunity.

In the story of the bishop and his wife, the prelate was lost, but his wife saw possibilities and used the situation to return respect to her husband and bring herself to a position of special recognition. Similarly, Billy Mills was given a great opportunity and made the most of it. The Hebrews had trammeled God's law and because of their actions had been exiled to Babylon, but through it all the Lord had not abandoned them. Rather, a message of hope was sent through the prophet Jeremiah that the people must make the most of a difficult situation and do what they can to flourish. Likewise, we must not become disheartened when events, however they come to pass, place us in a situation less than desirable. On the contrary, today's lesson beckons us to put our best foot forward, as suggested in the Pastoral Epistles (2 Timothy 4:7), so we can fight the good fight and win the race. In this way we can find joy today and the eternal presence of God tomorrow.

---

1. Paraphrased from "The Bishop's Wife," in William R. White, ed. *Stories for the Gathering* (Minneapolis, Minnesota: Augsburg Fortress Press, 1997), pp. 146-147.

Proper 24
Pentecost 22
Ordinary Time 29
Jeremiah 31:27-34

A Personal Commitment To God

One morning at a missionary church deep in the rain forest of South America, the Sunday worship service was being celebrated. As the scripture readings were being proclaimed, a loud crash interrupted the service as a group of armed guerrillas broke down the side door of the church and, with machine guns in hand, approached the sanctuary. The minister and congregation were horrified and filled with fear. The soldiers dragged the minister outside to be executed. There was a roar of gunfire. The leader of the guerrillas then returned to the church and demanded, "Anyone else who believes in this God stuff come forward!" Everyone was petrified and stood frozen. There was a long silence.

Finally after what seemed several minutes one man came forward, stood before the guerrilla chief, and simply said, "I love Jesus." He was summarily roughed up and taken outside for execution. After this several others came forward and said the same thing. They too were taken outside and the sound of the machine gun was once again heard. When there were no more people left who were willing to identify themselves as Christians, the guerrilla chief returned to the sanctuary and told those remaining, "Get out! You have no right to be here!" And with that he herded them out of the chapel, where they were astonished to see their pastor and the others standing there very much alive.

The minister and those with him were ordered back into the church to continue the service, but the others were angrily warned to stay out. "Until you have the courage to be committed and stand up for your beliefs," said the guerrilla chief, "you have no right to worship." He and his troops then quickly disappeared into the jungle.

This apocryphal story presents us with a challenge of immense proportions. Those in the church who came to worship that Sunday morning were, I am sure, sincere in their commitment to the church, their faith, and the worship of God. If this was not the case they would not have been present. But when the guerrilla chief challenged them to move to the next level, to a personal demonstration of their commitment to God, all hesitated and some completely failed the test. The story provides a good illustration of the challenge God, through the prophet Jeremiah, presented to the Hebrews in Judah at the time of the exile. It is a challenge that we must face and negotiate as Christian people if we are to be true disciples and follow Christ, whose commitment to his mission and his Father were absolute.

The Hebrew Torah, what Christians call the Pentateuch or first five books of the Old Testament, presents two crucial themes: the presentation and the maintenance of the law and covenant. The law was formalized in the book of Exodus when Moses spoke with God on Mount Sinai and was presented with the two stone tablets, the Decalogue, or as it is commonly known, the Ten Commandments. The rest of Exodus and the books of Numbers, Leviticus, and Deuteronomy lay out in detail the many requirements and proscriptions of the Law. While the Law was fundamental to the day-to-day living of the Hebrew faith, this tradition would not have been possible had not God first made a covenant with his people whom the Lord considered "peculiarly his own." God initiated the covenant with the first Patriarch, Abraham. In Genesis (15:5-6) we hear, "God brought him [Abraham] outside and said, 'Look toward the heavens and count the stars, if you are able to count them.' Then he said to him, 'So shall your descendants be.' And he believed the Lord; and the Lord reckoned it to him as righteousness." The Hebrews were to be special to God and would be provided all that they needed.

Over the course of many centuries, the covenant between God and his people was severely tested and broken on numerous occasions. The lack of fealty of the Hebrews to their agreement with

444

Yahweh often placed them in less than desirable circumstances. The judges were sent to Israel because the Hebrews often broke the covenant by their transgressions of the law. Later the prophets were sent, one-by-one, to both the Northern Kingdom of Israel and the Southern Kingdom of Judah, to tell the people, especially the religious leaders, about their failures and to warn them that consequences would arise from their continual failures.

In today's lesson God, through the voice of his servant and prophet Jeremiah, announces a new covenant to the people. In exile in Babylon, the Hebrew community most probably felt estranged from God and at a loss as to what to do or what the future would hold. Jeremiah provides a message of encouragement for the people, saying that although God in the past had brought destruction and evil to the community as a whole, as a consequence of their failures to uphold the covenant, nevertheless God will now build and plant. In other words, God will restore the community. No longer will people fear collective punishment from God, but rather individuals will be responsible for their own transgressions.

Jeremiah then introduces God's new covenant, one that is written on the hearts of the people. No longer will God's agreement with the Hebrews be collective; rather, it will be an individual and personal covenant, with each member of the community. God is telling the people that they must take personal responsibility for their relationship with the Lord. No longer can one hide under the umbrella of the collective whole, but rather, people must be willing to come forward and make a personal commitment to God. While the people can now be assured that God will not judge all because of the errors of a few, nonetheless more is now expected of the individual, who now, like those challenged in the chapel in the rain forest, must overtly step forward, if not physically then psychologically and spiritually, and profess faith and commitment in the Lord. The new covenant which God inaugurated with the Hebrews was the interiorization of their original collective commitment.

The message in today's reading requires significant reflection for all of us. Too often I suspect, if we are honest with ourselves, we hide behind the fabric of many institutions, whether it be our family, business, or faith community, hoping that the work, perseverance, and faith of others will hold the ship together and we will be able to sail rather smoothly and not have to demonstrate our personal effort, persistence, or commitment. Today we are encouraged to come out of the shadows and move into the light which is the level of personal commitment. This may necessitate a more active role as decision maker in our home or it may entail being more pro-active at work and not simply putting in our eight hours and exiting the scene at the stroke of five. Our commitment to God can no longer be simply a peripheral attachment to the parish community. God is asking, even challenging, us to take a more active role and to demonstrate in word and deed one's commitment to God, whom we all know as the Father, Son, and Holy Spirit.

Personal commitment and responsibility must become an endemic part of our day-to-day life. We can see the need in both dramatic and everyday events which can be illustrated by two short but profound stories. During World War II, while the Nazis marched through almost every country on the continent of Europe, King Christian of Denmark stubbornly resisted Hitler's regime. Because Denmark was small and its military resources few, the King realized that his people could never win on the battlefield, but they could fight a valiant moral struggle. One day the King observed a Nazi flag flying atop one of the nation's public buildings. He reminded the German occupation commander that such an action was contrary to the treaty signed between Germany and Denmark, and that the flag had to be removed by twelve noon or a Danish soldier would be sent to remove it. At five minutes to noon the Nazi flag was still flying and, thus, the King informed the military commander that a soldier was being sent to remove it. The Nazi official warned the King that the soldier would be shot, but the King responded, "I think I should tell you that the soldier will be me." King Christian demonstrated his personal commitment.

On a more day-to-day level our personal responsibility can also be shown. One morning, early in his career, a young teacher arrived early at school and found to his surprise a youngster eagerly waiting at the classroom door. The little boy said, "It's locked." The teacher reached into his pocket and pulled forth the key. "You are a teacher!" the boy enthusiastically proclaimed. "How do you know that?" asked the teacher. "You have the key," the child answered. The teacher always remembered that small incident throughout his career, for the event crystallized in his mind the personal responsibility of his vocation.

The Christian life calls us to a personal relationship with Christ and, therefore, a special, personal, and individual commitment to our baptismal promise of service to God and our neighbor. Jesus challenged his followers when he stated, "If any want to be my followers, let them deny themselves and take up their cross and follow me" (Matthew 16:24). It will not always be easy to demonstrate our commitment and faith, for many obstacles seek to impede our progress. When such realities come our way, we must recall the admonition in the pastoral epistles (2 Timothy 4:1c-2), "I solemnly urge you: proclaim the message; be persistent whether the time is favorable or unfavorable; convince, rebuke, and encourage, with the utmost patience in teaching." Let us today renew our relationship with God by making a personal pledge of commitment to our common Christian vocation to holiness and manifest that faith by responding to the needs of our world. God has given us time and opportunity; let us respond in a personal way to the God who created us, Christ who redeemed us, and the Spirit who brings us to sanctification, today and each day of our lives.

God Provides The Path To Life

Today people throughout the world refer to the Hawaiian islands as "paradise." Visitors come to enjoy the plush beaches, the warm weather, and the friendly atmosphere that has become a trademark of the islands. In the mid-nineteenth century, however, Hawaii, especially the island of Molokai, was not so inviting. The northwest section of this little island was home to victims of Hansen's Disease, commonly known as leprosy. People throughout the world were ferried to this spot by ships that were more like prisons than vessels of transportation. Ship captains maneuvered close enough to shore so that the unlucky passengers had at least a chance to make it to land. Because lepers were believed to be highly contagious the ship did not dock. Passengers were thrown over the side. Those who could swim made it to shore; many others drowned.

A small settlement, Kalapapa, was started on the island by the lepers themselves. Their daily existence was one of true misery as they slowly, day-by-day and one-by-one, succumbed to the debilitating and disfiguring effects of their common affliction. The outside world cared little for the plight of these people. Molokai's isolated location was a perfect spot, it was thought, to keep these people away from society.

There was one man who cared, one person who was willing to demonstrate that God had compassion and would provide direction for all, not merely those without leprosy. Joseph de Veuster, a Belgian missionary priest who took the name Damien, came to Molokai in the early 1870s to minister to those who had been abandoned by society. Damien was not only the priest of the settlement,

449

he was the doctor, social worker, and possibly most importantly the friend of all in the Kalapapa settlement. Daily Damien would attend to the needs of his brothers and sisters. He dressed their wounds, dried their tears, listened to their stories, and prayed with them and for them. Each Sunday in his sermon Damien began, "You the lepers of Kalapapa...." His message spoke to the people of how the power of God was with them in their time of trial. God would always remain faithful and never abandon them, for God could act in no other way.

One day, after many years of labor among the lepers of Molokai, Father Damien mounted the pulpit to address his people. His usual opening contained a subtle but very important difference. He began, "We the lepers of Kalapapa...." Father Damien had become one with the people he served in every way. Damien died in April 1889, a victim of the very disease that had claimed so many to whom he ministered faithfully.

Father Damien was a minister of God who accepted people for who they were. He was not concerned that they were sick or had been judged by society as unworthy of care. He realized that all who seek God, listen to his voice, and do their best to carry out the Lord's commands are members of God's family. All can be brother and sister to the Lord.

The life and ministry of Damien de Vuester is a good example of God's work related in today's lesson from the Prophet Joel, a book drawn from the apocalyptic literature of the Hebrew Scriptures. Written in the wake of the Babylonian exile, the prophet promises new life and a special path to God for the people of Israel. In the beginning of his book of prophecy, Joel describes a massive plague of locusts, which is a harbinger for the day of the Lord. The plague stimulates a holy fear of Yahweh and because of this, the people turn to penance and prayer. Thus, Joel provides the people with a consoling message that God will provide for the Hebrews. Rains will come to replenish the land; vats will overflow with wine and oil. God will repay Israel for the destruction wrought by the swarming locusts. The people will eat plenty and will always be satisfied; they will never be put to shame again. God will dwell with Israel and the people will be blessed by the presence of the

Spirit. Joel says that all who call on the name of the Lord will be saved and there will be a new and glorious day in the land.

The new day that Joel predicts is the time that God will provide for the people the direction they need in their lives. Throughout salvation history God has always been there, ever faithful, to provide whatever the people need to find the proper road. The action of the judges and the prophets was God's way of telling the people that they had not been abandoned. On the contrary, God continually showed the way by providing people who knew the proper direction. Unfortunately, the people often did not follow or they followed for a short period of time and then returned to their former ways which were inconsistent with the law, the great bulwark for the Hebrews and the source of their direction home to God. Despite the problems, failures, and outright faithlessness of the Hebrews, God continues to show the path to life.

The action of God's loving concern and faithfulness, demonstrated in the Old Testament, is manifest time and again by Jesus, our brother, Savior, and Lord. As Father Damien showed love and gave direction to the lepers of Molokai and Joel prophesied a new day for Israel, so Jesus of Nazareth pointed people toward the Father. We recall Jesus' encounter with the Samaritan woman (John 4:1-42) at Jacob's well. She had no idea what the Lord meant by "living water," but through her discussion with Jesus she was placed on the path of life. In the famous Parable of the Prodigal Son (Luke 15:11-32), possibly better titled the Parable of the Forgiving Father, Jesus shows how God patiently waits for us to return. All we need do is make the mental shift in our mind, realizing our need to return home, and God will take care of the rest. The story of the woman caught in adultery (John 8:1-11) also demonstrates Jesus' caring nature. When confronted and challenged by the Pharisees to make a judgment on the woman's guilt or innocence, Jesus responds, "Let anyone among you who is without sin be the first to throw a stone at her" (John 8:7b). When all have drifted away Jesus asks, " 'Woman, where are they? Has no one condemned you?' She says, 'No one, sir.' And Jesus replies, 'Neither do I condemn you. Go your way, and from now on do not sin again' " (John 8:10b-11). In all these cases Jesus provides the path to life.

451

The best example of Jesus' action to reach out, provide direction, and care for another is seen in his encounter with Peter in chapter 21 of John's Gospel, a section of the Evangelist's work that is considered by scripture scholars to be an addendum to the original text. Jesus comes to Peter and three times asks, "Simon, son of John, do you love me more than these?" (John 21:15b). The three questions were poised, most assuredly, to counter the three denials that Peter voiced in the early morning of the day of Christ's crucifixion, a time when the Lord needed him the most. Jesus gave Peter a chance to redeem himself. Once this was accomplished, then the Lord told him precisely where the path of life would take him: "Very truly, I tell you, when you were younger, you used to fasten your own belt and to go wherever you wished. But when you grow old, you will stretch out your hands, and someone else will fasten a belt around you and take you where you do not wish to go. (He said this to indicate the kind of death by which he would glorify God.) After this he said to him, 'Follow me' " (John 21:18-19).

As God never gave up on and provided direction for the Hebrews and Jesus did likewise with many he encountered, so we must never give up on others, but rather be a light, like Father Damien was to the lepers of Molokai, that provides direction to life eternal. The common Christian call to holiness and discipleship mandates that we follow Christ's lead in providing for others the path of life. Saint Teresa of Avila, the famous Carmelite mystic, articulated our common mission in a famous prayer: "Christ has no hands in the world, but yours, no hands no feet, but yours. Yours are the eyes with which Christ looks with compassion for the world. Christ has no hands, but yours." Yes, we are the hands, the feet, the eyes, and the ears of Christ in this world. We are, as Saint Paul tells us (1 Corinthians 12), the Body of Christ.

We must do Christ's work. We must do our share to complete the Master's work by never giving up on another person and doing our best to provide the direction that will place people on the correct path that leads to God and eternal life. Parents must never give up on their children. Today's society provides many wonderful opportunities but also many dangers and pitfalls for young people.

Parents, therefore, must be ever vigilant to help and guide the children along the right path. And if or when they leave the correct road and use an alternative path, parents must be there to welcome their children back when they return and point them again in the correct direction of life. We cannot give up on co-workers or neighbors whom we find troublesome or don't like. As diligently as God searches for lost souls and works to keep others on the correct path, so we must be willing to assist others. We too often give up on others who we feel are unqualified, possess insufficient skill, or don't fit the mold for the task at hand. We even give up on ourselves and allow others, including the world, to dominate us. What God created in us is beautiful and, thus, we must never give up on ourselves, for in essence we are giving up on God. Spouses should make every reasonable effort to work together as a team so that their marriage is not only solid and fulfilling for them, but also serves as a great witness to others. As Christians we simply must do our best to complete Christ's work by providing people the proper direction to life.

Damien de Vuester demonstrated by his life of sacrifice that what is truly important is to care for others, meet their needs, and point people in the direction that will lead them to life. Similarly, the prophet Joel spoke of a new day for the Hebrews where God would provide the direction and the people would never again be put to shame. It is our task to continue the work of Christ, who like Damien and Joel, spent his life directing others to his Father. Let us do what we can today to be more Christ-like and, by our actions and words, work to bring others to God and, thereby, to eternal life.

God Knows What God Is Doing

There is an apocryphal story told that after completing his masterpiece, the *Mona Lisa*, the famous Italian Renaissance artist Leonardo da Vinci went to a nearby tavern to celebrate the event with his friends. While in conversation and sipping a little of the local wine, Leonardo noticed that many in the tavern were making sport of an ugly fool who made his living going from tavern to tavern, entertaining patrons for a spare coin or a crust of bread. This man truly was an ugly person; he seemed to be more of a troll than a man. His small beady eyes were not centered in his over-sized head. His ears were like cauliflower and his nose was as large as a gourd, with an ugly mole on its tip. His mouth and jaw were locked in a perpetual grimace.

As those in the tavern continued to mock the fool, a contentious rival artist hurled a challenge at the great da Vinci. "You are a master," said the man, "can you make in paint a beauty of this ugly fool?" Leonardo could not avoid the challenge, to do so would forever place him in doubt with his followers. "Why not?" responded Leonardo. "If I can paint the most beautiful woman in the world in my 'Mona Lisa' then I can certainly make an Adonis of this ugly fool. Return here tonight at the call of vespers and I will reveal the work I have done." Leonardo had little time, far less than normal for such a project, so he began in earnest.

Several hours later the bell in the cathedral church rang for vespers and the crowd began to assemble at the tavern. It was filled to overflowing; it seemed that the whole city of Florence had heard the challenge and had come to see what the master had accomplished. Leonardo stood before his new painting, which was covered by a curtain, and called for quiet. Patrons continued to murmur, "What would the painting reveal? Would the fool's eyes now be blue and centered in his face? Would his nose be noble and Roman? Would his lips be gentle but firm? Would his large ears now be petite and soft?" When the noise subsided Leonardo called out, "Behold my masterpiece!" He slowly withdrew the curtain to reveal his work; the crowd held its breath. The painting was an exact image of the ugly fool — not one hair or expression was out of place. The silence in the tavern was deafening. The rival artist cried out, "The ugly fool was too much of a challenge, even for the great Leonardo da Vinci." "Not so," responded Leonardo. Then pointing to the face of the fool he said, "This face was painted by the hand of God and only a fool would dare change what God had created."[1]

Da Vinci was wise enough to be able to distinguish between what could and what could not be changed. Yes, the fool was an ugly man, and there was lots of pressure from his rival artists to create an Adonis figure from the man, but Da Vinci realized that some things come from God and should not be challenged or changed while there are some human things that can be changed. Unlike the rival artists who may have perceived ugliness in the man, Da Vinci saw beauty, for who can do more or greater than God the Creator. In a similar way the prophet Habakkuk, as we heard in today's First Lesson, was taught the idea that although it might not be clear, God really does know what God is doing.

Habakkuk prophesied to the Southern Kingdom of Judah shortly before the community's exile to Babylon. At the outset of this less well-known book in the Hebrew Scriptures we hear a dialogue between God and the prophet. Habakkuk has grave concern over the presence of evil in the world; he finds it extremely difficult to understand and accept what he perceives is God's toleration of wickedness. To him justice seems to be disregarded. He simply cannot understand why God will not act and punish those responsible for injustice and the creation of evil in society.

Habakkuk was not alone, for a century prior Amos and Hosea had decried the injustice perpetrated against the poor by the religious leaders of Israel. Isaiah, speaking to the people of Judah in his famous Song of the Vineyard (5:1-7), announced God's displeasure with the community, having been given everything and still producing bad grapes. One of the primary timeless messages of the Hebrew prophets is speaking against injustice in all forms, but most especially when it ill-affects the weakest, the *anawim* of society.

Habakkuk's cry is heard and the Lord responds in a manner that demonstrates not only that God knows what to do, but that the Lord is just and can discriminate between those who should be punished and those who should not. The prophet tells God he is ready and alert and, thus, the Lord tells him to write down the message he will receive. The Lord's words are not meant solely for the prophet, but for all people. God tells Habakkuk that the wicked will come to a bad end, but for those who are good there is the prospect of a long and fruitful life. God can and will judge rightly.

The prophet also speaks of the reward for the person of faith, the one who holds to the law and finds the proper direction of life. Those who possess the gift of faith are the ones whom God brings to greatness by choosing them to go forward to do God's work and more importantly to place people on the correct path that leads to life.

The ability to discriminate while simultaneously and precisely controlling all situations was demonstrated by Jesus in the Parable of the Wheat and the Tares (Matthew 13:24-30). We recall how the farmer sows good seed, but an enemy comes and plants weeds in the soil as well. The workers ask if the weeds should be pulled when they appear, but the wise owner says that it is too dangerous to pull the weeds for the good wheat may be lost as well. Rather, the owner says that the good and the bad, the wheat and the tares, must be allowed to grow together. At the harvest the two will be separated; the good wheat will be placed in the barn, God's house, while the tares will be collected and burnt. God is able to discriminate, as he did during the period of the great prophets, expressed powerfully by Habakkuk today. God knows what God is doing.

The Christian community today must, in many ways, feel like Habakkuk, when its members cry out to God expressing their disappointment at the multiple injustices in the world. We may at times think that God does not hear the cry of the poor, the *anawim*, but God, we believe, listens to all who in faith call out for assistance. We may feel frustrated with the presence of so much evil in the world and wonder why in our perception, God does nothing to stem the tide. We want God to take action in the way we want and the time frame we set. We grow impatient; we cannot seem to allow God to be God and, thereby, to guide the course of events.

In our personal lives we seek justice as well, especially if we perceive we have been wronged. If evil has been perpetrated against us, we seek a swift and permanent answer. We often show little patience with God and how the Lord might handle the situation. Like those who challenged Leonardo da Vinci to recreate the facial features of the fool, so we too often want things our way and are not content until it happens. We are confident that we know what is right; we never consider that others, especially God, will have a broader picture from which to view the situation and make prudent decisions. We ask why God has not taken care of our problem, eliminated our enemies, saved our dying relative or friend, and vanquished all evil and sin. We must come to the conclusion, as God promised Habakkuk, that the Lord is fully in charge and knows all things for all time. "Why do things happen the way they do?" is a perennial and unanswerable question. As Saint Paul says, "For who has known the mind of the Lord? Or who has been his counselor?" (Romans 11:34).

We must never doubt that God is in charge and knows precisely what needs to be done and when to do it. A little story shows how God keeps on top of things: One day a man was walking through a field, lost in his dreams and meditation. He stood in awe before a large oak tree and noticed the tiny acorns lying around the base of the tree. He then looked across the fence at a huge field of pumpkins, each growing on a tiny vine. Suddenly he thought, "Surely God made a mistake. Why should huge pumpkins be on a tiny vine and tiny acorns grow on a huge oak tree? It doesn't seem to make sense." Just then a puff of wind arose and an acorn fell from the tree and struck him on the top of his head. He managed a wry smile and said, "Maybe God was on top of things after all!"

We might not understand why things happen and we might even ponder why it appears God does not act in our world. One day a holy hermit, thinking these same thoughts, was passing along a street and encountered a cripple, a mother begging for food for her pathetically malnourished child, and the victim of what seemed to be a severe beating. Seeing this, the holy man gazed toward heaven and exclaimed, "Great God, how is it that such a loving creator can see so much suffering and yet do nothing about it?" And deep within his heart he heard God's reply. "I have done something about it. I made you."

Let us take up the challenge and do what we can today to lighten the load of another. Let us truly see our responsibility to assist in the work of salvation. Let us know in our hearts that God truly knows what is happening and be confident that the Lord is in charge. Our confidence and reliance upon God will not be lost, but will rather, in the end, bring us to the eternal life that is God's promise for all who believe.

---

1. Paraphrased from "The Fool," in John Aurelio, *Colors! Stories of the Kingdom* (New York: Crossroads, 1993), pp. 149-150.

God Restores Us To Life

I fled Him, down the nights and down the days;
I fled Him, down the arches of the years;
I fled Him down the labyrinthine ways
Of my mind; and in the midst of tears
I hid from Him, and under running laughter.
Up vistaed hopes I sped;
And shot, precipitated
Adown Titantic glooms of chasmed fears,
From those strong Feet that followed, followed after.
But with unhurrying chase
And unperturbed pace,
Deliberate speed, majestic instancy;
They beat — and a Voice beat
More instant than the Feet —
"All things betray thee, who betrayest Me."

"The Hound of Heaven," from which this opening stanza is taken, was written in 1890 by Francis Thompson, a British poet, who knew all about the underside of life, yet experienced how God, with the tenacity and perseverance exhibited by a bloodhound, searched for his soul, found it, and restored him to a new life in Christ.

Thompson was born in Lancashire, England, in 1859, and grew up a product of his middle-class environment. His father was a physician, but he gravitated to his mother's side with her love of literature. He was educated at Ushaw and then through

461

the influence of his father, attended Owens College where he studied medicine. He hated what he was doing, however, and, rather than face his father, he disappeared for some time, arriving in London. In 1879, he fell ill with a lung ailment that led eventually to his addiction to opium. Between 1885 and 1888 he spent the majority of his time as a homeless vagrant, a situation that left him in a state of incipient disease. He was employed for short periods of time as a bookselling agent and a shoemaker and earned a few pence by selling matches and calling cabs for the elite of the city. He was often famished and cold and he periodically received alms. When the weather was extremely inclement, he migrated to the public library. Thompson dabbled in poetry and, having seen an advertisement in a new magazine, "Merry England," he sent his poems to the editor, Wilfrid Meynell in 1888. The editor was impressed, but because there was no adequate return address, his only way to contact Thompson was to publish the works and hope that he would come forward. Thompson saw his poems in print and responded to the query in the paper. When the editor found Thompson, the latter's destitution ended. After some time Thompson was returned to health and his drug habit was remedied. He continued to write poems that were often collected, especially his three volumse, *Poems*, *Sister Songs*, and *New Poems*. Thompson died in London in November 1907, a victim of tuberculosis that he most probably contracted during his homeless years on the streets of London. God had rescued this talented man and restored him to health so he could give to the world the great talent of words that he possessed. In a similar way, today's reading tells us how God will restore our lives, making them whole and preparing us for our task of building the Kingdom of God in our world.

The prophet Haggai wrote to the restored nation of Israel some 500 years before Christ. At the outset of his ministry he reports that King Darius has commanded that the Temple in Jerusalem, which lies in ruins, be rebuilt. After fifty long years of captivity and with the shock of seeing their most sacred place in ruins, the Hebrews were most assuredly disheartened, even to the extent that some may have thought God had forever forsaken the people. God's voice, however, is heard through the prophet (2:3), "Who is left among you who saw this house in its former glory? How does it look to you now? Is it not in your sight as nothing?" Despite the sadness and distress that many might have felt, the reality of God's abiding presence among his people comes through forcefully. The people are told to take heart and have courage, for God is with them every step of the journey, as the Lord promised so many generations earlier when the Israelites escaped from Egypt and the clutches of Pharaoh. God's spirit abides with the people and, thus, they should have nothing to fear. God will shake the heavens, the earth, the sea, and the dry land, gathering a treasure from all nations that will be brought to Israel so that the house of the Lord will be filled with splendor. The greatness of the restored Jerusalem will exceed its earlier grandeur. Israel will prosper; the people, the land, and the nation will be restored.

The restoration of Francis Thompson's talent and productivity and the clear message from Haggai of God's unconditional acceptance of his people challenges us in turn to know and accept the many ways God restores us in this life. How often in our prayers do we ask God to restore the health of a family member, close friend, or colleague at work? We ask that God renew and revitalize our own health, in mind and body. We also ask God to restore those we know in the grip of addictions. This is most dramatically illustrated by the work of Alcoholics Anonymous, founded in Akron, Ohio, in 1935, by Bob Wilson, a former New York stockbroker, and Dr. Bill Smith, a surgeon in Akron. Both men were hopeless alcoholics, but working together they gained sobriety so that they, in turn, could assist millions, directly and indirectly, to restore dignity, health, and pride to their lives. God restores us in spirit as well. Through our daily prayer we are renewed to the reality of the multiple and magnificent ways that God buoys our lives, filling our spiritual shells with the special gifts of grace that can only come from God. As exercise renews our bodies and gives us added strength, endurance, and energy, so God restores us to spiritual wholeness. In line with our spiritual renewal is the restoration we all must seek in our need to be reconciled with the Lord. We know better than anyone when our relationship with God needs healing, and we can be totally confident that God, like the father in the

463

Parable of the Prodigal Son, stands ever ready to grant the forgiveness we seek and need, thereby providing wholeness and restoration to our lives. Our lives are too often thrown off stride by many peoples, events, and circumstances, many of which are beyond our control. God, however, is the great equalizer who restores life in every aspect.

As God restores us in mind, body, and spirit, so must we be willing to do our share to assist the Lord through our efforts, doing what we can to lighten the load and bring to greater fullness the lives of our sisters and brothers. We are called to reach out to the poor and destitute in our society and do what we can to restore them to a more dignified existence of life. Our assistance may be through direct aid and service, such as donations of material things or time; we may be an advocate for systemic change and lobby legislators to enact laws that protect the poor, children, the elderly, and other more vulnerable members of our society. We must also seek to do our part to restore the lives of those whose existence is shattered by death, divorce, loss of job or economic prosperity, a major family crisis, or a host of other problems that people experience on a daily basis. We cannot be like the priest and the Levite in the Parable of the Good Samaritan (Luke 10:25-37) who simply passed by when given the opportunity to restore life to another occurred. No, we must exemplify the attitude of the Samaritan and take the time and expend the necessary energy and effort to do our share to restore others to life.

Relationships are an integral ingredient and necessary aspect of our lives, and we must never shirk our responsibilities to maintain those intact and restore those broken relationships that need to be made whole once again. Often the cause of the strain in relationships is the inability of one or both parties to admit their errors and the stubbornness that generally accompanies such behavior. To admit error is for some a sign of weakness, yet for the Christian to admit error, whether it be one of omission or commission, is the recognition that as humans we are incomplete and desperately need the wholeness and reconciliation of God. Thus, it takes a big person and one filled with faith to admit error, especially with respect to our relationships. Only by admitting our imperfections and seeking wholeness can we move in the proper direction to bring restoration through reconciliation to damaged relationships. As we restore our relationship with our sisters and brothers, so too must we be mindful to renew our relationship with God. Through personal prayer, the process of reconciliation, and our personal participation, in whatever way we can, depending on time and talent, we must work to better our relationship with the Lord. As God seeks to restore us, so must we do what we can to find God and revitalize our love affair with the Lord.

In his epic poem, "The Hound of Heaven," Francis Thompson wrote of how God would leave no stone unturned in a diligent search for our souls. He understood this reality in his own life. Destitute and addicted to drugs, Thompson was restored to life, and thereby granted the opportunity to utilize his talent for the betterment of society. In a similar way God is always present to break down barriers, pave roads, and make crooked paths straight in an effort to find us and restore us to the fullness of life. We, in turn, must do what we can to assist the Lord in his mission of restoration. Let us, therefore, seek the wholeness of God and do what we can to make similar inroads in the lives of others. By our actions we imitate Jesus, the one who was born, lived, and died to set us free, the one who will bring all who believe to eternal life.

Supporting Others
As God Supports Us

In 1921 Lewis Lawes became the warden at New York's infamous Sing Sing Penitentiary. No prison in the country was tougher with more incidents of violence recorded during the period, but when Warden Lawes retired some twenty years later, Sing Sing had become a humanitarian institution. Those who studied prison reform in the period gave the credit for the institution's turn around to Lawes, but when he was asked about the transformation he had a different story. He once stated, "I owe it all to my wonderful wife, Catherine, who is buried inside the prison walls."

Catherine Lawes was a young mother with three small children when her husband became the warden. Everyone warned her from the very first day that she should never set foot inside the prison. But that didn't stop Catherine. When the first prison basketball game was held, she walked into the gym with her three children and sat down in the crowd with the inmates. Her attitude was simple but very profound: "My husband and I are going to take care of these men and I believe they will take care of me. I have nothing to fear or to worry about." Catherine wanted to know the prisoners and their case histories. She discovered that one convicted murderer was blind, so one day she paid him a visit. Holding his hand in hers, she asked, "Do you read Braille?" "What's Braille?" he asked. His response prompted her to learn Braille and teach the prisoner how to read in this manner. Later, Catherine discovered a deaf mute in the prison. She went to school to learn how to sign so she could communicate with the man.

Catherine Lawes was to many in Sing Sing Prison between 1921 and 1937 the Body of Christ. She did everything for all people and never feared for her safety. She was a true disciple who never counted the cost, but rather was always present to encourage, support, and bring light to situations shrouded in darkness. One day Catherine was killed in an auto accident. The next morning Lewis Lawes did not come to work and the acting warden took his place. Almost immediately all in the prison knew something was terribly wrong. The following day Catherine's body was resting in a casket in her home, about a mile from the prison's main gate. As the acting warden was taking his morning walk, he was shocked to see a large crowd of the toughest, hardest-looking criminals gathered like a herd of animals at the main gate. He came closer and noted tears of sadness and grief; he knew how much they loved Catherine. He turned, faced the inmates, and said, "All right, men, you can go and pay your respects. Just be sure and check in tonight!" The acting warden opened the gate and a parade of criminals walked without escort the mile distance to the warden's house. They filed by one-by-one and offered their condolences to the warden and his family. And everyone of them checked back in. Every one!

Catherine Lawes was one woman who changed the lives of many hardcore criminals and allowed them to see the face of God in a truly powerful way by the manner of her life and the support she gave. She created a new environment where men convicted of the most vicious and heinous crimes could, even for a moment, change their views and make a break from their sordid past. For the inmates of Sing Sing she was a savior who brought light to those in darkness and through her actions created a new world with all sorts of possibilities and opportunities.

The life and work of Catherine Lawes illustrate the central message of today's lesson, namely that God will create a new life in us if we are open and ready to receive the manifold gifts of God. In the third and final section of the book of Isaiah, chapters 56-65, the prophet writes to the Hebrews after their return to Jerusalem. The disgrace and shame of the Babylonian Exile has ended and now the prophet declares a new day for the people. God says through Isaiah, "For I am about to create new heavens and a new earth. The former things shall not be remembered or come to mind" (65:17). God will bring joy to Jerusalem. No more will there be the sound of weeping in the streets or the cry of distress. No more will an infant live but a few days or another not live out the fullness of one's lifetime. The people will again live in prosperity as before. They will build houses, plant vineyards, and enjoy the work of their hands. No longer will people labor in vain or hear children in calamity. No, there is a new day, one of changed lives, where the wolf and the lamb shall feed together and the lion and the ox shall eat straw.

Isaiah's description of the new Israel can and must be the understanding that we have in considering how God holds us close, always ready to mold us and change us into the likeness of God in which we are created. We must believe that God stands ready to change us and create a new life for each person. Salvation history is the story of the up and down relationship God experienced with the Hebrews. They turned away from God on numerous occasions, but each time they returned, confident that God was present and waiting for their return. The multiple failures of God's chosen people to live according to the law did not stop them from doing what they could to make amends and get back on the right road. There is a need in our lives to know and experience failure so as to appreciate the second or third chance we might receive. This idea is illustrated by the lives of two men, both famous for their accomplishments and the gifts they gave to society.

Jonas Salk, whose discovery of the polio vaccine transformed the world of medicine and wiped out a terribly crippling disease, was once asked how this one great accomplishment could be related to his 200 other failures. Salk responded, "I never had 200 failures in my life, for my family never thought in terms of failure. We spoke in terms of experiences. It was such an attitude that made my 201st experience a discovery. But it could not have been done without the 200 previous experiences."

Winston Churchill, the famous British statesman, also was not intimidated by errors. When he made one, he simply thought the situation through again. Once he was asked, "Sir Winston, what in your school experience best prepared you to lead Britain out of its darkest hour?" Churchill thought for a moment and then replied, "It was the two years I spent at the same level in high school." "Did you fail?" he was asked. "No," the statesman replied, "I had two opportunities to get it right."

God gave the Hebrews a second, a third, a hundredth chance to get it right, and God will do the same for us. As Christians who seek to follow Jesus, who like the Father was always ready to assist those in need and get their lives back on track, we must do what we can to make the lives of others better. We must do our share to create a new heaven and a new earth for our brothers and sisters, especially those who in small or great ways are in special need. Parents provide a special environment in their home where children can rejoice, be safe, and grow in wisdom, grace, and knowledge. It may not be an idyllic setting — none really is. But it must be a supportive place where love reigns. At work we must support our colleagues, both our peers and those who work below and above us. Each has a special and important role, and we must do what we can to create an environment that supports and fortifies our gifts. Daily life provides many special opportunities to assist others and thus transforms lives, both one-on-one aid and more collectively through systemic change. Like Catherine Lawes, we must be willing to use the gifts we have to bring out the best in others. In essence we must encourage others to be the best they can be in every aspect of their lives. A true anecdote about the famous nineteenth-century poet and artist Dante Gabriel Rosetti illustrates perfectly the challenge that lies before all of us.

One day as Rosetti was sitting on a park bench reading a newspaper, an older gentleman approached and asked if the master would look at some paintings he had recently completed and evaluate their quality. Rosetti stopped what he was doing and looked the art over from every dimension. Although he wanted to be kind and gentle, he had to be honest as well and, thus, he told the older man that the paintings were not that good and were of very little value. The man thanked Rosetti for his time, but before he departed he asked if the master would take a few minutes more and review some sketches made by a younger man. Rosetti reviewed the art with great delight. He told the older man that the artist possessed great talent, that he should receive significant training, and that the potential for greatness was truly present. "Were these done by your son?" the artist asked. "No," said the man, "they were completed by me forty years ago. I wish someone then would had said what you did today. It would have changed my life, but I gave up and never pursued art as my vocation."

Catherine Lawes touched the lives of people, the likes of whom the majority of us will never encounter, because of circumstance, situation, and desire. She made an overt effort to reach out to those whom others had discarded, cast aside as irredeemable. God could easily have cast aside the Hebrews due to their persistent lack of faithfulness, yet time after time God reached out and new life was given to the community of Israel. For the Hebrews, God, through the words of Isaiah, proclaimed a new heaven and a new earth. As Catherine Lawes brought light to those in darkness and God provided new life and support to the Hebrews, so must we be confident that God stands ready to assist us. Basking in the knowledge and experience of God's love and support for us, we, in turn, must do what we can to bring a new day to those troubled in mind and spirit. Let us be grateful of God's call, the certainty of God's love and support, and may we answer the call and challenge to bring the light to others and to support them as God supports us!

Reformation Sunday
Jeremiah 31:31-34

Living A Transformed Life

Reformation Sunday provides the opportunity to recall the great events of the sixteenth century that transformed Christian thought and practice. The courage of people like Martin Luther, John Calvin, Ulrich Zwingli, and numerous other pioneers has transformed the lives of countless men and women over the past 500 years, but the great events which we commemorate must have relevance in our lives today if we are to apply the message of history. Fortunately through today's powerful First Lesson we have the encouragement we need to move forward as individuals and a society transformed into a new life in Christ.

Jeremiah, writing to the Hebrews who have recently returned from exile in Babylon, says that God will forgive the iniquity of the people and remember their sin no longer. It is a new day for the nation and its people. The sign of this new day is the covenant God now makes with the Hebrews. Unlike the old covenant, written on tablets of stone, the new covenant is inscribed on the hearts of the people. Thus, the law is now within the person. In order for people to see the newness and greatness in this special contract with God there is a need for transformation. Now God asks more of them; they must be a new creation. As God says through the prophet, "No longer shall they teach one another or say to each other, 'Know the Lord,' for they shall all know me, from the least to the greatest" (31:34a). God will give the Hebrews another chance, a new city. Now it is up to the people to respond, transforming their lives and doing what they can to transform the lives of others.

The transformation that we need is provided by God. Sometimes we are open to this charge and other times we resist. But we generally find that even when we resist, God has a way of entering our lives and getting us to do what is needed. This situation is illustrated by a story of a sculptor and his master creation.

A well-known sculptor had a burning desire to create the greatest statue of Jesus Christ ever made. He began one day in his oceanside studio by shaping a clay model into a truly triumphant and regal figure. The head was thrown back and the arms were upraised in a gesture of great majesty. It was the artist's conception of how Christ would be — strong and dominant. During the night, however, a heavy fog rolled into the area and sea spray seeped through a partially opened window. The moisture affected the shape of the clay figure so much that in the morning the sculptor did not recognize it as his master work. Droplets of moisture had formed on the model creating an illusion of bleeding. The head had drooped and the facial expression was transformed to one of great compassion. The arms had also drooped into a posture of welcome. It had become a wounded Christ figure. The artist stared at the figure agonizing over the wasted time and effort. Then inspiration came over him to change his attitude and mood. He began to see that this second image of Christ was by far the more true one. Thus, he carved into the base of the figure, "Come unto me."

The sculptor believed he knew what God wanted, but in an unexpected way he was transformed to a new view of his master creation. The sculptor realized that what God had planned, although not his original intent, was the best option. In a similar way, God molds and fashions us, like the popular image of the potter in Jeremiah (18:1-12), into what we should be. This process is seldom easy; in fact, generally there is some pain involved. But the end product is well worth the effort. After God is done with us, we are a more beautiful vessel and better able to continue the process in another.

God's loving plan to transform the world cannot be done alone, however. As disciples of God's son, Jesus, we have an obligation to do what we can to transform our world. The great religious reformers of the sixteenth century in many ways turned the world upside down. They forced people to think about God and their relationship to the Almighty. We often have no concept of how powerful our witness value can be and how we can, even unconsciously at times, positively influence others.

One day a businessman in a hurry tossed a dollar into the cup of a man selling flowers and rapidly went on his way. Half a block down the street, he stopped, turned about, and walked back to the flower seller. "I am sorry," said the man as he picked his favorite flower. "In my haste I failed to make my purchase. After all, you are a businessman like myself. Your flowers are of high quality and fairly priced. I trust you will not be upset with my forgetting to pick out my purchase." Then with a smile he continued down the sidewalk.

A few weeks later, while at lunch a nicely-dressed man approached the businessman's table and introduced himself. "I am sure you don't remember me and I don't know your name, but I will never forget your face. You are the man who inspired me to make something of my life. I was a vagrant selling flowers on a street corner until you gave me the self-respect and sense of personal dignity I needed. Now I am a businessman, too."

We have the opportunity to transform lives in many and varied ways. We can work on the systemic level and make efforts to assist the poor, work for social justice, and promote human rights in ways that will benefit people on the large scale. We can also work on the local and personal level to bring transformation to people. We may be able to assist a person to see another side of another individual and thus transform a problematic relationship into a positive and beneficial one. We may be able to help a person see that addiction is an end road to destruction and, thus, see the need to transform actions from those that lead to death to ones that bring life. We may as well be able to show a person who is estranged from God, by our words and actions, that God can and even must be the source of our sustenance and hope.

Let us on this Reformation Sunday rejoice that God stands ready to transform our lives, molding them into the image of his Son, Jesus. May we, in turn, do what we can to transform our world as Jesus would ask us. He is the one who came, died, rose, and set us free. He is the way to God and eternal life.

475

Sainthood Means Overcoming Obstacles

In 1989 an 8.2 magnitude earthquake flattened much of the state of Armenia and killed over 30,000 people in less than four minutes. In the midst of the utter devastation and chaos, a man left his wife in the security of others at home and rushed to the school where he had taken his son that morning, only to discover that the building was damaged almost beyond recognition. After he recovered from the trauma of his discovery, the man remembered a promise he had made to his son a few years earlier: "No matter what, I will always be there for you!" The man's eyes filled with tears as he looked at the pile of debris that once was the school. Despite the apparent hopelessness of the situation, the commitment he had made continued to haunt him.

The father concentrated on where his son might be in the building, remembering where he had dropped him off that morning. When he felt he knew the location, he began to dig through the rubble. As he was digging, other forlorn parents, clutching their hearts and crying out the name of their child, tried to pull him off the pile, saying, "It's too late! They are dead; you can't help them now." To each parent he only responded, "Are you going to help now?" and then he continued to dig, stone by stone. The fire chief of the city arrived and tried to pull him away from his effort, stating, "Fires are breaking out and explosions are imminent. You are in danger. We will take care of things. Please go home." But in response the loving father said, "Are you going to help now?" The police then came and said to the father, "You are distraught and angry, but in your actions you are endangering others. Go home;

477

we will handle it." But again the father responded, "Are you going to help now?" No one was willing to help.

Courageously the man continued with his task, for he needed to know for himself if his son was dead or alive. He dug for eight hours — twelve hours — 24 hours — 36 hours and then, in the thirty-eighth hour, he pulled back a huge boulder and heard his son's voice. He screamed his son's name, "Armand!" The boy called back, "Dad, it's me! I told the others here not to worry. I told them that if you were alive you would save me because you had promised, 'No matter what, I will be there for you!' You did it, Dad." The boy and thirteen companions had been saved when a triangle-like wedge formed when the building collapsed. The father called his son, "Come out, boy!" "No, Dad," said the son, "let the other kids out first, because I know you will get me. No matter what I know you will be there for me!"

This true account is an excellent illustration of how one man refused to give up as he negotiated through what all others believed to be an impossible hurdle in life. Things were very grim and the possibility for success from his endeavors was slim, but the loving father was not about to give up, even if all others had. This man was not one to allow adversity to triumph, but rather found a way to negotiate not around but over this major hurdle that entered his life.

On this All Saints' Sunday we celebrate the lives of men and women, some who are famous and countless others who, although unknown to most, have negotiated the obstacles of life and found their eternal reward with God. They have experienced precisely what God promised as articulated so beautifully by Saint Paul: "What no eye has seen, nor ear heard, nor the human heart conceived, what God has promised for those who love him" (1 Corinthians 2:9). As contemporary disciples still on the path to the Lord, we must follow where these giants of the past have previously trod.

The apocalyptic literature of the Hebrew Scriptures, from which today's First Lesson from the book of Daniel is drawn, is filled with imagery, and is therefore a significant challenge to understand. In the seventh chapter of Daniel we read the vision which the prophet had concerning four great beasts. Biblical scholars today tell us that the four beasts represent the four successive pagan empires that dominated the Near Eastern world before the time of Christ — the Babylonians, Medes, Persians, and Greeks. The four winds scatter the influence of these peoples to the four cardinal points of the earth: north, south, east, and west. The winds create a cosmic tempest that disrupts the whole world.

Although not part of today's reading, the judgment of God against these civilizations is described by the seer of the vision. We hear of the Ancient One, that is, God, who takes his place on the throne, clothed in white, and destroys the beasts, wresting their dominion from them. God is victorious, for the Lord's dominion is everlasting and his kingdom will not pass away. The victory won by God will be enjoyed by the holy ones who will receive and possess the kingdom forever. Those who are able to endure these periods of great trial will, in the end, find the victory given by God to the faithful who believe.

When we think of saints, what virtues and ideas come to mind? First, we must acknowledge that saints were never perfect. We can look at the life of one of the greatest saints, Augustine of Hippo, who wandered rather aimlessly for many years before finding himself and becoming the great defender of the faith that he was. We certainly think of saints as holy, generally courageous, obedient, trustworthy, and faithful to God's call. We could enumerate many additional virtues descriptive of the saints. However, in essence, saints, those who have successfully returned to God, have done three things exceptionally well: 1) overcome obstacles, 2) taken advantage of the numerous opportunities that have come their way, and 3) always been conscious of the need to do things for others.

We can all relate to stories we have heard and personal experiences of those who have negotiated great trials and obstacles in life. The Armenian father was one, but we could enumerate many more — people whose heroics have become legendary and others whose courage is known to only a few. Beethoven overcame deafness to compose his famous Ninth Symphony; Wilma Rudolph, the famous American track star, overcame childhood paralysis to win three Olympic gold medals; Harry Truman overcame the pollsters who said he had no chance in the 1948 election to upset Governor Thomas Dewey of New York.

Taking advantage of the opportunities we have been given is also an integral part of finding eternal life with God, and thereby, becoming a saint. Often we are given opportunities, but we do not respond. Sometimes the reasons may be proper, but other times things get in the way. A little story illustrates what we lose in failing to respond and what we gain when we do.

There is a town that has four separate neighborhoods. The first neighborhood is called "Yabuts." The people who live there think they know what must be done. As a matter of fact they speak about what they do in a very convincing way. When told they have an opportunity for something, the conversation generally goes like this, "Ya, but." The "Yabuts" have an answer, but it is the wrong answer. The second neighborhood calls itself the "Gunnados." Some of these folks are the best intentioned people you can find. They truly understand what needs to be done, but they usually do not follow through on their intentions. They realize what they were "gunnado," but it is often too late.

Another neighborhood is called the "Wishawoodas." These folks have an excellent perspective on things — hindsight. They say "I 'wishawooda' this or 'wishawooda' that...." They know everything that should be done, only its after the fact.

The last neighborhood is know as the "Gladidids." They are truly a special group of people. The "Wishawoodas" drive by the "Gladidids" homes and admire them. The "Gunnnados" want to join them, but they just cannot quite get around to it. The "Yabuts" could have been "Gladidids," but destiny simply did not smile on them. The "Gladidids" are pleased that they are disciplined enough to do what they know they should do, instead of always doing what they wanted to do.

Besides taking advantage of opportunities, another important quality of saints is actively assisting others in the daily Christian journey. Too often we not only miss opportunities, like the "Yabuts," "Gunnados," and "Wishawoodas," but even consider our position or state in life as excuses for not helping others. We say we cannot

480

be bothered; what we are doing is too important or our time too valuable to sacrifice some to assist another. Such an attitude, however, is inconsistent with Christian ethics, and therefore, not in keeping with the path to sainthood. One famous American never let his position get in the way of assisting a person in need.

One cold and wintry evening many years ago in northern Virginia, an old man stood alongside a road waiting for a ride across the river. He waited anxiously for many hours and then he watched as several horsemen approached from a distance. He let the first two pass without an effort to get their attention. Finally the last rider came upon the man, who by this time was more like a stone statue than a human. "Sir," said the old man, "would you mind giving me a ride to the other side of the river?" Reining the horse, the rider said, "Sure, hop aboard." Seeing the man was unable to move well, the rider dismounted and helped the man onto the horse. The horseman took the man not only across the river but to his home a few miles further. As they approached the tiny cottage, the rider asked, "Sir, I noticed that you let other riders pass without asking them for a ride. Then I came along and you asked immediately. I am curious why on such a bitter cold night you would wait and ask the last rider." The old man dismounted and said, "I have been around these parts a long time and know people rather well. I looked into the eyes of the others but saw no compassion or concern for my situation. I knew it would be useless to ask for a ride. But when I looked into your eyes I saw compassion and knew immediately that your gentle spirit would say yes to my request." The words touched the horseman deeply. "I am grateful for what you have said. May I never be too busy that I fail to respond to the needs of others." With that Thomas Jefferson turned his horse around and rode back to the White House.

All Saints' Sunday provides an opportunity for us, that is God's people, to be thankful for the countless men and women whose examples have been formative in building our Christian lives along lines consistent with the gospel message. While there are many things that encompass sainthood, certainly the ideas of negotiating obstacles, taking advantage of opportunities given, and doing what we can to assist others are significant goals for any who seek union

481

with Christ and eternal life with the Father. The aim of the saint is well illustrated in a little story.

One day a second grade Sunday school teacher decided to begin her lesson by introducing her students to Jesus. She began, "I want to tell you about the most wonderful man in the world. He is kind and compassionate; he will do anything he can to assist you. He will always listen and will never fail you." As the teacher was speaking, a little girl in the back of the classroom began to wave her hand excitedly, but before the teacher could call upon her, she burst out with great enthusiasm, "I know who you are talking about. He is my neighbor next door." My friends, may any of us be so fortunate that others, upon seeing what we do and hearing what we say, could say the same thing about us!

Christ The King
Jeremiah 23:1-6

Conversion To Christ

Once upon a time there was a beautiful garden that was owned by an ugly and unfriendly Giant. This was truly a lovely spot — the flowers bloomed in abundance, the peach trees always seemed to have their springtime blossoms, and the birds sang sweetly in the trees. Each day after school, children came and played in the Giant's garden.

One day the Giant, who had been away visiting his friend the Cornish Ogre for seven years, returned to his home and garden. He grew angry when he observed the children playing in his garden. "This is my garden," he shouted. The children ran in fear. Immediately the Giant hung a sign which read, "Trespassers will be prosecuted!" and then hurriedly built a wall around his garden. Now the children had no place to play. They tried to play in the street, but they found it was too dangerous. The Giant was selfish; he was not open to the beauty the children brought.

Meanwhile spring came to the land, but not to the Giant's garden. The birds did not come to sing and the trees refused to blossom. One flower popped its head above the earth, but when it read the sign and observed no children in the garden, it slipped back beneath the ground. The snow and frost were the only ones who were happy about this situation. "Spring has forgotten this place!" they exclaimed. The snow covered the ground and the frost painted the trees silver. The Giant could not understand why spring had not come to his garden; he was confused. The spring came and went to the land, but not to the Giant's garden. Summer passed and autumn came, but the garden remained in winter.

One day the Giant awoke to the sweet song of a bird. He looked out the window and beheld a beautiful site. Children had crawled through a small opening in the garden and were playing. The trees were in their autumn glory, the flowers were in bloom, and the birds were flying around the garden as they sang. There was one small corner of the garden which was shrouded in winter. In the corner a little boy was trying to climb a tree but he was unable to due to his small stature. The Giant bounded down the steps and ran into the garden. The children were initially afraid and ran in fear, but they returned when they saw the Giant had a smile of his face. He walked across the garden to the little boy, picked him up, and placed him on the branch of a tree. Instantly the tree blossomed and birds sang in its branches. The child was overjoyed and hugged and kissed the Giant. "I have been so selfish," the Giant said. "Now I know why spring never came to my garden."

From that time forward the children played each day in the garden. The Giant loved all the children, but especially the little boy, because the child had kissed him. But although the children came daily, the little boy did not return. Over many years the Giant grew old and feeble, but the little boy never returned to the garden. One spring day the Giant awoke and looked out his window. There was the little boy. He hurried downstairs as fast as he was able and walked to the boy who stood in the garden. But when the Giant came close to the boy he grew angry. The boy's palms were red with nail marks in them, and so too were his feet. "Who has done this?" asked the Giant. "I will slay him." "No," said the boy, "these are wounds of love." "Who are you?" asked the Giant. The child only responded, "Years ago you allowed me to play in your garden. Today I will take you to my garden in paradise." That afternoon when the children came to play in the garden they found the Giant lying dead all covered with white blossoms.

Oscar Wilde's classic tale, "The Selfish Giant," shows how Christ can convert the hearts of all, even those who appear to be oriented away from God and the betterment of God's people. As the Church year draws to a close and we look forward to a new season of grace in Advent, it is appropriate to take time to reflect on our lives, to judge how our words and actions have been seen, heard, and interpreted by others. How badly we all need the conversion which only Christ can bring. We need Christ the King.

The concept of conversion to a new way of life is illustrated well in today's First Lesson from the prophet Jeremiah. Writing to the Hebrews during their fifty-year exile in Babylon, the prophet wants the people to know that despite their pain, possible humiliation, and uncertainty about the future, God is and always has been with them. God is not blind to the sins of those whose actions have led the people of Judah astray, culminating in their exile. Jeremiah says that God will punish those responsible for Israel's fall. The Lord knows that not all are responsible; God can distinguish between the shepherds, Israel's religious leaders, and the sheep. It is the leaders who have provided poor witness and example. It is their sins of commission and omission that have landed the nation in exile.

Once the Lord has attended to those responsible for the downfall of the nation, he will bring conversion and restoration to the faithful of the land. We hear that God will gather the remnant of the flock, that is the faithful of Judah, and return them to their homeland. The people will be able to rebuild their lives through the renewal of their families and appointing new leaders to guide them. Those in exile should have no fear nor live in dismay, for there will come a day when God will raise up from the branch of David one who will reign as king. This king will deal wisely with people and will execute justice and righteousness in the land. Judah will be saved and the people will live in security.

While scripture scholars debate the symbolism of the prophet's message we can surely recognize in today's First Lesson a missive of hope for us who have been brought to its height and fulfillment in Christ. The conversion and restoration needed by the Hebrews in exile is just as badly needed by the Christian community today. We can have absolute confidence that as Yahweh walked with his chosen people, so Christ, our brother, friend, and Lord is with us at every moment. During his public ministry Jesus demonstrated numerous times his desire to restore people to wholeness. The Gospels recount how he raised to life Lazarus (John 11:1-44), the widow of Naim's son (Luke 7:11-17), and Jairus' daughter (Luke 5:21-24,

35-43). Numerous times Jesus cured the physical ailments of those who sought his healing touch: the ten lepers (Luke 17:11-19), Bartimaeus, the blind man (Mark 10:46-52), and many cases of paralytics (Matthew 9:2-8, Mark 2:1-12, Luke 5:17-26). Jesus was also the one who restored hope and dignity to those in despair. He converted the heart of the Samaritan woman at Jacob's well (John 4:1-42) and forgave the woman accused of having committed adultery (John 8:1-11). Even on the cross, Jesus was ready and willing to listen and bring conversion to the thief who asked his assistance (Luke 23:39-43).

Traditionally in our society, when a calendar year ends, we make some resolutions. As Christians we should do similarly with the onset of a new liturgical year. What do we need? The answer will be different for each person. There are, however, a couple of areas that need our common restoration. One is the area of admitting our errors and seeking wholeness. The dramatic effect such an act of humility can have on ourselves and others is illustrated in a popular tale from Native American culture.

One day a twelve-year-old Indian boy died from a snake bite. The poison took away his life and the grieving parents carried his body to the holy man of the village and laid it before him. The three sat around the boy's body for some time. Then the father rose from his seated position, stood over the his son's body, and stretched his hands over the boy's feet and said, "In all my life I have not worked for my family as I should have done." And the poison left the feet of the child. Then the mother rose and stretched her hands over the heart of the child, saying, "In all my life I have not loved my family as I should." And the poison left the heart of the child. Then the holy man stretched out his hands over the boy's head and said, "In all my life I have not believed the words I have spoken." And the poison left the head of the boy. The child rose up, along with the parents and the holy man. The village rejoiced that day. By admitting their faults and omissions the parents and holy man brought new life to the boy. We can bring new life to others if we have the courage to admit our shortcomings.

A second area of common necessity is our need to get involved. Too often opportunities come our way and we, like the priest and

Levite in the Parable of the Prodigal Son (Luke 11:15-32), simply "pass by," and in the process we often miss the presence of God that passes before us. We need to minister actively to others, to be the Christ present on earth.

Contemporary life brings many challenges and questions that require answers. Because they are tangible, usually straightforward and available, we gravitate toward human solutions. We seek the answers we need from people — family, friends, politicians, professionals in various fields, and even the clergy. We seek solutions from the material world. Some believe that money or other "things" can satisfy our needs and bring answers to the questions of life. Some as well believe the answers to life's challenges are found in ideas or institutions, whether it be a political or economic understanding or a specific group or permanent institution to which we give our loyalty. In the end, however, all of these solutions — people, things, or ideas — are empty; they cannot provide the answers we need. The one true solution to the challenges and questions of contemporary life is Christ. He is the one who can convert hearts and bring us to wholeness. He is the one who brings peace to troubled lives and nations. He is the King who brings those who believe to eternal life.

Thanks Be To God

Once upon a time there was a woodcutter who spent the majority of every day in the woods. He knew every trail and basically every inch of the forest. One day the woodcutter was preparing to fell a tree when he heard a cooing sound not far away. He followed the sound and found two white doves that were caught in a wooden trap. He felt sorry for the birds and thus opened the trap door and allowed them to fly to freedom. He then returned to his job of felling the tree and forgot all about the birds.

As the days and even years went by, the woodcutter fell in love and married the woman of his dreams. The couple moved to a small city ten miles from the forest where they began to raise a family. Twenty-five years passed quickly and though he prospered in his new work in the city, the woodcutter was at heart a man of the forest. Thus, one day he kissed his wife and children good-bye and went off to the forest, saying that he would return by supper time the next day.

The ten-mile journey seemed like only a few hundred yards to the woodcutter, so excited was he at the prospect of returning to his roots. He instantly recognized the old pathways he had earlier walked and saw a few old and gnarled trees that were just where he remembered them. He walked about, moving further and further into the forest. After some time he realized that he was lost. This had never happened to him before, and he was a bit afraid. He continued to walk until dark came. He figured he would have to bed down for the night on the ground, but then he saw a light and followed it to a small cottage. He knocked on the door and after a few moments the door opened from the inside. Standing behind the door was the strangest woman the woodcutter had ever seen. Her skin was whiter than snow, but her eyes shone like burning coals. Her long black hair flowed below her waist. "May I help you?" the woman asked. "I am lost, cold, and hungry," the woodcutter replied. The woman invited him in and, although uncomfortable, he accepted the invitation, for the food on the stove smelled wonderful and he had no place to go. The woman offered him a meal and he ate everything in sight. He wanted to thank his hostess, but when he turned about he did not see her. Instead he heard a hissing sound and from the corner of the room he saw a huge black snake approach. When the serpent reached him, it raised up on its tail and looked at him. The snake had the face of the woman. "You have returned at last," hissed the snake. "I have waited 25 years for you. Do you remember the two doves you set free? They were going to be my dinner. When I saw you release them, I swore an oath that I would one day kill you." "I did not know they were yours," said the woodcutter. "If you had said something, I would never have opened the trap." "Then you admit that you set them free. I have the right man," the serpent hissed. "Tonight at midnight I will kill you." "Is there anything that can save me?" asked the woodcutter. "Yes," said the snake. "If the bell in the old church tower rings twelve times before midnight, you will be set free."

The woodcutter was filled with fear and began to panic. He wanted to escape, but the house was locked up tightly; there was no way out. As he slumped on the floor, the woodcutter thought of his wife and family. He had been a fortunate man and now his life was to end. After a long time, the woodcutter looked at the clock on the wall; it read five minutes to midnight. The snake stood ready to strike, but in the distance could be heard a faint sound; the church bell was ringing. It rang and rang — nine, ten, eleven, twelve times. With the last peal of the bell, the house and the snake disappeared. With no place to go, the woodcutter, grateful for his reprieve from death, curled up in a soft place and went to sleep. The next morning he made his way toward the old church. When he arrived, he found the stairs to the belfry and climbed to the top. As he peered at the old bell, he noticed small spots of blood. On the floor of the bell tower he found many feathers and then the bodies of two white doves. They had thrown their tiny bodies at the bell twelve times in order to free the woodcutter, repaying him for their rescue by his hand so many years earlier. The woodcutter quickly picked up the doves. Their bodies were bruised and broken, but they were alive. He ripped his shirt and wrapped the small creatures tenderly. He stayed with the doves, feeding and nursing them until they were once again healthy. Then one morning he opened the church door and again set the birds free. The woodcutter then returned to his wife and children and all lived happily ever after.[1]

The story of the woodcutter and the doves demonstrates the need for gratitude in our lives. The doves were so grateful that they had been freed that they were willing to die in order to assist the woodcutter, who, in turn, was grateful for their totally unselfish action and nursed them back to health. This story, our lesson from Deuteronomy, and the national holiday we celebrate suggest that we must always demonstrate gratitude in our lives, to one another and most especially to God.

The Hebrews sojourned in the desert for forty years due to their disobedience and lack of faithfulness, but God never forgot or abandoned them. In order for the people to demonstrate in some way that they, despite their past inconsistency, wanted to follow Yahweh, the Lord instructs the people, as we hear in the reading, how they are to celebrate the harvest and the goodness of God to them. This festival will be a sign of their commitment to God and a realization that all the blessings of the Israelite community have their origins in God.

Scripture scholars suggest that this passage from Deuteronomy refers to the spring festival of Azymes, which was established in the new "promised" land as a way to demonstrate faith and thanks-giving. In opposition to the fertility cults that dominated the land when the Israelites arrived, and the practices that gave thanks to the gods for the fruitfulness of the earth, Yahweh asked his people to demonstrate that the fruitfulness of the land comes from the one eternal God. The possession of the land and its fruitfulness is the fulfilment of God's divine promise. God's faithfulness to the people requires the community as a whole and its members individually to respond in praise and thanksgiving.

In a similar way we all recall from our grammar school history lessons the story of the first Thanksgiving. The first year for the Pilgrims in Massachusetts was very hard. All suffered greatly and many died. The preparation of the land, creation of a community, and the need to find peace with the native peoples took a toll on those first residents of Plymouth Colony. Yet, despite the hardship, failures, and problems, the people possessed great faith and realized their need to give thanks to God who had provided all the opportunities and possibilities of their new lives, as well as the fruit of the land.

It is no secret to any of us that the United States is a land of great plenty that has been blessed by God in numerous ways. One might rightly ask, why are any of us so privileged to be born here or for others to have emigrated to America's shores? Why after the end of the Cold War is the United States the only world super power? Yes, we have our problems, but relative to all other nations, the obstacles and difficulties we face are minor, compared with our brothers and sisters in most lands.

The needs of the peoples of the world cry out to us and we must respond. The United States has been generous in its support of other nations, but there is a need to do more. We live in a land of plenty, but despite the plentitude there are some among us who need our assistance today. The response in our local community to the needs of the poor and disadvantaged has been good, but again we can most assuredly do more. As a community of faith, as individuals who seek to follow in the footsteps of the Lord, are we not obligated to assist others? Can any of us think of a better way to give thanks to God for the privileges and material possessions we have than by sharing with others? Distributive justice is the term used to describe an environment where those who have an abundance can share with those who have too little. Should not this basic premise of social justice become a hallmark of the way we do business in our personal, corporate, and religious lives?

The abundance that we as Americans enjoy should cause us to pause and reflect upon what is truly important in life. We have opportunities, talent, material possessions, and time. We live in a land of freedom — politically, religiously, and socially. With all that we have the big picture might be lost, but a series of short stories can bring us back to earth as to what is most important in life.

On the battlefield a chaplain encountered a wounded soldier lying in pain in a foxhole. "Would you like me to read to you from this good book, the Bible?" The man could only respond, "I'm so thirsty." The chaplain dutifully ran off, found a canteen, and poured the soldier a drink of water. The wounded man was shifting around as if he were very uncomfortable. Thus, the chaplain found a bed-roll and placed it under the man's head as a pillow. The soldier then began to shiver. Without thinking the chaplain stripped off his own field jacket and laid it over the wounded man. The soldier then looked the chaplain in the eye and said, "Now if there is anything in that book of yours that will allow a man to do more for another than you have already done, then please read it, because I would like to hear it."

Three students were discussing various versions of the Bible. One said, "I like the New American Bible. It is easier to read than the older versions." A second student commented, "I like the Jerusa-lem Bible. It too is easier to read and it is poetic in its style. I can use it in my daily prayer." The third student stood and said, "I like my mother's version the best. She translated the Bible into action so I can use it in my daily life."

An international gathering of youth met for a full week to dis-cuss how better to promulgate Christ's message to the world. Those assembled for the conference read many informative essays, heard many fine speakers, watched a few videos, and had ample time to discuss with each other. As the conference was beginning to break up and the those attending were packing to leave, a young woman from East Africa arose and said, "In my country when we hear that a pagan village is ready to accept the Gospel we don't send books, videos, a Bible or even an evangelist. Rather we send the best Chris-tian family we can find because we have found that the example of a good family speaks louder and more clearly than all the books, speeches, and videos in the world."

The truly important things in life are generally the intangibles, like the way we present ourselves to others. The one that is often forgotten and undoubtedly the most important is our faith. It is only through faith that we come together as a community to give thanks to God this day. It is our faith in peoples, institutions, and ideas which allows our society to progress. As we gather around the dining room table and celebrate with family, friends, and loved ones, sharing the produce of the land, let us be mindful of the great gifts God has given us. The words of a popular Christian hymn appropriately express what our feelings and attitude should be:

> *For the fruits of all creation, thanks be to God.*
> *For the gifts to every nation, thanks be to God.*
> *For the ploughing, sowing, reaping,*
> *silent growth while men are sleeping,*
> *future needs in earth's safe keeping, thanks be to God.*
> — F. Pratt Green

---

1. Paraphrased from "The Woodcutter and the Doves," in William J. Bausch, *A World of Stories for Preachers and Teachers* (Mystic, Connecticut: Twenty-Third Publications, 1999), pp. 31-33.

Lectionary Preaching After Pentecost

The following index will aid the user of this book in matching the correct Sunday with the appropriate text during Pentecost. All texts in this book are from the series for the First Readings, Revised Common Lectionary. (Note that the ELCA division of Lutheranism is now following the Revised Common Lectionary.) The Lutheran designations indicate days comparable to Sundays on which Revised Common Lectionary Propers or Ordinary Time designations are used.

(Fixed dates do not pertain to Lutheran Lectionary)

Fixed Date Lectionaries *Revised Common (including ELCA)* *and Roman Catholic*	Lutheran Lectionary *Lutheran*
The Day of Pentecost	The Day of Pentecost
The Holy Trinity	The Holy Trinity
May 29-June 4 — Proper 4, Ordinary Time 9	Pentecost 2
June 5-11 — Proper 5, Ordinary Time 10	Pentecost 3
June 12-18 — Proper 6, Ordinary Time 11	Pentecost 4
June 19-25 — Proper 7, Ordinary Time 12	Pentecost 5
June 26-July 2 — Proper 8, Ordinary Time 13	Pentecost 6
July 3-9 — Proper 9, Ordinary Time 14	Pentecost 7
July 10-16 — Proper 10, Ordinary Time 15	Pentecost 8
July 17-23 — Proper 11, Ordinary Time 16	Pentecost 9
July 24-30 — Proper 12, Ordinary Time 17	Pentecost 10
July 31-Aug. 6 — Proper 13, Ordinary Time 18	Pentecost 11
Aug. 7-13 — Proper 14, Ordinary Time 19	Pentecost 12
Aug. 14-20 — Proper 15, Ordinary Time 20	Pentecost 13
Aug. 21-27 — Proper 16, Ordinary Time 21	Pentecost 14
Aug. 28-Sept. 3 — Proper 17, Ordinary Time 22	Pentecost 15
Sept. 4-10 — Proper 18, Ordinary Time 23	Pentecost 16
Sept. 11-17 — Proper 19, Ordinary Time 24	Pentecost 17
Sept. 18-24 — Proper 20, Ordinary Time 25	Pentecost 18

Sept. 25-Oct. 1 — Proper 21, Ordinary Time 26	Pentecost 19
Oct. 2-8 — Proper 22, Ordinary Time 27	Pentecost 20
Oct. 9-15 — Proper 23, Ordinary Time 28	Pentecost 21
Oct. 16-22 — Proper 24, Ordinary Time 29	Pentecost 22
Oct. 23-29 — Proper 25, Ordinary Time 30	Pentecost 23
Oct. 30-Nov. 5 — Proper 26, Ordinary Time 31	Pentecost 24
Nov. 6-12 — Proper 27, Ordinary Time 32	Pentecost 25
Nov. 13-19 — Proper 28, Ordinary Time 33	Pentecost 26
	Pentecost 27
Nov. 20-26 — Christ The King	Christ The King

Reformation Day (or last Sunday in October) is October 31 (Revised Common, Lutheran)

All Saints' Day (or first Sunday in November) is November 1 (Revised Common, Lutheran, Roman Catholic)

U.S. / Canadian Lectionary Comparison

The following index shows the correlation between the Sundays and special days of the church year as they are titled or labeled in the Revised Common Lectionary published by the Consultation On Common Texts and used in the United States (the reference used for this book) and the Sundays and special days of the church year as they are titled or labeled in the Revised Common Lectionary used in Canada.

Revised Common Lectionary	Canadian Revised Common Lectionary
Advent 1	Advent 1
Advent 2	Advent 2
Advent 3	Advent 3
Advent 4	Advent 4
Christmas Eve	Christmas Eve
Nativity Of The Lord / Christmas Day	The Nativity Of Our Lord
Christmas 1	Christmas 1
January 1 / Holy Name of Jesus	January 1 / The Name Of Jesus
Christmas 2	Christmas 2
Epiphany Of The Lord	The Epiphany Of Our Lord
Baptism Of The Lord / Epiphany 1	The Baptism Of Our Lord / Proper 1
Epiphany 2 / Ordinary Time 2	Epiphany 2 / Proper 2
Epiphany 3 / Ordinary Time 3	Epiphany 3 / Proper 3
Epiphany 4 / Ordinary Time 4	Epiphany 4 / Proper 4
Epiphany 5 / Ordinary Time 5	Epiphany 5 / Proper 5
Epiphany 6 / Ordinary Time 6	Epiphany 6 / Proper 6
Epiphany 7 / Ordinary Time 7	Epiphany 7 / Proper 7
Epiphany 8 / Ordinary Time 8	Epiphany 8 / Proper 8
Transfiguration Of The Lord / Last Sunday After Epiphany	The Transfiguration Of Our Lord / Last Sunday After Epiphany
Ash Wednesday	Ash Wednesday
Lent 1	Lent 1
Lent 2	Lent 2
Lent 3	Lent 3
Lent 4	Lent 4
Lent 5	Lent 5
Passion / Palm Sunday (Lent 6)	Passion / Palm Sunday
Holy / Maundy Thursday	Holy / Maundy Thursday
Good Friday	Good Friday
Resurrection Of The Lord / Easter	The Resurrection Of Our Lord

Easter 2	Easter 2
Easter 3	Easter 3
Easter 4	Easter 4
Easter 5	Easter 5
Easter 6	Easter 6
Ascension Of The Lord	The Ascension Of Our Lord
Easter 7	Easter 7
Day Of Pentecost	The Day Of Pentecost
Trinity Sunday	The Holy Trinity
Proper 4 / Pentecost 2 / O T 9*	Proper 9
Proper 5 / Pent 3 / O T 10	Proper 10
Proper 6 / Pent 4 / O T 11	Proper 11
Proper 7 / Pent 5 / O T 12	Proper 12
Proper 8 / Pent 6 / O T 13	Proper 13
Proper 9 / Pent 7 / O T 14	Proper 14
Proper 10 / Pent 8 / O T 15	Proper 15
Proper 11 / Pent 9 / O T 16	Proper 16
Proper 12 / Pent 10 / O T 17	Proper 17
Proper 13 / Pent 11 / O T 18	Proper 18
Proper 14 / Pent 12 / O T 19	Proper 19
Proper 15 / Pent 13 / O T 20	Proper 20
Proper 16 / Pent 14 / O T 21	Proper 21
Proper 17 / Pent 15 / O T 22	Proper 22
Proper 18 / Pent 16 / O T 23	Proper 23
Proper 19 / Pent 17 / O T 24	Proper 24
Proper 20 / Pent 18 / O T 25	Proper 25
Proper 21 / Pent 19 / O T 26	Proper 26
Proper 22 / Pent 20 / O T 27	Proper 27
Proper 23 / Pent 21 / O T 28	Proper 28
Proper 24 / Pent 22 / O T 29	Proper 29
Proper 25 / Pent 23 / O T 30	Proper 30
Proper 26 / Pent 24 / O T 31	Proper 31
Proper 27 / Pent 25 / O T 32	Proper 32
Proper 28 / Pent 26 / O T 33	Proper 33
Christ The King (Proper 29 / O T 34)	Proper 34 / Christ The King / Reign Of Christ
Reformation Day (October 31)	Reformation Day (October 31)
All Saints' Day (November 1 or 1st Sunday in November)	All Saints' Day (November 1)
Thanksgiving Day (4th Thursday of November)	Thanksgiving Day (2nd Monday of October)

*O T = Ordinary Time

498

About The Authors

Steven E. Albertin is the pastor of Christ Lutheran Church of Zionsville, Indiana. He previously served parishes in Indianapolis and Fort Wayne, Indiana. Albertin has received degrees from Concordia College (B.A.), Concordia Seminary in Exile, St. Louis (M.Div.), Christ Seminary - Seminex (S.T.M.), and the Lutheran School of Theology at Chicago (D.Min.). He is the author of *Against The Grain — Words For A Politically Incorrect Church* (CSS).

Charles D. Reeb is currently the associate pastor of the largest United Methodist congregation in Florida, the First United Methodist Church in Lakeland. He has previously served churches in Atlanta and Athens, Georgia, and Plant City, Florida, and also served as a chaplain and devotional speaker for the Georgia Senate. Reeb's work has appeared in *Preaching* and *Circuit Rider* magazines, and he is in demand as a preacher and speaker for conferences and retreats. Reeb is a graduate of Florida Southern College and Candler School of Theology at Emory University.

Richard E. Gribble, CSC, the author of 15 books and over 150 articles, is an associate professor in the department of religious studies at Stonehill College in North Easton, Massachusetts. Father Gribble is a graduate of the United States Naval Academy, and served for five years on nuclear submarines before entering the priesthood. Gribble earned his Ph.D. from The Catholic University of America, and has also earned degrees from the University of Southern California and the Jesuit School of Theology at Berkeley. He is the former rector/superior of Moreau Seminary at the University of Notre Dame. Among Gribble's previous CSS publications is a three-volume series on *The Parables Of Jesus*.